D0782499

WITHDRAWN

ESSENTIAL STRUCTURAL TECHNOLOGY FOR CONSTRUCTION AND ARCHITECTURE

Burl Dishongh, Ph.D., P.E.

Department of Construction Management
Louisiana State University

Merrill
Prentice Hall

Upper Saddle River, New Jersey
Columbus, Ohio

[redacted]

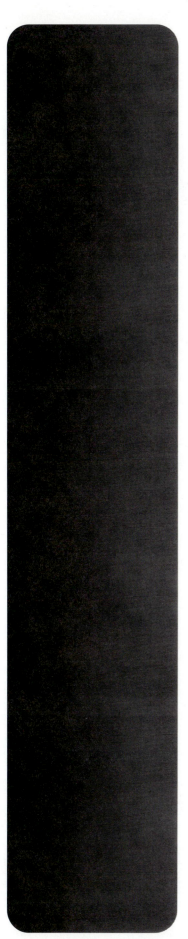

Library of Congress Cataloging-in-Publication Data

Dishongh, Burl E.
Essential structural technology for construction and architecture/Burl E. Dishongh.
p. cm.
Includes index.
ISBN 0-13-012858-9
1. Building. 2. Structural engineering. 3. Architecture. I. Title.

TH846 .D57 2001
624--dc21

00-031345

Vice President and Publisher: Dave Garza
Editor in Chief: Stephen Helba
Executive Editor: Ed Francis
Production Editor: Christine M. Buckendahl
Production Coordinator: Karen Fortgang, *bookworks*
Design Coordinator: Robin Chukes
Cover Designer: Tom Mack
Cover Photo: FPG
Production Manager: Matthew Ottenweller
Marketing Manager: Jamie Van Voorhis

This book was set in Caslon Book by York Graphic Services, Inc., and was printed and bound by R.R. Donnelley & Sons Company. The cover was printed by Phoenix Color Corp.

Copyright © 2001 by Prentice-Hall, Inc., Upper Saddle River, New Jersey 07458. All rights reserved. Printed in the United States of America. This publication is protected by Copyright and permission should be obtained from the publisher prior to any prohibited reproduction, storage in a retrieval system, or transmission in any form or by any means, electronic, mechanical, photocopying, recording, or likewise. For information regarding permission(s), write to: Rights and Permissions Department.

10 9 8 7 6 5 4 3 2 1
ISBN 0-13-012858-9

Merrill
Prentice Hall

Preface

The study of structural technology forms a major component of the professional training of engineers, architects, construction contractors, construction project managers, inspectors, and others involved in the construction of buildings, bridges, and other structures. The focus of structural technology is to efficiently use building materials–primarily concrete, steel, and timber–to safely resist all loads applied to a structure. Though most professionals involved with construction are not structural engineers, they nonetheless need to know the basic structural technology that structural engineers are concerned with, including structural loads, how they are carried through the structure into the ground, and how to communicate this information with other professionals.

Essential Structural Technology for Construction and Architecture is written for students and practicing professionals who need to develop a basic understanding of structural analysis and design. The book provides a concise presentation of structural technology, from the determination of structural loads all the way through to the sizing of foundations. The book may serve either as a student textbook or as a compact reference for practicing construction professionals wishing to gain, or regain, a grasp of the subject.

In *Essential Structural Technology for Construction and Architecture,* we focus on the key concepts of structures taken from traditional engineering courses in statics, mechanics of materials, structural analysis, timber design, steel design, reinforced concrete design, soil mechanics, and foundation design. The reader will find that the basics of structural analysis and design are a reasonable application of natural laws that may be presented with a minimum of mathematical rigor. Readers will gain a sufficient working knowledge of structures enabling them to envision how structures resist loads, as well as to collaborate with other construction professionals while analyzing, designing, and constructing structures.

We begin with a discussion of the natural forces that act on structures. We look at how these loads make their ways through a structure member by member. These loads set up proportionate forces in each member that cause it to stretch, compress, rack, twist, bend, and/or buckle. We see the relationships between the intensity of forces in members and their deformation effects in order to select appropriate proportions and materials for structural elements. Like most other things in nature, structural loads end up going back into the earth, and so we will look at properties and behavior of soil with a focus on structures.

The intent of *Essential Structural Technology for Construction and Architecture* is to present concisely all the essential topics of the field of structural technology in a compact manner that is accessible to as many readers as possible. It is not meant to be a structural engineer's handbook; it is more like a liberal paraphrase of such a volume. Simple principles are observed in order to develop fairly sophisticated relationships between structural loads and their many load effects. Chapters of the book are used both to develop a group of related structural principles and to apply these principles in typical structures problems.

Many engineering books provide numerous problem exercises for each subject that is presented, but such books are usually intended to ground the reader intensively in the detailed theory of one specific field, such as strength of materials, steel design, or soil mechanics. On the other hand, *Essential Structural Technology for Construction and Architecture* provides an overview of the entire field of structural technology in which the reader progresses through ever-broadening application examples that continually build upon and reinforce previously presented principles. As such, the author feels that readers will experience sufficient repetition as they carefully go through the entire book, especially if they spend time working a few of the suggested exercise problems included with many of the application examples.

Contents

1 Forces and Structures

1.1 Basic Structural Loads

A structure must efficiently and safely resist all applied loads. Structural loads are the result of natural forces. The common materials of construction–concrete, steel, and timber–are fabricated into elements such as beams, columns, arches, and trusses. These elements must be arranged into forms that best serve the function of the structure, yet still safely support all loads.

The most basic structural loads are gravity loads that act vertically on a structure and result from the earth's gravitational pull. These loads include dead loads and live loads. *Dead load* is simply the weight of the structure itself–the roof, the walls, the floor, beams and columns, and so on. *Live loads* consist of people, movable furnishings, forklifts, cars and trucks, snow, temperature changes, or anything else that may temporarily act on the structure.

Lateral loads due to wind and earthquakes are live loads that push horizontally on structures. When the wind blows against the projected area of a structure, the structure will be forced to lean sideways. In an earthquake, the ground upon which a massive structure sits is rapidly shaken side to side and large earthquake forces are generated in the structure as its huge mass resists the sudden lateral motion. Structures that retain soil, such as retaining walls and basements, also experience lateral loads from the soil as it resists being confined.

Throughout this book, we discuss the active and reactive loads on elements of structures, such as beams, cables, arches, trusses, frames, and shearwalls. With the exception of dead loads that are simply the self-weight of the structure, it would be extremely difficult to know the exact magnitude of these highly variable and uncertain forces of nature that act on a structure. Instead, we consider nominal loads that accurately represent the actions of the variable gravity live loads and lateral loads that are most probably expected for a given structure. The word *probably* in the last sentence is significant, since load data is often collected from surveys of hundreds of structures, and statistical analyses are employed to verify that nominal loads used in design are indeed accurate indicators of the actual loads that occur.

1.2 Equilibrium of Forces and Moments

We can begin our discussion of structural equilibrium by looking at forces. A *force* is a push or a pull that is exerted on an object. When you are standing on the ground, your weight is an active force (action) pushing downward on the earth. If you want a total experience of this force, let someone stand on you! You can stand still because the ground is pushing on you with an opposing reactive force (reaction) equal to your weight. Note that the terms–force, load, action, and reaction—all refer to the push or pull of one thing on another. Like your weight, force is expressed in units of pounds. Equilibrium exists when all actions are equally opposed by reactions.

When loads act on members of structures, it is necessary to determine what reactive forces are established to hold the active forces in equilibrium. In a multimember structure, the reactive force of one member becomes the active load on a supporting member. And, we need to know all forces acting on a member if we are to limit the intensity of the internal forces (stresses) and associated deformations. Finally, we must safely deliver all member loads through a foundation and into the soil.

We usually represent the push or pull of a force by an arrow in the direction of the push or pull. Figure 1.1 depicts a 150-pound person standing on a beam that rests on blocks at either end. The arrow lengths here are drawn relative to their force magnitudes. The two upward reaction forces at the beam supports must oppose the downward force of the person's weight. The weight of the beam will be ignored for this discussion.

Concentrated forces are exerted at a point, but in reality, no force can be applied at a point, which by definition has no area. Instead, loads must act over a finite area, which is most conveniently considered to be a point when investigating force equilibrium. The person standing on the beam of Figure 1.1 is considered to exert a concentrated force of 150 lb at a point on the beam between the feet. However, we see that the 150-lb force is actually spread over the area defined by the footprints on the beam. The weight force of the person standing relaxed and upright effectively acts at a point known as the center of gravity on a line of action that passes through the center of the area of the footprints termed the area centroid. We will have more to say about center of gravity and area centroid later in the book.

If the person stands at the middle of the beam, each reaction is clearly seen to equal $\frac{1}{2} \times 150 = 75$ lb. When, as in the figure, the person stands nearer to one end, the nearby reaction is greater than that at the farther support. But how do we determine the reactions in this case?

For equilibrium of an object to exist, the net sum of all forces acting on the object must be zero. The sum of vertical forces and the sum of horizontal forces must be zero or the object is sliding in the direction of the net

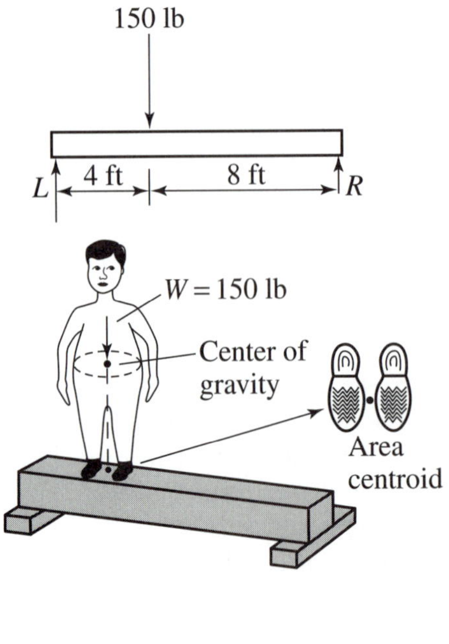

FIGURE 1.1

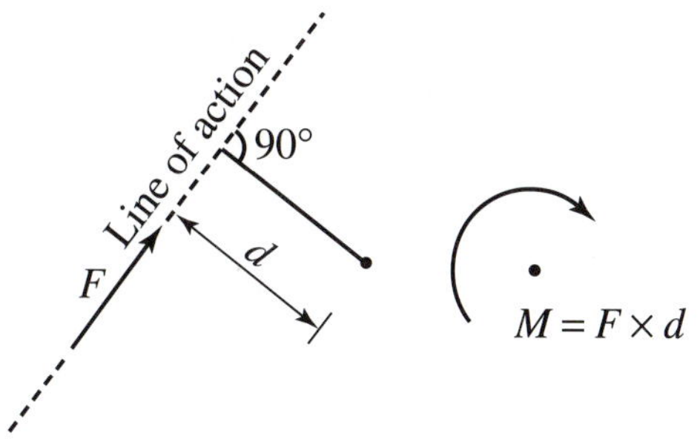

FIGURE 1.2

unbalanced force. These two conditions of force equilibrium are necessary to ensure equilibrium, but there is another necessary condition.

Referring to Figure 1.2, the line of action of a force is the line formed by extending the force arrow in both directions. A force has leverage about any point that lies off its line of action. We call leverage of a force about a point the moment of the force, or simply the moment.

Moment is the tendency for a force to rotate about a point. The magnitude of the moment is the force multiplied by the shortest distance between the point and the force line. This shortest distance is called the lever arm, or moment arm, and it is perpendicular to the force line of action as shown. The units of moments are foot-pounds (ft-lb).

If an object is in equilibrium, then it is not moving with respect to any reference point. Select any point, and the moments of all forces acting on an object must oppose one another, so that the net tendency to rotate is zero. This has to be true of any point you may choose, otherwise, the object will actually rotate relative to the point. So in addition to the two conditions of force equilibrium, we need a third condition of moment equilibrium–the net sum of all of the moments about any point must be zero.

The three conditions of equilibrium lead to three equations of equilibrium. In Figure 1.1, there are no horizontal forces acting on the beam, so a trivial equation would state that the sum of all horizontal forces (zero) is equal to zero. If the downward weight is 150 lb, then the left and right reactive forces, L and R, must together oppose the vertical load with a net total force of 150 lb and we write a vertical force equilibrium equation,

$$L + R - 150 = 0$$

We usually refer to the upward and rightward directions as positive. The equation simply states that all vertical forces add up to zero.

The beam is 12 ft long, and the person is standing 4 ft from the left. Arbitrarily choose any point, such as the point where the person is standing on the beam. Then the lever arms about this point are 4 ft for the left reaction, L, and 8 ft for the right reaction, R. We write a moment equilibrium equation,

$$4 \times L - 8 \times R = 0$$

Clockwise moment rotations are usually considered positive. By rearranging and substituting the terms, we find the solution of the preceding two equilibrium equations is $L = 100$ lb and $R = 50$ lb, which answers our question from the previous section.

Because the line of action of the 150-lb force passed through the point we chose for moment summation, it had no leverage about this point. We could have written a different moment equation by summing the moments about a point at the left end of the beam. In this case, the clockwise moment of the person's weight is $150 \times 4 = 600$ ft-lb and is opposed by the counterclockwise moment of $12 \times R$, thus,

$$600 - 12 \times R = 0$$

From this we again find that $R = 50$ lb. Since the force L passes through the left end of the beam, it has no lever arm and so creates no moment about the point.

For another example, consider the ladder in Figure 1.3. The person's vertical 150-lb weight is opposed by the vertical reaction of the concrete floor, A, so that $A = 150$ lb. This is the same as writing

$$A - 150 = 0$$

Friction between the rough concrete floor and the base of the ladder allows a horizontal reaction, B, to resist the horizontal reaction, C, that the smooth wall applies to the top of the ladder that is pushing into the wall. The two horizontal forces must be equal and oppose one another, so

$$B - C = 0$$

We choose the bottom of the ladder as a point to sum moments. This is convenient, since both forces A and B have their lines of action passing through this point and so they create no moment about the point. Remember that the moment of a force about a point is the force multiplied by the shortest distance between the force line of action and the point. Therefore, the weight creates a clockwise moment of 2 ft $\times$ 150 lb $=$ 300 ft-lb. We have a counterclockwise moment of $12 \times C$ from the wall reaction, so,

$$300 - 12 \times C = 0$$

We find $C = 25$ lb. And from $B - C = 0$, we find that $B = 25$ lb.

The preceding examples are typical of how equilibrium conditions allow us to determine the forces acting on objects. The exact same process is applied to structural members, or even entire structures, in order to determine the magnitudes of forces that must be dealt with. In the next section we look at means to simplify situations where the forces are not exactly vertical or horizontal.

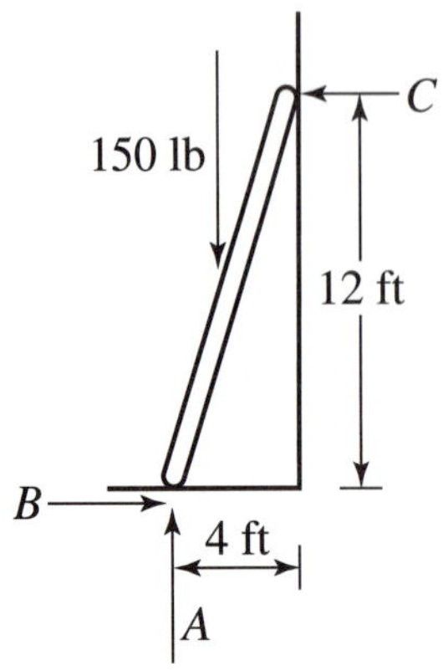

FIGURE 1.3

1.3 Force Components

Often, a force will be inclined with respect to the horizontal and vertical directions, as in Figure 1.4. To facilitate use of equilibrium equations, it is most convenient to replace the single inclined force by its horizontal and vertical projections. These two projections are called *force components.* The two force components are a totally equivalent replacement for the single inclined force, and vice versa.

If we measure the acute angle that an inclined force F makes with a vertical line and call that angle z, we can say,

$$F_{\text{HORIZONTAL}} = F_{\text{H}} = F \times \sin(z)$$

$$F_{\text{VERTICAL}} = F_{\text{V}} = F \times \cos(z)$$

Recall from trigonometry that the cosine of an acute angle of a right triangle is the ratio of the adjacent leg to the hypotenuse and the sine of the angle is the ratio of the opposite leg to the hypotenuse. The ratio of the opposite leg to the adjacent leg is the tangent of the angle. These relationships are shown in Figure 1.4.

If we replace all inclined forces by their two components before doing anything else, the steps for checking force and moment equilibrium can be systematically applied as we saw with the beam and ladder. For example, Figure 1.5

FIGURE 1.4

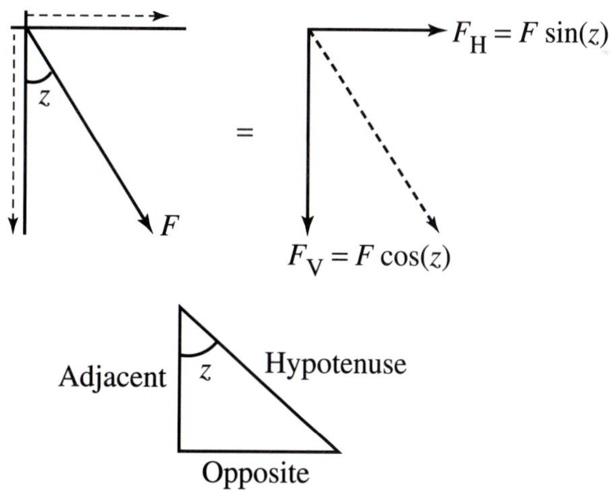

$$\cos(z) = \frac{\text{adj}}{\text{hyp}}; \quad \sin(z) = \frac{\text{opp}}{\text{hyp}}; \quad \tan(z) = \frac{\text{opp}}{\text{adj}}$$

FIGURE 1.5

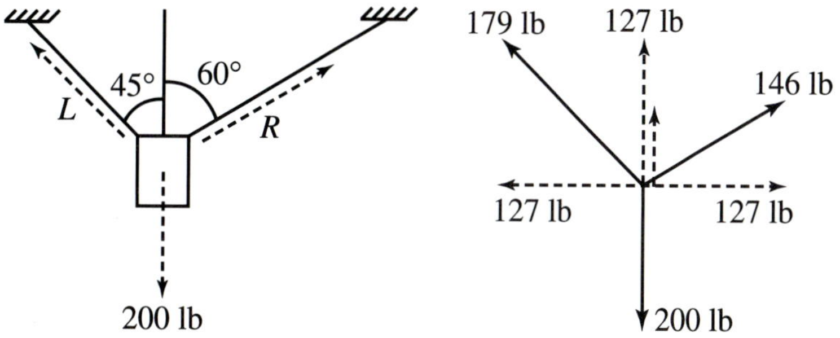

shows a 200-lb weight being supported by two ropes. The three forces acting on the weight essentially meet at the same point. When this occurs, the forces are said to be concurrent, and they have no leverage on the object. With concurrent forces, we consider only the two force equilibrium conditions since the sum of the moments is zero.

From a vertical line, the left rope is inclined 45° and the right rope is inclined 60°. The active 200-lb weight sets up reactive forces in both ropes, as shown. The vertical components of the reactive rope forces can be seen to oppose the 200-lb vertical load. The horizontal rope force components must oppose one another to ensure horizontal force equilibrium. We write the vertical force equilibrium equation,

$$L_V + R_V - 200 = 0$$
$$L \times \cos(45°) + R \times \cos(60°) - 200 = 0$$
$$0.707(L) + 0.5(R) = 200$$

In similar fashion, we write the horizontal force equilibrium equation,

$$L_H - R_H = 0$$
$$L \times \sin(45°) - R \times \sin(60°) = 0$$
$$0.707(L) = 0.866(R)$$

The solution of the two force equilibrium equations is $L = 179$ lb and $R = 146$ lb. The rope forces and the values of their components are shown in the figure.

In the case above, we knew the inclination angles of both inclined forces. If we have a force, but do not know its magnitude or its inclination angle, we simply replace the force with its vertical and horizontal components, F_V and F_H. When these two components are subsequently determined from an equilibrium analysis, we may determine the force, F, and its inclination angle, z, by

$$F = \sqrt{(F_V^2 + F_H^2)}$$
$$z = \arctan\left(\frac{F_H}{F_V}\right)$$

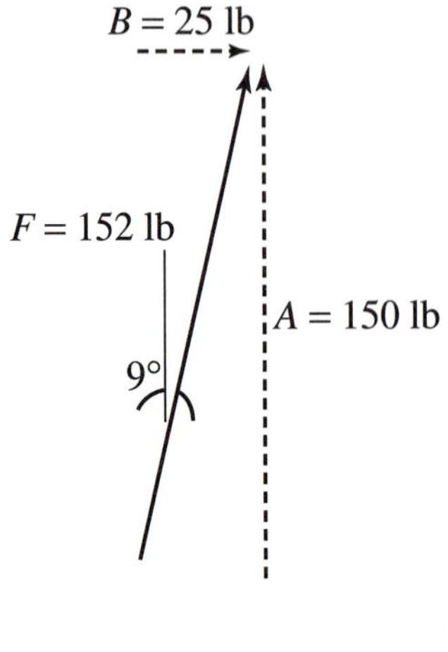

FIGURE 1.6

In the case of the ladder of Figure 1.3, for example, we have already used this concept. We designated A and B as the reaction components at the ladder base. Figure 1.6 shows these two forces are really the components of an unknown reactive force magnitude, F, and force inclination, z. With $A = 150$ lb, and $B = 25$ lb, we see that F and z are 152 lb and 9°, respectively.

1.4 SIGN SUPPORT

Let's see how the concepts of force equilibrium and force components can be applied to a very simple structure for which the only active load is that due to its self-weight, or dead load. The wood sign of Figure 1.7 is attached to the side of a building and is equally supported by two cable and strut assemblies as shown, with each assembly carrying half the weight of the 300-lb sign. To determine the adequacy of its members, we would want to know the force in the cables and the compression in the struts that attach the sign to the wall.

Joint C of assembly ABC is isolated and a load diagram is sketched as shown. This load diagram is often called a free-body diagram because the object is isolated free from its surroundings, and all known and unknown active and reactive forces are applied to the object to replace the effects of its former environment. The load diagram also includes any dimensions and/or angles needed to write equilibrium equations.

In this case, the cable tension force, B, the strut compression force, A, and half the sign weight, 150 lb, are concurrent at joint C. In a concurrent force problem, all forces are assumed to pass through a common point and the forces have no moment arms to create rotations, so moment equilibrium is automatically satisfied. The two force equilibrium equations are needed to determine the forces and their inclination angles. Force A acts horizontally and the 150-lb sign half-weight acts vertically, while from the problem geometry, force

FIGURE 1.7

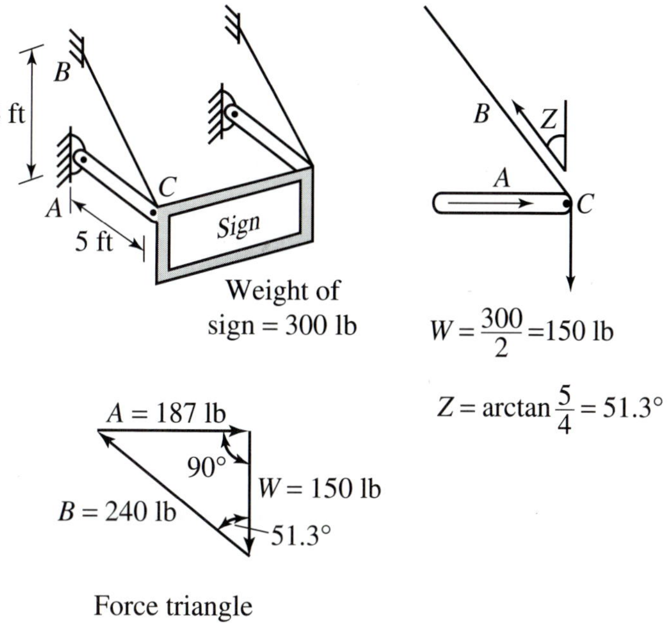

Exercise Rework this problem assuming that the distance between points A and B is

a. 3 ft

b. 8 ft ■

B acts at an angle of $z = \arctan(5/4) = 51.3°$ from a vertical axis. From vertical force equilibrium we see that

$$B = \frac{150}{\cos(51.3°)} = 240 \text{ lb}$$

From horizontal force equilibrium

$$A = 240 \times \sin(51.3°) = 187 \text{ lb}$$

It is often useful to form a closed triangle with three concurrent forces that are in equilibrium as shown in the figure. Such a force triangle is useful to observe graphically the relationships among the three forces, as we will see in other situations to come.

1.5 Friction on an Inclined Slope

Now we will look at another concurrent force equilibrium problem, and at the same time discuss some basic ideas about the nature of friction, which is the active-reactive force that occurs between rough surfaces of objects in mutual contact. In general, the rougher the surfaces of the contacting objects, the greater the friction that is created between them. We will see that some types of structures, especially foundation elements, rely on friction to remain in equilibrium.

The wood crate of Figure 1.8 has a loaded weight of 1,000 lb. We wish to determine the force P needed to pull the crate up the concrete surface with a 20° slope. The load diagram of the crate shows that in order to move it up the slope, the applied pulling force must overcome the friction force, F, on the surface between the wood and concrete as well as overcoming the component of weight in the direction of the slope, W_P, where

$$W_P = 1{,}000 \times \sin(20°) = 340 \text{ lb}$$

The friction force, F, which opposes the motion of the crate, is proportional to the force, N, that acts to clamp together the two rough surfaces of wood and concrete. Equilibrium of forces acting perpendicular to the slope indicates that this clamping force is equal to the component of the weight perpendicular to the sloping surface, W_N, where

$$W_N = N = 1{,}000 \times \cos(20) = 940 \text{ lb}$$

As the force P is slowly increased, the opposing friction force will increase proportionately until the maximum possible friction between wood and concrete is overcome–then the crate can slide. The maximum possible friction force in the case of these particular two materials is about 70% (less if the surfaces are wet) of the clamping force, so $F = 0.7 \times N$. The value, 0.7, is referred to as the friction coefficient, which must be experimentally determined for any

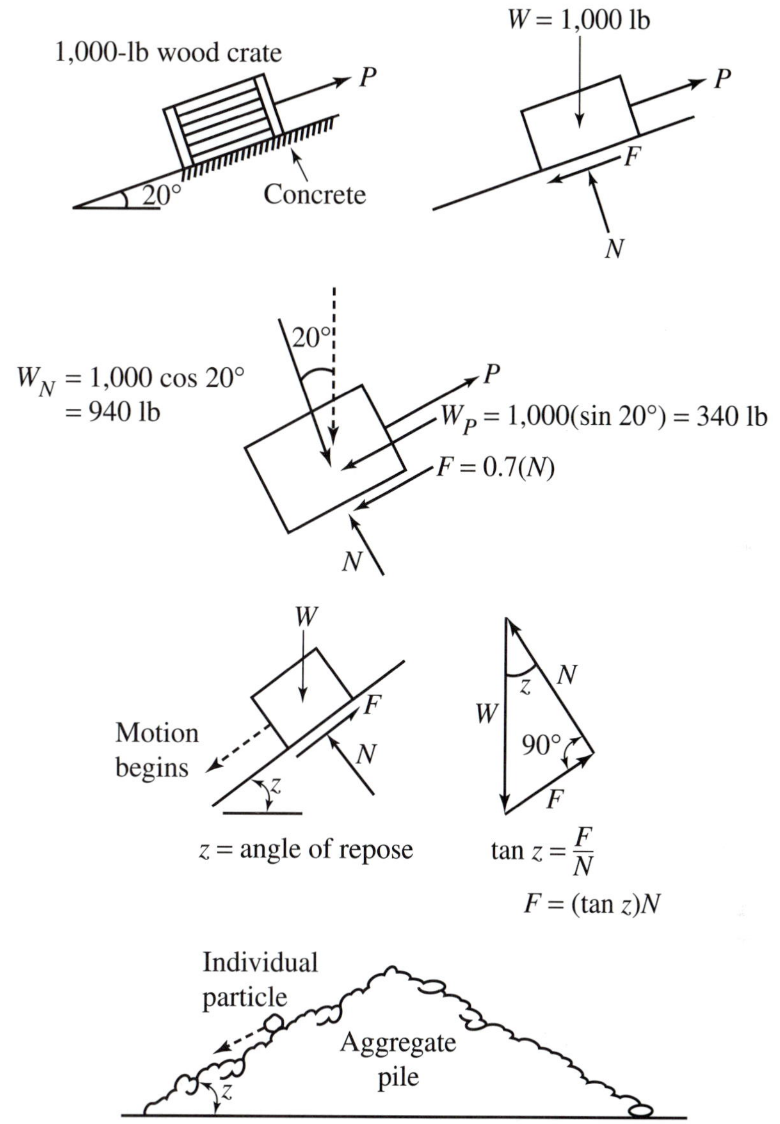

FIGURE 1.8

two materials in mutual contact. This coefficient generally ranges from 0.1 for smooth, slippery contact surfaces, to 0.9 when the contact surfaces are both rough.

From the load diagram, we see that the forces acting on the crate, W, F, N, and P form a concurrent force system. Just before the crate slides, it is motionless, and so we can write two force equilibrium equations. The two components of the known weight are shown and the friction is expressed in terms of the unknown clamping force N. The two unknowns are thus P and N.

We add the forces in the direction perpendicular to the inclined surface and equate them to zero:

$$N - 940 = 0$$

Thus $N = 940$ lb, and $F = 0.7 \times 940 = 660$ lb. We then sum forces in the direction of P:

$$P - 340 - 660 = 0$$

Exercise In the problem we just looked at, what force is required to push the crate down the slope?

In a more personal matter, consider what friction force is required between your feet and the shingles of a roof to prevent you from sliding off of a roof with a 7 on 12 slope? ■

So we see that we need to pull the crate with a force $P = 1{,}000$ lb to overcome friction and start the crate sliding up the incline.

The coefficient of friction between any two material surfaces is easily determined if one of the materials forms a flat plane that can be adjusted to any slope and the second material can be block-shaped. In particular, we might be interested in this coefficient when the two materials are both the same, such as between concrete and concrete. The plane is tilted at increasing values of angle, z, as shown in the figure, until the block just begins to slide. If the block and plane are both of the same material, the value of the angle z at this point is termed the angle of repose, or friction angle, of the material.

As we see in the figure, the three concurrent forces, W, N, and F, are in equilibrium just prior to the sliding motion, and they form a right triangle that includes the angle z. By trigonometric definition, the tangent of angle z is the ratio of the opposite to the adjacent legs of the right triangle:

$$\tan(z) = F/N$$

which means that

$$F = \tan(z) \times N$$

Comparing this to what we have discussed with the wood crate problem, we see that the coefficient of friction of a material is simply determined as the tangent of its friction angle.

This angle may be observed for a material such as soil or some pile of aggregate, by forming a pile, as shown in the figure. As the height of the pile increases, it is evident that there is an upper limit to the slope angle of the sides of the pile, and it is the material friction angle, z. Any additional particle placed on the pile must behave like the inclined block and slide down the side of the pile–the plane–so that the pile forms an ever-increasing conical shape with sides that retain a constant slope. This information is especially important as we will see for soils and foundations, since the friction angle of soil is an important aspect related to the ability of soil to support structural loads.

1.6 Tilt-Wall Panel

Figure 1.9 illustrates the technique of tilt-wall construction, which is a popular building method that allows for quick erection of low-rise structures that have many feet of perimeter walls, such as discount department stores and warehouses. We will see that the concept of moments enters the analysis of forces acting on a tilt-wall panel since the forces are no longer concurrent.

A rectangle of wood form boards is laid out on the concrete floor slab of the building under construction, so that the slab can temporarily serve as the bottom of the form for the concrete wall. A debonding chemical is sprayed

FIGURE 1.9

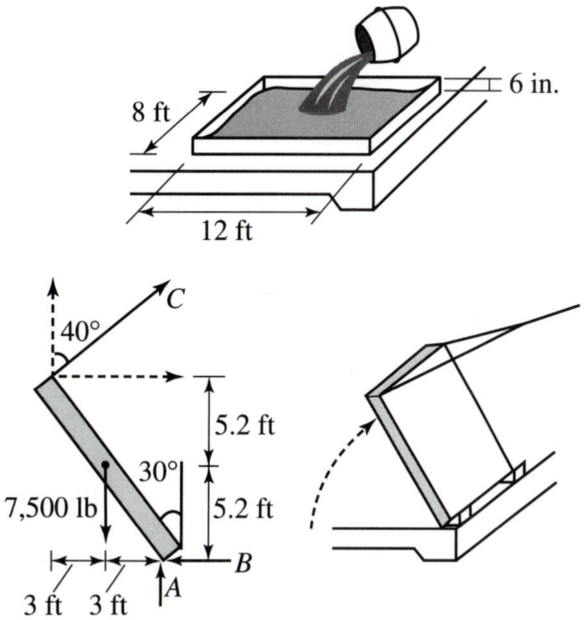

on the concrete slab to prevent the new concrete wall pour from adhering to the slab; then, reinforcing steel is placed inside the formed rectangle and wet concrete is poured until level with the top of the form boards. This creates a wall that is typically 6 to 12 in. in thickness. Once hardened, the toe end of the wall panel is blocked against sliding, and a crane tilts the panel upward with a cable attached to hardware that was inserted in the wet concrete.

At one point in the tilt-up phase of the 6-in.-thick, 8-ft-wide, and 12-ft-tall wall panel shown, the panel is 30° from vertical and the lifting cable makes an angle of 40° with a vertical axis. We need to determine all the forces acting on the wall. The unknown forces acting on the tilted wall are the lifting cable force *C*, the upward reaction of the ground *A*, and the force the blocks provide to resist lateral sliding at the panel base *B*. The active force is the wall weight, *W*, which is determined knowing that the unit weight (density) of concrete is 150 lb/ft^3. Thus, we can compute the panel weight and locate it at the center of the panel (known as the center of gravity). Adding about 300 lb to account for uneven concrete finish, the weight is

$$W = 150\ \text{lb/ft}^3 \times \left(6\ \text{in.} \times \frac{1}{12}\ \text{ft/in.} \times 8\ \text{ft} \times 12\ \text{ft}\right) + 300 = 7{,}500\ \text{lb}$$

The forces (and force components) acting on the wall are shown on the load diagram in the figure. Summing moments about the base of the wall,

$$C \times \cos(40°) \times 6 + C \times \sin(40°) \times 10.4 - 7{,}500 \times 3 = 0$$

From this we get $C = 1{,}370$ lb. Summation of vertical forces yields the equation

$$1{,}370 \times \cos(40°) - 7{,}500 + A = 0$$

Thus, $A = 6{,}450$ lb. Finally, equilibrium of horizontal forces indicates that

$$B = 1{,}370 \times \sin(40°) = 880\,\text{lb}$$

Exercise Rework this problem assuming that the wall panel is 10 in. thick and it is at an angle of 60° from the vertical direction. What about 89°?

Also, what force is required to completely lift the panel from the ground? ■

1.7 Center of Gravity of a Truck on a Bridge

To apply equilibrium principles to analyze structures, we need to know about the term center of gravity. The *center of gravity* of an object is the point about which the object may be perfectly balanced. Because the weight of an object is a primary structural load, we need to locate where this weight effectively acts–this is its center of gravity. Regardless of how the object is oriented, a rope attached at this point can lift it up without any tilting. Center of gravity is often shown abbreviated as c.g. We may treat a group of loads as an object and again, the c.g. is the point about which the total force of these loads may effectively be assumed to act.

A truck rolling across a bridge as shown in Figure 1.10 will serve us well in visualizing the concept of center of gravity. Note that the five axle weights of the 50,000-lb truck may be determined by slowly advancing the vehicle and successively taking readings from the scale of a roadside weigh station each time an additional axle comes onto the scale.

We will locate the center of gravity of the truck with respect to the front axle, *X*. Then, we can use this information to determine where the front

FIGURE 1.10

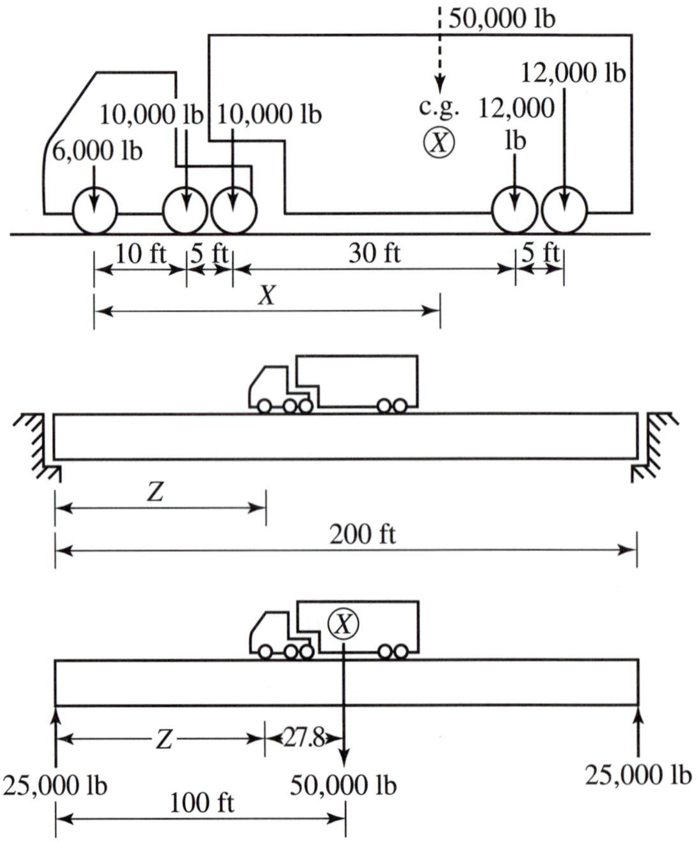

Exercise Using the left abutment as a reference point, verify that the sum of the moments of the five axles is equal to the moment of the total 50,000-lb weight.

Rework this problem removing the last axle of the trailer, and determine where should the lead axle of this truck be located to create the greatest reaction at the left support? ■

axle of this truck should be located, Z, from the left abutment of the 200-ft span bridge so as to cause equal support reactions of $50{,}000/2 = 25{,}000$ lb at the left and right abutments.

By definition, the center of gravity (shown as c.g.) is the point where the full 50,000-lb weight of the vehicle is effectively located. Thus to locate this point, we observe that the moments of all the individual axle weights with respect to the front axle must equal the moment of the total weight taken about the front axle, as follows:

$$10{,}000(10) + 10{,}000(15) + 12{,}000(45) + 12{,}000(50) = 50{,}000(X)$$

From this, $X = 27.8$ ft from the first axle.

To locate the truck's lead axle on the bridge span so as to create equal reactions at the abutments, we merely observe that the two vertical reactions are equal when the center of gravity of the truck is in the middle of the 200-ft span. From the figure, we see that

$$Z = 100 - 27.8 = 72.2 \text{ ft}$$

1.8 Distributed Gravity Loads

One of the most commonly occurring structural situations is that of distributed loads. We will see many such loads as we progress through the book. Instead of being concentrated at a specific point, a load may also be distributed all along the body as a series of forces whose total effect can be said to occur at the c.g. of the distributed load.

The floor beam *AB* shown in Figure 1.11 is a good example of such a situation. It supports a concentrated load due to the wall that it supports as well as a uniformly distributed series of loads made up of the floor joists that deliver their reaction forces. We want to determine the magnitudes of the support reactions that the foundation blocks must provide to support beam *AB*, and in the process of doing so we will begin to gain an insight as to how the loads of a structure are supported by its many individual elements. For the time being, we are only considering the dead weight of the wall and floor in this example.

The beam *AB* is 18 ft long and supports a wall at a point 6 ft from end *A*. The wall has a unit weight of 8 lb/ft^2(psf), so that a concentrated load P equal to one-half the total wall weight is delivered to *AB* via another beam that directly supports the wall and

$$P = \frac{1}{2} \times (8 \times 9 \times 20) = 720 \text{ lb}$$

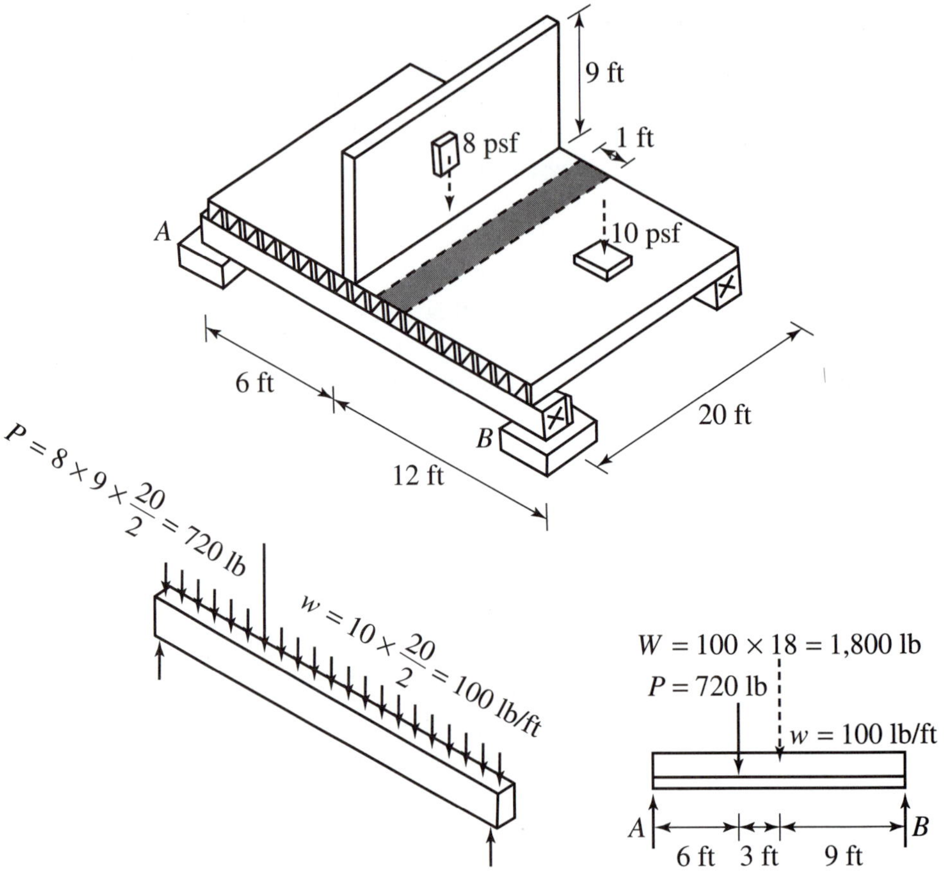

FIGURE 1.11

In addition, beam *AB* supports floor joists (smaller beams) at every foot along its length. Each joist carries its share of the total floor load. This is known as tributary area and shown in the figure as the shaded foot-width strip of floor. Every foot along each of the joists carries half of the floor between itself and its neighbor joists to either side. Since the joists are 1 ft apart, each foot of joist thus carries a tributary floor area of 1 ft $\times$ ($\frac{1}{2} + \frac{1}{2}$) ft = 1 ft^2 of floor. At a unit floor weight of 10 lb/ft^2, we see that the total load carried by a 20-ft-long joist is 1 ft^2 $\times$ 10 lb/ft^2 $\times$ 20 ft = 200 lb. Since the joist is supported at each end, half of this load is delivered to beam *AB*. Beam *AB* supports similar joist loads at every foot along its length, creating a uniformly distributed load of

$$w = \frac{200}{2} = 100 \text{ pounds per linear foot (lb/ft, or plf)}$$

To determine the support reactions at *A* and *B*, we sketch the load diagram for *AB* as shown in the figure. We replace the 18 feet of distributed load by its total force effect positioned at its center of gravity, which is clearly at the middle of the load–9 ft from either end. We could count the joists resting on *AB*, or more simply state that the load per foot times the length of the load gives the total equivalent distributed force

$$W = w \times L = 100 \text{ lb/ft} \times 18 \text{ ft} = 1{,}800 \text{ lb}$$

Exercise Rework the problem with the wall completely removed, but place a live load of 40 psf on the floor, in addition to the given dead load.

Rework this problem assuming that, in addition to the given dead loads, there is a live load on the floor of 40 psf, and the wall height is 12 ft. ■

Finally, we apply the moment and the vertical force equilibrium equations. Summing moments at A,

$$720 \times 6 + 1{,}800 \times 9 - B \times 18 = 0$$

From this $B = 1{,}140$ lb. Summing vertical forces will show that

$$A = 720 + 1{,}800 - 1{,}140 = 1{,}380 \text{ lb}$$

1.9 Distributed Lateral Loads

Figure 1.12 depicts a multistory structure that is subjected to a lateral load induced by the rapid back and forth ground motion of an earthquake. The lateral loads are the result of the huge resting mass of the building resisting the sudden lateral ground movement. This causes a lateral load on the structure that for severe quakes could actually be as great as the weight of the building itself!

FIGURE 1.12

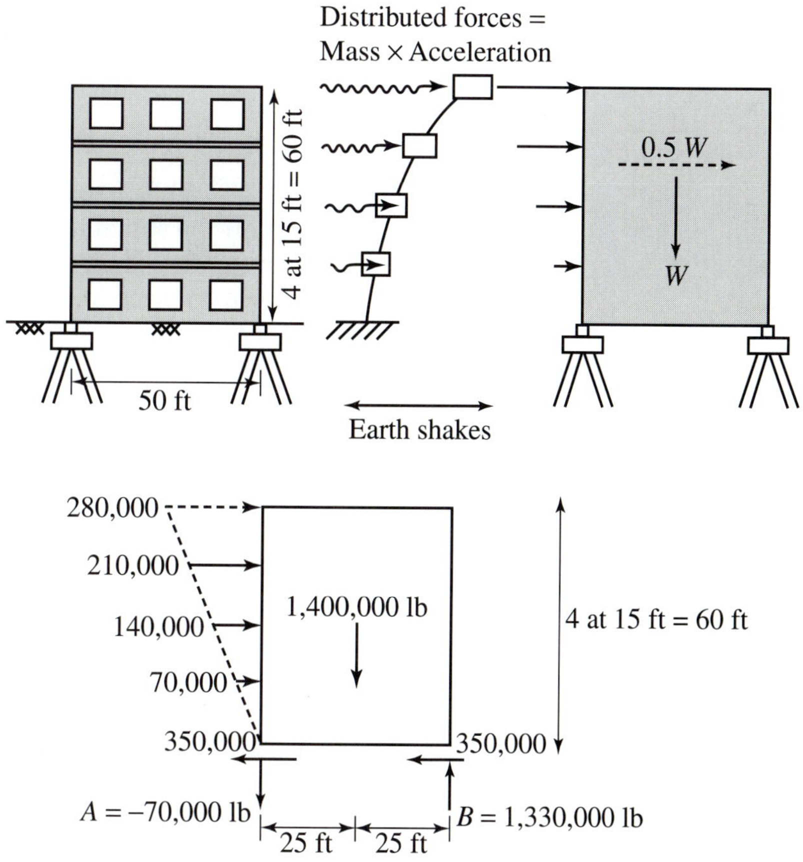

During the ground shaking of the earthquake, the massive building will begin to rapidly sway back and forth with the upper levels experiencing the greatest back and forth movement. When moving first one way and then another, an object must undergo sudden changes in velocity, which is called acceleration, and from physics we know that an accelerating mass is being acted upon by a force.

In the case of a massive building, the to-and-fro acceleration of its mass results in a lateral load that is distributed at the level of the roof and each floor along the height of the building, since this is where concentrated roof and floor masses exist. The higher stories receive greater portions of the total lateral load because they experience the greatest accelerations as the structure sways back and forth.

For this building subjected to a strong earthquake, the total lateral force is expected to equal 50% of the structure's self-weight. The lateral forces at each level of the four-story building are shown in the figure along with the building dimensions and overall weight. We want to know what force is required to keep the building connected to its foundation at point A, and what percentage increase in foundation load occurs at point B as a result of a left to right sway due to the quake.

The load diagram is shown with the reaction at A assumed here to be pulling down on the structure, which has a tendency to tip in the direction of the lateral loads. The building weighs $W = 1{,}400{,}000$ lb with its center of gravity at the center of the building volume. The total lateral load expected from the worst possible quake is $0.5 \times W = 700{,}000$ lb, and it is vertically distributed as shown. The total lateral load is assumed to be equally resisted by the foundations at A and B, and we may determine vertical foundation forces at A and B by summation of moments at B:

$$70{,}000(15) + 140{,}000(30) + 210{,}000(45) + 280{,}000(60) + A(50) - 1{,}400{,}000(25) = 0$$

From this we find $A = -70{,}000$ lb. This indicates that the foundation at A is pushing upwards to support the structure rather than pulling down to prevent overturning, as we had presumed. Thus, even if it were only resting on support A with no vertical tie-down connection to the foundation, the building would not tip over as a result of this quake. Summing vertical forces, we see that

$$B - 1{,}400{,}000 - (-70{,}000) = 0$$

The vertical reaction at B is 1,330,000 lb.

With no lateral loads, both A and B equally share the 1,400,000-lb weight of the building. Therefore, the earthquake increased from $B = 700{,}000$ lb to $B = 1{,}330{,}000$ lb, which is an increase of

$$\left(\frac{1{,}330{,}000}{700{,}000} - 1\right) \times 100\% = 90\%$$

You may be interested to know that lateral loads due to wind can be of the same order of magnitude as moderate earthquake forces, especially for tall structures that are subject to the increasing wind speeds that occur at greater heights. For tall structures, the wind loads are distributed similarly as

Exercise Instead of working with the four individual lateral forces, rework this problem by locating the total lateral load at the c.g. of the four distributed loads.

Rework this problem assuming that the building is six stories tall, and its weight increases proportionately.

Rework the problem if the distance between the supports is reduced from 50 ft to 40 ft. ■

for earthquake forces. For shorter buildings of only a few stories, the wind is usually uniformly distributed along the building height.

1.10 Retaining Wall

A retaining wall, such as that shown in Figure 1.13, establishes and maintains a difference in ground elevations. We will learn later that this type of retaining wall structure composed of a vertical wall stem rigidly attached to a wide horizontal base is called a cantilever wall. In this example where 12 feet of difference in elevation is maintained, the structure is acted upon by lateral earth pressure caused by the tall soil mass behind the vertical wall that resists being unnaturally held at a steep vertical slope. This lateral soil pressure tends to tilt the wall outward from the retained soil. The result is that the portion of the base behind the wall, called the heel, tends to lift up, and the base in front of the wall, called the toe, tends to push down, much like a person's foot in a step forward.

A linear foot slice of the wall is usually considered for analysis. The lateral pressure of the soil on the wall increases with each foot of depth be-

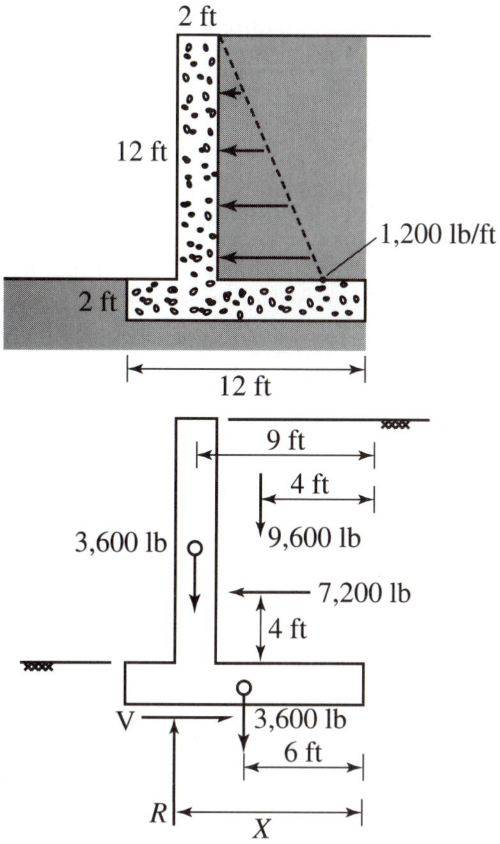

FIGURE 1.13

low the upper ground surface and in this instance reaches a maximum load of 1,200 lb/ft as shown. The total lateral force may be computed as the "area" of the triangularly distributed load:

$$V = \frac{1}{2} \times 12 \text{ ft} \times 1{,}200 \text{ lb/ft} = 7{,}200 \text{ lb}$$

This force is located at the center of gravity of the triangular distributed load which is one-third the distance from the large end of a triangle, or 4 ft above the base. (See if you can verify that as the location of the c.g.) The other loads that act on the structure are the weights of the wall and base, computed to be 3,600 lb each, and the 9,600-lb block of soil behind the wall above the heel that will be pushing down and preventing the heel from lifting.

As for reactive forces, the lateral force, $V = 7{,}200$ lb, must be resisted by an equal and opposite friction force between the base and the soil. All downward forces are resisted by the vertical reaction, R, shown in the figure. The main concern is to locate the position of this vertical reaction. We will see later that this reaction should act within the middle third of the width of the base, or else the heel base will actually be lifting off of the soil, and this increases the likelihood of the retaining structure overturning. Summing forces vertically, we find

$$R = 3{,}600 + 3{,}600 + 9{,}600 = 15{,}800 \text{ lb}$$

We can locate the reaction, R, at a distance, X, from the heel by summing moments about the tip of the heel

$$15{,}800(X) - 9{,}600(4) - 7{,}200(4) - 3{,}600(6) - 3{,}600(9) = 0$$

We see that $X = 7.7$ ft, and to be within the middle third, we see that the value for X could range from 4 ft to 8 ft. Thus the reaction just lies within desirable limits.

Exercise Rework this problem assuming that the stem is 16 ft tall and the lateral soil pressure at the base of the stem is 1,000 lb/ft.

Rework the problem assuming that the toe portion is removed to give an L-shaped structure. ■

2 Structural Components

2.1 Structural Members

There are two primary types of structural members that will concern us in a basic study of structures: two-force members and transversely loaded members. We have already seen examples of both members in the previous chapter. We see in Figure 2.1 that two-force members have only two forces acting on them. The two forces share the same line of action, are equal, and they oppose one another. The two forces are directed along the longitudinal axis (i.e., along the length of a straight member) and are called axial loads.

If the forces are pulling the member at both ends, the member is in tension. Ropes, cables, chains, or other slender elements can support only tension loads–you cannot push with a rope. If the two forces are pushing on the ends, the member is in compression and is called a *column.* To support compression loads, a member must be stocky–it must have a substantial cross-sectional area relative to its length–or else it will tend to buckle. Notice in the figure that tension members react by pulling on the two objects that they connect, while compression members push on the two objects.

We see in the figure that transversely loaded elements support loads that act at some angle to the longitudinal axis of the member. Straight structural members that are transversely loaded are called *beams,* which by far constitute the majority of transversely loaded members. Beams go by many names, such as joist, girder, rafter, and purlin. Beams may support axial forces, and if the axial force is compressive, the element is called a *beam-column.*

Unlike two-force members, there have to be more than two forces on a beam, since the distance between two transverse forces forms a relative lever arm and moment that must be countered by another moment-producing load. Thus we see in the figure that at point *A* of the beam, the clockwise moment of the applied distributed load is countered by a moment due to the reactive force at *B.* Likewise, taking moments at *B,* we see that the counterclockwise moment of the distributed load must be equilibrated by the clockwise moment due to reaction *A,* indicating that there need to be more than just two transverse loads on the beam.

Structures are systems composed of the assemblage of two-force members and/or transversely loaded elements. Members are generally straight, though this is not always the case with members in arches and frame structures. In this chapter we deal with the common structural components: beams, cables, arches, and columns. We also briefly discuss the various types of connections that are used to bring the elements together into a complete load-resisting structural

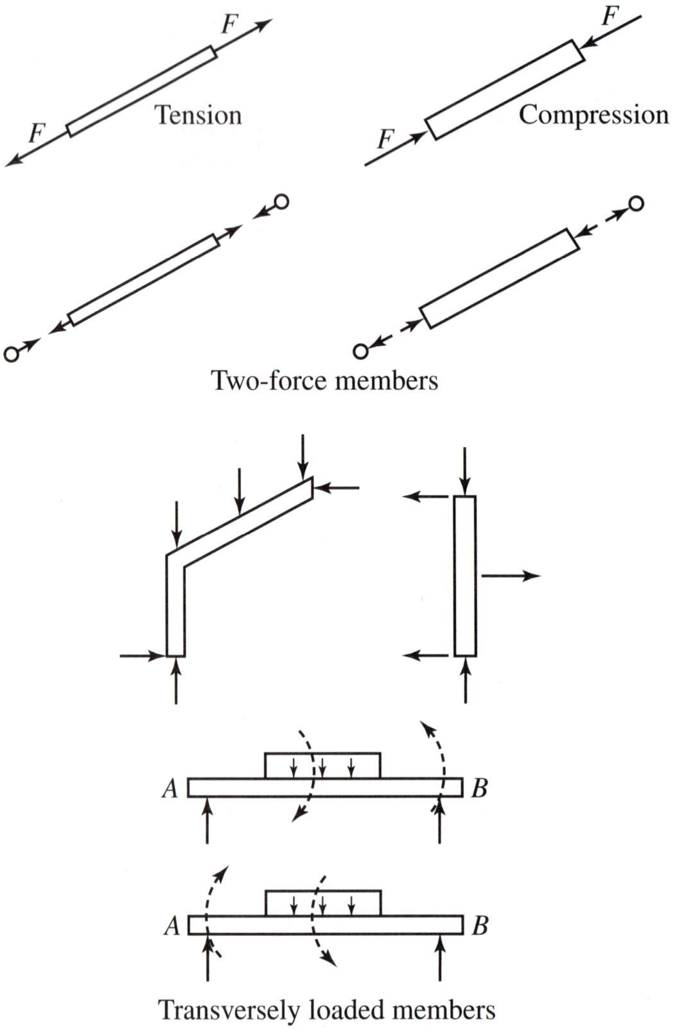

FIGURE 2.1

system. In the next chapter we look at the most common structural assemblages of these elements: truss, frame, and diaphragm structures.

2.2 Beams

Beams support loads over a distance called the span. The behavior of other structural elements and assemblies, such as cables, arches, trusses, frames, and diaphragms, is often explained by first drawing analogies with beams. We have already discussed equilibrium analysis of some simple beams and we will merely elaborate a bit.

What basically distinguishes beams from one another is the placement of loads along the span(s), and the location and type of supports. Figure 2.2 shows several ways that a load of 3,000 lb could be applied to a simple beam. Beam loads can be a concentrated force or forces, or a load distributed over some portion of the beam. The end support reactions happen to each equal 1,500 lb for all the beams shown. Can you verify this? While the active and reactive loads are the same for each beam, the way in which load is distributed

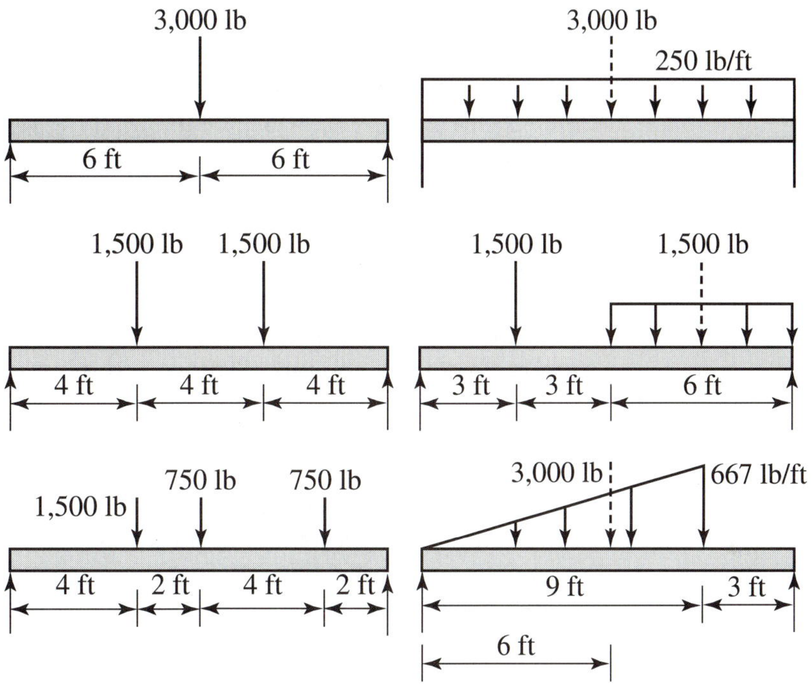

FIGURE 2.2

on a beam affects the intensity of internal forces and the deformation that the beam material will undergo. Generally speaking, concentrated loads are harder on a beam than distributed loads.

Figure 2.3 shows several possible beam support types and arrangements and their associated support reactions. The triangle represents what is called a *pin support.* The pin sets up transverse and longitudinal reaction force components. A pin cannot resist rotation, so there is no reactive moment at a pin. The circle represents a *roller,* which provides a transverse beam reaction, but which cannot provide a reactive force in the longitudinal direction or a moment reaction. The most common structural member is a beam that is pin-supported at one end of its span and roller-supported at the other end. This is called a *simple beam.* The roller allows the beam to expand and contract in response to temperature changes, and thus it is common to see such supports on beams exposed to the elements, such as bridge girders.

The heavy line represents a support that totally restrains the beam called a *fixed end.* The fixed end provides transverse and longitudinal reactive force components as well as a reaction moment. This reaction moment that

FIGURE 2.3

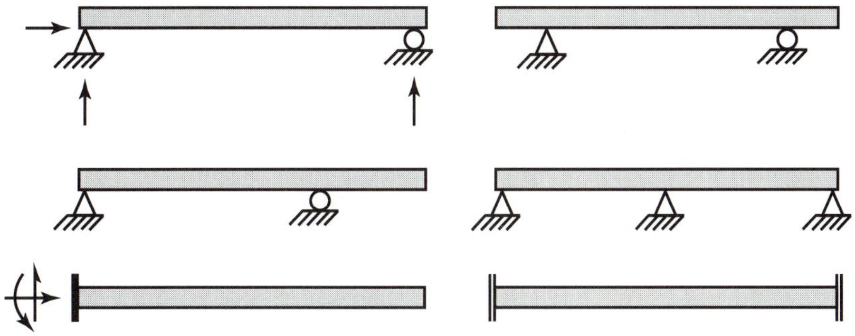

resists rotation is actually a pair of parallel opposing forces, *F*, that are separated by a lever arm, *d*, to form what is called a *moment couple.* The name refers to the moment, $M = F \times d$, created by a pair, or couple, of equal forces as shown in Figure 2.4. A beam supported by a fixed end with the other end free is called a *cantilever beam.* We look at the actual details of pin, roller, and fixed supports when we discuss connections later in the book.

The combinations of beam load and support arrangements are endless. We will investigate only beams with three unknown support reaction forces and/or couples. These are called *determinate beams,* because the three support reactions can be determined by applying the three equilibrium equations. With more than three support reactions, a beam is said to be indeterminate, and the three equilibrium equations are insufficient to solve for all of the reactions.

In Figure 2.3, the two-span beam with three pins is called a continuous beam and has six unknown support reactions. The beam that is fixed at both ends (called fixed-fixed) also has six support reactions. Since there are more than three reactions in these cases, the beams are indeterminate. Such beams require an advanced analysis approach or use of simplifying assumptions, as we see later in the book.

Suppose we analyze the cantilever beam of Figure 2.4. It has a height (depth) of 12 in., spans 6 ft, and carries a 500-lb concentrated load at its end. There are no axial loads applied to the beam, which is usually the case. The sum of the horizontal forces must be zero, and so there is no axial force reaction at the wall. The vertical force reaction at the wall, *V*, must be 500 lb upward to oppose the applied load. If we choose to sum moments at the wall, we see that the force, *V*, creates no moment. The moment couple, $M = F \times d$, must oppose the 500-lb force acting with a 6-ft lever arm, so that $M = 500 \times 6 = 3{,}000$ ft-lb, which is equivalent to $M = 36{,}000$ in-lb.

We see later that the couple lever arm of a beam with a solid rectangular cross section, *d*, is two-thirds the beam height, $h = 12$ in., so

$$d - \frac{2}{3} \times 12 - 8 \text{ in.}$$

FIGURE 2.4

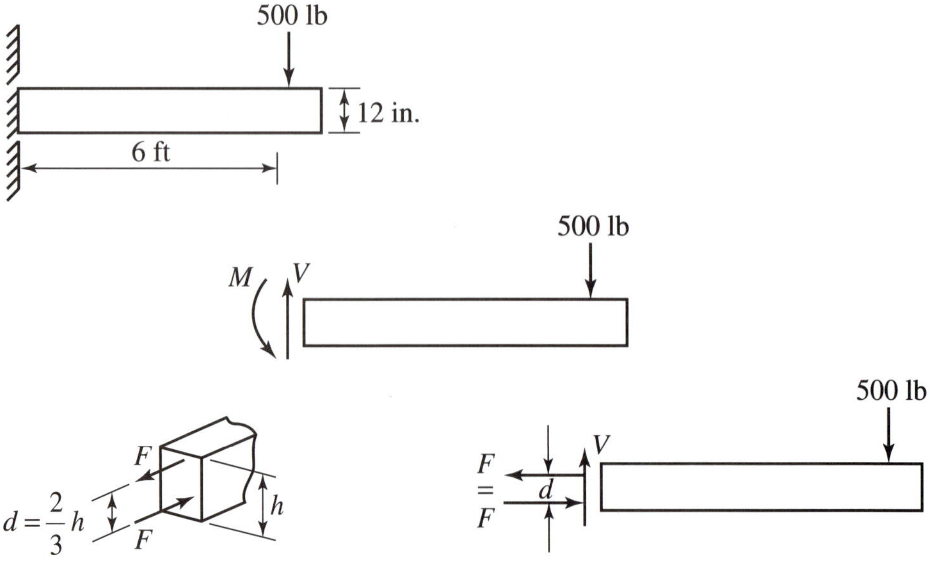

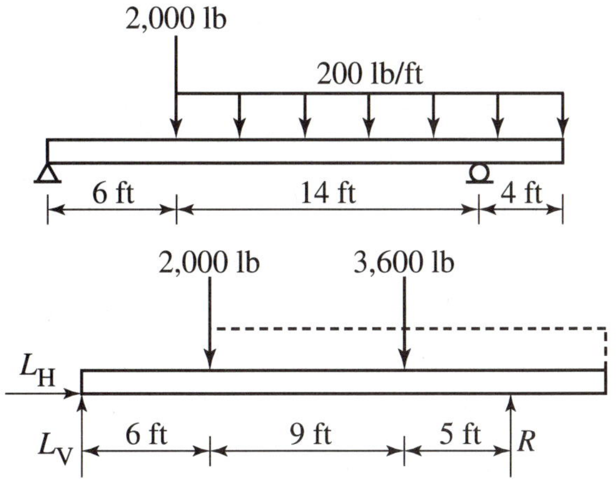

FIGURE 2.5

The two couple forces are both

$$F = \frac{M}{d} = \frac{36{,}000}{8} = 4.500 \text{ lb}$$

Thus, the applied load creates shearing reaction $V = 500$ lb at the wall support and a surprising bending couple force $F = 4{,}500$ lb. If the beam height, h, increases to 24 in., what would the forces of the couple become?

Let's consider another beam as shown in Figure 2.5. The overall length is 24 ft and there is a 4-ft overhang at the right end. The left support, L, is a pin and the right, R, is a roller. A concentrated downward load of 2,000 lb is located 6 ft from the left support, and a uniformly distributed load of 200 lb/ft (plf) begins 6 ft from the left support and extends to the right end of the member.

The beam is redrawn with all actions and reactions represented as concentrated forces. The distributed load is replaced by an equivalent force of 200 lb/ft × 18 ft = 3,600 lb placed in the middle of the uniformly distributed load range, which puts it 15 ft from the left support. Once again, the horizontal reaction component at the left pin, L_H, is zero because there are no horizontal forces acting on this beam. This uses up the horizontal force equilibrium equation. We are thus left with two available equations, enough to solve for the remaining two unknown reactions, L_V and R. The equations of the vertical forces and moments about the left support are, respectively,

$$L_V - 2{,}000 - 3{,}600 + R = 0$$

$$(6)(2{,}000) + (15)(3{,}600) - (20)(R) = 0$$

From this, $L_V = 2{,}300$ lb and $R = 3{,}300$ lb.

What happens when the 4-ft overhang is extended another 10 ft and the 2,000-lb concentrated load is removed?

2.3 Internal Reactions by Method of Sections

We see later in the book that in order to analyze and/or design beams, we need to know what is going on at every point along the member. Once we know support reactions for a beam, we can zoom in on any point along the member and determine internal reactions. If the entire beam is in equilibrium, then so must be any portion of the member. At some section along the beam,

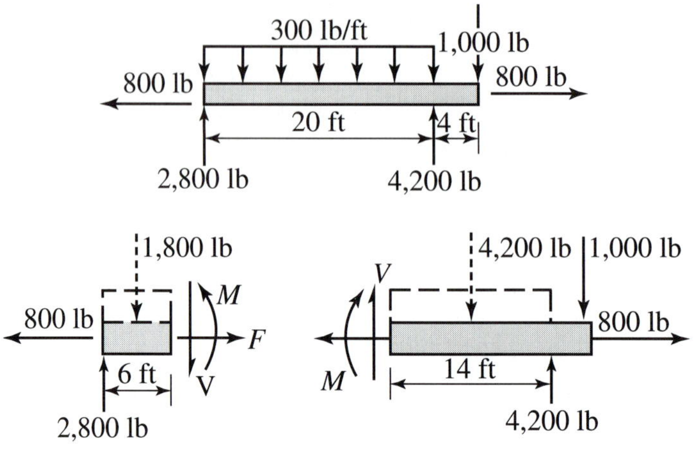

FIGURE 2.6

we may fictitiously cut the member into two parts as in Figure 2.6. The left half is restrained from horizontal, vertical, and rotational movement by the right half, and vice versa.

Cutting a structural member at a section in this fashion to determine the three unknown internal reactions is known as the *method of sections.* Using either the left or right half (left, usually), three equilibrium equations are solved for the three internal reactions. The three internal reactions exposed by cutting the member are the longitudinal force (axial force, F), the transverse force (shear force, V), and the internal couple or bending moment, M.

The three unknown internal reactions, F, V, and M at a section 6 ft from the left support are determined by applying the equilibrium equations for horizontal forces, vertical forces, and moments about the cut section of the left half of the beam as follows:

$$F - 800 = 0: F = +800 \text{ lb}$$

$$2{,}800 - 1{,}800 - V = 0: V = +1{,}000 \text{ lb}$$

$$2{,}800(6) - 1{,}800(3) - M = 0: M = +11{,}400 \text{ ft-lb}$$

The internal reactions are shown acting in a positive manner: axial tension forces are positive; shear that pushes downward on the left half of a cut beam is considered positive; and moment that rotates the left half counterclockwise is likewise positive. If the solution for a reaction is negative, this merely indicates that the reaction acts opposite to the assumed positive direction.

You may wish to practice the method of sections by determining the internal reactions at several points along this beam.

We will be especially concerned with the mutually dependent values of the shear, V, and the bending moment, M, and how they vary along the beam. The axial force, F, is independent of these two reactions, and we treat it separately. We can plot the values of V and M along the beam axis, in which case the two graphs that result are called *shear and moment diagrams.* In Figure 2.7, we see a simple beam, its two applied concentrated forces, and its computed support reactions. The beam is shown being sectioned at six locations and the internal reactions, V and M, are determined from the equations of equilibrium of vertical forces and of moments about the cut section.

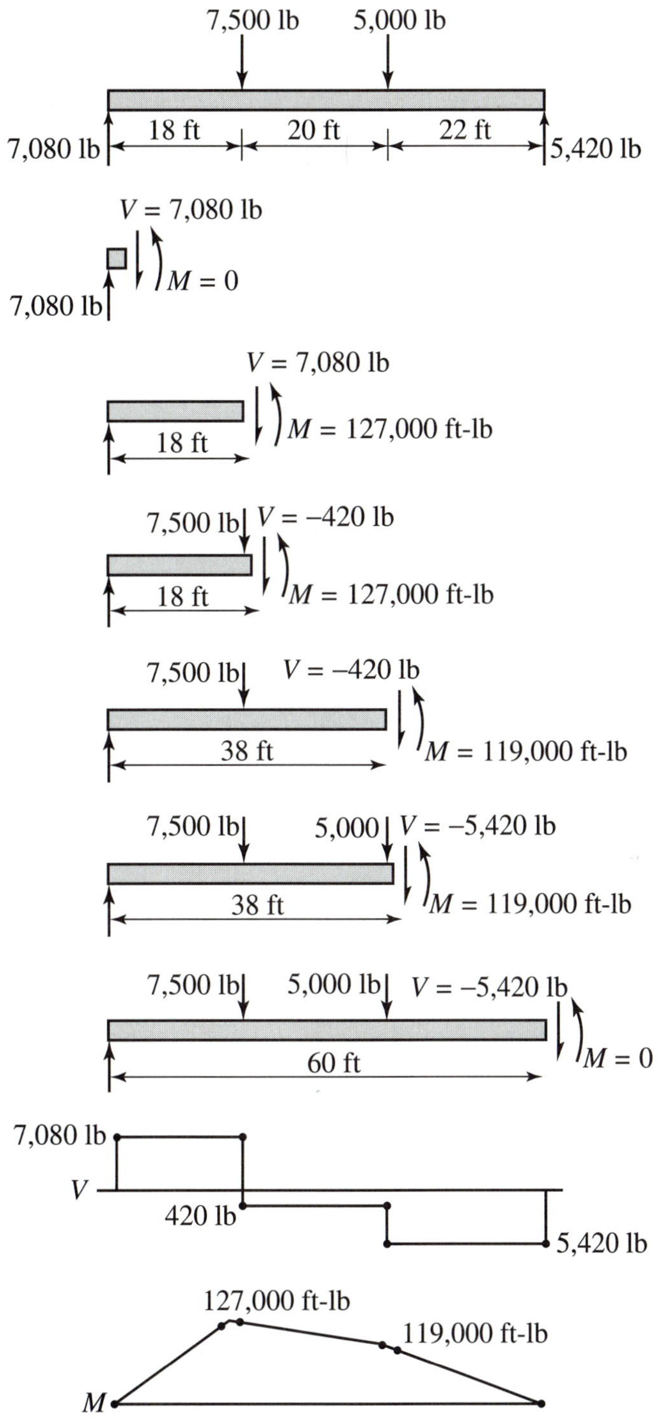

FIGURE 2.7

At the first section cut at a negligible distance from the pin support, we see that $M = 0$ and $V = 7{,}080$ lb. At a section just to the left of the 7,500-lb force, we find no change in V, but

$$M = 7{,}080 \times 18 = 127{,}000 \text{ ft-lb}$$

To the right of the 7,500-lb load, essentially still 18 ft from the pin support, M does not change, since the 7,500-lb force has no moment arm about the moment point, but the shear abruptly changes to

$$V = 7{,}080 - 7{,}500 = -420 \text{ lb}$$

At the section 38 ft from the pin, V is still -420 lb and

$$M = 7{,}080 \times 38 - 7{,}500 \times 20 = 119{,}000 \text{ ft-lb}$$

The other two sections are shown in the figure and you may wish to verify their values for added practice. The computed internal V and M reactions are plotted and the points connected to yield a shear and a moment diagram as shown.

With simple beams, we usually see that shear is highest at the supports, and bending moment is highest at the middle of the beam. Much can (and will be) said about V and M diagrams as we go on.

2.4 Overhead Crane Girder

Not only do the internal reactions, V and M, vary along a beam, but under the effects of a moving load, they will vary at the same section of a beam as the load is repositioned. Consider two side-by-side 60-ft simple span steel girders. Each supports two of the four wheels of a moveable overhead crane, as shown in Figure 2.8. Each acts as one of two rails for the rolling crane that can move from left to right to lift and relocate heavy parts and equipment in an industrial building.

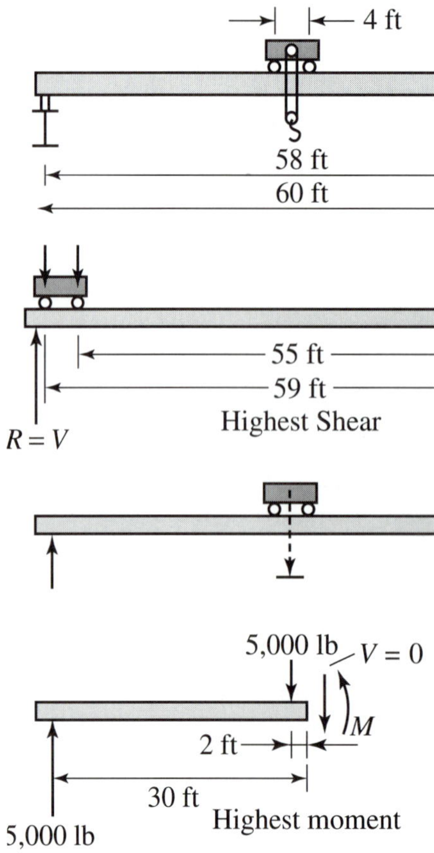

FIGURE 2.8

Exercise Assume that the two 60-ft crane rail girders are 3 ft apart. For the longitudinal girders that span 100 ft out of the page and support the two adjacent crane rail girders, what is the maximum shear and bending moment? ■

Wheels at the ends of these two rail girders rest on 100-ft simple span longitudinal rail girders (the I-shaped supports shown) at both of their ends that allow the crane to also be rolled from front to back of the building (in and out of the page). Thus, an object may be lifted at one corner of the facility, and be set down in the corner diagonally opposite from it.

We will focus on the pair of adjacent 60-ft span crane rail girders. When designing each girder, it is important to know the highest girder shear that the moving crane load could create, as well as the highest bending moment. The crane has a lifting capacity of 10 tons (20,000 lb), with half going to each of the two parallel rail girders. The crane can move only on the inner 58-ft portion of the girder.

The worst shear will occur when the crane is positioned to cause the highest support reaction. The resulting reaction is the shear force in the girder. From the figure, we get the reaction R by summing moments at the right end of the girder:

$$55(5{,}000) + 59(5{,}000) - 60(R) = 0$$

From this $R = V = 9{,}500$ lb. By summing vertical forces we can easily see that the right support reaction would be only 500 lb.

The highest bending moment occurs when the crane is approximately at the center of the girder span as shown. By cutting a section of the beam at midspan, we find the moment M as follows:

$$M + 2(5{,}000) - 30(5{,}000) = 0$$

And we find $M = 140{,}000$ ft-lb.

2.5 Overhanging Deck Beam

The 20-ft-long floor beams for a timber deck shown in Figure 2.9 span 16 ft with an additional 4-ft overhang. We will try our hand at constructing a shear and moment diagram in order to determine what the maximum shear and moment are, as well as where they occur. The deck supports a dead plus live load of 10 psf and 40 psf, respectively, for a total load of 50 psf. The dead load is the weight of the deck boards and the four support beams averaged over the entire floor area. The live load, which is specified in building design codes, represents a nominal estimate of the maximum weight of people and furnishings that might exist on the deck, also averaged over the entire floor area.

Each floor beam carries its share of the load, so the floor load that one beam must support is defined as that area halfway between itself and the adjacent beams. In this case, one of the interior 20-ft beams carries the floor load $6/2 = 3$ ft on both sides, so that it supports a tributary area of $20 \times (3 + 3) = 120$ ft^2 of floor. At 50 psf, the beam supports 6,000 lb, which amounts to a uniformly distributed load, $w = 6{,}000/20 = 300$ plf, as shown. One could arrive at the same figure by saying that each foot of the 20-ft beam

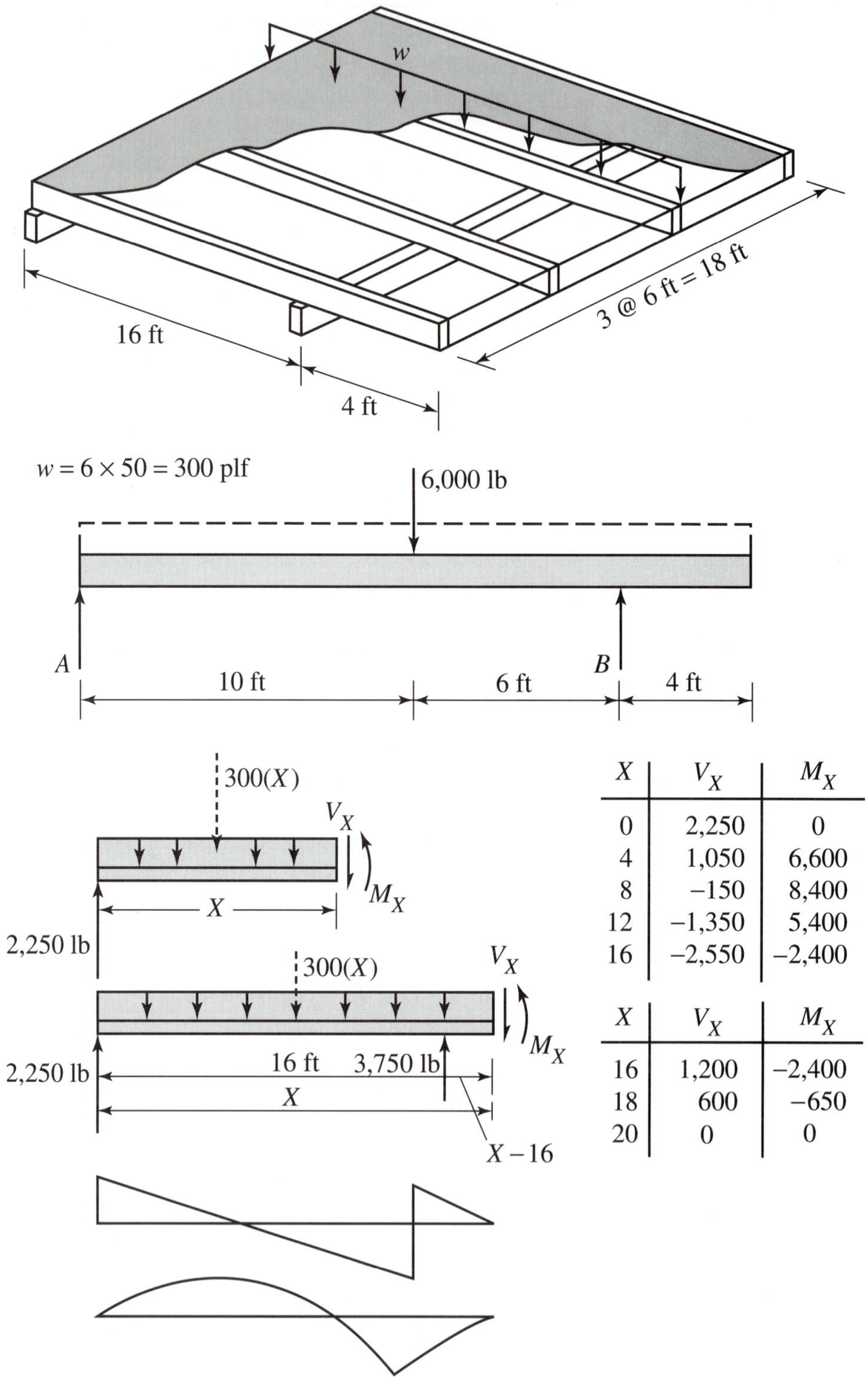

X	V_X	M_X
0	2,250	0
4	1,050	6,600
8	−150	8,400
12	−1,350	5,400
16	−2,550	−2,400

X	V_X	M_X
16	1,200	−2,400
18	600	−650
20	0	0

FIGURE 2.9

picks up $1 \times (3 + 3) = 6\ \text{ft}^2$ of floor, and at 50 psf, each foot of the beam is supporting 300 pounds, or $w = 300$ plf.

Knowing the uniformly distributed load, we may determine the support reactions by first replacing the distributed load with its equivalent concentrated force effect acting at its center of gravity. This 6,000-lb force acts 10 ft from either end of the beam. Next, we can write two equilibrium equations, first summing moments at the right support to get the left reaction, and then we sum vertical forces to get the right support:

$$6(6{,}000) - 16(A) = 0\text{: } A = 2{,}250 \text{ lb}$$

$$2{,}250 - 6{,}000 + B = 0\text{: } B = 3{,}750 \text{ lb}$$

By cutting a beam in two, we can solve for the internal shear and bending moment at any section along the member. In this case of a uniformly loaded beam, we can look at a section with a variable length, X, as shown in the figure. By definition, positive shear acts downward and positive moment rotates counterclockwise on a left section of a beam. The load diagram of the isolated left section is shown in the figure with shear, V_X, and moment, M_X, acting in the positive sense. The subscript X indicates that these two internal reactions vary at each value of length X.

We sum vertical forces on this section and get the following equation for shear at X:

$$V_X = 2{,}250 - 300(X)$$

Likewise, when we sum moments at the cut section, where the force, V_X, creates no moment, we get the following equation for moment at X:

$$M_X = 2{,}250(X) - 300(X)\left(\frac{X}{2}\right) = 2{,}250(X) - 300\left(\frac{X^2}{2}\right)$$

We may substitute different length values for X into both equations, which effectively cuts the beam at each length and solves equilibrium equations for the shear and moment at the section. V_X and M_X for different X values between supports A and B are shown in the table next to the first section of the beam.

For the beam overhang, a second section must be cut between support B and the free end of the beam as shown. The shear and moment equations for this segment of the beam are different than for the stretch between supports A and B because the reaction $B = 3{,}750$ lb is now included on the left section. The result is that a term is added to the previous shear and moment equations that are, respectively,

$$V_X = 2{,}250 - 300(X) + 3{,}750$$

$$M_X = 2{,}250(X) - 300(X)\left(\frac{X}{2}\right) + 3{,}750(X - 16)$$

Values of X are substituted into these relationships and the resulting shears and moments at X are given in a table next to the sketch of the second section.

A graph of all these shears and moments at values of X now gives us a picture of the shear and moment variation along the entire beam. We may observe that peak values of the bending moment occur where the shear changes signs. We see that where $X = 16$ ft, the shear changes sign and the moment has a peak negative value of $M_X = -2{,}400$ ft-lb. A peak positive bending moment occurs where $V_X = 0$. We can use the shear equation associated with this section of beam to solve for the specific value of X as follows:

$$V_X = 0 = 2{,}250 - 300(X)$$

We find that $X = 7.5$ ft. We then get the peak positive moment value by substituting this value of X into the appropriate moment equation as follows:

Exercise Rework this problem assuming that the overhang is (a) 5 ft long, and (b) 0 ft in length. Verify by applying the method of sections at several specific locations.

Don't skip this one! Show that for a simple span beam of length L and with a uniformly distributed load along its full length w, the maximum shear is $V = wL/2$ at the supports and the maximum moment is $M = wL^2/8$ at the midspan. ■

$$M_X = 2{,}250(7.5) - 300\left(\frac{7.5^2}{2}\right) = 8{,}440 \text{ ft-lb}$$

Readers familiar with calculus may recognize that the shear equation is the derivative of the moment equation, and this means that the shear and moment are interdependent with one another. Plotting graphs of shear and moment can be simplified by understanding the mathematical relationships between shear and moment, but the straightforward method of cutting the beam at several sections along the beam is usually sufficient to determine critical V and M values. As we progress through the book, we will mainly deal with simple span beams for which maximum shear exists at a support and maximum moment at the midspan.

2.6 Cables

A very efficient means of spanning distances with loads is the cable structure. For instance, Figure 2.10 depicts the Golden Gate Bridge in San Francisco for which just two large cables support a six-lane highway that weighs 10 tons per foot along the center 4,200-ft span between the two support towers. The cables sag down 470 ft from the tower peaks. What is the tension in each of the cables? Maybe we should cover a few more things before you answer this question.

FIGURE 2.10

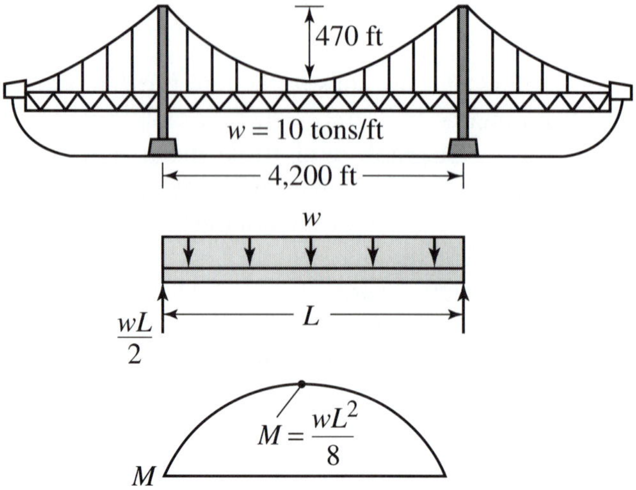

Every portion of a cable structure is in axial tension. Because of their inherent lightness, these tension structures are often too flexible to meet structural needs unless they are used in tandem with another stiffening structural system (such as the deck truss in the case of the Golden Gate Bridge). Also, because cables only resist tension, they cannot be used in cases where applied loads could change and require the member to resist with compression or bending.

For a particular cable length and placement of loads, a simple flexible cable must take on a unique shape in order to support the loads in equilibrium. Change the relative magnitude and/or placement of the loads and the cable must assume a new shape. It can be shown that the sag at any point of a simple loaded cable is proportional to the internal bending moment along the length of a simple beam with the same horizontal span and load placement. With this analogy, we can determine the geometry of the cable structure. Observe the similarity between the cable sag of the bridge and the simple beam moment diagram in Figure 2.10, and between the moment diagram of Figure 2.7 and the sag geometry of the cable structure of Figure 2.11.

Figure 2.11 shows a simple cable that supports two traffic signal lights that weigh 75 lb and 50 lb. The cable has a horizontal span of 60 ft. In cable structures, we must know at least one of the sag distances and we can determine the others. Since the two loads are proportional to those of the beam of Figure 2.7 and have the same horizontal spacing as the beam loads, we can determine the unknown sag indicated as s in the figure:

$$\frac{4\text{ ft}}{127{,}000\text{ ft-lb}} = \frac{s}{119{,}000\text{ ft-lb}}$$

From this, $s = 3.74$ ft. We now have the geometry of the cable using the beam analogy.

As shown, each of the three segments of the cable structure is a two-force tension member with values T_1, T_2, and T_3. From the given dimensions, the inclination angles of the three segments are

FIGURE 2.11

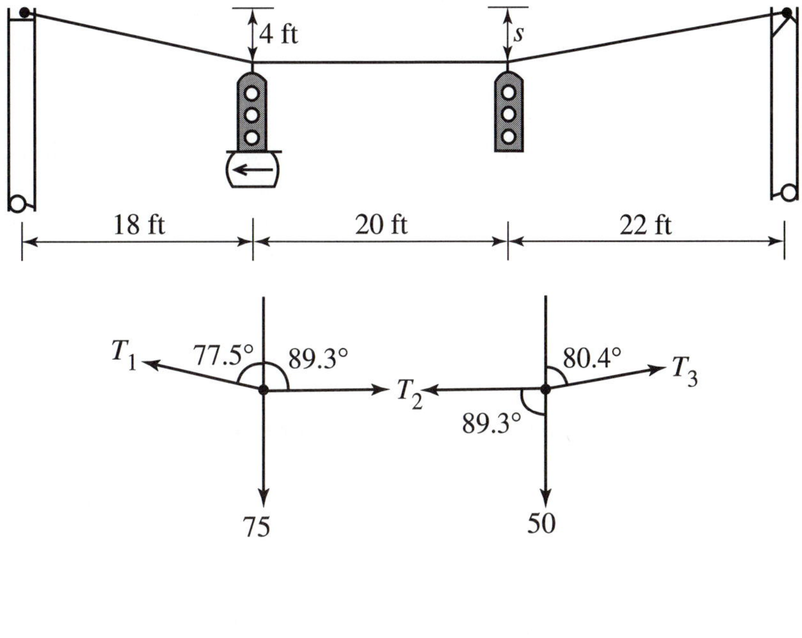

$$z_1 = \text{arc tan}\left(\frac{18}{4}\right) = 77.5°$$

$$z_2 = \text{arc tan}\left(\frac{20}{4 - 3.74}\right) = 89.3°$$

$$z_3 = \text{arc tan}\left(\frac{22}{3.74}\right) = 80.4°$$

At each point of load application, there are three concurrent forces: the applied load, the tension load in the left cable segment, and the tension in the right segment. To ensure equilibrium of concurrent forces, we write two force equilibrium equations, which lets us solve for the left and right cable tensions. For the concurrent force system that includes the 75-lb signal head, the vertical and horizontal force equilibrium equations are, respectively,

$$\cos(77.5°) \times T_1 + \cos(89.3°) \times T_2 = 75$$

$$\sin(77.5°) \times T_1 = \sin(89.3°) \times T_2$$

From these we get $T_1 = 328$ lb and $T_2 = 321$ lb. For the 50-lb force group, we need to write only one equation, since we need to know only T_3. The horizontal components must be equal, so we have

$$\sin(80.4°) \times T_3 = \sin(89.3°) \times 321$$

From this we get $T_3 = 326$ lb.

2.7 Rope Suspension Bridge

When a nearby bridge is undermined from flash flood waters, a U.S. Peace Corps Volunteer devises a suspension bridge to temporarily allow for pedestrians to cross a ravine during the remainder of the rainy season. Figure 2.12 shows the bridge that consists of a 5-ft-wide deck fashioned from small wood logs and suspended from two ropes tied to large trees at the ends of the bridge. There is enough rope to allow for an estimated effective 5-ft sag of the middle relative to the ends, as shown. The thick nylon rope is rated to take a tension force of 10,000 lb before snapping in two. The designer needs to know what safety factor exists against a rope failure.

The designer figures that the deck timber weighs about 10 lb/ft^2, which creates a uniform dead load of 50 lb/ft along the span. The designer thinks it is possible that as many as 40 people might be on the bridge at one time. With an estimated weight of 150 lb per person, a uniform live load of 150 lb/ft would be created on the 40-ft span. With the total load estimated at 50 + 150 = 200 plf, and assuming that the suspension hanger ropes, *A*, *B*, and *C*, each carry their 10-ft share of the load along the deck length, we see that the two ropes together carry three equal concentrated loads of 2,000 lb. Note that the 5-ft portion of deck load at the ends goes directly to the ground.

To get the highest tension in the rope, which occurs at the end segments, *AD* and *CE*, we need to know the sag distance *s*, so we can determine

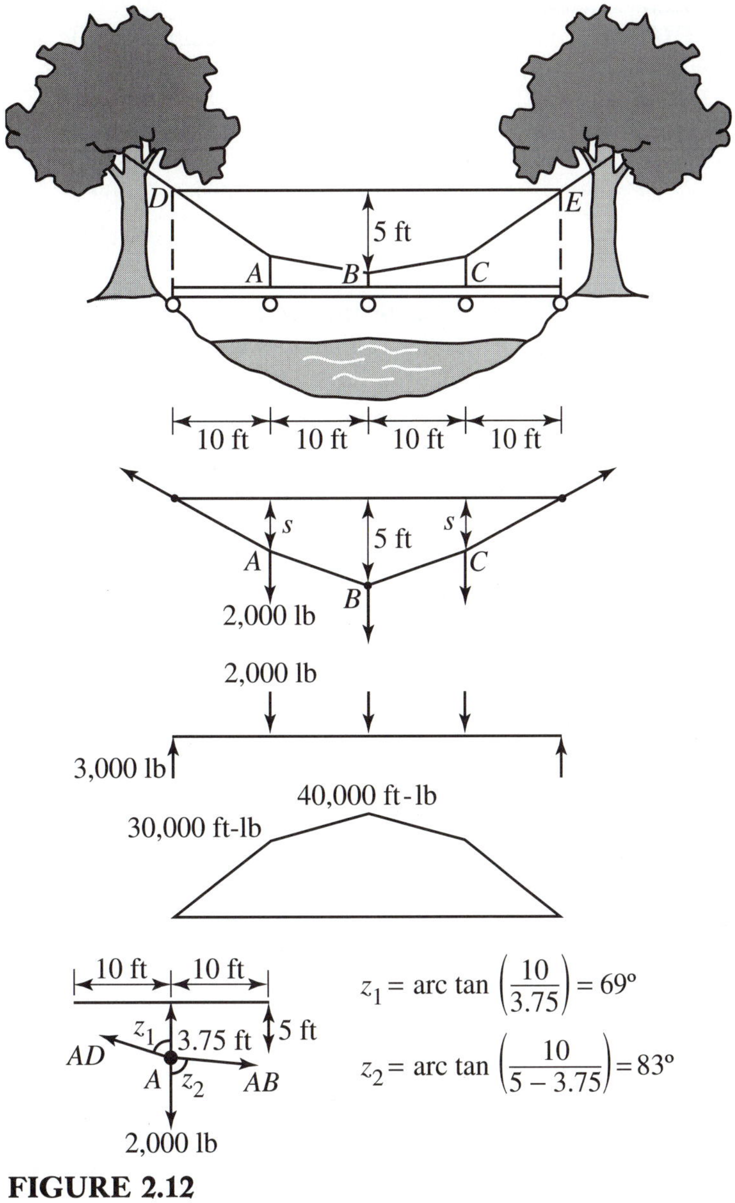

FIGURE 2.12

the angles of the rope segments, *AE* and *AB*, shown in the figure as z_1 and z_2, respectively. Making an analogy to a simple 40-ft span beam with three 2,000-lb loads, we see that the associated moment diagram is as shown. Proportions then obtain the sag distance

$$\frac{s}{30{,}000} = \frac{5}{40{,}000}$$

From this, $s = 3.75$ft, and the rope geometry is determined.

The concurrent force system at hanger *A* is shown with the unknown rope segment forces, *AD* and *AB* and angles $z_1 = 69°$ and $z_2 = 83°$ computed from the known geometry. We write the vertical and horizontal force equilibrium equations, respectively, for point *A* as follows.

Exercise What is the factor of safety against rope failure if the center sag is 12 ft instead of 5 ft? Would you walk across this bridge? ■

$$AD \times \cos(69°) - 2{,}000 - AB \times \cos(83°) = 0$$
$$AD \times \sin(69°) - AB \times \sin(83°) = 0$$

The solution of these equations gives us the maximum tension in the rope, $AD = 8{,}200$ lb. Since we have been looking at the total bridge load, this is the force carried by both ropes, so each rope only carries $8{,}200/2 = 4{,}100$ lb. The safety factor against rope failure would then be

$$\text{Factor of Safety} = \frac{10{,}000}{4{,}100} = 2.4$$

2.8 Arches

A very convenient and interesting observation of cable structures is that when they are inverted, their shape forms the ideal shape for an arch that has similar loads and load placements over the same horizontal span. This ideal arch structure must be pin-supported at its two ends like the corresponding simple beam and is referred to as a two-hinged arch. For an ideally shaped arch, every segment of the arch is in pure compression, just the inverse of the cable structure where every segment is pure tension.

So there is an elegant similarity between the inverted shape of the cables of a suspension bridge with the shape of an arch bridge, and both the cable and arch shapes are analogous to the moment diagram of a beam with similar load and span as shown in Figure 2.13. The analysis of an ideal arch is thus the same as for a cable structure. The beam analogy of arches and cables

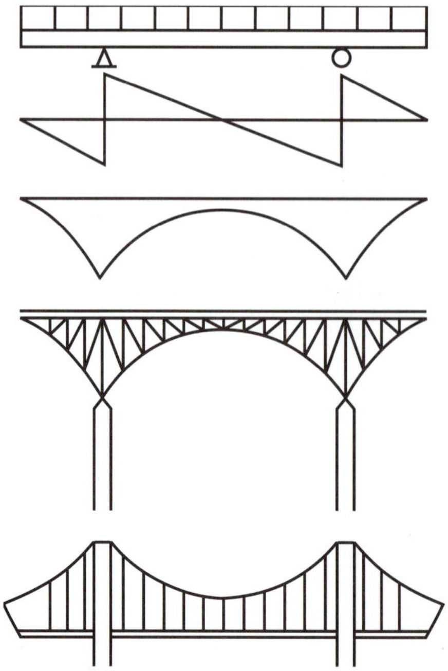

FIGURE 2.13

tells us that the shape of these structural elements should conform to the moment diagram of a similarly loaded beam.

In Figure 2.14 we see a beam, a cable, and an arch along with a free body diagram of their half-sections. We let s denote the maximum sag of a uniformly loaded cable or the rise of a uniformly loaded arch. For all three elements, the vertical reaction components are $V = wL/2$.

Unlike the beam, the arch and cable must have horizontal reaction components to maintain equilibrium. Equilibrium of the half-sections of the members indicates that the horizontal reaction components must be constant throughout the member length. We see that for a simple beam, $H = 0$, and the maximum moment is $M = wL^2/8$. For cables and ideal arches, $M = 0$ and $H = wL^2/(8s)$, which is the ratio of the simple beam moment to the sag or rise, s. For cables, this force is the horizontal component of the tension in the cable at any point, and it is the horizontal component of the compression (thrust) at every point of the ideal arch. The expression, $H = wL^2/8s$, may be

FIGURE 2.14

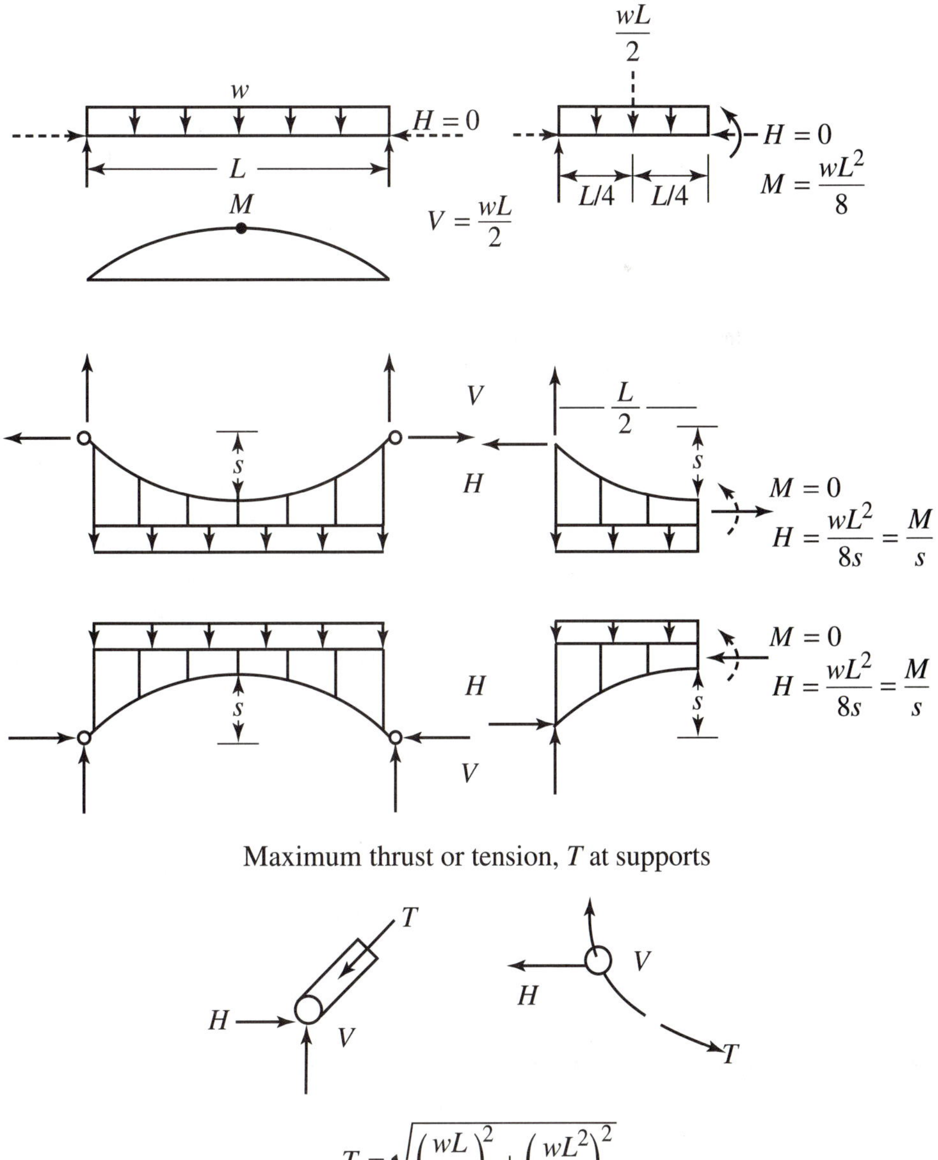

$$T = \sqrt{\left(\frac{wL}{2}\right)^2 + \left(\frac{wL^2}{8s}\right)^2}$$

used to approximate the horizontal thrust of three hinged arches, as we will see when we look at frames.

Finishing our discussion of arches, we have said that if the loads on a cable are changed, the shape of the cable must change; however, if the loads on the arch change, the shape will not be able to change. This is because to keep from buckling, compression members must be stiff and stocky with substantial cross sections that resist shape changes. When the ideal arch loads change, the arch is no longer in pure axial compression, it is also subjected to internal shear and bending reactions. In this case, the arch is analyzed as a frame structure.

Remember the question about the maximum tension in the cables of the Golden Gate Bridge at the beginning of Section 2.6? From the figure we have that

$$T = \sqrt{\left(\frac{wL}{2}\right)^2 + \left(\frac{wL^2}{8s}\right)^2}$$

For the maximum tension in one of the centerspan cables, which carries half of the 10-ton/ft distributed load over a 4,200-ft span with a sag of 470 ft, we have

$$T = \sqrt{\left(\frac{5 \times 4{,}200}{2}\right)^2 + \left(5 \times \frac{4{,}200^2}{8 \times 470}\right)^2} = 25{,}700 \text{ tons}$$

2.9 Columns

Before leaving this chapter on structural members, it may be of interest to some readers to note another member type that can be studied using beam analysis–columns. Remember that a column is a two-force member in compression that must be stocky (and stiff) or it will buckle when loaded by a large compressive force.

In Figure 2.14 we see how the simple beam moment to the arch rise/cable sag ratio, M/s, is used to determine the force, H, which acts along the axis between the supports of arch and cable members. We will see later in the book that for a beam of length, L, and stiffness, EI, the ratio of simple beam moment, M, to corresponding deflection, D (deflection is the slight amount of sag caused by transverse load), is a constant given by

$$\frac{M}{D} = \frac{10EI}{L^2}$$

We will also discover later that the critical buckling load, which is the largest axial force that a straight column can support without failing by buckling, is given as $F_{CR} = 10EI/L^2$, the same as the ratio of M/D of a beam. Thus, all the common structural elements, beams, cables, arches, and columns, may be studied by means of beam analysis. Don't be surprised if the same isn't true of entire structural assemblies.

2.10 Connections

For a structural system to be functional, load paths (which we discuss in the following chapter) must be created throughout the structural elements via connections that are able to transfer loads from one to another. In discussing types of beam supports earlier, we described three primary types of support connections–rollers, pins, and fixed–and we noted that the support types and locations defined the way that beams were classified–simple, cantilever, continuous, and so on. The same may also be said for more complex structural systems. To a large extent, we classify and model structural behavior based on the connections used and whether the structural assemblies are connected to allow for temperature expansion between elements, to transfer only forces between members, and/or to allow for the transfer of both forces and bending moments.

There are as many ways to make connections among structural elements as there are people to think up the details. A few illustrations of typical connections are presented in Figure 2.15. A roller connection, which is generally used only at the structure supports, provides only restraint against motion in a single direction, usually perpendicular to the member that is supported. A bearing pad used between a beam and its support, especially common for bridge girders, is a common form of a roller support. The rubberlike pad prevents vertical movement of the girder end, but offers little resistance to horizontal girder movement and thereby allows for temperature expansion and contraction.

A pin connection, also called a hinge or a simple connection, prevents joined members from any relative horizontal or vertical movement, thus two unknown restraint force components are present. A pin connection is most notable for the lack of rotational restraint that it provides, that is, members connected by pins are free to rotate relative to one another and so no moment is transferred through the connection, only a force represented by its horizontal and vertical components. Pin connections are typically fabricated with nails or bolts. Even when a group of large steel bolts are used to form a somewhat rigid looking joint, the bolt placement and the fact that the bolt holes are slightly larger than the bolts creates enough slack in the joint to prevent the transfer of moment between the connected elements.

FIGURE 2.15

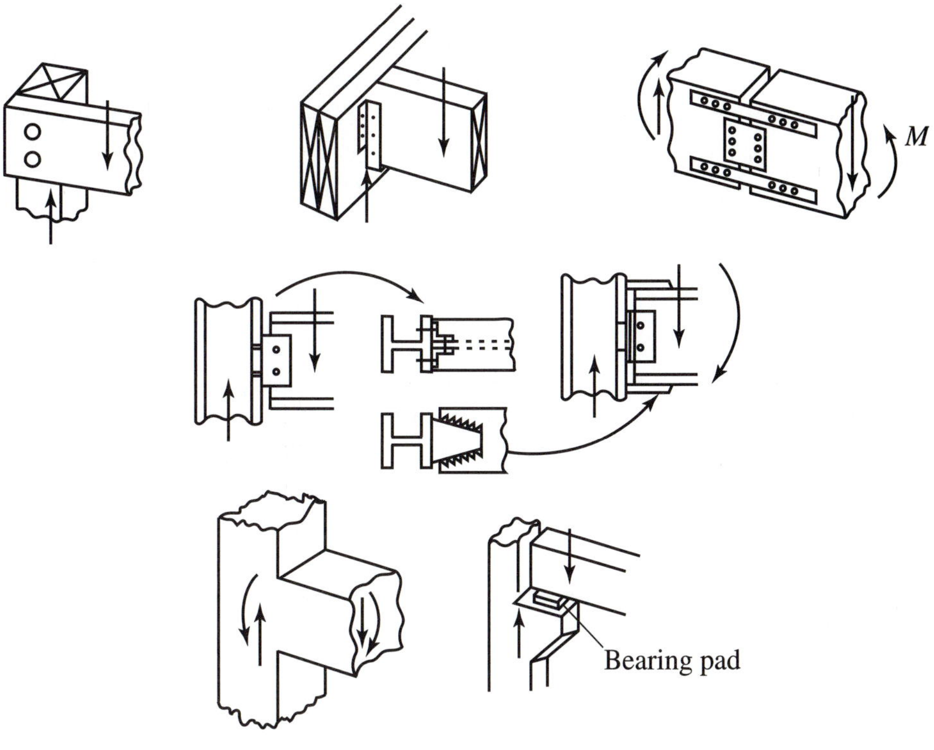

The fixed, or rigid, connection is assumed to be a complete fusion of the connected elements. The connected members are completely locked together and no relative movement is possible–no relative horizontal movement, no relative vertical movement, and no relative rotation. There are thus three unknown reactions between any two members so joined: a horizontal force component, a vertical force component, and a moment couple.

In any given structure, the member material type–wood, steel, and/or concrete–play a decisive role in the type of connections that are used. Most timber structures use pin connections; cast-in-place reinforced concrete structural connections tend to all be fixed, while steel and precast concrete structures use connections that are evenly divided between simple pins or rigid moment resisting types. Rigid joints are rare in timber construction, and usually require use of steel plates. Rigid steel connections can appear sleek or bulky, depending on whether numerous bolts or, more suitably, lines of welds are the dominant connector. Rigid joints in reinforced concrete are very common and are a natural for this construction material. Steel reinforcing is placed in formwork and then concrete is poured to form a monolithic structural joint between structural members that is very rigid. The steel carries any tension and the concrete resists any compression that occurs at the joint.

Generally, when loads are transferred from horizontal beams to vertical columns in structures, using rigid connections instead of simple connections will result in material savings as smaller beams and slightly larger columns are required. The disadvantage is in the extra time and cost to construct rigid connections. Soil conditions play a big role in determining what system is appropriate, as we will see later in the book.

The analysis of structural connections is very complex. We will investigate forces (and stresses) associated with bolts and welds later in the book. While standard connection details are available, unique structural designs often necessitate unusual connections that will require considerable analysis effort. Insufficient care taken with connection details has led to many unfortunate failures. It is essential that all professionals involved–design architect, structural engineer, structural fabricator, construction manager, and building inspector–be in agreement as to who is responsible to develop the connection details and to approve any changes that are required.

3 STRUCTURAL ASSEMBLIES

3.1 DESIGN LOADS

We have briefly discussed structural loads and tributary areas in previous sections. Now we go into more detail to gain a better feel for how structural assemblages do their jobs of resisting loads. We have seen that structural loads may generally be grouped as vertical dead and live load forces due to gravity as well as lateral wind and earthquake forces.

We begin with the most accurately determined of structural loads, dead loads, which are simply the weight of the materials that compose the structure. Whether designing a new structure, or analyzing an existing one, we can accurately determine the dead weight that any component of the structure supports. It is merely a matter of knowing unit weights of materials, and how many units are involved.

Suppose a steel beam spans 30 ft and supports 500 ft^2 of 6-in.-thick concrete floor slab, we can determine that every square foot of floor occupies a volume of $1 \text{ ft} \times 1 \text{ ft} \times \frac{6}{12} \text{ ft} = \frac{1}{2} \text{ ft}^3$ of concrete. Since the unit weight of concrete is 150 lb/ft^3, we figure that the steel floor beam supports a slab dead load:

$$W = 150 \text{ lb/ft}^3 \times \frac{1}{2} \text{ ft}^3/\text{ft}^2 \times 500 \text{ ft}^2 = 37{,}500 \text{ lb}$$

If this load is uniformly distributed along the beam length, it creates a linear load, w:

$$w = 37{,}500 \text{ lb} \div 30 \text{ ft} = 1{,}250 \text{ lb/ft(plf)}$$

In addition to the slab weight, the steel beam must support itself. Suppose that the beam has a cross-sectional area of 20 in^2. A linear foot of this beam occupies a volume, V:

$$V = \frac{1 \text{ ft} \times 20 \text{ in}^2}{(12 \text{ in/ft})^2} = 0.14 \text{ ft}^3$$

Since the unit weight of steel is 500 lb/ft^3, the linear steel beam weight is w:

$$w = 500 \text{ lb/ft}^3 \times 0.14 \text{ ft}^3 = 70 \text{ plf}$$

The total weight of the 30-ft-long beam would simply be $30 \text{ ft} \times 70 \text{ plf} = 2{,}100$ lb.

We may always compute structural dead load as the product of material unit weight times the units of material supported, as we have just shown.

However, common building wall, roof, and floor elements are composed of several materials, such as interior plasterboard on wood stud walls, concrete on steel deck floors, asphalt shingles on plywood decking on wood rafters with fiberglass insulation, and so on. For these cases, it is more convenient to simply state the dead weight per square foot of various building elements.

For example, typical residential wood floors and roofs weigh 10 psf, and walls weigh about 5 psf. The weight of steel floor and roof systems common to commercial structures varies quite a bit, with typical values ranging from 30 to 50 psf. For concrete structures, the material unit weight times volume procedure is normally used to compute dead loads of all elements.

Vertical live loads are the weight of anything that is not a fixed-in-place part of the structure. Examples of structure vertical live loads are people, furniture, forklifts, cars, trucks, pounding rain, snow, and movable equipment. Because of the uncertainty of the live load that exists on a building or a bridge at any given time, it is necessary to design structures for live load levels–called *design live loads*–that will reasonably match the level of the worst probable loading that could be expected. Thus, we do not design the living room floor of a residence for the same occurrence of people as we would for the hallway forming the fire escape route of a large office building. Likewise, we do not design every roadway lane of a bridge for a bumper-to-bumper string of the heaviest truck that exists.

Structural designers usually refer to building codes that establish reasonable design live load levels based on the typical load capacity provided by structures that have withstood the test of time. Suppose the structural analysis of numerous older parking garages indicates that those structures that have performed well over time can support a uniform floor live load of 100 psf without overstressing the building material or exhibiting excessive deformations. If structures researchers perform load tests to failure on several such structures, and results indicate that these structures have a reasonable factor of safety against failure, then 100 psf would appear to be a proven and realistic nominal design live load for parking garages.

Similarly, if calculations for the typical spacing and spans of floor joists for houses used for the last 100 years indicate that the floors can support 40 psf without excessive movement or overstressing of the timber members, then building codes will reflect this when establishing a design live load. Thus, experience over time has led to standard construction practice for various types of building and bridge structures, and the inherent safe load capacity of these structures has evolved into building code provisions for design live loads.

It is impossible to design for the exact live loads that exist on a structure. We cannot know the exact amount of snow that will fall on the roof of a building, or exactly how many and at what location people and pieces of furniture will occupy a floor area, or the exact axle loads of trucks and cars on a bridge. For this reason, design live loads are usually nominal values expressed as distributed load per square foot, or load per linear foot. These nominal loads mimic the load effect of the actual live loads that most probably can be anticipated in specific structural cases. Nominal design live loads reported in building codes, and used in example problems throughout this text, indicate that the intensity of nominal design live loads varies depending on such things as regional climate, building type and usage, bridge span length, and bridge location.

In addition to vertical gravity loads, structures must also withstand the natural effects of wind and earthquakes that create lateral forces. Structures

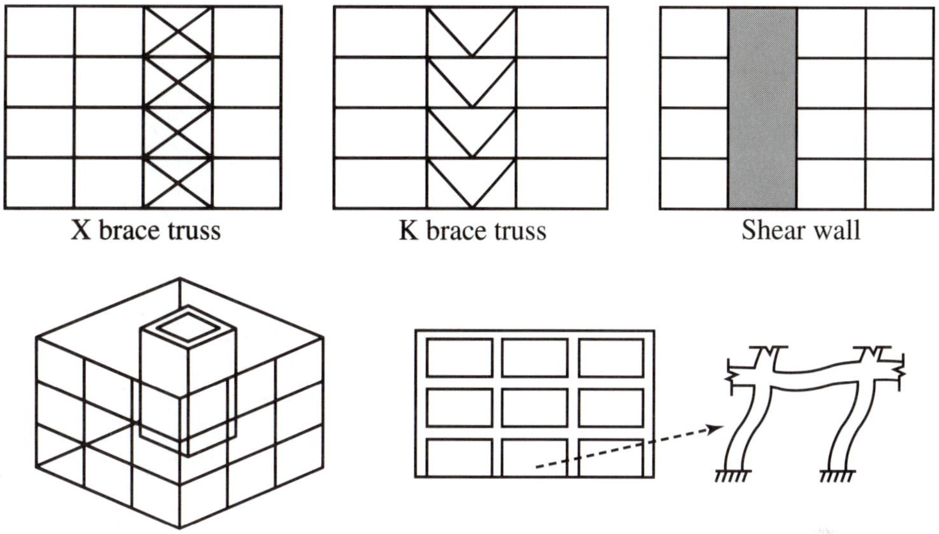

FIGURE 3.1

must be braced against these lateral loads. As we will later see in design examples, and as exemplified in Figure 3.1, shearwalls, elevator core shafts, vertical trusses formed by X or K bracing, or moment resisting frames are the commonly used systems to brace structures against lateral collapse.

Wind and earthquake forces are highly variable and their actions on structures are so complex that we must employ simplifying models to examine how these natural forces affect structures. For instance, when a structure is in the path of a fast-moving stream of air (wind), the air must flow around the obstruction (structure) with the effect that inward and outward pressures are established. The forces acting on structures due to wind are computed as the nominal design pressures multiplied by the surface areas over which they exist. The direct pressure on a windward wall is

$$q = 0.003(V)^2$$

where q is lb/ft^2 and V is wind speed in miles per hour.

Figure 3.2 shows the design pressures that model the effect of a 100-mile-per-hour wind acting on structures with different geometric configurations. Notice in the figure that the majority of the structure is subject to outward suction pressures. In the case of relatively flat roofs, suction pressures can generate forces that overcome the weight of the roof and actually lift it from the building. The lateral load that the structural system must resist is the sum of the lateral forces created on the windward and leeward walls. The wall and roof elements themselves, such as window panes, curtain wall connections, and roof tie-down connections must all be designed for inward and outward pressure effects.

Earthquakes create extremely variable load effects on structures depending on such factors as foundation conditions, height of structure, structural framing systems (shearwall, trussed, or moment resisting frame), density of the mass of the structural material (wood, steel, or concrete), and proximity of the structure to the quake epicenter. The rapid lateral ground-shaking motion of an earthquake soon forces the huge mass of any structure to begin a side-to-side swaying movement that generally increases with the duration of

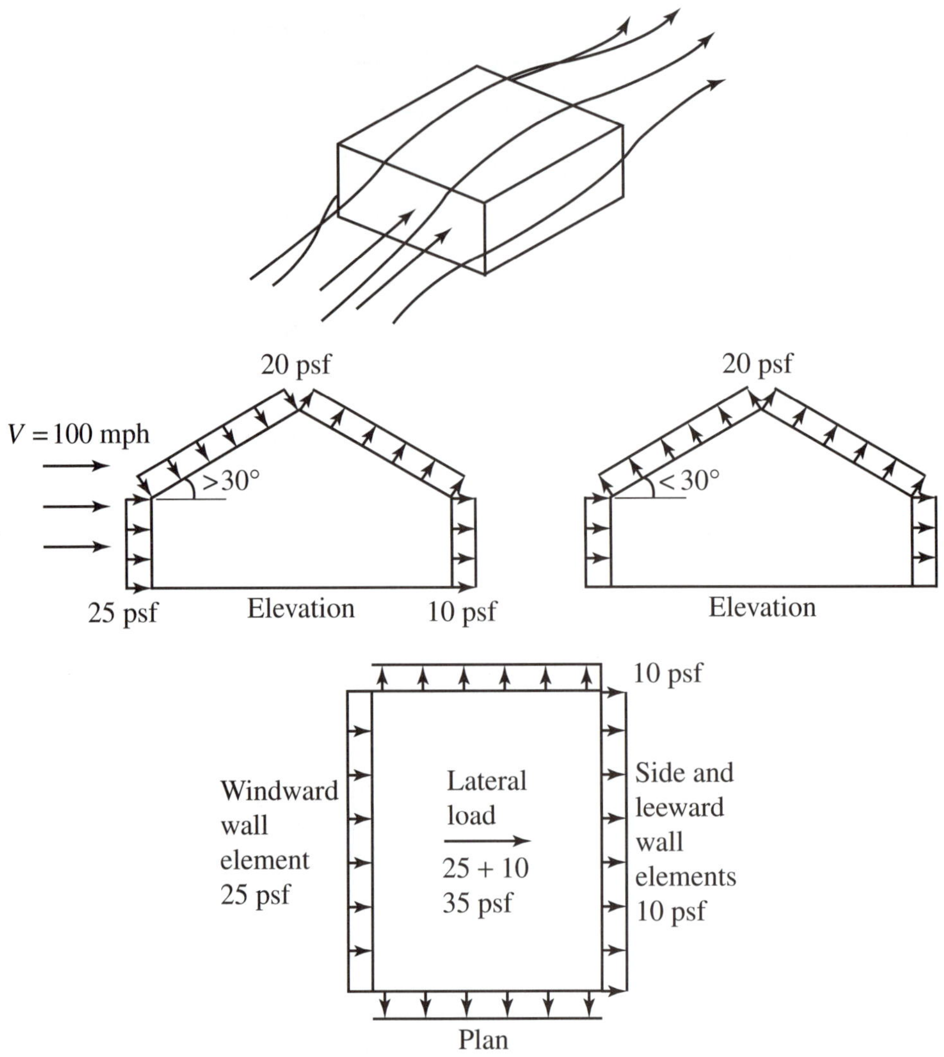

FIGURE 3.2

the earthquake, which may last over a minute. Any massive object that rapidly moves first one way and then another must be undergoing rapid acceleration and deceleration in the process.

From physics, we know that Newton's second law of motion states that an accelerating mass equals a force–in our case, the force is a lateral earthquake load on the structure. The lateral forces on a structure caused by earthquakes are expressed as a fraction of the vertical structural weight, and this fraction may be as high as $\frac{1}{2}$ to 1 for the most severe situations possible. Thus, a structure may experience a large fraction of its own weight as a lateral load!

For analysis and design, the magnitude and distribution of lateral earthquake loads are similar to the lateral loads imposed by hurricane force winds, and so similar lateral bracing systems are required in both cases. These lateral forces increase with the structure height, and as shown in Figure 3.3, these forces are usually assumed to act at the level of each floor and at the roof level. For wind loads, the total force at each floor level is the sum of windward and leeward design wind pressures times the tributary projected area of each floor. For earthquake forces, the loads model the design earthquake acceleration at each level times the mass of the floor or roof and the walls at that level.

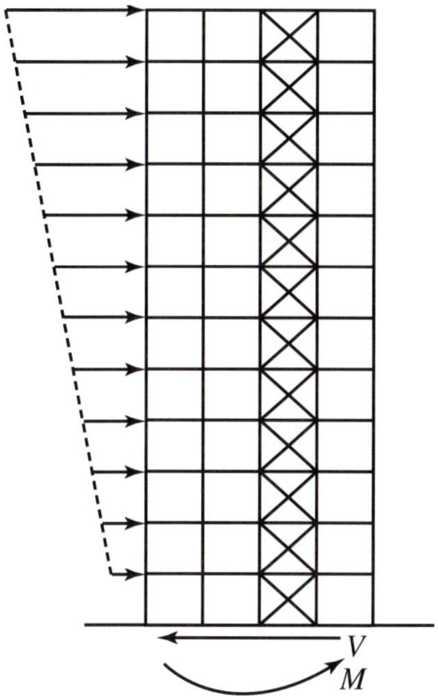

FIGURE 3.3

The response of lateral load resisting structural systems to earthquakes and high wind gusts is a complex subject studied in the field of structural dynamics. In general, structures are designed to avoid resonating with continuously applied bursts of lateral load. A structure that resonates with each additional wind gust or earth shake will experience lateral swaying motions that tend to synchronize with the load pulses and then the swaying will continue to increase in magnitude until the structure collapses. To prevent this, designers create "tuned" structural systems that resist resonating with the repeated loads by using the structure mass to "damp out" or delay the load response and thus break up the rhythm of the dynamic forces.

3.2 Tributary Areas and Load Paths

When analyzing or designing the various components of a structural system, we must first identify the portion of load that each such element supports. We do this by applying the concept of force equilibrium to the entire structure as well as to its various structural subsystems and individual members. Later in the book we see how to apply stress and deformation relationships to determine appropriate member sizes that limit the intensity of force and deformation to safe and reasonable levels.

To identify the loads that act on individual elements of a structural assemblage, we need to envision the area of floor, roof, or wall that a particular element is responsible for–this is called its *tributary area.* To determine the tributary area of an element such as a beam or a column, we need to trace the path of the loads from the roof and upper floors, down through the skeletal framework (or load-bearing walls), and on into the foundation–called the *load path.* Thus, tributary area and load path are basically synonymous, with the latter term most often associated with determining the cumulative tributary areas for an element in a complex structural system, such as the lower interior column of a multistory building.

FIGURE 3.4

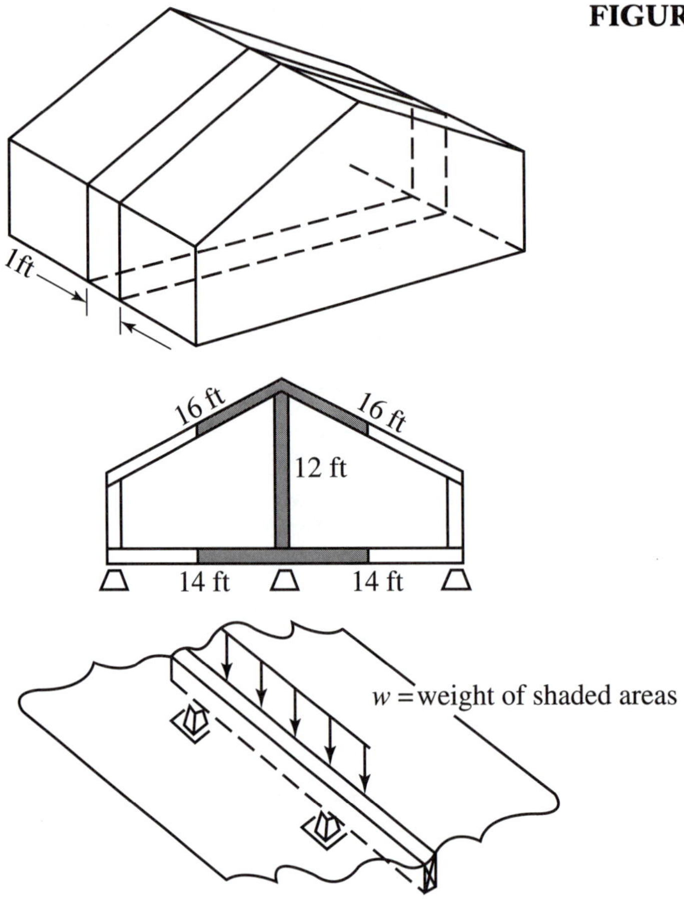

To demonstrate simple tributary areas and load paths, in Figure 3.4 we see a house on pier supports and we wish to determine the dead load per foot along the center floor beam. One of the many ways to look at such a situation is to imagine the house as a loaf of bread out of which we take a 1-ft slice, as shown. Since each sloping half of the roof is equally supported by the interior and the exterior walls, it follows that the middle half of the entire roof is supported by the inner load-bearing wall, which in turn is directly supported by the center floor beam. The same may be said of the two halves of the floor, so that the center floor beam also picks up half of the entire floor.

The dead load per foot along the center floor beam equals the weight of the shaded portions of the structural elements in the figure, so we simply figure out the number of square feet of each element (roof, wall, and floor), and multiply this by the unit weight of each. If the unit weights are $q_{\mathrm{ROOF}} = 10$ psf, $q_{\mathrm{WALL}} = 6$ psf, and $q_{\mathrm{FLOOR}} = 12$ psf, then from the dimensions shown in the figure, the dead load that each 1-ft slice of house places on the center floor beam, w, is

$$w = (8 + 8)(10) + (12)(6) + (7 + 7)(12) = 400 \text{ plf}$$

Live, wind, and earthquake loads are handled in similar fashion, as we will see in many application problems throughout the book.

3.3 Load Path in a Multistory Building

For more complex structures, the load path must be traced from top to bottom, accumulating all tributary areas associated with a particular element of the structure. For example, in Figure 3.5 we see a 120-ft-long by 100-ft-wide four-story office building with a parking garage space at the ground floor level. The dead load + live load for both the roof balcony and floors is 30 lb/ft^2 + 70 lb/ft^2 for a total design load of 100 psf.

From the upper levels plan view, it is apparent that from the roof and each upper floor level, the interior columns support a tributary area of $30 \times 33.3 = 1{,}000$ ft^2, with boundaries as indicated by the dashed lines. It also shows how typical exterior columns support half this tributary area, and the corner columns get a quarter.

From the elevation view of the four-story building, following the load path down column lines, we see that the interior columns of the second story support the load from the roof level, the fourth-floor level, and the third-floor level and deliver it to transfer girder *AB*. The load that each of the upper levels brings to a column is

$$P = 1{,}000 \times (30 + 70) = 100{,}000 \text{ lb}$$

We often abbreviate 1,000 lb as 1 kilopound, or 1 kip (1 k), so that $P = 100$ k. The cumulative load on the second-story column is $3 \times P = 300$ k. The X's shown in the plan view of girder *AB* indicate the three 300-k loads that the second-story interior columns deliver to the transfer girder.

Looking at the interior four columns of the first story, they must support the cumulative load of the three exterior upper-level columns, which would be half the load of the interior columns, or 150 k, as well as the reactions of the transfer girder. We see in the plan view and load diagram of *AB* that the

FIGURE 3.5

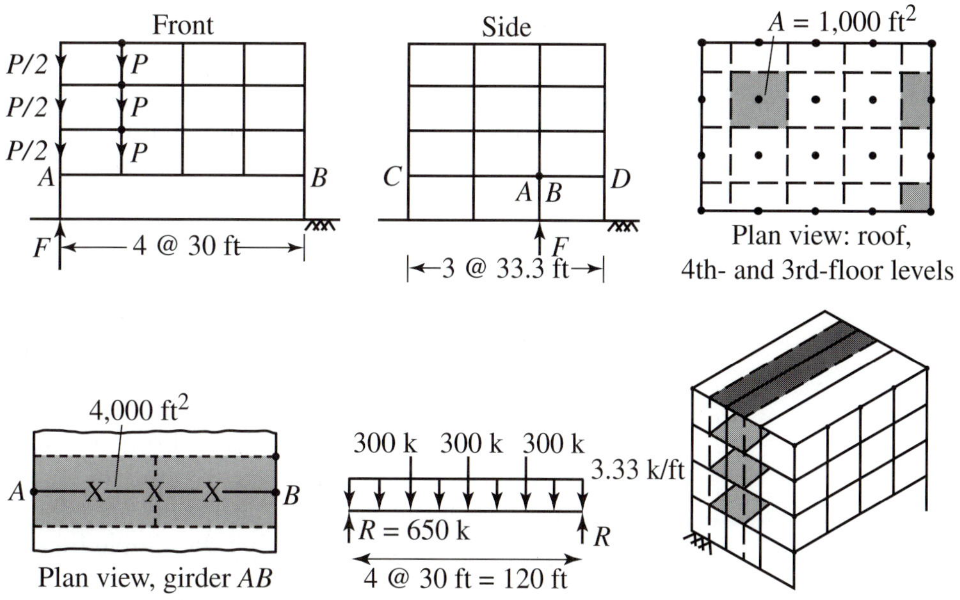

Exercise If the inner columns are removed from the ground floor and *CD* becomes a transfer girder, what is the load diagram for this girder, and what load, *F*, is supported by each of the only four remaining ground-floor columns? ■

120-ft transfer girder supports three 300k concentrated loads and a distributed load from the 4,000 ft^2 tributary area of the second floor:

$$w = \frac{4{,}000 \times 100}{120} = 3{,}330 \text{ plf} = 3.33 \text{ klf}$$

The transfer girder thus delivers a reaction to the ground-floor columns at *A* and *B* equal to

$$R = \frac{1}{2} \times [3 \times 300 + 3.33(120)] = 650 \text{ k}$$

The path taken by the vertical loads from the roof level down to the inner ground-floor columns (and on into the foundation) accumulates to

$$F = 150 + 650 = 800 \text{ k}$$

Alternatively, as seen in the figure, we could have simply taken a typical interior slice of the building that includes four levels of 4,000 ft^2 at 100 psf for a total of 1,600 k, and apportioned half the load, $F = 800$ k, to each of the two ground-floor columns.

3.4 Structural Systems

A structural system is made up of individual elements and/or subassemblies connected together to resist loads as a single entity. The connections used to transmit vertical loads through the structure must be selected in light of the structural system used to resist lateral loads. If simple pin connections are used to transmit vertical loads from beam to column and into the foundation, then lateral bracing systems are required to deliver lateral forces to the foundation. If moment resisting rigid connectors are used, they may serve as the fixed connections in a lateral load resisting moment frame, but will most certainly have to be strengthened and larger beam and column elements will be needed.

Floor and roof subsystems in timber structures support vertical loads and are almost always formed with plywood on joists that are pin-connected with nails and bolts to other wood girders, columns, or load-bearing walls. As we will see, these horizontal subsystems are often structurally detailed to act as large rigid plates called diaphragms that bring lateral forces to vertical plywood diaphragms, called shearwalls. The shearwalls will often double as vertical load-bearing walls.

Like timber structures, steel or precast concrete structures can also be designed as a system of horizontal roof and floor diaphragms laterally braced via vertical X or K brace steel trusses, and/or concrete shearwalls. Designers often design the concrete core shafts used for elevators and mechanical service as large rigid columns that the simple framed structure may "lean" against. In all these cases, floor and roof subsystems form large diaphragm plates and need not transfer moment to vertical columns so that simple beam to column connections can be used. Simple connections also connect the horizontal diaphragms to the bracing trusses or to the concrete walls that carry lateral forces.

On the other hand, if a structure must be free of X or K bracing or of solid shearwalls in order to maintain open bays, the structural skeleton itself may resist both vertical and lateral forces as a rigid frame, or moment frame. In this case, beam to column connections all transfer forces and bending moments through rigid moment connections. Moment frames require considerably larger beams and columns, especially at the lower levels of tall structures. All elements in a moment frame are actually beam-columns, and stress interaction and column slenderness (subjects we address later in the book) must be considered in the analysis and design of these elements.

For very tall structures or in intense seismic regions, hybrid lateral redundant load-resisting systems may be created where moment frames are coupled to truss, shearwall, and/or core shaft lateral bracing systems. Redundancy provides multiple load paths in a structural system, so in a sense, one system acts as a backup to the other in the event of a structural distress. Also, by using multiple types of bracing systems, each with different load response characteristics, designers may alter the dynamic response of a structure so that it is better "tuned" to resist resonating with dynamic wind and earthquake loads.

When we discuss the analysis of different structural assemblages and systems later, we will see that they are classified as indeterminate if they contain more unknown reactions than the applied equations of equilibrium can determine. Indeterminate structures have more members and/or more connections than are absolutely necessary for the structure to stand in equilibrium. The result is that there are redundant load paths for vertical and lateral loads to follow into the ground. Structural redundancy is desirable, since loads can bypass points of distress as they make their way through the structure. The analysis of indeterminate redundant structures is inherently more complex than for nonredundant structures, and we will generally make reasonable simplifying assumptions to carry out noncomputer analyses of such structures.

3.5 Trusses

A truss is a structural assemblage made of two-force members connected together into any of a vast number of possible arrangements of triangles. A few examples of trusses are shown in Figure 3.6. Trusses can be made to span any

FIGURE 3.6

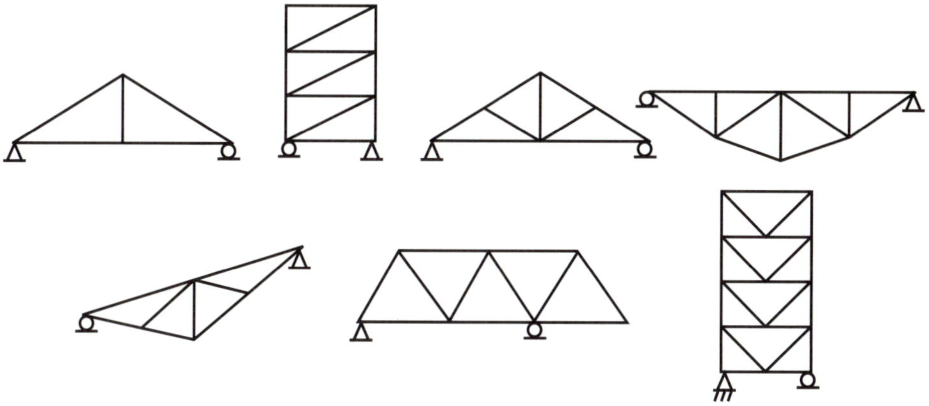

distance and are especially common for use in buildings with large roof and floor spans and for long bridges. While most structural elements and structural assemblies are covered by ceiling, floor, and wall finishes, because they can be quite dramatic and aesthetic, trusses are often intentionally left exposed to lend added architectural appeal to a structure. There are many historical, rustic, covered wooden bridges that dot the landscape of rural regions. These structures usually conceal wonderful old timber trusses that can be viewed from the inside of the structure, which no doubt is one of the reasons people are drawn to enter them as much as to see them from afar.

Ideally, truss loads are applied only at the connection point of members, called *joints*. Trusses are constructed so that the longitudinal axis of each connected member meets at the joint, so that each joint may be considered as a concurrent force system. Trusses are assumed to behave as though a pin connects all the members and any applied loads at each joint, usually referred to as a *pin connection*. While there may in fact be many fasteners required to form a single large truss joint, the fact that all the connected loads are concurrent results in members that are assumed to transfer negligible moments among themselves at the idealized pin connections.

Every two-force member of a truss is either pulling its two end joints together (tension member), or it is pushing against its two joints (compression member). In Figure 3.7 we see a truss separated into its joints and members. To design a truss, we can determine the forces in every member using

FIGURE 3.7

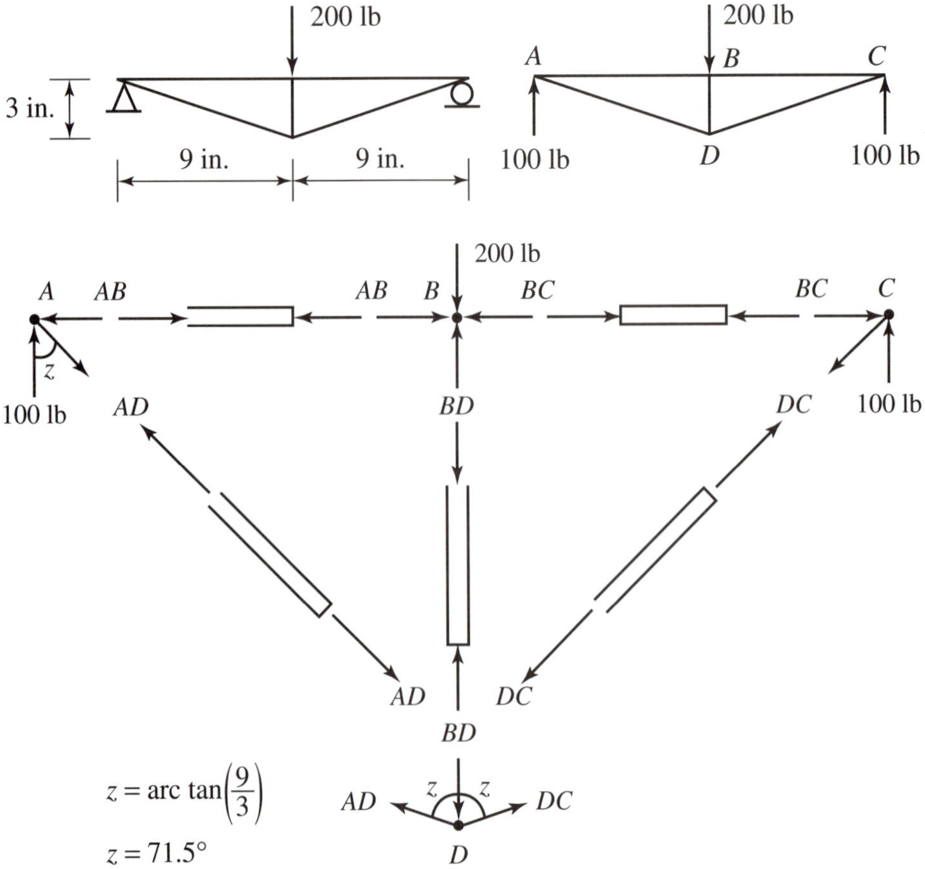

$z = \text{arc tan}\left(\frac{9}{3}\right)$

$z = 71.5°$

a joint-by-joint concurrent force analysis approach. If for some reason we need to analyze the forces in a just a few members of a large truss, we will use the method of sections similar to the beam section method for determining internal shear and moment.

In a joint-by-joint analysis of a truss, the support reactions are first determined by using the three equilibrium equations of the entire truss. These reactions are then treated as joint loads just like the applied joint loads. We usually begin with a support joint, and proceed joint by joint, solving vertical and horizontal equilibrium equations for two unknown member forces at each separate joint. The solution of the equations at every joint will provide the force in every member.

When choosing each successive joint to analyze, you must pick one with no more than two unknown members, since there are only two available equations per joint. When a member is assumed to be in tension and is found to have a negative value, the member is in compression and vice versa.

For example, the disassembled truss in the figure supports a single 200-lb load. A separate drawing shows the labeled joints and computed support reactions equal to half the 200-lb load in this symmetrical loading case. The angle $z = 71.5°$ is also shown computed from the truss geometry. This inverted king post truss somewhat models the commonplace step of a wooden ladder reinforced with a steel rod. Members *AB* and *BC* form the wood step, *AD* and *DC* the steel rod, and *BD* is a wood block. With larger dimensions and loads, the truss could just as easily model a small bridge, and you will see many exposed king post roof trusses in old churches and in the great rooms of many elegant structures.

The member forces are assumed to act as shown. The vertical and horizontal force equilibrium equations for joint *A* are, respectively,

$$100 - \cos(71.5°) \times AD = 0$$

$$\sin(71.5°) \times AD - AB = 0$$

This tells us that AD = 315-lb tension and AB = 299-lb compression. At joint *B*, the equations tell us that

$$BD - 200 = 0$$

$$AB - BC = 0$$

We see that BD = 200-lb compression, and since AB = 299 lb, so does *BC*. We can proceed to joint *C* or *D* to verify that CD = 315-lb tension as did *AD*.

It should be pointed out that if the number of equations (2 × number of joints) is less than the number of unknowns (number of members + 3), then the truss is indeterminate so there are not enough equilibrium equations available to solve for all unknown member forces. Sometimes, we can make an indeterminate truss determinate if we can identify members that are not supporting load and ignore them. This is commonly the approach taken with cable or light steel framing members that go limp when subjected to compression under certain structural loading situations (this is common for wind brace trusses as the wind shifts).

The method of joints is good for small trusses, but the method of choice for determining the force in selected truss members–especially for large trusses–is to use the method of sections discussed for beams. A truss may be

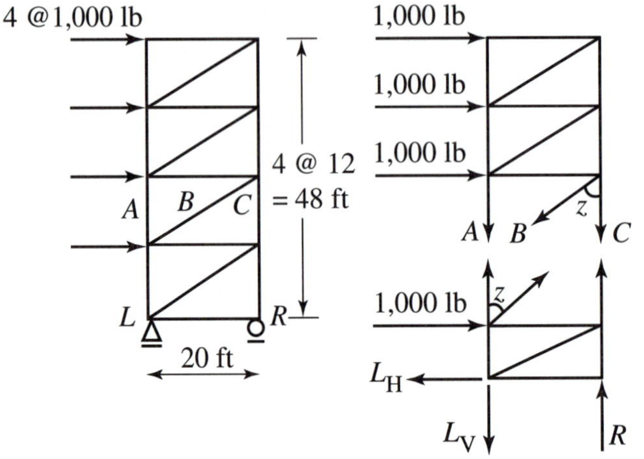

FIGURE 3.8

considered to be a large beam. As shown in Figure 3.8, after first determining support reactions, we can cut the truss into two halves by cutting through no more than three members. We can then determine the three unknown member forces using vertical force, horizontal force, and moment equilibrium equations applied to one of the half-sections.

The vertical cantilever truss in the figure might be used to brace a building against wind loads. If we want to know the forces in members marked *A, B,* and *C,* we can cut the truss in two, exposing the three forces as shown. If we work with the top portion of the truss, we do not even need to compute the reactions because they are not acting on the top half-section. The angle z is computed as $z = \text{arc tan}(20/12) = 59°$. The horizontal force equilibrium equation is

$$3 \times 1{,}000 - B \times \sin(59°) = 0$$

from which $B = 3{,}500$-lb tension. If we sum the moments at the joint where B and C meet, the only unknown in the equation is A:

$$1{,}000 \times 12 + 1{,}000 \times 24 - A \times 20 = 0$$

$A = 1{,}800$-lb tension. Finally, the vertical force equilibrium equation is written for C as follows:

$$-C - A - B \times \cos(59°) = 0$$

$$-1{,}800 - 3{,}500(0.515) = C$$

$$C = -3{,}600 \text{ lb} = 3{,}600\text{-lb compression}$$

We assumed that C was in tension when we drew it pulling on the joints. Since we found it to be a negative force, it is in compression and it pushes on its end joints.

3.6 Roof Truss

A common form of light roof construction for residential and small commercial structures involves the use of prefabricated timber trusses made from boards that typically have 2-in. × 4-in. cross sections such as that shown in Figure 3.9.

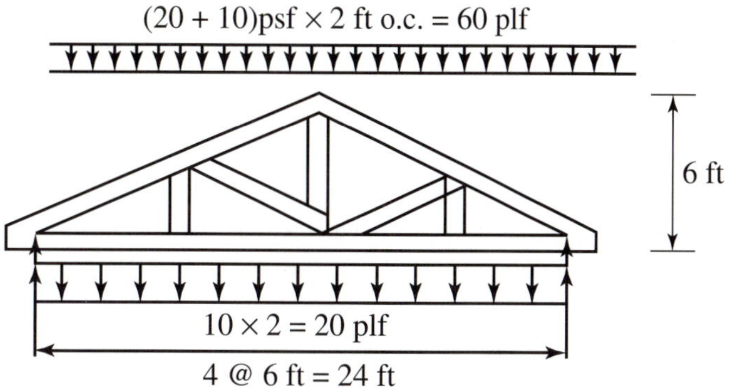

$$z = \arctan \frac{12}{6} = 63.4°$$

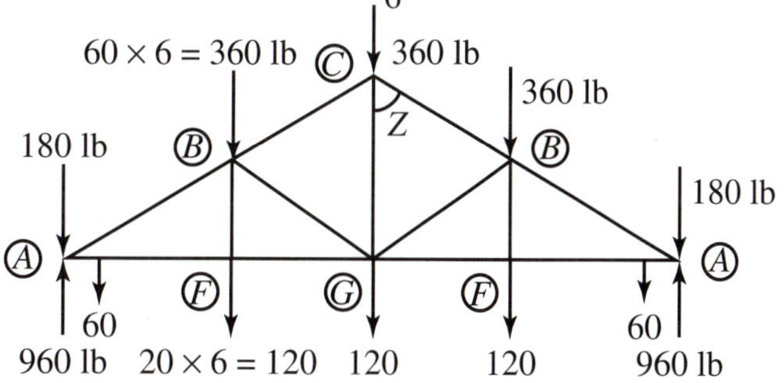

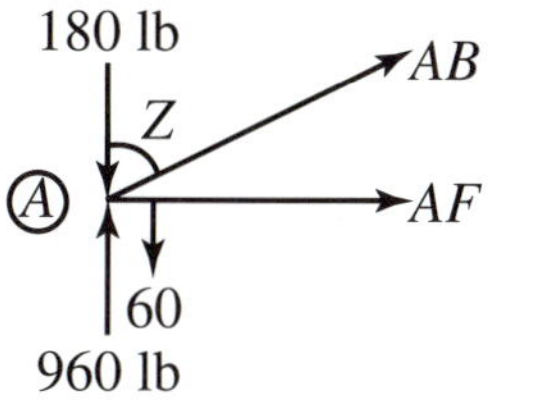

$960 - 180 - 60 + AB \cos Z = 0$
$AB = -1{,}610 = 1{,}610$ lb C
$(-1{,}610) \sin Z + AF = 0$
$AF = 1{,}440$ lb T

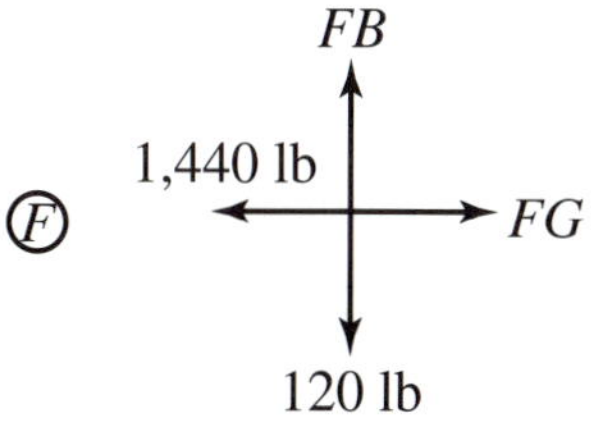

By inspection:
$FB = 120$ lb T
$FG = 1{,}440$ lb T

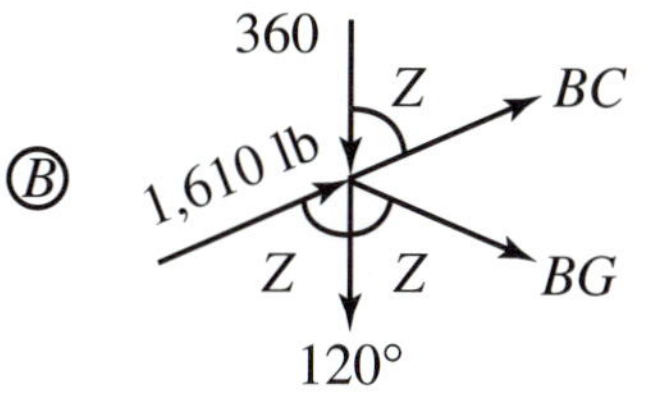

$1{,}610 \sin Z + BC \sin Z + BG \sin Z = 0$
$1{,}610 \cos Z + BC \cos Z - BG \cos Z = 480$
$BC = -1{,}070 = 1{,}070$ lb C
$BG = -540 = 540$ lb C

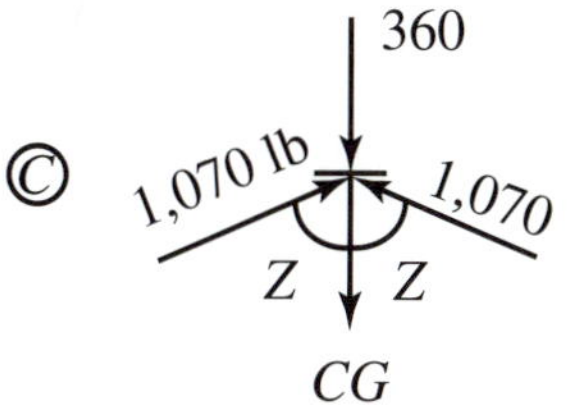

$2 \times 1{,}070 \cos Z - 360 - CG = 0$
$CG = 600$ lb T

FIGURE 3.9

Exercise Remove the two members labeled *BF* and remove the 10 psf attic load, then reanalyze this truss. ■

These pre-built units replace the individual joists rafters, and braces needed for common stick-built roofs put together one element at a time, so the added expense of prefabricating the trusses may overcome the extra field labor costs associated with the slower stick-built approach. Prefab trusses are typically spaced 2 ft apart, similar to joists and rafters that are usually spaced 16–24 in., on-centers (o.c.).

The roof and ceiling decking is nailed all along the sloping roof and horizontal ceiling truss members, and thus the loads delivered to the trusses are not concentrated at the joints. However, to perform a truss analysis, we may assume equivalent joint loads by placing half of the load carried by each member at each of its two end joints. The roof load specified by most building codes is 20 psf, and it is nominally placed on the horizontal roof projection along with the estimated dead load, typically 10 psf. The ceiling dead plus live load is only 10 psf, since the attic space does not allow people to freely move around and is thus only available for light storage. The resulting joint loads for this situation are shown in the figure.

We wish to determine the force in all members, noting that truss symmetry will cut the analysis work in half. The external support reactions at each end are obtained first–they are merely half of the entire downward load on the truss, or

$$A = 24 \text{ ft} \times (60 + 20) \text{ plf} \times \frac{1}{2} = 960 \text{ lb}$$

The angle that all sloping members make with a vertical line is shown to be $z = 63.4°$.

Beginning at support *A*, the known concurrent forces are applied at the joint and the unknown member forces are arbitrarily assumed to be in tension, and hence pulling on the joint. The equilibrium equations are written beside joint *A* as shown in the figure, and the unknown forces are $AB = -1{,}610 = 1{,}610$ lb C (compression), and $AF = 1{,}440$ lb T (tension). Note how the negative sign of *AB* is carried through the equations when determining *AF*. We cannot proceed directly to joint *B*, since it has three unknowns, but joint *F* provides obvious answers for the unknown members, $FG = 1{,}440$ lb T and $FB = 120$ lb T.

Now we proceed to joint *B*. All known forces are correctly applied and two equations of two unknowns must be solved simultaneously to find that both *BC* and *BG* were assumed incorrectly, and we find $BC = 1{,}070$ lb C and $BG = 540$ lb C. Finally, at joint *C*, horizontal symmetry and vertical equilibrium indicates that the last unknown member force must be $CG = 600$ lb T.

3.7 Load Rating of a Deck Truss Bridge

Figure 3.10 shows a narrow deck truss bridge that a private logging company constructed to allow their equipment to cross the 90-ft span over a stream. The state highway department has obtained permission to let the public use

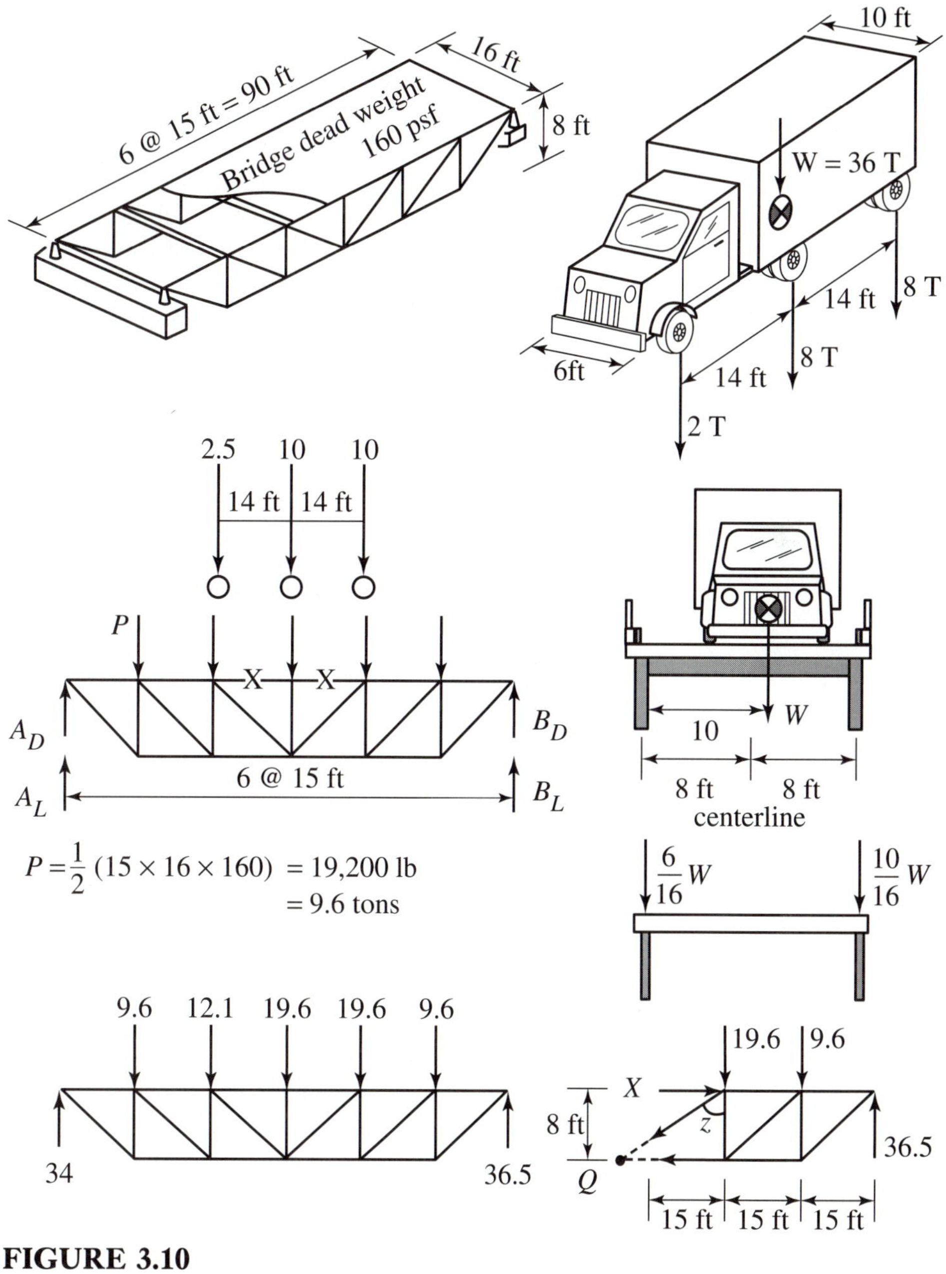

FIGURE 3.10

the bridge as a detour while the nearby state bridge is closed for emergency repairs after being damaged by a mudslide. To ensure safety, before the public can use this structure, the state bridge engineer must perform a load rating of the structure to determine if it is adequate to carry the 36-ton legal design truck, shown in the figure with its dimensions and wheel loads.

The bridge consists of two trusses spaced 16 ft apart to form a roadway that essentially allows only one lane of traffic. The trusses are under the roadway deck (hence the name, deck truss) that consists of concrete slab panels that span 15 ft in the direction of the roadway. These slabs are supported by cross beams that deliver half the deck weight to each truss at its joints connecting members along the top of the truss–these members form what is known as the top chord.

When the dead weight of the entire bridge, including deck, cross beams, and trusses, is averaged over the deck area, it comes to 160 psf. This averaged bridge dead load creates joint loads of 19,200 lb = 9.6 tons along the top chord.

Depending on roadway width and truck dimensions, the truck live load applied to one of the two trusses can be greater than half the 36-ton truck weight. This is because the truck can travel away from the roadway centerline and the truck center of gravity will be closer to one truss as shown in the figure. By summing moments about the far truss, we find that instead of having to support only half (50%) of the truck weight, one truss must carry $\frac{10}{16}$ of the weight, or 63%. This number represents what bridge engineers call the live load distribution factor, and it tells us that a critically loaded truss supports 63% of the legal truck axle loads of 4 tons front, 16 tons center, and 16 tons rear. Thus, the truck live load for the truss consists of three concentrated loads 2.5 tons, 10 tons, and 10 tons spaced 14 ft apart.

The total load applied along the top chord joints is shown along with the computed truss support reactions. The truck is placed at the center of the span to create the highest force in the members that concern the engineer the most and which are marked by an "X". These critical members carry the highest compressive force of any of the members and are known to have a safe compressive load capacity of 240,000 lb, or 120 tons. With the center axle of the truck placed at the bridge midspan the outer truck axles are close enough to be considered directly over the nearest joints. From horizontal equilibrium at their shared joint, we see that the two top chord members carry the same load.

When we need to check the force in only one or two members of a large truss, we use the method of sections. Cutting the truss in two and working with the right half, we may sum moments at the point labeled Q, and we have

$$X(8) + 19.6(15) + 9.6(30) - 36.5(45) = 0$$

From this we get $X = 132$ tons, which is more than the safe member capacity of 120 tons, so the bridge cannot carry the full legal load, and the bridge will have to be posted for a safe legal load less than 36 tons.

In Figure 3.11, the method of sections is applied separately so that the total force in the critical member, $X = 132$ tons, is broken down into that force caused by dead load, $X_D = 81$ tons, and that which the 36-ton truck live load creates, $X_L \approx 51$ tons. The available capacity of the critical member to support live load is

$$X_{CAP} = 120 - 81 = 39 \text{ tons}$$

This means that the fraction of a complete 36-ton truck that the member can safely support is

$$\frac{X_{CAP}}{X_L} = \frac{39}{51} = 0.76$$

This tells us what portion of the safe legal load a bridge can be posted to carry, which in this case is

$$\text{posted load} = 0.76 \times 36 \text{ tons} = 27 \text{ tons}$$

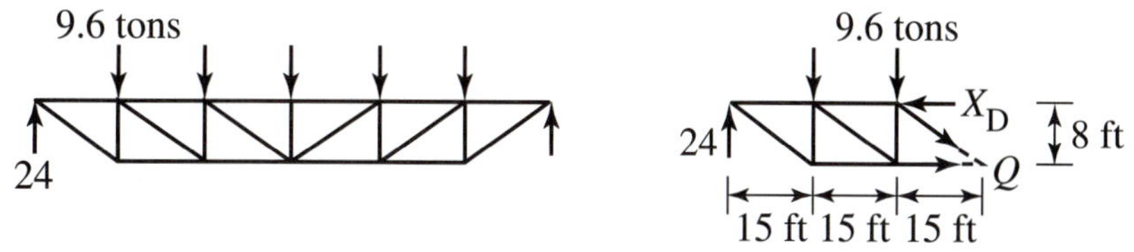

$$X_D = \frac{-9.6(15) - 9.6(30) + 24(45)}{8} = 81 \text{ tons}$$

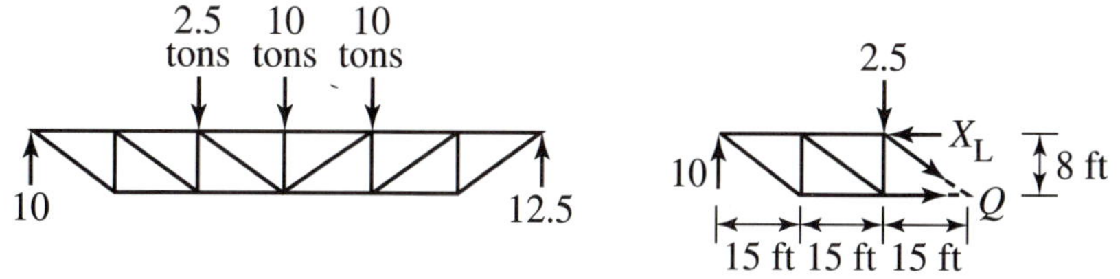

$$X_L = \frac{-2.5(15) + 10(45)}{8} = 51 \text{ tons}$$

FIGURE 3.11

Exercise Rework this problem assuming that the trusses are 20 ft apart, instead of 16 ft. ■

Thus, the bridge engineer will open the bridge to the public, but with a load limit sign stating that the structure is posted for trucks with three axles weighing over 27 tons.

3.8 FRAMES

Frames are what most people think of when the word *structure* is used. Structure conjures up images of the steel skeletons of high-rise skyscrapers under construction, and indeed, the steel skeleton of these buildings is a frame. On a simpler scale, the structures in Figure 3.12 through Figure 3.15 are also frames. The more complex frames associated with large structures are best analyzed by specialized computer programs and are beyond our immediate interest.

A frame is a structural assemblage of all types of members: two-force members, and transversely loaded elements such as beams and irregular-shaped elements. Even cables, arches, and trusses can be subassemblies of frames. With such a wide array of possibilities, we will have to limit our discussion of these assemblages and look at only those with pin connections–often called *hinges* in framed structures. Like the joints of a truss, negligible moments are being transferred between two frame members at a hinge. We will limit our analysis of frames to those with hinges that connect no more than two members, so that at each hinge, the two connected members exert a force on one another that is usually represented by its two unknown force components. Figure 3.12 shows several hinged frame structures.

Because determinate frames may have more than three support reactions (frames in parts (b) and (c) in the figure each have four support reaction components), we cannot usually apply equilibrium equations to the entire

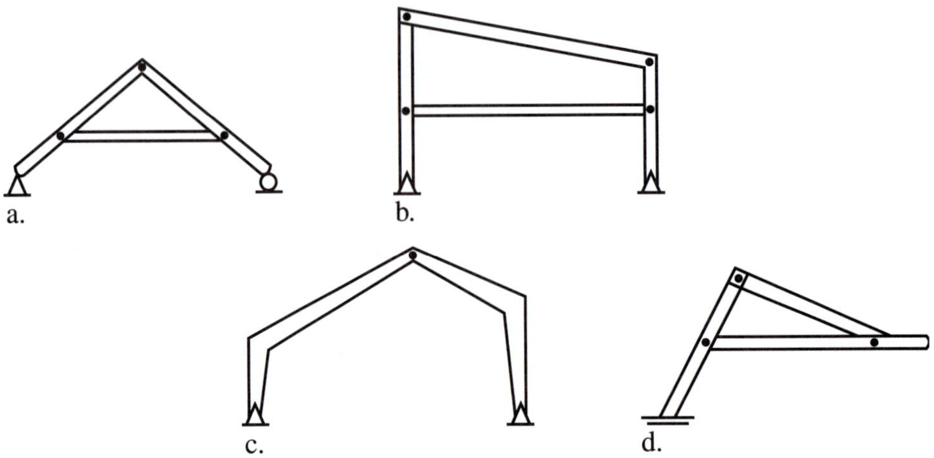

FIGURE 3.12

frame, as we do for determinate beams and trusses. Also, unlike trusses that are loaded only at the joints, applied loads can occur anywhere along members of frames. To analyze the forces in each element of a frame, we must disassemble the structure at its hinges and separate the individual members as shown for the unsymmetrical three-hinged gable frame in Figure 3.13.

Three equilibrium equations are written for each separated member. These equations are used to solve for the unknown force components at each hinge. Frames will be indeterminate if the number of equilibrium equations

FIGURE 3.13

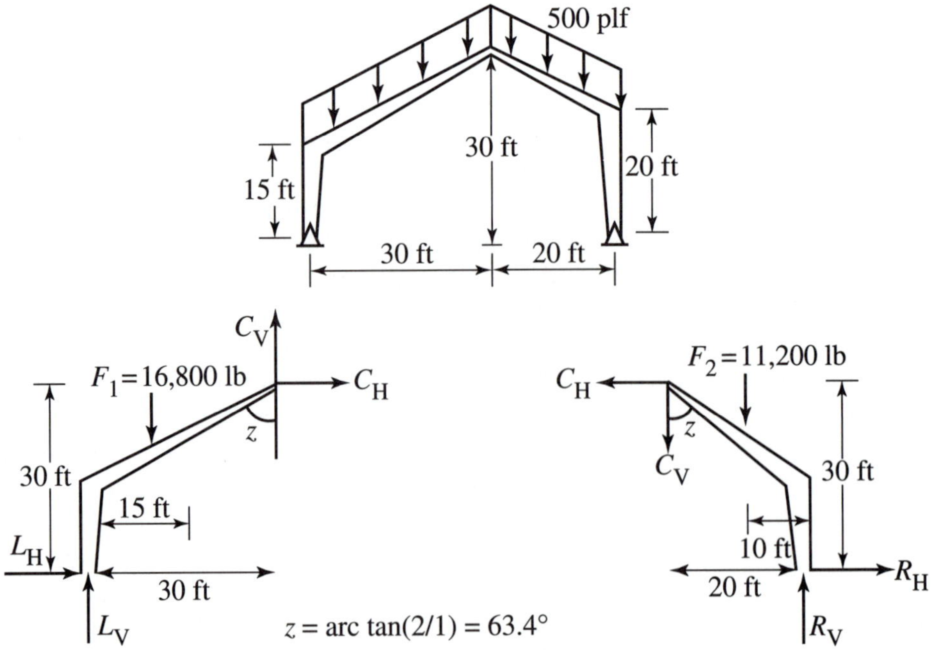

$z = \text{arc tan}(2/1) = 63.4°$

$$F_1 = 500 \times \frac{30}{\sin(63.4°)} = 16{,}800 \text{ lb}$$

$$F_2 = 500 \times \frac{20}{\sin(63.4°)} = 11{,}200 \text{ lb}$$

(3 × number of members) is less than the number of unknown force components (2 × number of hinges + number of support reactions). All the frames of Figure 3.12 are determinate.

The gable frame of Figure 3.13 is a determinate structure with three hinges–one at the left support, one at the right support, and one at the crown. There are four support reaction components, so we cannot apply three equilibrium equations to the entire frame to determine reactions. We will separate the structure into its left and right members, each of which is acted upon by part of the roof load and by the two hinge force components at each pin connection, as shown. Notice that at the crown, the components of the shared hinge force must act equally and oppositely on the joined members. To solve for the six unknowns, we will write three equilibrium equations for both members.

The equilibrium equations for vertical forces, horizontal forces, and moments about the support for the left member are, respectively:

$$L_V - 16{,}800 + C_V = 0$$

$$L_H + C_H = 0$$

$$16{,}800(15) - C_V(30) + C_H(30) = 0$$

And for the right member, we similarly have

$$R_V - 11{,}200 - C_V = 0$$

$$R_H - C_H = 0$$

$$-11{,}200(10) - C_V(20) - C_H(30) = 0$$

Unfortunately, none of these six equations directly yields a solution for one of the six unknowns. The two moment equations can be solved simultaneously to give $C_V = 2{,}800$ lb and $C_H = -5{,}600$ lb. The negative value for C_H tells us that the two members are not pulling horizontally on one another, they are laterally pushing against one another. Substituting these two values (retaining the negative sign on C_H), we find that $L_V = 14{,}000$ lb, $L_H = 5{,}600$ lb, $R_V = 14{,}000$ lb, and $R_H = -5{,}600$ lb. We see that R_H does not pull on the right member, it pushes against the member to restrain the outward thrust, similar to the reaction of L_H.

Many times we will see frame structures with connections that are not hinges, especially for cast-in-place concrete frames, and for many steel frames as well. If frame members are rigidly connected to one another (i.e., they transfer moments at connection joints), the structure is called a *rigid frame,* and it is usually indeterminate. Rigid frames, such as those in Figure 3.14, require computer analysis; otherwise, simplifying assumptions are needed in order to render them suitable for hand analysis (i.e., make them determinate).

If we are able to identify points where internal bending moments are zero along frame members, a fictitious hinge can be assumed to connect two distinct members at the point. Such points are indicated on the rigid frames in the figure. The location of such "hinges" of a frame varies for different loads as seen for the two loaded bents in the figure. For complex rigid frames, additional assumptions regarding load distribution may also be needed. Before computers were available to analyze indeterminate frames, the approximate methods of frame analysis were all that was available to design many great and complex structures.

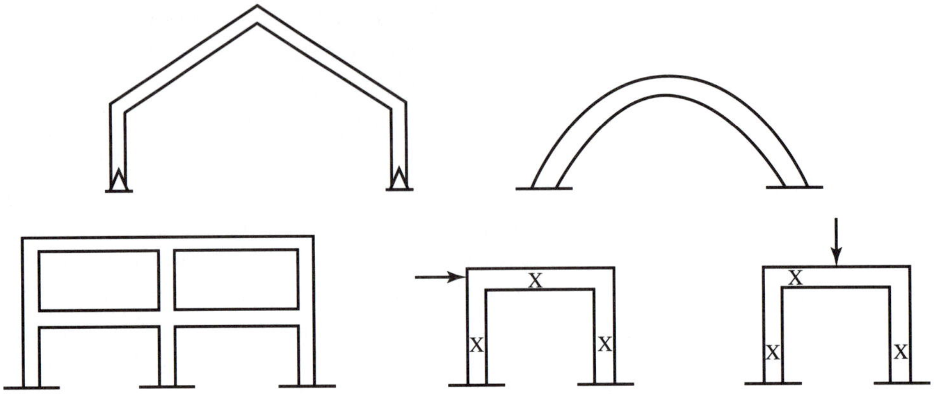

FIGURE 3.14

3.9 Three-Hinged Radial Arch

Figure 3.15 shows a radial three-hinged arch, so named because the shape of the two-member structure is an arc of a circle with a 42-ft radius that is pinned at its two external supports with a third pin connecting the two members at the crown of the arch. Such frames are commonly used to form circular dome and barrel arch buildings and, as in this case, arch bridges.

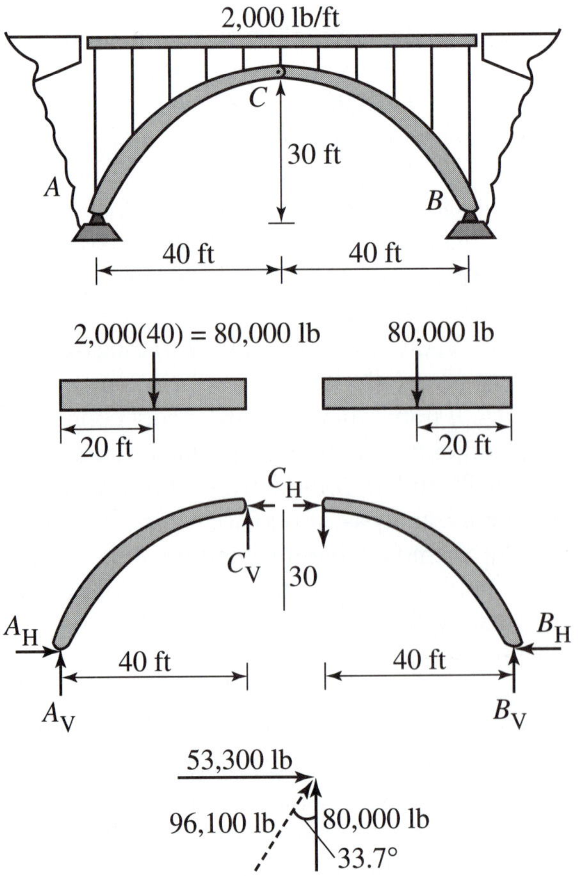

FIGURE 3.15

This bridge structure consists of four arches spaced 18 ft apart, with each supporting a roadway deck having a uniform dead (including allowance for the arch self-weight) plus averaged live load of 2,000 plf. As shown, this horizontal load is delivered to the arch through vertical columns spaced 8 ft apart, each delivering the same vertical load to the supporting arch. In this instance, or whenever four or more uniformly spaced equal concentrated loads act on a structural element, it is reasonable to assume the element is uniformly loaded.

We want to know the external reaction components at supports *A* and *B*. Since there are four support reactions–two per hinge–we cannot simply determine them by application of the three equilibrium equations to the entire 80-ft structure. By taking it apart at pin *C*, however, we see that we have a total of six unknowns (two per pin) and three equations of equilibrium for each of the two separated members–six equations and six unknowns. Note that the two components of the force in hinge *C* must be assumed to be equal and opposite on the left and right members.

By summing moments at *A* and *B*, respectively, we get the following two equations with the two unknown components of force in pin *C*:

$$80{,}000(20) - C_H(30) - C_V(40) = 0$$
$$-80{,}000(20) + C_H(30) - C_V(40) = 0$$

From these, $C_H = 53{,}300$ lb and $C_V = 0$. Summing vertical forces on each arch element shows us that $A_V = B_V = 80{,}000$ lb, and summation of horizontal forces on both members indicates that the outward kick of the arch members, called the horizontal thrust, is

$$A_H = B_H = C_H = 53{,}300 \text{ lb}$$

Thus, the force with which the foundation reacts to support the arch bridge is given as

$$F = \sqrt{(80{,}000^2 + 53{,}300^2)} = 96{,}100 \text{ lb}$$

This force makes an angle with a vertical axis of

$$z = \text{arc tan}\left(\frac{53{,}300}{80{,}000}\right) = 33.7°$$

Actually, we could have made quick work of determining the arch reaction components by applying the simple arch equations discussed in the last chapter. Since it is uniformly loaded, the vertical component of the reaction at *A* would be $V = wL/2 = 2000(80)/2 = 80{,}000$ lb. The horizontal component would be $H = wL^2/8s = 2000(80^2)/(8 \times 30) = 53{,}300$ lb.

Exercise Rework this problem where members *AC* and *BC* are straight, so that the radial arch becomes a uniformly loaded A-frame structure.

Rework the arch problem by placing the live load on only one side of the structure, so that the uniform load over the 40-ft horizontal span of member *CB* is 1,000 plf instead of 2,000 plf. ■

3.10 DIAPHRAGM STRUCTURES

A diaphragm structure is an assembly of large platelike elements that act much like deep thin beams to resist lateral loads. These load-resisting plates are called diaphragms. With diaphragms, a skeletal framework is not used to carry loads; instead, the structure's skin–the roof, floors, and walls–is designed to deliver horizontal wind or earthquake loads to the foundation. Even in structures that use frames to support loads, the large floor and roof elements are often treated as load-resisting diaphragms that transfer lateral forces to the frame members.

Figure 3.16 shows a basic diaphragm structure. In a sense, such a structure reminds one of a "house of cards," but this image does not do justice to a well-designed diaphragm structure that is capable of resisting very large lateral forces. In the figure, we see that the roof of the building is a deep, thin uniformly loaded simple beam that spans the length between the two end walls.

The roof diaphragm is laterally loaded with a distributed load that acts along the roof length and in the plane of the roof. The load could be due to wind blowing against the long wall that attaches to the roof, or it might also be due to the inertial reaction (resistance to movement) of the mass of the roof to a sudden lateral ground movement caused by an earthquake. In any case, the roof diaphragm is held in equilibrium by the reaction of the two end wall diaphragms. The lateral load delivered to the end walls is then held in equilibrium by the foundation that reacts with an opposing force and a couple. The end wall diaphragms are called shear walls because the racking effect of the opposing top and bottom shear forces is the critical load on these elements.

The shear walls act like cantilever beams fixed to the ground. The fixed end reactions are the horizontal shear force, $F/2$, and the moment couple, M, formed by the vertical tension and compression forces, T and C, respectively. At the top free end, the cantilevers are loaded with a concentrated force equal to the lateral shove of the roof diaphragm, also $F/2$.

For example, say the building in the figure has dimensions $L = 30$ ft, $B = 12$ ft, and $H = 8$ ft. A lateral wind load of 120 plf is applied along the 30-ft roof edge. What is the force in a tie-down connector that resists uplift of

FIGURE 3.16

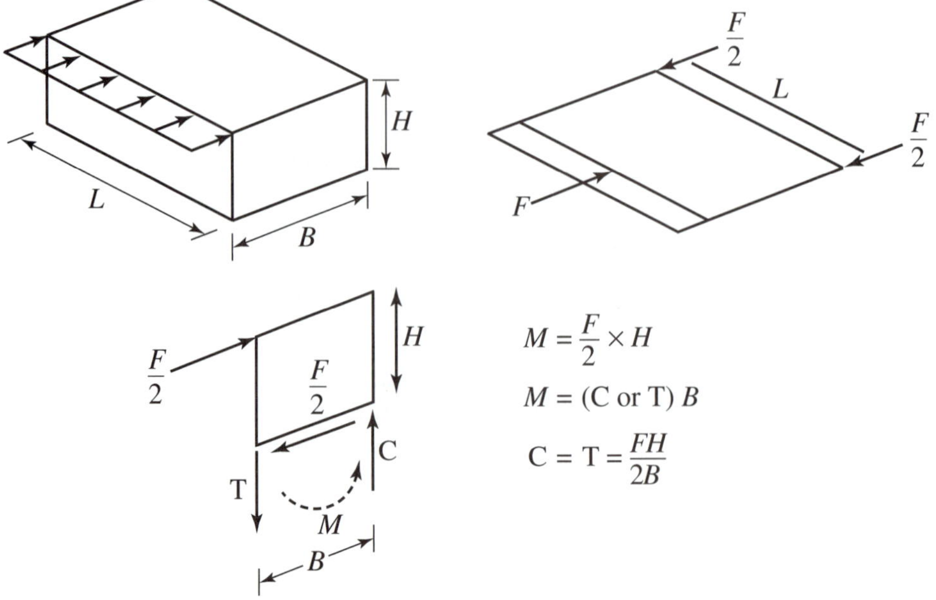

$$M = \frac{F}{2} \times H$$

$$M = (\text{C or T})\,B$$

$$\text{C} = \text{T} = \frac{FH}{2B}$$

the end shear walls? We are looking for T, caused by a total lateral force acting in the plane of the roof, $F = 120 \times L = 3{,}600$ lb, and

$$T = \frac{F \times H}{2B} = \frac{3{,}600 \times 8}{2 \times 12} = 1{,}200 \text{ lb}$$

Thus, lateral loads can cause fairly substantial uplift forces, even on a modest-size structure.

3.11 Interior Shear Walls

In Figure 3.17 we see a simple diaphragm structure with interior and exterior shearwalls. The lateral load of 200 plf acting along the 74-ft roofline represents the inertial force caused by the mass of the roof and the walls as an earthquake causes ground shaking in the 25-ft direction of the building. The two full-length exterior shearwalls and the two interior shearwalls with openings must each resist their share of this lateral earthquake loading. The dashed lines in the plan view mark off each wall's tributary portion of load. We see that each exterior wall carries a small portion of the 14,800-lb lateral load when

FIGURE 3.17

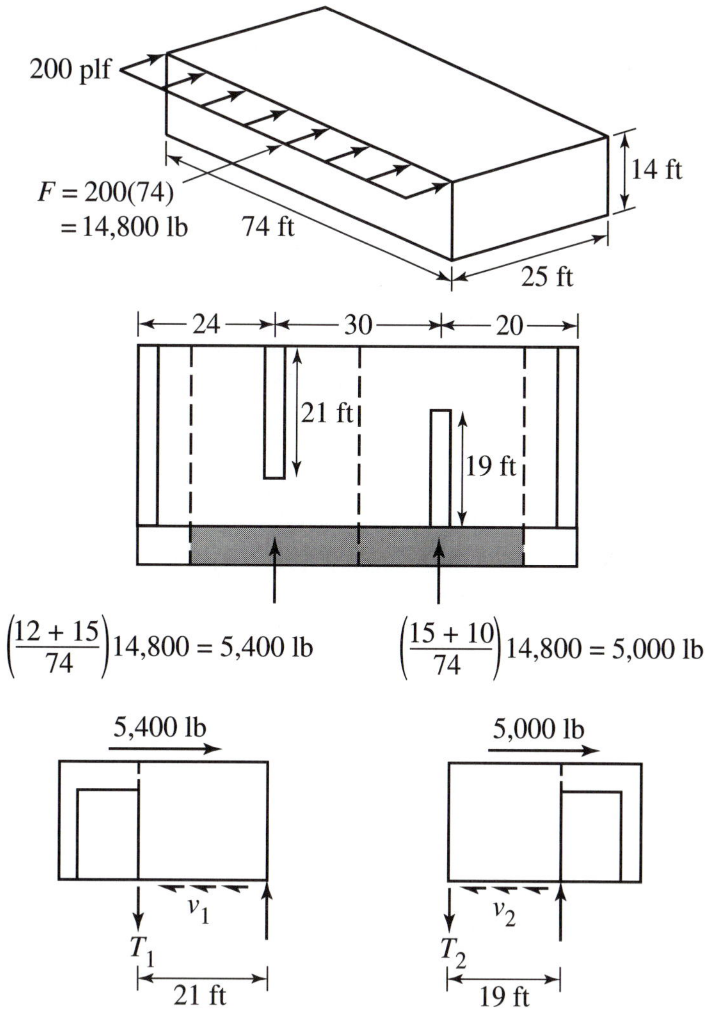

compared to the 21-ft-long interior wall, which picks up 5,400 lb, and the 19-ft wall, which gets 5,000 lb.

Building codes specify the allowable unit shear strength of various types of diaphragm construction. The unit shear is simply the total shear force on the wall divided by the length of the wall. The codes also specify the allowable tensile force that various tie-down fasteners may withstand. If the shearwalls of the figure are rated for 275 plf unit shear capacity, and tie-down bolts are rated for 5,000 lb, are the interior walls adequate to withstand the earthquake force?

For the 21-ft interior shearwall, the unit shear is

$$v_1 = \frac{5{,}400}{21} = 257 \text{ plf} < 275 \text{ plf} \qquad \text{OK}$$

The tie-down force required to hold the wall in place is determined by summing moments at the opposite corner of the wall

$$5{,}400(14) - T_1(21) = 0$$

$$T_1 = 3{,}600 \text{ lb} < 5{,}000 \text{ lb} \qquad \text{OK}$$

For the 19-ft shearwall, the unit shear is

$$v_2 = \frac{5{,}000}{19} = 263 \text{ plf} < 275 \text{ plf} \qquad \text{OK}$$

The tie-down force is

$$5{,}000(14) - T_2(19) = 0$$

$$T_2 = 3{,}680 \text{ lb} < 5{,}000 \text{ lb} \qquad \text{OK}$$

Exercise Add a second story to this structure and recheck the interior shearwalls of the ground floor. Assume that the walls are strengthened to resist a unit shear of 500 plf. ■

4 STRESSES AND DEFORMATIONS IN STRUCTURES

4.1 STRESS, STRAIN, AND DEFORMATION

As we have seen, we connect members and/or subassemblies into structural systems in order to safely resist the vertical and lateral loads caused by natural forces. Each element of such systems is fashioned from a common building material, such as concrete, steel, or timber, into a structural member with a specific length and cross-sectional measurements. In structural technology, *stress* is defined as the intensity of force acting within the material of a structural member. Stress is the ratio of the force to the area over which the force is distributed, so that

$$\text{stress} = \frac{\text{force}}{\text{area}}$$

A force pulling longitudinally on each end of a length of thin steel wire will create much more tension stress in the steel than if the same force is applied to the same length of a solid steel rod. This is because the area of the wire is much smaller than that of the rod, and so the intensity of the two equal forces–the force per unit area–is greater. If the force is gradually increased in the two elements, the stresses in both members will grow proportionately with the force increase, with the more highly stressed thin wire being the first to reach a point of overstress and then fail.

Deformation is the overall dimensional change that occurs in a structural member subjected to stress. *Strain* is the rate of this deformation, or the deformation per member length:

$$\text{strain} = \frac{\text{deformation}}{\text{length}}$$

In Figure 4.1, we see a short member of length, L, with a cross-sectional area, A, being compressed between two rigid plates by an axial force, F. Measurements indicate that as the compressive axial force increases, so does the deformation of the member, D. The axial stress in the member material is $f = F/A$. This stress is seen to act perpendicular to a cross section of a member and is uniform if the axial force is centric. (Axial forces are generally idealized to be centric, which implies that the force line of action passes through the centroid of every cross section of the member–we will discuss this in more detail later). The uniform strain that results from the uniform stress is $d = D/L$.

For the member of length, L, we consider a cube of the stressed material with unit dimensions, 1 in. × 1 in. × 1 in. The axial stress in the member,

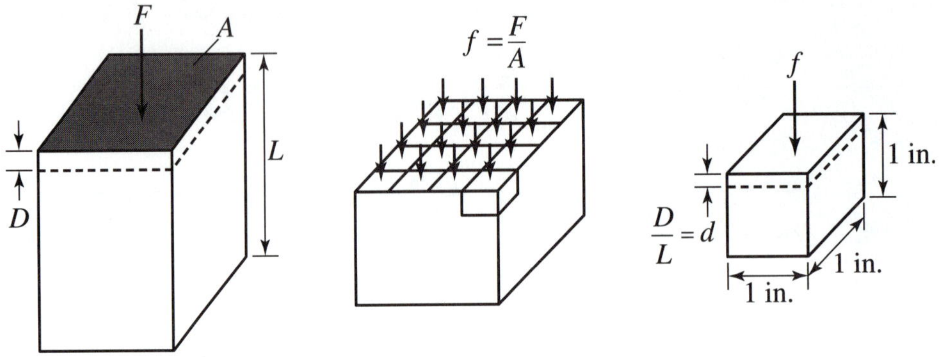

FIGURE 4.1

f, is a small force acting on the 1-in^2 unit cross-sectional area, and the member strain, d, is actually the deformation of the 1-in. unit length cube. Thus, stress and strain are, respectively, the unit force and unit deformation of a loaded member. Stress is reported as force per area, typically pounds per square inch, or psi, and strain is dimensionless, since it is a ratio of deformation to length, typically inches to inches, or in./in.

The graph shown in Figure 4.2 is a generalized plot of the type of data that would be obtained from a specimen like that of Figure 4.1. A measured load is gradually applied to a member (causing stress = force per member cross-sectional area), while at the same time measuring total deformation (from which the strain is computed as deformation per original member length). The plot of corresponding stress versus strain data pairs yields a graph known as the stress-strain curve for the specific material tested. By dividing force by member area and deformation by member length, we are looking at unit force and unit deformation, so that the influence of the member size is eliminated and we are then focusing on the member's material characteristics only. A unique curve will be obtained for each different structural material.

Initially, before the applied stress reached the level called the elastic limit, the load could have been removed and all stress and strain would have gone away—this is termed *elastic loading*. The initial portion of the curve leading up to the elastic limit is a line. The slope of this line is the ratio of the

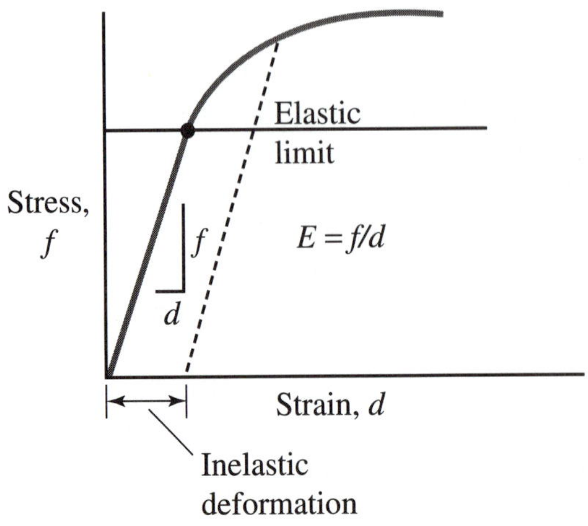

FIGURE 4.2

stress to strain that is unique for each material, and this ratio is called the modulus of elasticity, E:

$$\text{modulus of elasticity} = \frac{\text{stress}}{\text{strain}}$$

As its name implies, E is a measure of the elastic stiffness of the material. For the most common building materials, practical values of E for timber, concrete, and steel are 1,600,000 psi, 3,500,000 psi, and 30,000,000 psi, respectively.

If a force stresses the material of a member beyond the elastic limit, gradual removal of the force will result in the stress and corresponding strain following the dashed line down to zero stress, and some unrecoverable strain will then exist. The member is then said to have been *inelastically stressed.* Further elastic loading and unloading of a material that has been inelastically stressed would follow the dashed line shown. The slope of the dashed line is still E, which means the material retains its elastic stiffness. Inelastic loading is generally undesirable in structures, because as a result, the structure will be permanently deformed.

When the stress-strain curve for a material extends well beyond the elastic limit, we say the material is ductile. Steel is a very ductile material. Common structural steel, for example, has an elastic limit (generally called the steel yield stress) of $f = 36{,}000$ psi at an elastic strain of

$$d = \frac{f}{E} = \frac{36{,}000}{30{,}000{,}000} = 0.0012 \text{ in./in.}$$

The inelastic strain that steel can withstand is well over 100 times its elastic strain. Concrete may be considered ductile in compression, but it is brittle (and quite weak) in tension. Timber is not particularly ductile, since its stress-strain curve is mainly linear.

In design, we will see that material stresses in structures are kept well below the elastic limit to ensure safe and functional structures that respond elastically to all loads. To analyze and design structural members, the following useful relationship can be derived from the definitions of stress and strain:

$$D = \frac{F \times L}{A \times E} = \frac{f \times L}{E}$$

For a known axial force (or stress) in a particular structural member, we can compute its deformation. The relationship also indicates that axial deformation varies directly with force (or stress) and member length, and inversely with area size and material stiffness.

An illustration of these relationships will be helpful. In Figure 4.3, the load on a 28-in. × 28-in. ground-floor column of a 10-story building is shown to be

$$F = 10 \times 100{,}000 = 1{,}000{,}000 \text{ lb}$$

The 16-ft- (192-in.-) tall concrete column has a cross-sectional area of

$$A = 28 \times 28 = 784 \text{ in}^2$$

Knowing that for concrete, $E = 3{,}500{,}000$ psi, we see that the column will shorten,

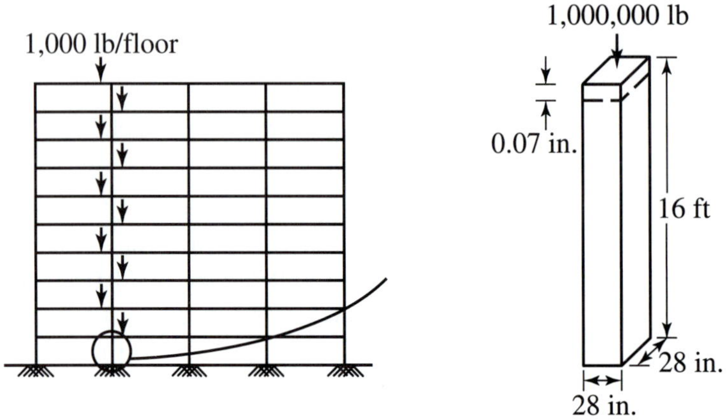

FIGURE 4.3

$$D = \frac{1{,}000{,}000 \times 192}{784 \times 3{,}500{,}000} = 0.07 \text{ in.}$$

You might think that if the building were 20 stories tall, then the ground-floor column would shorten twice as much, since the column load would double with 10 more stories and become very problematic for 100 stories. This would indeed occur were it not a fact that we must change the cross section of the lower columns for the taller structure. If we do not make these column areas larger for any additional stories that are added, the added stress due to the extra load per floor will become excessive and crush the concrete in these columns.

The stress in the column of the 10-story structure is

$$f = \frac{F}{A} = \frac{1{,}000{,}000}{784} = 1{,}280 \text{ psi}$$

This is about as high a stress level as we can allow in concrete columns. In order to maintain the same stress level in the 20-story building, we need a cross-sectional area that would give us the same stress. Since $f = F/A$, we have $A = F/f$, so that

$$A = \frac{2{,}000{,}000}{1{,}280} = 1{,}560 \text{ in}^2$$

Not surprisingly, the ground-floor column cross section for the taller building must be twice as large. The column cross section dimensions would need to be $\sqrt{1{,}560}$. This requires a 40-in. × 40-in. column.

From the deformation formula, since the stress is the same in both cases, the ground floor of both buildings must shorten the same:

$$D = \frac{1{,}280 \times 192}{3{,}500{,}000} = 0.07 \text{ in.}$$

Furthermore, if we keep the same stress in the columns at every floor level by varying the column areas at each floor level of each building, then each floor of each building shortens 0.07 in. And, overall, the 10-story building will shorten $10 \times 0.07 = 0.7$ in., and the 20-story building will shorten 1.4 in.

Perhaps we want to compare concrete with a steel alternative based on a common story deformation of $D = 0.07$ in. Since $D = (f \times L)/E$, we would need the steel to withstand a stress of

$$f = \frac{D \times E}{L} = \frac{0.07 \times 30{,}000{,}000}{192} = 11{,}000 \text{ psi}$$

This is a reasonable value for the design stress of a steel column. The required steel cross-sectional area would need to be

$$A = \frac{2{,}000{,}000}{11{,}000} = 182 \text{ in}^2$$

With basic definitions of material stress, strain, and elastic stiffness, as well as an understanding of their relationships to the force, area, and length of structural members, we can proceed to investigate a few simple applications of these principles.

4.2 DETERMINING TIMBER MODULUS OF ELASTICITY

Before being replaced by a new wider bridge, an old timber bridge, for which construction plans were no longer available, was loaded to failure as part of a university research project. In order to analyze the load-deformation data collected during the researcher's field tests of the structure, the modulus of elasticity E of the unknown timber species must be determined.

The lab technicians in the materials testing laboratory used the concrete compression testing machine to get the material stress-strain relationship, since timber in compression has a similar failure strength to that of normal strength concrete. Timber samples 5 in. × 5 in. × 12 in. were cut from the large bridge beams, since these dimensions are similar to the standard concrete test cylinder with a 6-in. diameter and 12-in. height.

A sketch of the test sample appears in Figure 4.4 along with a sketch of the load machine. The large dial of the load machine tells what compressive load, F, the hydraulic loading jack puts on the specimen. Each time a reading of F is taken, the corresponding shortening deformation D is also read from the small dial on the deformation measuring device called a dial extensometer. The load and deformation readings from the test of a specimen are shown in the figure. These F and D values are converted to their corresponding stress, f, and strain, d, values by dividing each by the specimen cross-sectional area, $A = 25$ in^2, and total length, $L = 12$ in., respectively. A plot of the stress-strain data is shown.

The material elastic stiffness, or modulus of elasticity, E, is the slope of the initially straight portion of the plotted data. We see that the highest stress in the material for which the strain-strain relationship follows a straight line was about 4,300 psi. This is the elastic limit, beyond which a nonlinear relationship exists between stress and strain until the specimen crushes at an ultimate compressive stress of 4,900 psi, in this case.

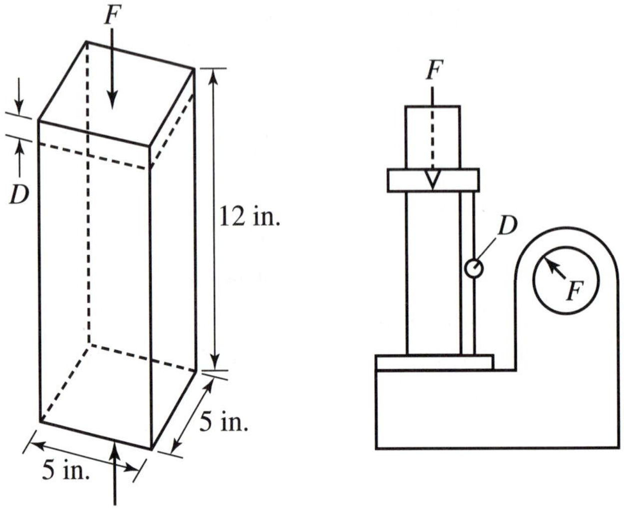

F	D
0	0
37.5 k	0.011
75 k	0.022
100 k	0.029
108 k	0.032
115 k	0.045
123 k	0.059

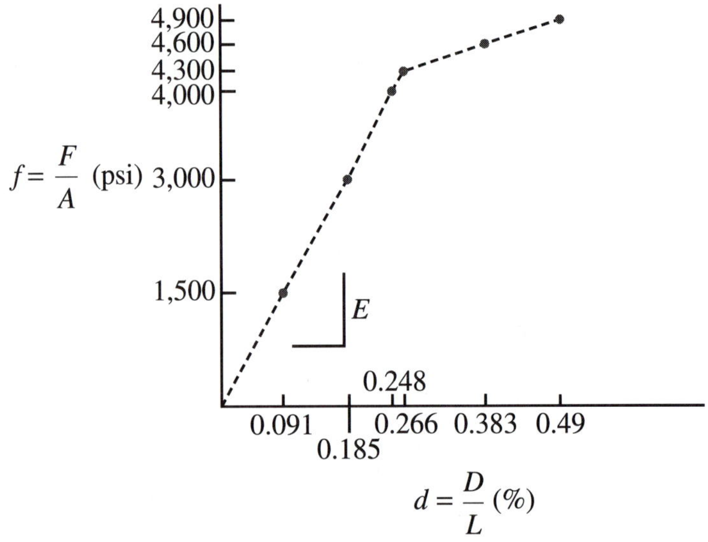

FIGURE 4.4

Exercise An elongation of 0.012 in. was measured over a 2-ft length of an element that was elastically stressed to 5,000 psi in tension. What is the modulus of elasticity of this material?

How much stretch would occur in a 30-ft length member of this material if the cross-sectional area is 4 in^2 and it supports an axial load of 12,000 lb? ■

E may be determined from the ratio of the elastic limit stress, $f = 4{,}300$ psi, to its corresponding strain of $d = 0.00266$ in./in., thus

$$E = \frac{f}{d} = \frac{4{,}300}{0.00266} = 1{,}620{,}000 \text{ psi}$$

We will see that in addition to axial stress and deformation, *E* is important in the study of beams and columns.

4.3 Post-tensioned Floor Slabs

To prevent excessive cracks from forming in concrete slab floors, especially when expensive ceramic tiles are glued to the slab as the finished interior floor covering, slabs may be post-tensioned as depicted in Figure 4.5. Post-tensioning effectively compresses the slab so that tension and shrinkage cracks that routinely occur in such structural components can be reduced.

During the forming of the slab, parallel $\frac{1}{2}$-in.-diameter high-strength steel strands encased in plastic sheathing are stretched across the length of the slab formwork. Special anchoring hardware is used to secure one end of the strand and to allow the other end to be stretched. The concrete slab is poured and allowed to harden.

At the unanchored end of the strand, a special tool is used to stretch the strands out of the slab by jacking them against it and then special hardware is clamped to the free end of each strand. The tensioned strands are then released to immediately bear against the end of the slab and thus compress it as the cable acts to try to pull the two anchored ends together. The strand is free to stretch along its full length because it is encased in a plastic tube and does not bond with the hardened concrete.

The manufacturer of the special hardware used in this operation recommends that the strands should be safely stressed to $f = 80{,}000$ psi tension. For the long direction of a 50-ft × 30-ft slab, how much will the strands be stretched and what stretching force is created?

Since stress is force per unit area, the stretching force is simply

$$F = f \times A = 80{,}000 \times \pi\left(\frac{1}{2} \times 0.5\right)^2 = 15{,}700 \text{ lb}$$

FIGURE 4.5

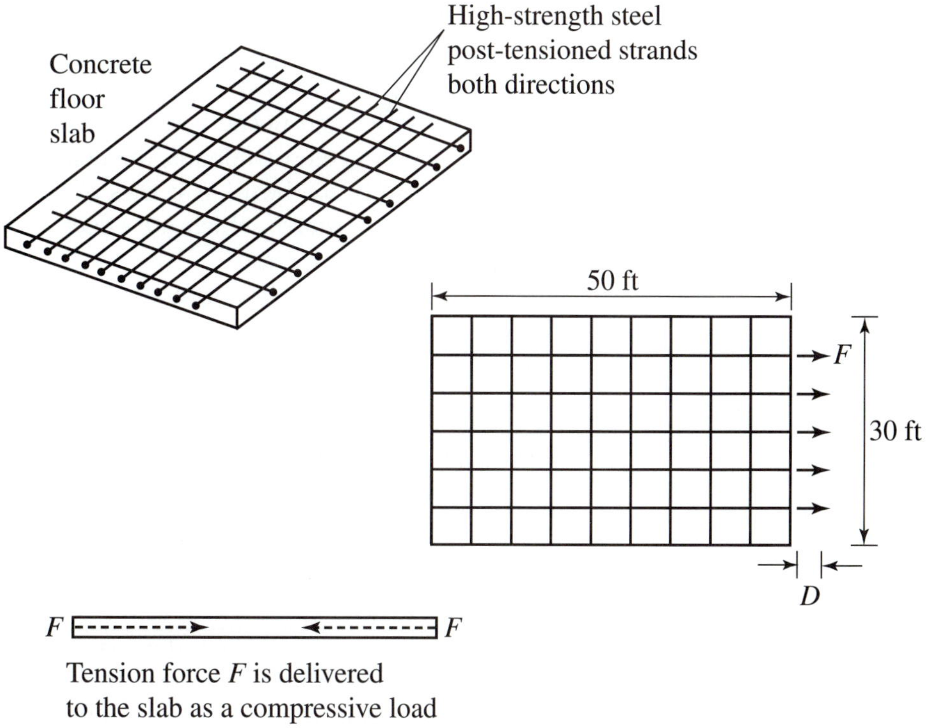

Exercise How much stretch is required for cables that are oriented in the 30-ft direction?

Rework the problem assuming that fiberglass-reinforced plastic strands stressed to 10,000 psi are used instead of the steel strands. The modulus of elasticity of this composite is $E = 2{,}500{,}000$ psi.

If the rule of thumb is to stretch the cables 1 in. for every 12-ft length of cable, what is the stress and strain in the steel? ■

The required strand stretch to achieve a stress of 80,000 psi is

$$D = \frac{F \times L}{A \times E} = \frac{f \times L}{E} = \frac{80{,}000 \times 50 \times 12}{30{,}000{,}000} = 1.6 \text{ in.}$$

4.4 Temperature Stress and Deformation

When the temperature rises or falls, building materials expand or contract. If the members are free to expand, like for a simple beam with its roller at one end, nothing noteworthy comes of the temperature change. If the beam were pinned or fixed at both ends, the change in temperature could have serious results, especially for massive steel and concrete structures.

A property of materials called the *coefficient of thermal expansion, c,* is the unit deformation (strain) that the material will undergo for a 1° change in temperature. For both steel and concrete this coefficient is approximately $c = 0.000006$ in./in./°F. For example, the unit deformation in a steel beam due to a 25°F rise in temperature is

$$d = 25 \times 0.000006 = 0.00015 \text{ in./in.}$$

Suppose a 150-ft- (1,800-in.-) long steel bridge girder is subjected to a 25°F temperature rise. It will need to expand

$$D = d \times L = 0.00015 \times 1{,}800 = 0.27 \text{ in.}$$

Thus, if the roller end of the beam is working correctly, and if the expansion joints are not clogged with debris, the beam will expand about $\frac{1}{4}$ in. Otherwise, stress will build in the beam as it tries to freely expand but must push against its end supports instead, which are effectively axially compressing the girder with a large counterforce.

If the girder cannot expand and the strain is $d = 0.00015$ in./in., then the stress must be

$$f = d \times E = 0.00015 \times 30{,}000{,}000 = 4{,}500 \text{ psi}$$

If the girder has a cross-sectional area of $A = 90 \text{ in}^2$, then the axial compression force exerted against its supports is

$$F = 4{,}500 \times 90 = 405{,}000 \text{ lb}$$

This is 200 tons of force! Clearly, we cannot overlook the potential of temperature to create a significant affect on structures.

When the temperature drops by 25°F, everything stated above is merely reversed. The beam will freely contract 0.27 in. or else pull on its supports with a tension force of 200 tons.

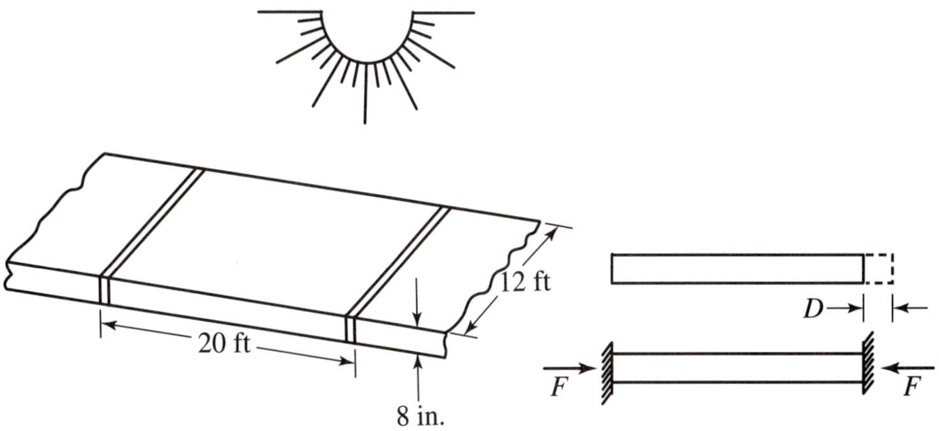

FIGURE 4.6

4.5 HEAT BUCKLING OF HIGHWAY PAVEMENT

You may have witnessed the aftermath of the temperature-induced structural failure that follows, especially if you live in a hot climate. Suppose that on very hot days, the temperature of a highway pavement may rise by 30° or more. The expansion joints of roadway slabs are often spaced every 20 ft or so as shown in Figure 4.6. These joints may be unable to allow for the pavement to expand, either because they become filled with debris, or because extreme heat has caused all joints to be compressed to their limit. In this case, very high thermal stresses will build up in a pavement section, causing pavement cracking or possibly even explosive buckling of the slab.

How much expansion would occur for a 25°F rise in temperature if the joints allow for free expansion? How much compressive axial stress is created if this temperature rise occurs with totally restrained expansion due to failed expansion joints?

The expansion deformation is the product of the thermal strain times the member length, which is equal to the thermal coefficient × temperature change × member length, or

$$D = 0.000006 \times 25 \times (20 \times 12) = 0.036 \text{ in.}$$

This free expansion is depicted in the figure. If this expansion is prevented by the restraining forces of adjacent slabs as shown, the stress created as the adjacent slabs effectively compress and shorten a freely expanded slab by $D = 0.036$ in. equals the compressive strain times the material modulus of elasticity, or

$$f = D/L \times E = 0.036/(20 \times 12) \times 3{,}600{,}000 = 540 \text{ psi}$$

In a 12-ft-wide by 8-in.-thick slab, this stress corresponds to a tremendous compressive force of

$$F = f \times A = 540 \times \{12 \times (12 \times 12)\} = 933{,}000 \text{ lb}$$

Exercise Suppose that the expansion joints allow some expansion, say, 0.02 in. What stress is created in the pavement in this case?

Also, rework the problem assuming the joints occur every 30 ft. ■

4.6 COMPOSITE MEMBERS

A composite structural member is made up of two different materials that work in parallel to support a load. High-performance automobiles and aircraft are fabricated from modern day high-tech composites of carbon fibers mated with special resins. When subjected to heat and pressure, the fibers and resin fuse and harden to create materials stronger and lighter than steel.

On the low-tech end of things, all reinforced concrete members are a composite of concrete and steel that work together to resist bending stresses in beams and compression stress in columns. Also, we often see timber beams stiffened with steel side plates to add additional bending capacity to the element. Figure 4.7 shows a hollow steel pipe section with a wall thickness of $\frac{1}{2}$ in. and an inner diameter of 9 in. This short compression member is a composite of the steel pipe and the concrete that fills the inner hollow void of the tube.

Both the steel and concrete each carry a portion of the applied 100,000-lb compressive load, but how much for each? We will try to determine the axial compressive load resisted by the steel and that resisted by the concrete. Notice that vertical force equilibrium indicates that the force in the steel, F_S, plus the force in the concrete, F_C, must equal the applied 100,000-lb load:

$$100{,}000 = F_S + F_C$$

This vertical force equilibrium equation alone will not yield the two unknown forces, and the horizontal and moment equilibrium equations cannot aid us here in the analysis of this compressive two-force member. Thus, the problem is indeterminate based on equilibrium, and we will need another relationship (equation) between the two forces if we want to solve for two unknowns.

By observing that deformation compatibility must exist we are able to develop this second relationship. Deformation compatibility simply tells us that with the two materials working compositely as one member, the 100,000-lb compressive force causes the steel pipe to shorten the same amount as does the concrete cylinder inside the pipe. We can then apply the relationship among deformation and member and material properties, $D = FL/AE$, as follows:

$$D = \frac{F_S \times L}{A_S \times E_S} = \frac{F_C \times L}{A_C \times E_C}$$

FIGURE 4.7

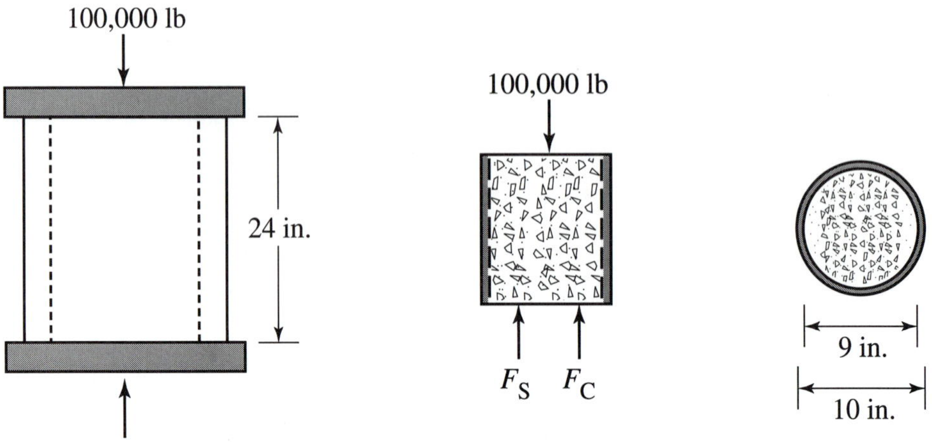

Exercise Rework this problem for a 13.5-in. × 13.5-in. wood column with a 10.5-in. × 10.5-in. hollow core that is filled with a stiff foam product with a modulus of elasticity of $E = 200{,}000$ psi. ■

In this relationship, the member length is $L = 24$ in., the moduli of elasticity for concrete and steel are $E_C = 3{,}600{,}000$ psi, and $E_S = 30{,}000{,}000$ psi, respectively. The concrete cross-sectional area is $A_C = \pi/4 \times 9^2 = 64\ \text{in}^2$, and the steel cross section is $A_S = \pi/4 \times 10^2 - 64 = 15\ \text{in}^2$. Substituting these values, we find

$$\frac{F_S \times 24}{15 \times 30{,}000{,}000} = \frac{F_C \times 24}{64 \times 3{,}600{,}000}$$

This reduces to

$$\frac{F_S}{18{,}750{,}000} = \frac{F_C}{9{,}600{,}000}$$

With further simplification, we see that $F_S \approx 2 \times F_C$, which means that the 15 in^2 of steel carries twice as much of the applied 100,000-lb compressive load as does the 64 in^2 of concrete. The denominators in the equation above represent the individual AE/L terms for the two materials.

The term AE/L is referred to as member stiffness, and we see that the steel portion of the composite member is twice as stiff as the concrete portion, and this is why the steel carries twice as much load as the concrete. This indicates a basic structural principle–*the stiffest part of a structure attracts the greatest share of the load.*

Combining the equilibrium equation and the deformation compatibility relationship, we can find the force carried by concrete:

$$100{,}000 = (2 \times F_C) + F_C$$

From this we get $F_C = 33{,}000$ lb and thus the steel force must be

$$F_S = 2 \times F_C = 67{,}000\ \text{lb}$$

4.7 Nonuniform Axial Stress and Centroids

Thus far, we have considered axial stresses to be acting uniformly on the cross section of a member. This will be the case when the line of action of the force is along the line forming the longitudinal axis through what is known as the centroid of each cross-sectional area.

If an axial force passes through the centroids of every cross section along a member, the force is said to be acting centrically. If the line of force action is different from the member centric axis, it is acting eccentrically and it will create nonuniform axial stress. In Figure 4.8, we see the distribution of axial stress as the line of force action moves closer to the bottom edge of a rectangular member. In each pictured case, the average stress is $f = F/A$. When the force acts at one-third of the member height from the bottom of

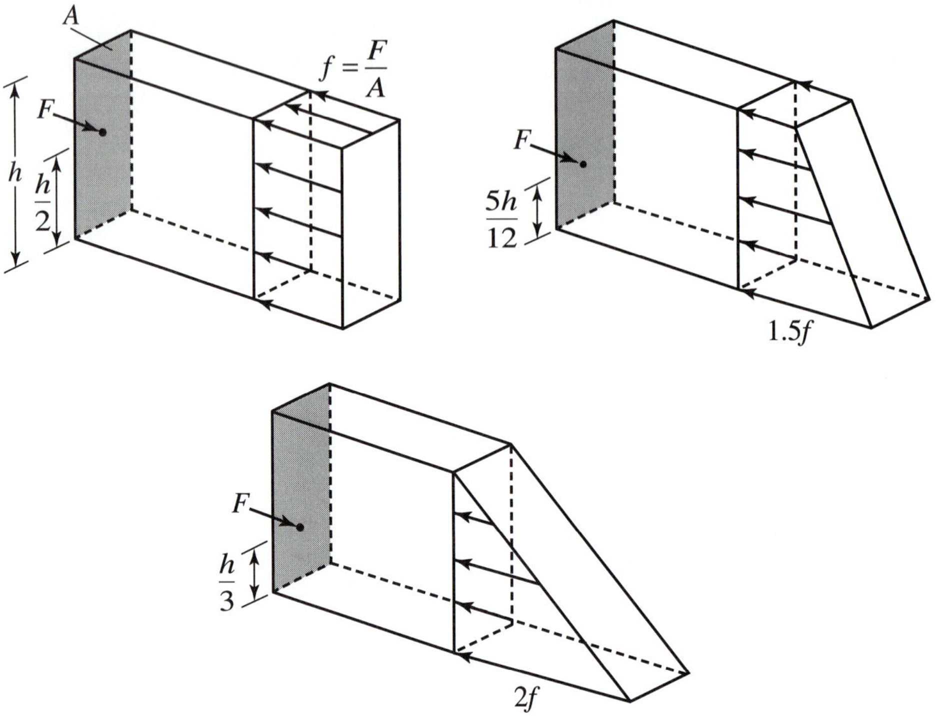

FIGURE 4.8

the section, the resulting stress variation forms a wedge with zero stress on the top edge and twice the average stress, $2 \times F/A$, on the bottom edge.

Figure 4.9 shows several cross-sectional areas of different structural members labeled with their centroidal locations. If we think of any one of these areas as a thin metal plate, the area centroid of the cross section coincides with the center of gravity of the plate. We recall that the c.g. is the point where the weight of the plate is effectively concentrated, so the area centroid is defined as the point at which the total area of a cross section is effectively concentrated.

The centroids of several different areas are shown in the figure and may be determined by subdividing the areas into subrectangles. We can choose an arbitrary baseline, and say that the total area times its centroidal distance to the baseline is equal to what is called the area moment. The sum of the individual sub-area moments times each of their centroidal distances to the baseline must equal the area moment of the total undivided area. As seen in the figure for the triangular area, by equating the area moment to the sum of the sub-area moments, we can determine the location of the centroid of the area relative to the baseline.

We make use of the location of cross-sectional area centroids when investigating structural members, particularly columns and beams. The two different areas shown in Figure 4.10 are the cross sections of prefabricated concrete beams. The first is called a double T beam, and the second is a hollow core slab panel.

Recalling what we said about the center of gravity and the centroid, the horizontal location of the centroids of the two areas is easily seen to lie

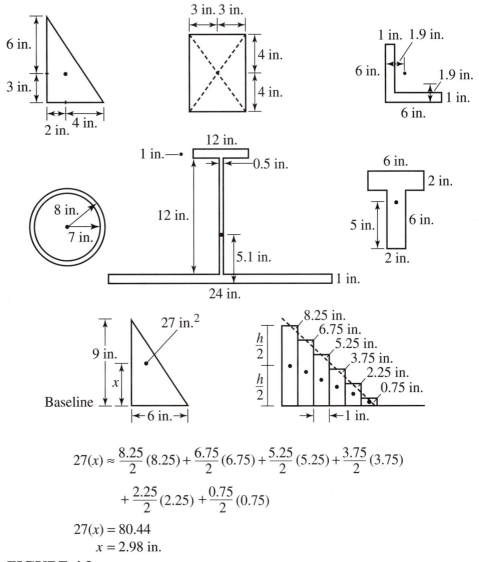

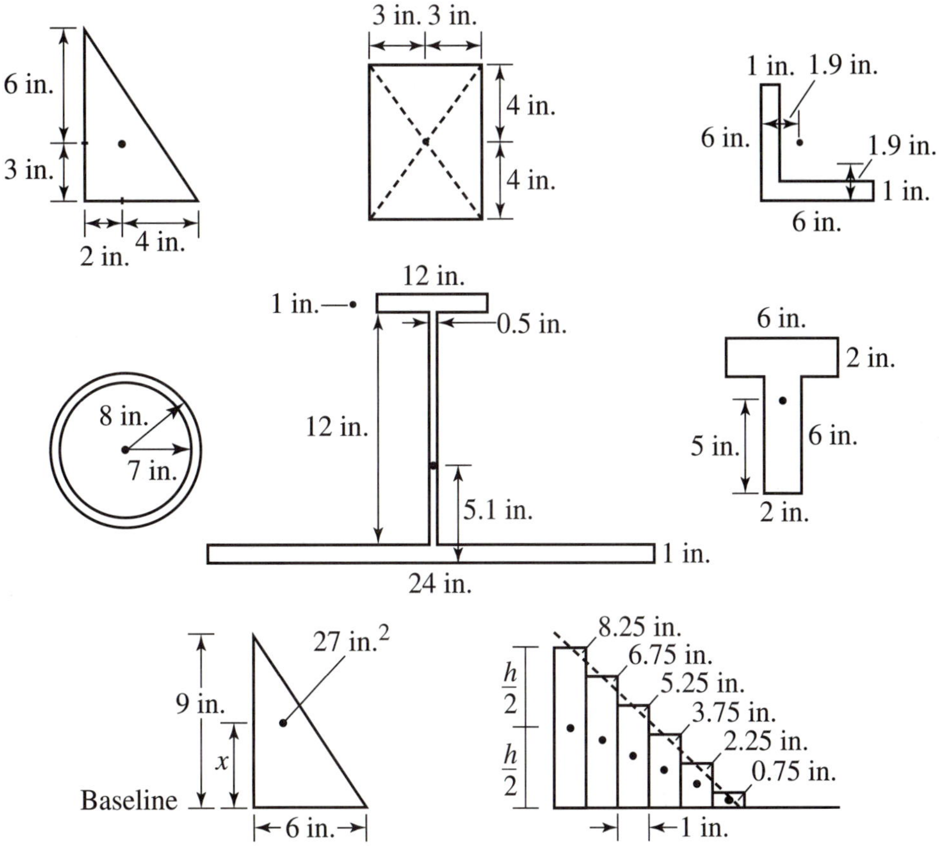

$$27(x) \approx \frac{8.25}{2}(8.25) + \frac{6.75}{2}(6.75) + \frac{5.25}{2}(5.25) + \frac{3.75}{2}(3.75) + \frac{2.25}{2}(2.25) + \frac{0.75}{2}(0.75)$$

$$27(x) = 80.44$$
$$x = 2.98 \text{ in.}$$

FIGURE 4.9

on a vertical line of symmetry as shown. This is the vertical centroidal axis. We can imagine that if the areas were thin plates of metal and the vertical centroidal axes were taut strings, then the plates could be perfectly balanced on the string. This is because the center of gravity–the point at which all the plate weight is effectively concentrated–is located at the centroid and is thus acting directly down on the string. Move the string over a bit so that the center of gravity is not directly over the string, and the plate weight would create an unbalanced moment that causes the plate to rotate and fall off the string. Thus, an axis of symmetry, such as the vertical axis in these cases, will be a centroidal axis.

We next want to locate the horizontal centroidal axis of each of these areas relative to their baselines. We thus need to determine the distance, Y, for each area. Looking first at the double T, the area is subdivided as shown with the centroids of each sub-area located in the figure. Keeping the idea of the area as a thin plate of metal, the moments that the

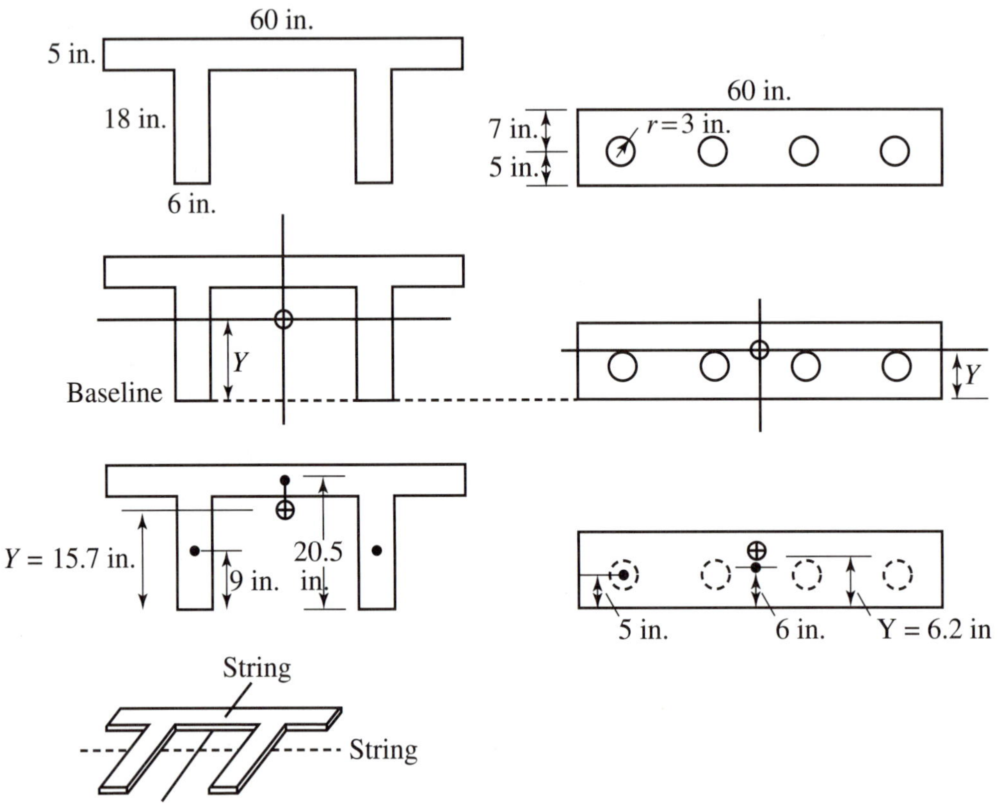

FIGURE 4.10

sub-areas create about the baseline must be the same as the area moment of the total undivided area that is concentrated at the centroid. For the double T we have

$$2 \times (6 \times 18) \times 9 + (5 \times 60) \times 20.5 = [5 \times 60 + 2 \times (6 \times 18)] \times Y$$

From this we get $Y = 15.7$ in.

For the hollow core slab, we subdivide the area into a large 12-in. × 60-in. rectangle minus the area of four 6-in.-diameter circles, and we have

$$(12 \times 60) \times 6 - (4 \times \pi \times 3^2) \times 5 = [(12 \times 60) - (4 \times \pi \times 3^2)] \times Y$$

From this, $Y = 6.2$ in.

For practice, you may wish to verify the centroidal axis locations for the areas presented in Figure 4.9.

4.8 Bearing Stress

When structural members transmit their loads to one another, the transfer of forces must occur over some area of mutual contact, and the area must be large enough to prevent overstressing at the contact points. In Figure 4.11, we see that *bearing stress* is the compressive stress between two members in contact–it may also be referred to as *contact pressure.* The elements in contact ex-

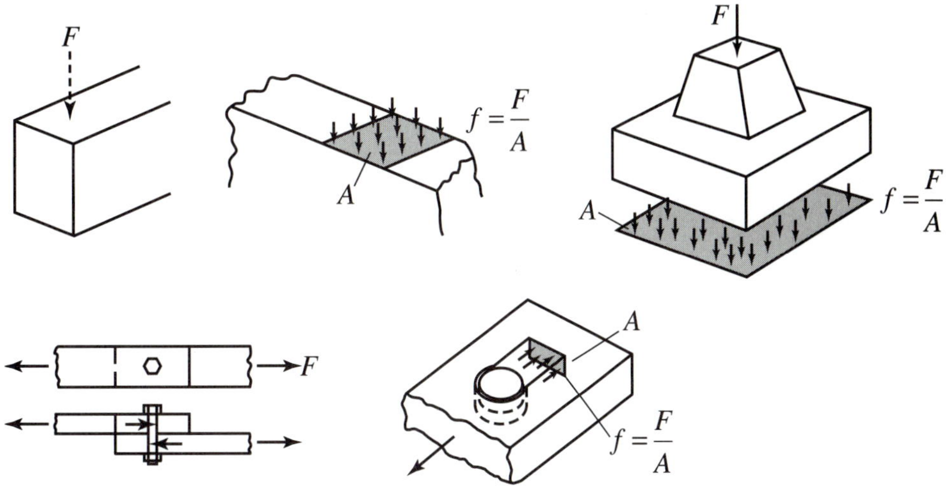

FIGURE 4.11

ert an equal and opposite force, *F*, on one another that creates a bearing stress, $f = F/A$, acting perpendicular to the area, *A*, of the contact surfaces. Bearing stresses between beams and their supports, footings and soil, and between members connected by bolts are the most common types of bearing stresses that we will encounter throughout the book.

As an example, suppose that for the pier support shown in the figure that the safe soil pressure under the footing is limited to no more than $f = 2{,}000$ lb/ft^2 (psf). If the downward load of the floor, walls, and roof is $F = 4{,}000$ lb on this pier that supports a house, what are the dimensions needed for a square concrete footing that delivers the pier load to the soil?

This is a rather easy problem to solve. Since $f = F/A$, we have

$$A = \frac{F}{f} = \frac{4{,}000}{2{,}000} = 2\ \text{ft}^2$$

The square footing dimensions are thus each $\sqrt{2} = 1.41$ ft (17 in.), and we would probably use a standard size 18-in. $\times$ 18-in. concrete pad.

5 SHEAR STRESS

5.1 SIMPLE SHEAR STRESS

In addition to the various forms of axial and bearing stresses that we have discussed, another mode of stress common to structural members is *shear stress.* Actually, there are two basic modes of stress: (1) stress perpendicular (or normal) to a surface–axial, bearing, and flexural bending stress; and (2) stress tangent to a surface–simple, torsional, and flexural shear stress. We will discuss flexural stresses later.

Shear forces are so called because of the "clipping" action that they create within a member (note that scissors and hair clippers are often called shears). Simple shear stress occurs when the action of a shear force is distributed over a cross-sectional area to which the shearing force is parallel (or tangent) as shown in Figure 5.1. The simple shear stress due to a shear force F, acting over a cross-sectional area A is

$$f_V = \frac{F}{A}$$

The subscript V is a common identifier of shearing stress to distinguish it from stresses that act perpendicular to cross sections.

The notched hanger in the figure suspends a tensile axial load, $F = 1{,}000$ lb, and the shaded area is $A = (2 \times h)$ in^2. If the wood shear strength on surfaces parallel to the grain should not exceed $f_V = 100$ psi, how long should we make dimension h? We answer this by simply rearranging the stress definition to find

$$A = 2 \times h = \frac{F}{f_V} = \frac{1{,}000}{100} = 10 \text{ in}^2$$

Therefore, $h = 5$ in. If h is less than 5 in., the possibility of shear overstress increases, and the protruding notch might be clipped off by the downward acting force, F.

Shear often exists on the contact area between separate objects connected through friction, adhesives, nails, bolts, welds, and so on. For instance, the concrete pile, a structural member commonly used in foundations to deliver loads into the soil, in the figure has a diameter, $d = 18$ in. (1.5 ft), and its length in the soil is $L = 20$ ft. The contact area between the pile and soil is $A = \pi dL$. We could test the pile to determine the frictional stress acting on its surface by simply pulling it from the ground with a force F. From this, we could determine the shear stress, f_V, between the soil and the pile, called adhesion or

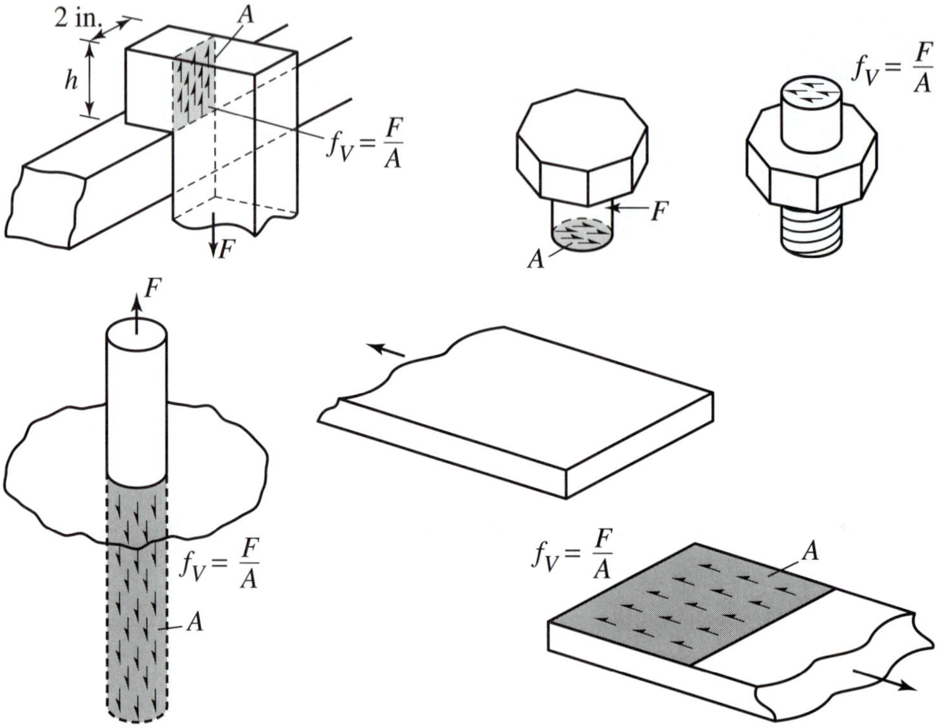

FIGURE 5.1

skin friction. If it takes 45,000 lb to break the pile free from the soil, the skin friction is determined to be

$$f_V = \frac{F}{A} = \frac{45{,}000}{\pi \times 1.5 \times 20} = 480 \text{ psf}$$

5.2 Bearing Stress and Shear on a Corbel

A *corbel,* or haunch, is a ledge attached to a column to support a beam. Figure 5.2 shows a corbel made from timber that transfers a 12,000-lb timber beam support reaction to a timber column. The column is notched so that bearing stress between the corbel and the column supports the beam reaction. There is also bearing stress between the beam and the corbel, but it is a lower stress, since the contact area is larger. The corbel can be seen to transfer the beam load to the column through shear stress that is parallel to the wood grain. To prevent the corbel from rotating and thus being pulled out of the notch, it would need to be securely attached to the column with large wood screws called lag bolts, but these are not our concern here.

Suppose that the allowable shearing stress parallel to wood grain is 80 psi, and the allowable bearing stress parallel to grain is about 1,000 psi. The bearing stress between the beam and the corbel acts perpendicular to the beam grain, and this bearing stress is limited to 500 psi. To check the adequacy of this simple beam-to-column connection, we need to answer a few questions. Is the 12-in.-deep corbel adequately sized to prevent a shear fail-

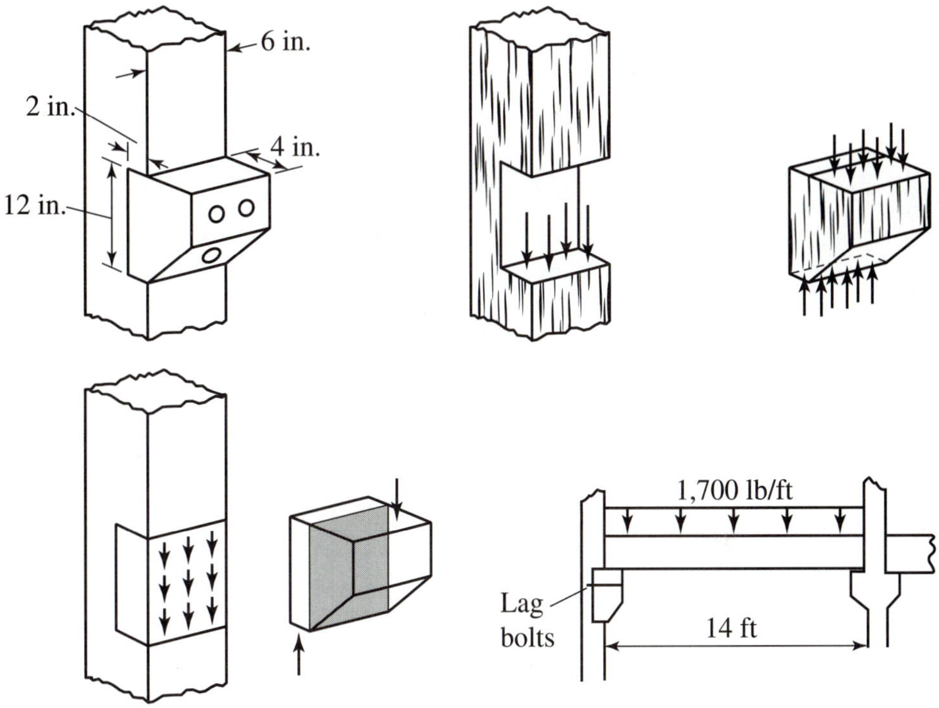

FIGURE 5.2

ure? Is the 2-in. notch deep enough to prevent column bearing overstress? Is the 4-in. corbel ledge wide enough to prevent bearing overstress of the beam?

The shearing stress in the corbel is

$$f_V = \frac{F}{A} = \frac{12{,}000}{12 \times 6} = 167 \text{ psi}$$

This shear stress is excessive. If the corbel is to be used, it will need a depth, h, sufficient to keep the shear stress at 80 psi and thus

$$\frac{F}{f_V} = h \times 6 = \frac{12{,}000}{80}$$

From this, $h = 25$ in.

The critical bearing stress in the corbel occurs on the bottom 2-in. $\times$ 6-in. bearing surface and is

$$f = \frac{12{,}000}{2 \times 6} = 1{,}000 \text{ psi}$$

This stress equals the allowable stress, so it is OK. The bearing stress perpendicular to the grain of the beam is given by the beam reaction divided by the contact area between the beam and its support ledge

$$f = \frac{12{,}000}{4 \times 6} = 500 \text{ psi}$$

Since this equals the allowable stress of 500 psi, it is also OK.

Exercise If the beam spans 10 ft instead of 14 ft in this problem, what notch size and corbel height are required? ■

5.3 Punching Shear Through a Footing

Figure 5.3 shows a concentrated column load, P, being spread out over a larger area, $B \times B$, through the use of a footing, another type of foundation used to "ground out" the loads of a structure. Through a footing, the contact pressure (bearing stress) on the soil is reduced from a large stress equal to the axial

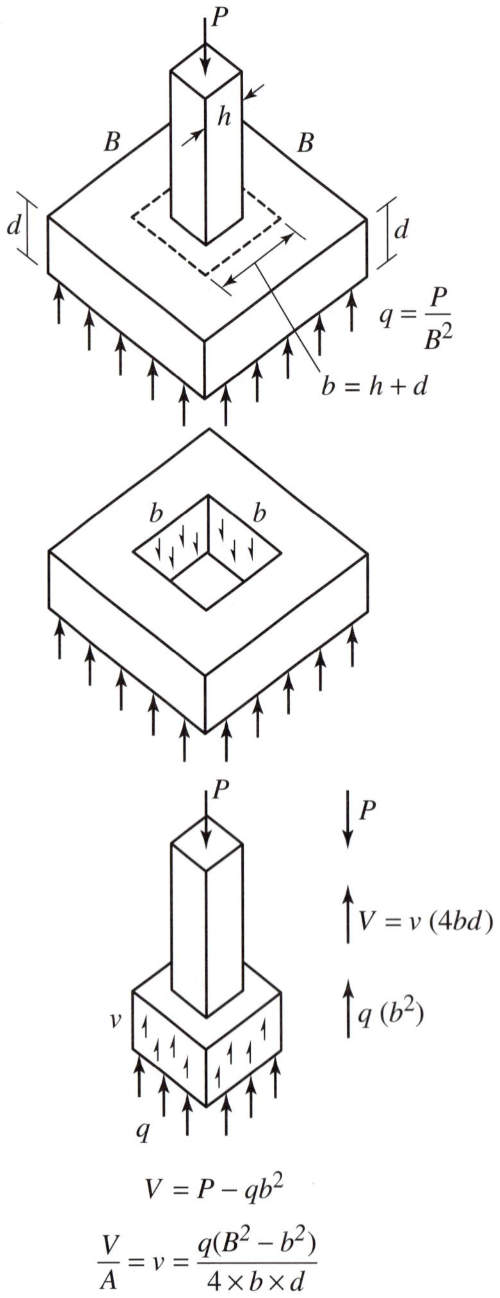

FIGURE 5.3

stress of the concrete column, $f = P/h^2$, to a much lower uniform pressure that the soil can sustain:

$$q = \frac{P}{B^2}$$

When we are given a value for the load to be grounded, P, and the allowable soil pressure, q, we determine the required footing size as

$$B = \sqrt{\frac{P}{q}}$$

The square footing dimension B required to support a column load P is thus determined by the allowable soil pressure, q.

The footing must also be thick enough to prevent the column from punching a hole through the footing as shown. The dimensions of this punched-through hole are generally assumed to be $b \times b$, where b is the column dimension, h, plus the footing effective thickness, d:

$$b = h + d$$

The required thickness of concrete footings is determined by limiting the punching shear stress that acts on the four sides of the potential failure hole with its shear area of $4 \times b \times d$.

The load diagram of a column that has punched through the footing is shown in the figure. Vertical force equilibrium indicates that the shearing force is the difference in the large downward column load and the small upward force due to the uniform soil pressure acting on the bottom of the punched-through portion of footing. The shear force is thus

$$V = P - q \times b^2 = q \times B^2 - q \times b^2 = q \times (B^2 - b^2)$$

The shear stress that this force creates on the four surfaces of the square punched-out portion of slab is thus

$$v = \frac{V}{A} = \frac{q \times (B^2 - b^2)}{4 \times b \times d}$$

If a 12-in.-square column delivers a 150,000-lb column load to a footing and the allowable soil pressure is 2,000 psf, what is the required dimension base width of a square footing? Is a 20-in. footing thickness sufficient if the punching shear stress is not to exceed 70 psi?

The required footing area is determined as

$$A = B \times B = \frac{F}{f} = \frac{150{,}000}{2{,}000} = 75 \text{ ft}^2$$

From this

$$B = \sqrt{75} = 8.66 \text{ ft} = 8 \text{ ft} - 8 \text{ in.}$$

Exercise Rework the problem if the allowable soil pressure is 6,000 psf.

Rework this problem using a 16-in. × 16-in. column carrying 225,000 lb to the ground. ■

The dimension of the square portion of the footing that is tending to punch through is

$$b = h + d = 12 + 20 = 32 \text{ in.} = 2.67 \text{ ft}$$

Thus, we compute the punching shear stress to be

$$v = \frac{q \times (B^2 - b^2)}{4 \times (b \times d)} = \frac{2{,}000 \times (8.66^2 - 2.67^2)}{4 \times (32 \times 20)} = 53 \text{ psi}$$

Since $v = 53$ psi does not exceed the allowable stress of 70 psi, the footing is thick enough to safely prevent a punching failure.

5.4 Torsional Shear Stress

Though not as common in buildings and bridges, another form of shear stress is that created by the twisting action of a torque, and it is called *torsional shear stress*. Probably the most common occurrence of torsional shear stress is in a circular drive shaft that couples an engine to the wheels of a vehicle or some equipment such as a pump or air compressor. The engine twists the shaft at one end, driving a device that resists with a counter twist–action equals reaction. The twist, called torque, is actually a moment acting about the shaft longitudinal axis. Figure 5.4 shows a shaft resisting torque, *T*.

We can see that a shaft cut into two sections exposes the torsional shearing stress that allows for the transfer of torque from one end to another. Remember that shear stress acts tangent to a surface–the shaft cross-sectional area in this case. For a solid shaft, the stress varies in intensity from zero at

FIGURE 5.4

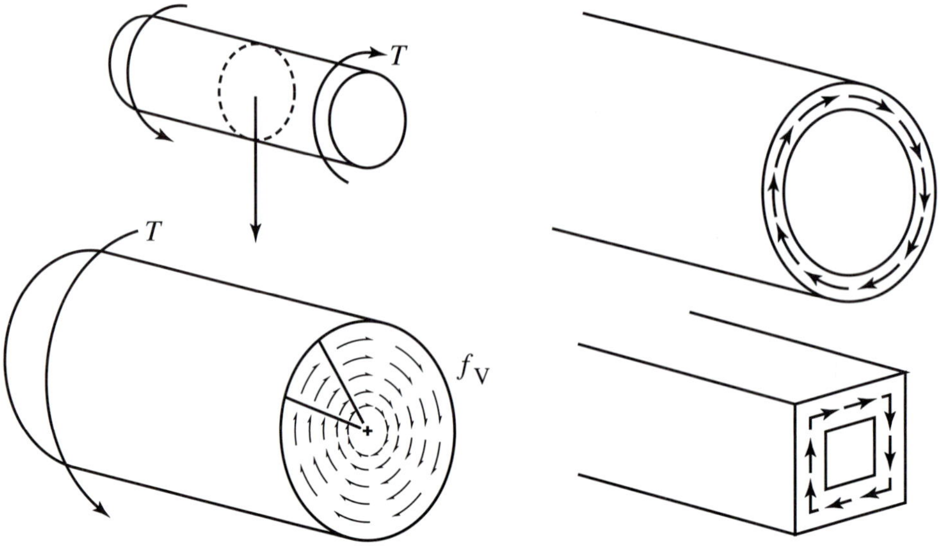

the shaft center to a maximum value at the outer radius, while for a hollow shaft, the stress is fairly constant around the ring section area, as shown.

Torsional stresses are created in structural members such as exterior building beams and horizontally curved bridge girders. These members usually have I-shaped or rectangular cross sections that must resist torsion by developing complex torsional shear and torsional axial stress (called *warping stress*) that are more severe than the simple torsional shear in circular cross sections. For this reason, we generally try to minimize torsion on structural members, and when we have torsion, we try to use round or at least closed shapes, such as rectangular beams or hollow tubes.

5.5 Bolts and Stress Concentration

There are an unlimited number of ways to connect structural members, and we will look at common connection details when we discuss design. The stresses that occur in connectors can be very complex. Even the most basic bolt and weld connections involve several stress modes.

For bearing-type bolted connections, including nails, wood pegs, steel reinforcing bars, or other dowel-like connectors, the force transmitted through the connected members acts as a shear force that tends to clip the bolt into a top and a bottom half when the shear stress, $f_V = F/A$, becomes excessive (Figure 5.1). The term *bearing bolt connection* refers to the fact that the force, F, in a member is transferred to another member through bearing between the bolt and one side of the hole in each member. The bearing stress is $f = F/A$, where A is the projected rectangle equal to the bolt diameter times the member thickness (Figure 4.11).

Friction-type bolted connections are so called because the bolts are tightened with such a high torque that the two joined members are clamped together and interlock in friction. The force F is transferred between members via this friction shear stress f_V, as though the members are glued together (Figure 5.1). These connections are often called slip-critical because they do not have the slack inherent in bearing connections, where the bolts must shift within their slightly oversized holes to bear against the connected members that contain the holes.

In Figure 5.5, we see the two basic configurations of bolted connections: single shear and double shear. In single shear, two connected members tend to shear the bolt in two on just one plane, whereas two planes of shear occur for bolts through three members. Single shear connectors usually connect a lightly loaded secondary element to a primary member. Double shear connections are used for the transfer of larger loads from a pair of similar members to a single member, or vice versa.

Suppose the double shear connection consists of four 1-in.-diameter bolts–two rows of two bolts–connecting three $\frac{3}{4}$-in.-thick plates and the force on the connection is $F = 12{,}000$ lb. What is the critical bearing stress, and what is the shear stress in the bolts? The critical bearing stress occurs in the main member where the 12,000-lb force is transferred in bearing on four projected areas, and each projected bearing area equals

$$A = 1 \times \frac{3}{4} = \frac{3}{4}\ \text{in}^2$$

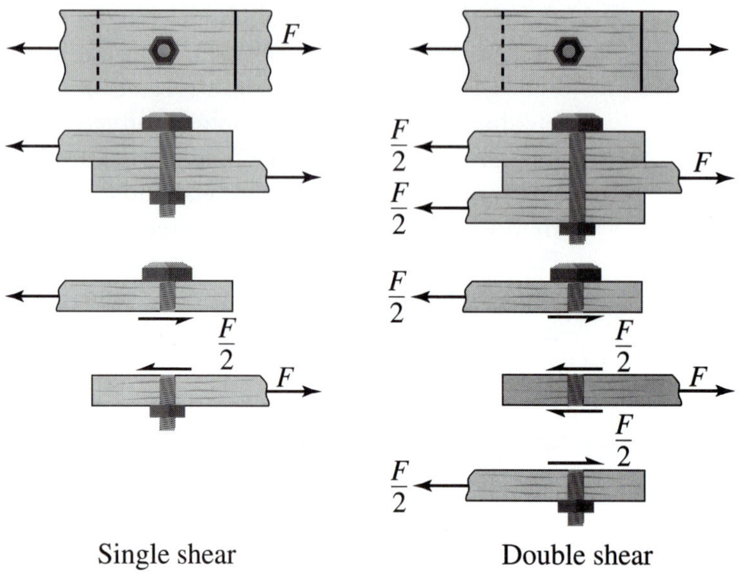

FIGURE 5.5

The bearing stress is

$$f = \frac{12{,}000}{\frac{3}{4} \times 4} = 4{,}000 \text{ psi}$$

The bearing stress on the eight bearing areas of the $\frac{3}{4}$-in. side members is merely half this value. The bolt shear stress occurs on two planes of each bolt, for a total of eight planes with a total area,

$$A = 8 \times \left(\pi \times \frac{1}{4} \times 1^2 \right) = 6.28 \text{ in}^2$$

The shear stress is therefore

$$f_V = \frac{12{,}000}{6.28} = 1{,}910 \text{ psi}$$

FIGURE 5.6

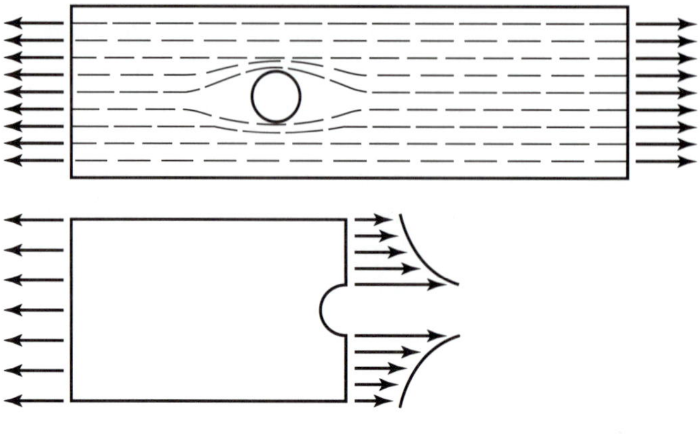

Obviously, bolt holes reduce the cross-sectional area A of the connected members. Since stress is force per area, member axial stresses increase near bolt holes because the net area is reduced. The actual analysis of stresses around bolts is quite complex. Stresses must "flow" around a bolt hole and stress concentration occurs at the perimeter of the hole as shown in Figure 5.6. Structural detailers must take care when dimensioning bolted connections to prevent the stress increases around bolts from becoming a problem.

5.6 WELDS

Welding is also a commonly used method for connecting steel members, especially those connections that can be performed in the shop, rather than in the field, where it is more advantageous to use bolts. In welding, the steel of two separate members is fused with that of a third steel element–a welding rod that the welder holds close to the two members while carefully passing it along the length of the connection. The three steels melt together under intense heat from an electric arc that is generated by an electric current that is made to jump the short distance from the tip of the steel welding rod to the steel of the two members being joined. Figure 5.7 shows the two major types of welds–a groove weld and a fillet weld.

A groove weld is oriented transversely to the longitudinal axis of two axially loaded members and transfers axial stress, $f = F/A$, between the members. This is referred to as a butt joint. If properly crafted, such a weld is stronger than the two joined members.

Fillet welds transfer the axial force of one member through shear in the weld to the second member. As shown in the figure, the weld shear stress is $f_V = F/A$, where the effective shear area is the total weld length, $2 \times L/2$ in this case, times the weld throat, which is $0.707 \times s$. Weld size is denoted by the weld leg dimensions, s. A common weld size is $\frac{5}{16}$ in. The shear stress of a

FIGURE 5.7

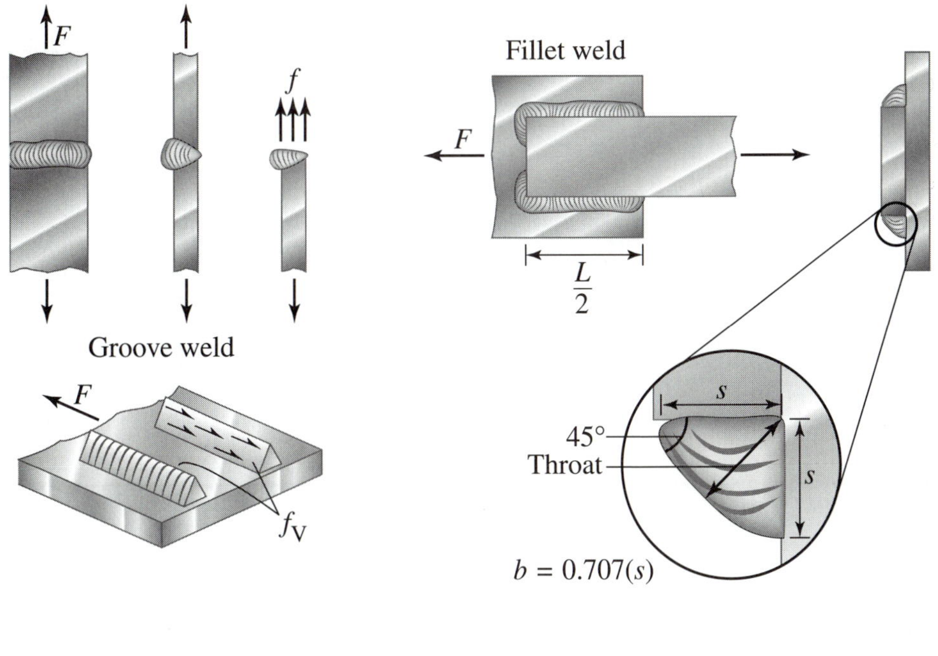

fillet weld is usually limited to f_V = 18,000 psi. Putting this together, the force that can be transmitted per inch of $\frac{5}{16}$-in. fillet weld is

$$F = f_V \times A = 18{,}000 \times \left(1 \times 0.707 \times \frac{5}{16}\right) = 4{,}000 \text{ lb/in.}$$

5.7 Bolted and Welded Connections

Circular cross sections are the most efficient shapes to use for columns, but we often use open sections like I-beams when selecting steel columns, because it is easier to make connections with the beams. If a hollow pipe or rectangular tube is used, beams cannot easily be bolted to these sections, so they must usually be welded. Since it is easier and more desirable to perform field erection with bolts instead of welds, a practical way to use field-bolted connections of a steel I-beam to a hollow steel pipe column is shown in Figure 5.8.

In this case, a 5-in. × $\frac{1}{2}$-in. plate is shop-welded all around its contact edges with the pipe for a total of 10 in. of $\frac{5}{16}$-in. fillet weld. In the field, two 1-in. diameter bolts will attach the I-beam through its $\frac{1}{4}$-in.-thick web. If the reaction that the beam delivers to the column is 36,000 lb, we want to determine if the fillet weld is adequate. Also, we can check the shear stress in the welds and bolts, and the bolt bearing stress on the I-beam web.

The strength of a standard $\frac{5}{16}$-in. fillet weld was shown to be 4,000 lb/in. Since the total weld length provided is 10 in., the weld capacity is 40,000 lb, which is greater than the required strength of 36,000 lb, and so the weld is OK. The actual shear stress on the weld is

FIGURE 5.8

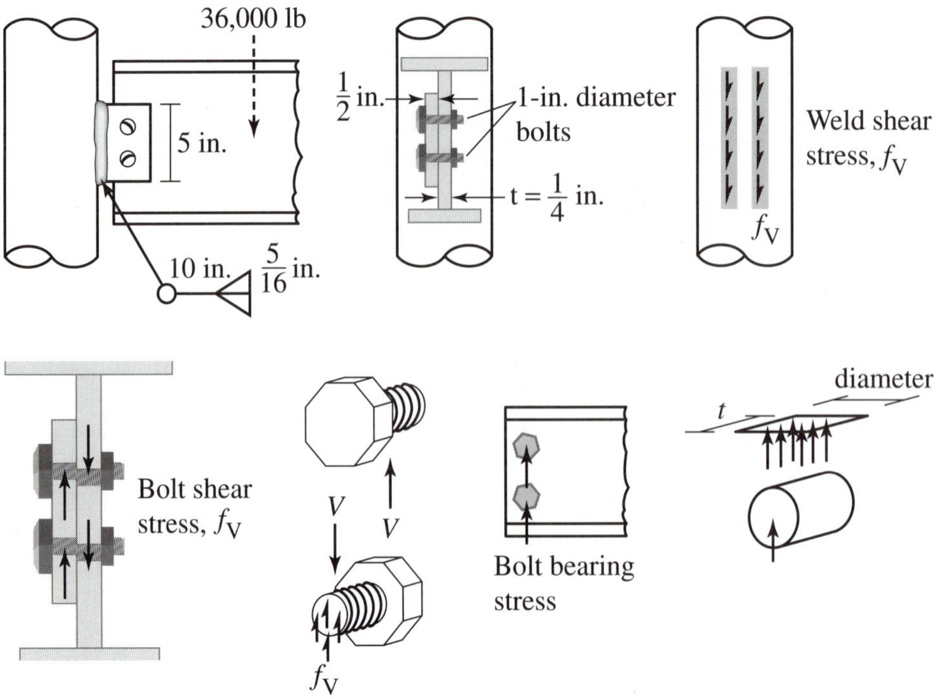

$$f_V = \frac{F}{A} = \frac{36{,}000}{10 \times 0.707 \times 5/16} = 16{,}300 \text{ psi}$$

The shear area of the two bolts in single shear is given as

$$A = 2 \times \left(\frac{\pi}{4} \times 1^2\right) = 1.57 \text{ in}^2$$

The shear stress in the bolts is thus

$$f_V = \frac{F}{A} = \frac{36{,}000}{1.57} = 22{,}900 \text{ psi}$$

This is near the maximum allowable shear stress range of high-strength bolts (27,000 psi for A325 bolts in bearing-type connections).

The bearing stress between the bolts and the web plate of the I-beam is determined as the total reaction force divided by the projected area of contact between the two 1-in. bolts and the $\frac{1}{4}$-in. web plate:

$$f = \frac{F}{A} = \frac{36{,}000}{2\left(1 \times \frac{1}{4}\right)} = 72{,}000 \text{ psi}$$

Allowable bearing stress of steel is very high, typically exceeding 90,000 psi, so we do not have a problem with the bolts bearing against the web. Notice that since the plate welded to the column is thicker than the web, the bearing stress will be less in the connection plate element.

Exercise It is usually desirable to have symmetry in connection details. Suppose that two $\frac{5}{16}$-in. × 5-in. plates are each fillet welded to the pipe with a 5-in. length of $\frac{1}{4}$-in. fillet weld for each plate. Now, two $\frac{3}{4}$-in. bolts are used to connect the I-beam to the two plates in a double shear connection. What are the stresses in the weld and the bolts, and what is the critical bearing stress due to the bolts? ■

6 Stress and Deformation of Beams

6.1 Bending Stress

Beams are to structures what interest rates are to the stock market–almost everything. Not only are beams ubiquitous throughout any structural system, but as we have discussed, even elements and subassemblies that are not beams, such as columns, cables, trusses, and diaphragms, are still treated as being beamlike. In the case of a bridge structure, we might even say that the entire structural system acts as a horizontal member supporting a load over a span–in other words, a beam!

At any section along a beam, there may be up to three internal reactions: an axial force, a transverse shear force, and a bending moment. We have previously shown how to determine the magnitude of these internal reactions using the method of sections. We now focus on the stresses due to the bending moment, then the stresses due to the transverse shear force, and then the sag, or deflection, created in a beam.

Of the three internal reactions, axial force, shear force, and bending moment, we have already discussed in detail the stress and deformation created by the axial force. The axial stress that occurs if there is an axial force is independent of the stresses due to shear force and bending. We will see that bending moment creates stress along the longitudinal axis of the beam member similar to axial stress, so that any such axial stress will superimpose with the bending stresses (we will discuss this subject in a later section).

A beam supporting transverse load is said to be in flexure, in reference to the noticeable bending or flexing that occurs in beams. The deformation due to bending is called *deflection.* The stresses due to both the bending moment and the shear force in beams are called *flexural stresses.* These two very different modes of stress are linked together–shear stresses derive from bending stresses, as we shall see. (In fact, in a mathematical analysis, we see from calculus that an equation expressing beam shear may be found as the derivative of the moment equation.)

For this discussion, we will focus on a beam with a rectangular cross section, shown in Figure 6.1. The width and height of the beam cross section are b and h, respectively. We locate a segment of the beam by drawing two parallel lines on the sides of the unloaded straight member separated by a unit distance, 1. We would observe on a deflecting loaded beam that the lines are now squeezed closer together at the top, where the segment is shortened to a length, $1 - d$, and the lines are stretched farther apart at the bottom, where the segment length has grown to length, $1 + d$. Remember that d is strain, or unit deformation. There is no change at the midheight of the beam, where the segment length is still the unit distance, 1.

Since d is strain, and we know that stress is proportional to strain, we conclude that the top half of the beam is subject to a wedge of compressive

$$F = \frac{f}{2}\left(b \times \frac{h}{2}\right)$$

$$M = F \times \frac{2h}{3} = f \times \frac{bh^2}{6} = f \times S$$

$$f = M/S$$

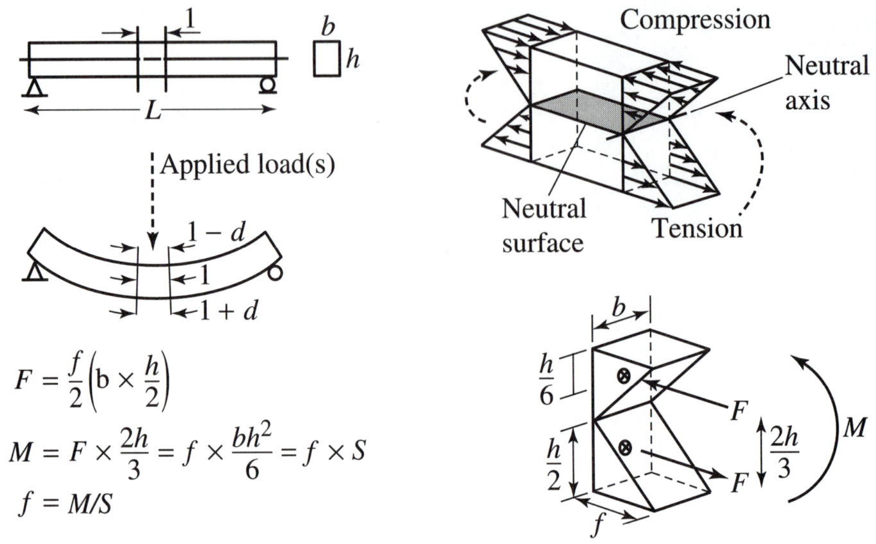

FIGURE 6.1

stress and the bottom half sees a wedge of tension stress. The bending stresses, f, have their greatest magnitude at the top and bottom of the beam. These bending stresses act perpendicular to the cross section and in the longitudinal direction of the beam. The midheight of the beam is a neutral surface where the two zero stress sides of the wedges meet. The intersection with this neutral surface at beam midheight with a cross-sectional area is called the neutral axis, as indicated in the figure.

The two wedges of stress create two equal opposing compression and tension forces determined as average wedge stress times area, or

$$F = \frac{1}{2} \times f \times b \times \frac{h}{2}$$

These equal and opposite forces act at the wedge centroids and so are separated by a lever arm of $2/3 \times h$. These equal and opposite forces separated by a lever arm create an internal bending couple that is equal to and resists the external bending moment, M, caused by loads on the beam. The internal couple moment is

$$M = F \times \frac{2}{3}(h) = f \times \frac{b \times h^2}{6}$$

The term $b \times h^2/6$ is called section modulus, S. Section modulus is a measure of the moment capacity of the rectangular beam cross section. The section modulus for any other beam cross-sectional shape besides a rectangular cross section can also be determined. In the case of steel I-beams, for instance, S is usually given in tables, but it can easily be computed, as we will see later. The units of section modulus are given in cubic inches. We may now write the flexure formula, which gives the bending stress, f, in terms of applied bending moment, M, and beam section modulus, S:

$$f = \frac{M}{S}$$

The formula is analogous to the basic stress formula, $f = F/A$, and is similarly used. By rearranging the three terms of the flexure formula, we can check the applied stress, determine required beam section size (S), or compare the moment capacities of beam alternates. Note that the maximum bending stress in a beam occurs at the top and bottom fibers of the beam at a section where the internal bending moment is highest (at midspan for most simple beams).

For example, suppose the beam of Figure 6.1 is 20 ft long, 18 in. high, and 6 in. wide, and carries a 10,000-lb load concentrated at midspan. The support reactions would each be 10,000/2 = 5,000 lb, and at a midspan section, the externally applied bending moment equals the reaction times 20/2 ft, or $M = 50{,}000$ ft-lb (600,000 in-lb). The beam section modulus is

$$S = \frac{6 \times 18^2}{6} = 324 \text{ in}^3$$

From the flexure formula, we compute the internal bending stress that results:

$$f = \frac{M}{S} = \frac{600{,}000}{324} = 1{,}850 \text{ psi}$$

As a second example, suppose the highest stress allowed is $f = 1{,}850$ psi, but the load on our 20-ft beam doubles to 20,000 lb. The applied moment would also double and we would need a beam with a section modulus of

$$S = \frac{M}{f} = \frac{1{,}200{,}000}{1{,}850} = 648 \text{ in}^3$$

If we want to keep the same 6-in. width, then we need a new beam height,

$$h = \sqrt{\frac{6 \times S}{b}} = \sqrt{\frac{6 \times 648}{6}} = 25.5 \text{ in.}$$

6.2 Flexural Shear Stress

We said that the internal transverse shear force is called flexural shear, and it is linked to the internal bending moment. Consider Figure 6.2 in which the left section of arbitrary length r is taken from a simple beam carrying a concentrated midspan load. As shown, the top half of the rectangular beam will be sheared off along the neutral surface at the beam midheight by the wedge force F, unless there is an equal and opposite horizontal force along the neutral plane to resist it. This force along the neutral surface creates horizontal shear stress f_V that is proportional to the transverse shear force V at each section along the member.

As before, the wedge force times the couple moment arm equals the internal moment resistance of the beam, so we see that the wedge force is

$$F = \frac{M}{\frac{2}{3} \times h}$$

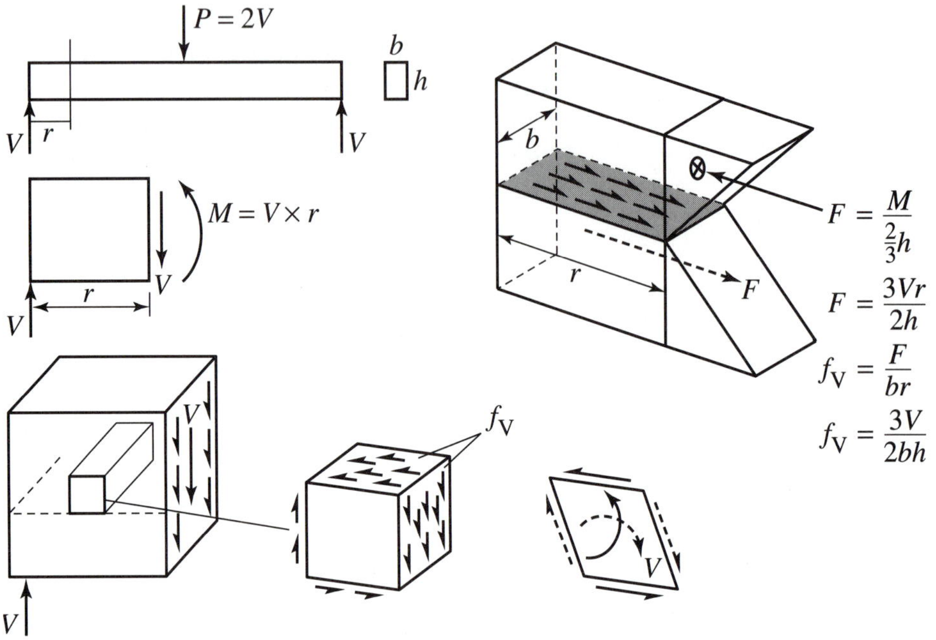

FIGURE 6.2

The equal force on the neutral surface resisting this wedge force is the product of the shear stress and the area over which it acts

$$F = f_V \times b \times r$$

This force is the shear stress times the shaded surface area of the neutral surface that is shown in the figure. From equilibrium of the left beam section, we find that the bending moment is

$$M = V \times r$$

As shown in the figure, when we put these three relationships together we get the flexural shear stress formula

$$f_V = \frac{3 \times V}{2 \times b \times h} = 1.5 \times \frac{V}{A}$$

The maximum shear stress f_V occurs in a beam at the section where the internal transverse shear force V is at a maximum–usually at a support. The flexural shear stress formula then tells us that the maximum flexural shear stress f_V at a section of maximum transverse shear force is 1.5 times this shear force V, averaged over the cross-sectional area A.

If the horizontal stress is computed on any other surface parallel to the neutral surface, the wedge of bending stress used to compute the shearing force F would be truncated and thus of smaller magnitude. As a result, we can conclude that the flexural shear stress is a maximum at the neutral axis, where the full wedge acts, and the shear stress drops off to zero at the top and bottom of the beam. The top and bottom of a beam are often called the outer fibers of the beam, and we see that shear stresses are zero at the points where we have previously found that the flexural bending stresses were at their highest–at the beam outer fibers.

It may seem odd that shear stress created on a horizontal plane results from a shear force that is transverse to this plane, but if we look at the small square element cored out from the beam as shown in the figure, we see why this is so. The shear stress acting on the horizontal surfaces of the little cored-out element must be associated with equal vertical stress on its vertical faces (which coincide with the beam cross sections). Otherwise, the little square element would rotate one way or another. Notice that the shears on its four faces are racking the element–this is the mode of deformation associated with shear.

Like the flexure formula for bending stress, the flexural shear relationship can be rearranged to suit the needs of the situation. For instance, recall our 20-ft-long 6 × 25.5 beam that supports a 20,000-lb load at midspan. The transverse internal shear force anywhere along the beam is a constant

$$V = \frac{20{,}000}{2} = 10{,}000 \text{ lb}$$

The cross-sectional area is

$$A = 6 \times 25.5 = 153 \text{ in}^2$$

and the maximum shear stress is simply

$$f_V = 1.5 \times \frac{10{,}000}{153} = 98 \text{ psi}$$

While rectangular beam cross sections are the most commonly used shapes for timber and concrete beams, steel beams are more often I-shaped. The flexural shear stress in an I-beam acts in the same manner as for a rectangular cross section. It is greatest at midheight, but unlike a rectangular cross section, the shear stress is basically constant along the full height, h, of the I-shaped cross section. The shear stress in I-beams is therefore generally approximated as

$$f_V = \frac{V}{A_W}$$

Here, $A_W = h \times t_W$, and t_W is the web thickness.

6.3 Deflection of Beams

We have already noted for a simple beam that the deformation associated with beam flexure results in a downward sag called deflection. If this deflection is excessive–even if stresses are within safe limits–the beam is not stiff enough and in order to be serviceable, a larger beam is needed. Excess deflection will cause ceiling plaster to crack, floors to squeak and bounce, doors to jam, bridge travelers to feel motion sickness, and so on. We will see that the nature of the deflection of a beam member is also very important in the analysis of columns and indeterminate structures.

The theoretical computation of beam deflection can be very tedious and can really provide only an estimate of the actual sag, since the assumed ideal conditions are not usually met in reality. There is no single practical formula that will exactly handle all the possible beam load and support configurations. Numerous deflection formulas are available that provide the deflection for common beam loading and support conditions, including cantilevered and indeterminate members. We will concentrate on the deflection of the most commonly encountered beam–the simple beam–and derive a useful approximate deflection formula.

The deflection D of a simple beam of span L occurs as the top half of the beam shortens while the bottom half elongates as shown in Figure 6.3, where we see that $CD < AB < EF$. It is assumed for now that every section of the beam is bending with the same moment, so that the curved element has a constant radius and so forms a segment of a circular arc.

As shown, the ends of the beam slope towards one another to form a very small angle, z. Let q denote the top compressive shortening deformation and the equal bottom tensile stretch of the beam fibers. Recall that overall deformation equals unit deformation times length, and unit deformation is strain, d, which is proportional to stress, $d = f/E$, and we have

$$q = d \times L = \frac{f}{E} \times L$$

The angle z is seen as the sum of these two axial deformations divided by the beam height h:

$$z = \frac{2 \times \dfrac{f}{E} \times L}{h}$$

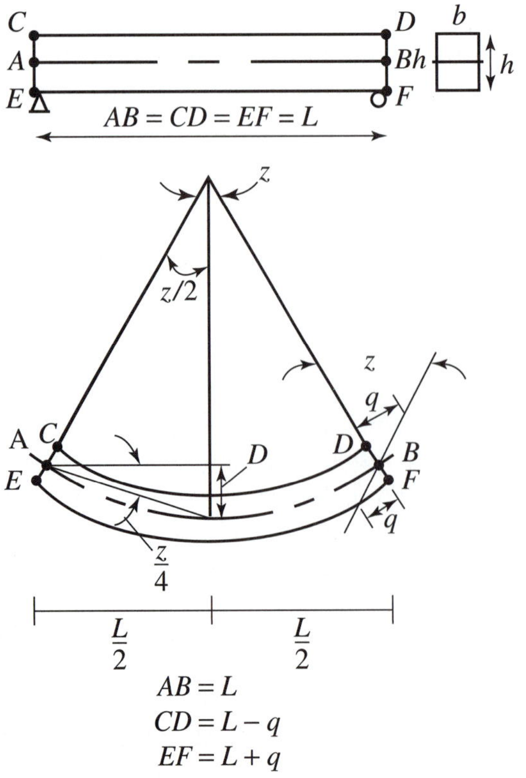

FIGURE 6.3

From the geometry of the curved beam shown, the angle formed by the ratio of the beam deflection D to half the beam length, $L/2$, is $z/4$, so that another expression for the angle z is

$$z = \frac{8 \times D}{L}$$

Equating the two expressions for the angle z, we get the beam deflection for a beam under uniform moment (and uniform bending stress) to be

$$D = \frac{f \times L^2}{4 \times E \times h}$$

This formula indicates that the deflection of a beam is proportional to the bending stress in the member and the square of the span, while it is inversely related to material elastic stiffness and beam depth.

An alternate form of this equation can be written if we replace the bending stress f with M/S, and identify a new cross-section property called the area moment of inertia I, which has units of in^4, and it is given as

$$I = S \times \frac{h}{2}$$

The alternate beam deflection formula is then

$$D = \frac{M \times L^2}{8 \times E \times I}$$

In this formula, the beam deflection is related to the applied bending moment in the member and the product $E \times I$, which is often called *beam stiffness,* or member rigidity.

Beam member stiffness EI is thus a result of its material stiffness E, and its cross-sectional profile, measured by I. For rectangular cross sections,

$$I = S \times \frac{1}{2} \times h = \frac{b \times h^3}{12}$$

For steel I-beams, the value of I is usually obtained from a table, but these reported tabular values are simply computed as the sum of positive and negative rectangular moments of inertia as exemplified in Figure 6.4. We will look at these types of computations when discussing steel design.

Thus far, the deflection formulas have been based on the assumption that every section of the simple beam experiences the same bending moment, M. Usually, the loading of a simple beam creates an average bending moment along the member equal to about 80% of the highest moment, so we can simply multiply the deflection formulas by 0.8, which results in the following approximate formulas for simple beam deflection:

$$D = \frac{f \times L^2}{5 \times E \times h} = \frac{M \times L^2}{10 \times E \times I}$$

These formulas give an adequate estimate of the beam deflection for most simple beams that support distributed loads or several concentrated loads

$$I = \frac{bh^3}{12}$$

$$S = I/(h/2) = \frac{bh^2}{6}$$

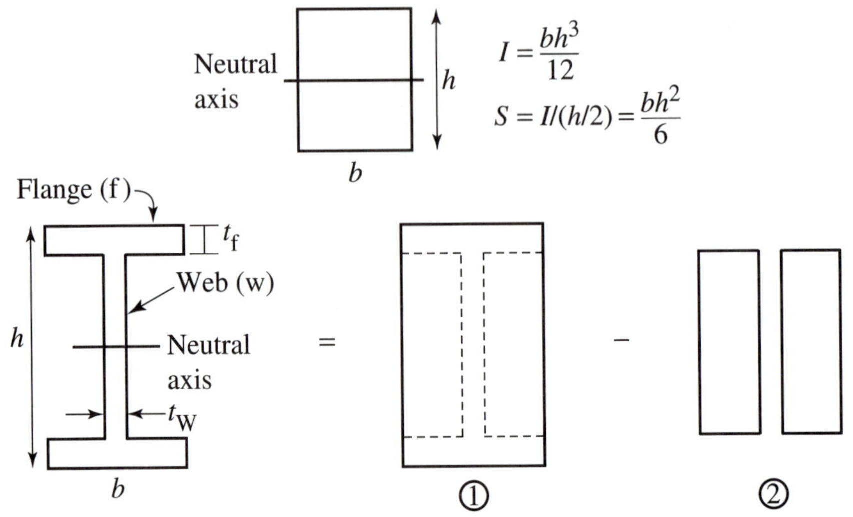

$$I_1 = \frac{1}{12}bh^3$$

$$I_2 = 2 \times \frac{1}{12}(b - t_W)(h - 2 \times t_f)^3$$

$$S = (I_1 - I_2)/(h/2)$$

$$I = I_1 - I_2$$

FIGURE 6.4

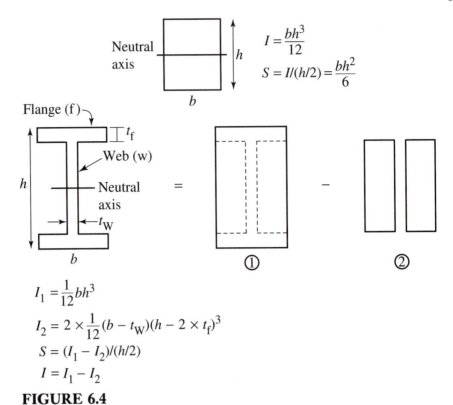

spread out over the span. When the only load on a beam is a single concentrated load at midspan, the resulting deflection will be 80% again as much as that given by these approximate formulas. This is because only a small segment of the beam directly below the midspan load is subject to the full bending moment and bending stress, whereas for uniformly distributed loads, high moments occur over a larger portion of the beam, as may be observed in Figure 6.5.

Let's look at our 20-ft- (240-in.-) long 6-in. \times 25.5-in. beam that supports a 20,000-lb load at midspan. As we have determined previously, it has a maximum moment at midspan of $M = 1,200,000$ in-lb and a corresponding bending stress of $f = 1,850$ psi. Assume the beam is timber with a modulus of elasticity, $E = 1,600,000$ psi. The moment of inertia is $I = bh^3/12 = (6 \times 25.5^3)/12 = 8,290$ in^4. We may substitute these values into either form of the deflection formula. Using the formula based on stress, and recalling that when only one concentrated load causes all the bending stress in a beam, the deflection will be 80% again as much as that given by the approximate formulas, we find our beam will sag

$$D = (0.80)\frac{1,850 \times 240^2}{5 \times 1,600,000 \times 25.5} = 0.4 \text{ in.}$$

You may wish to verify that the deflection formula using moment and beam rigidity provides the same result.

For another example, suppose a 50-ft simple steel I-beam is 36-in. deep and uniformly loaded where all dead plus live loads create a stress equal to the full allowable $f = 24,000$ psi. How much will it sag? The deflection is simply

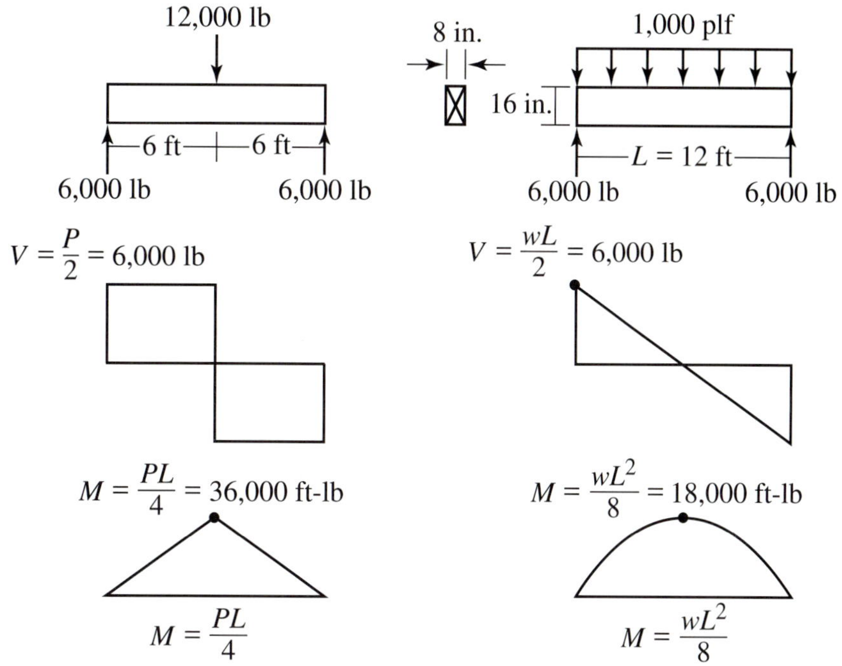

$$A = 8 \times 16 = 126 \text{ in}^2$$

$$S = \frac{1}{6}(8)(16)^2 = 341 \text{ in}^3$$

$$f_V = 1.5\frac{V}{A} = 1.5\left(\frac{6{,}000}{126}\right) = 70 \text{ psi}$$

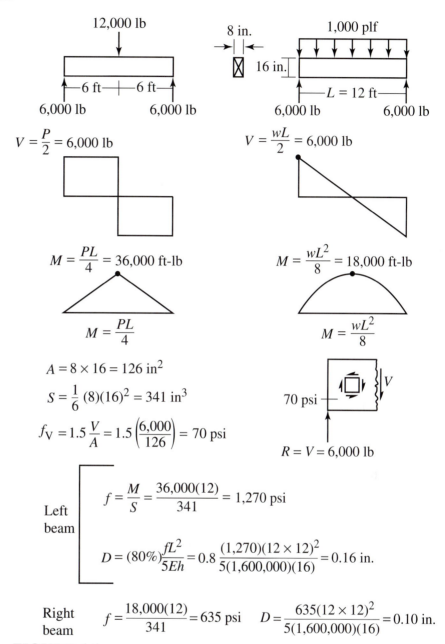

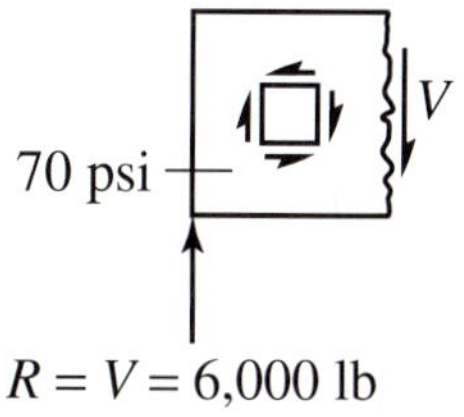

Left beam

$$f = \frac{M}{S} = \frac{36{,}000(12)}{341} = 1{,}270 \text{ psi}$$

$$D = (80\%)\frac{fL^2}{5Eh} = 0.8\frac{(1{,}270)(12 \times 12)^2}{5(1{,}600{,}000)(16)} = 0.16 \text{ in.}$$

Right beam

$$f = \frac{18{,}000(12)}{341} = 635 \text{ psi} \qquad D = \frac{635(12 \times 12)^2}{5(1{,}600{,}000)(16)} = 0.10 \text{ in.}$$

FIGURE 6.5

$$D = \frac{f \times L^2}{5 \times E \times h} = \frac{24{,}000 \times (50 \times 12)^2}{5 \times 30{,}000{,}000 \times 36} = 1.6 \text{ in.}$$

Beam deflections are usually limited to some fraction of the beam span L, such as $L/240$ for all loads, or $L/360$ for live loads alone. For the case above, where all loads are included in the total stress of 24,000 psi, $D = 1.6$ in. will be alright, since the allowable deflection would be $(50 \times 12)/240 = 2.5$ in. Usual beam proportions result in beam span-to-depth ratios L/h from 20 to 25, and when L/h values exceed this range, deflections may be quite large and possibly govern beam sizes.

From the deflection formula based on moment and member rigidity, we see that the ratio of moment to deflection is a constant given by

$$\frac{M}{D} = \frac{10EI}{L^2}$$

When looking at straight columns, we will see that this constant ratio represents a force called the critical buckling load, F_{CR}, the axial force that will hold deflection of a member, D, in equilibrium in the absence of the transverse loads that created the internal moment M. Put another way, for a transversely loaded beam member, the ratio of uniformly loaded simple beam moment to the resulting deflection equals the buckling load of the same member used as a column.

In the remainder of the chapter, we look at some simple examples of timber, steel, and concrete beams. This serves both to further illustrate the principles of beam stresses and deformation, as well as to prepare us later for a more intensive focus on the design of structures made from these materials. We close the chapter with a classic example of how deformation compatibility can be used to solve for the forces of an indeterminate beam.

6.4 Bending, Shear, and Deflection in a Timber Beam

We have been deriving general formulas for flexural beam stresses and deformation using a simple span beam with a rectangular cross section because it is the easiest shape to work with. Since most timber beams are rectangular in cross section, they tend to be the easiest with which to first learn basic structural principles.

In Figure 6.5, the values of the support reactions, the shear diagrams, and the moment diagrams have all been determined for two 12-ft simple spans timber beams with 8-in.-wide and 16-in.-deep cross sections. Each span supports 12,000 lb of load with the beam on the left supporting the 12,000 lb as a single concentrated load, while the beam on the right has the load uniformly distributed as a 1,000 plf load. We want to compare the maximum bending and shear stresses and deflections in each beam.

For both beams, we see from the shear diagrams that the maximum shear force is 6,000 lb, which is also the reaction at the beam supports. So in both cases, the maximum shear stress that occurs at the neutral axis at the beam section of maximum shear stress is $f_V = 70$ psi, as shown. This stress occurs at the neutral axis only at the ends of the uniformly loaded span, but it occurs all along the length of the beam with a concentrated load. If the stress were excessive, horizontal splits would form at the neutral axis at the ends of the uniformly loaded beam, and at the neutral axis all along the other. Remember that shear stress has equal values horizontally and vertically, and timber is weaker in shear along its grain (horizontally) than in shear across its grain (vertically).

The bending stress and the deflection is shown first for the beam on the left, then for the one at the right. Notice that the maximum moment at midspan is cut in half when the load is distributed all along the span instead of concentrating it at one point. This also means that the bending stress is cut in half, from $f = 1{,}270$ psi for the concentrated load, to $f = 635$ psi for the distributed load case.

Exercise The reader may wish to verify some useful design formulas for the maximum simple beam shears and moments. For a simple span beam with length L, with a midspan concentrated load P, $V = P/2$ and is $M = PL/4$. For the simple beam with a distributed load w, $V = wL/2$ and $M = wL^2/8$.

Rework this problem assuming the 8 × 16 timber beam is replaced with a steel I-beam with $\frac{1}{2}$-in. × 6-in. flanges and a $\frac{1}{4}$-in. × 16-in. web and assume a new span length of 20 ft. ■

Beam deflection is higher for the beam on the left, in this example, mainly because the bending stress is much higher than for the beam on the right. If the uniformly loaded beam has the same bending stress as the beam on the left, its deflection would double to 0.20 in., and thus exceed that of the concentrated load case.

6.5 Steel Plate Girder Stresses and Deflection

The 150-ft simple span steel I-shaped girder of Figure 6.6 supports five equally spaced loads of 30,000 lb each. This could be a bridge girder, in which case the loads represent floor beam reactions, or perhaps a transfer girder in a building, where the girder supports column loads and allows for a column-free space on the level below the beam. The member is called a plate girder because instead of being formed at a steel mill where hot steel is molded into one solid I shape by being forced through roller guides (hence the term rolled shapes), the girder I-shaped cross section is fabricated from three separate steel plates. The two 1-in. × 18-in. horizontal plates at the top and bottom are called flanges, and they are responsible for resisting most of the bending moment. The $\frac{1}{2}$-in. × 60-in. vertical plate is called the web, and it carries the beam shear.

The plates are attached by longitudinal fillet welds located along the four corners of the web plate and running the full length of the girder. As shown in the figure, this weld must be able to resist the horizontal shear stress at the interface of the flange and web plates. We will try to determine the maximum shear stress in the $\frac{5}{16}$-in. fillet welds, the maximum bending stress at midspan, and the deflection of the girder.

From the figure, we see that the maximum vertical (and horizontal) shear is equal to the 75,000-lb reaction and so the maximum shear stress in the web is

$$f_V = \frac{V}{h \times t_W} = \frac{75{,}000}{62 \times \frac{1}{2}} = 2{,}340 \text{ psi}$$

We will focus on a 1-in. length of the web/flange interface near the support where the maximum shear stress exists. The area of contact between the web and the flange plates along this 1-in. interface is $\frac{1}{2}$ in. × 1 in. = $\frac{1}{2}$ in^2, and so a unit shear force of $\frac{1}{2}$ in^2 × 2,340 lb/in^2 = 1,170 lb/in. must be transferred between the two plates. Since the two fillet welds have a combined capacity of 2 × 4,000 lb/in. = 8,000 lb/in., the welds are more than adequate.

The maximum bending moment is shown to be 3,375,000 ft-lb. From the given section modulus (which you should verify using the procedure shown

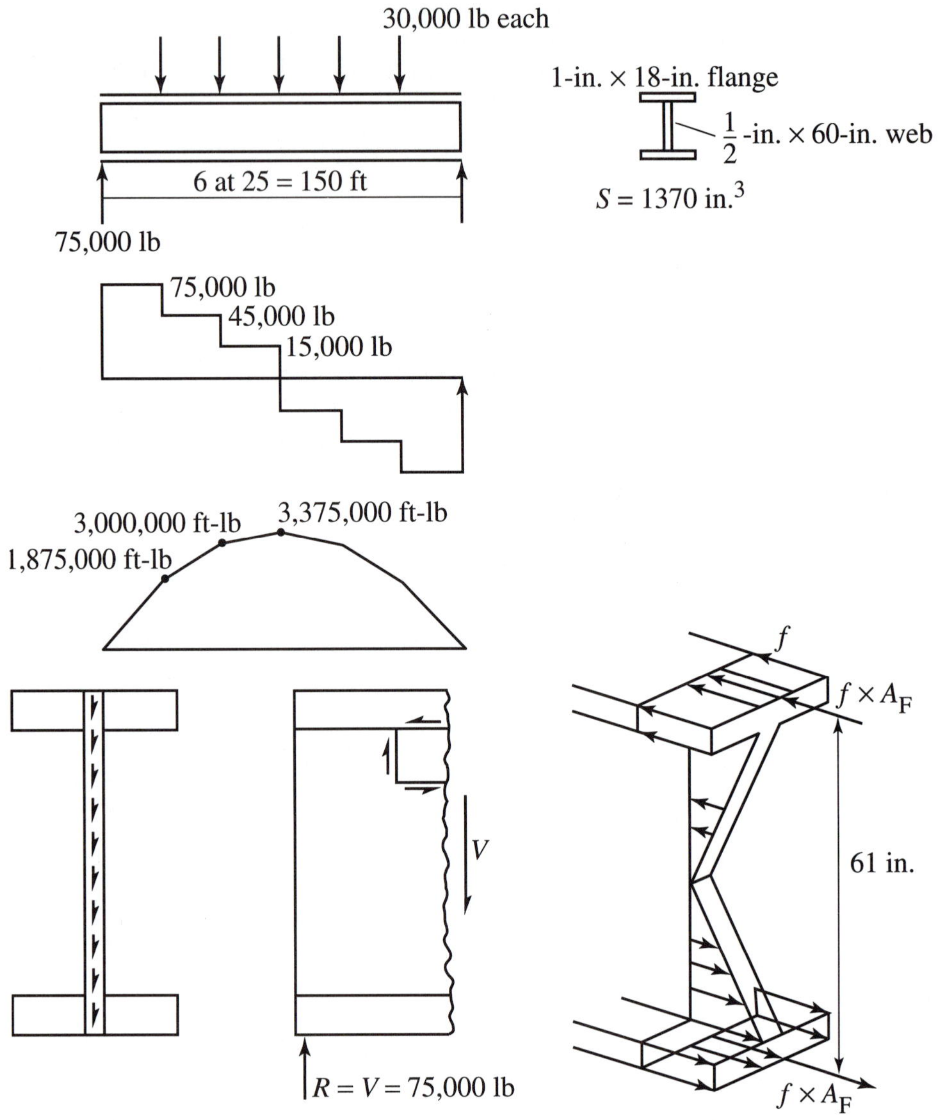

FIGURE 6.6

in Figure 6.4), we compute the maximum bending stress which occurs in both flanges to be

$$f = \frac{M}{S} = \frac{3{,}375{,}000 \times 12}{1{,}370} = 29{,}600 \text{ psi}$$

This stress is acceptable for steel with a yield strength of 50,000 psi, which is typically used in plate girders. In the figure, we see the distribution of bending stress on the cross section and note that the entire area of either flange, A_F, is practically stressed with the full maximum bending stress. With both flanges, the flange stress times flange area creates a pair of couple forces separated by a moment arm nearly equal to the girder depth, as shown. This couple resists the majority of the bending moment, with only a small amount being resisted by the web.

Steel plates do not come in 150-ft lengths, so shorter plates must be butt-welded to form long girder flanges and webs. Since the bending moment is less near the ends of the plate girder and a butt joint is required anyway, it is common to see a transition to smaller flange plates where bending moment is reduced. This will reduce girder weight and material costs. The web plate is generally kept the same size throughout the full girder length.

The deflection of this girder is computed as

$$D = \frac{f \times L^2}{5 \times E \times h} = \frac{29{,}600 \times (150 \times 12)^2}{5 \times 30{,}000{,}000 \times 62} = 10 \text{ in.}$$

This at first appears to be an alarming value. If, however, about half of the girder load is dead load (commonly the case for such large structures), then about 5–7 in. of the computed deflection would be cambered into the girder at the time of fabrication (camber is upward curvature of a beam). Now, under dead load only, there is no deflection or maybe even an inch or two of camber.

The additional 5 in. of anticipated live load deflection is within the standard allowance for buildings of

$$\frac{L}{360} = \frac{150 \times 12}{360} = 5 \text{ in.}$$

For bridge girders, the allowable live load deflection is $L/800 = 2.3$ in., so that the deflection of this girder is excessive and a deeper girder would need to be used. Increasing the web depth to 70 in. would make the new section modulus

$$S = \frac{I}{\frac{h}{2}} = \frac{\frac{18 \times 72^3}{12} - \frac{17.5 \times 70^3}{12}}{\frac{72}{2}} = 1{,}660 \text{ in}^3$$

And so the new bending stress is reduced to

$$f = \frac{M}{S} = \frac{3{,}375{,}000 \times 12}{1{,}660} = 24{,}400 \text{ psi}$$

The total deflection is then also reduced:

$$D = \frac{24{,}400 \times (150 \times 12)^2}{5 \times 30{,}000{,}000 \times 72} = 7.3 \text{ in.}$$

If half of this deflection, 3.7 in., is due to live load then the beam is still too flexible to meet the 2.3-in. allowable bridge live load deflection, and a still deeper beam is needed.

Exercise How much does the plate girder in the preceding example weigh?

Suppose the steel girder is replaced by a timber beam with a beam width of 12 in. The allowable bending stress is 2,400 psi and the allowable shear stress is 200 psi. What is the required beam depth? What is the deflection?

If half of the computed deflection is due to live load, will a 76-in. web satisfy the $L/800$ bridge deflection limit? ■

6.6 Reinforced Concrete Beam

As we have seen, when any simple beam bends in response to applied transverse loads, it will undergo flexural compressive stresses above its neutral surface, and flexural tension stresses below. The beam bending moment due to the applied loads is resisted by an internal couple created by the equal and opposite compressive and tensile forces that result from the flexural stresses acting over the area of the beam cross section.

In the case of concrete beams, the tension below the neutral surface causes the concrete to crack, as shown in Figure 6.7, and thus this concrete is unable to generate a tension force to couple with the compressive force above the neutral surface. Longitudinal reinforcing steel bars are placed near the bottom of simple span concrete beams to create what is termed reinforced concrete. These bars intercept the vertical cracks caused by the high moments along the center portion of the span. We will see later that smaller vertical bars, called stirrups, must be spaced along the ends of girders to intercept diagonal cracks caused by the racking effect of high shear. In any case, the steel

FIGURE 6.7

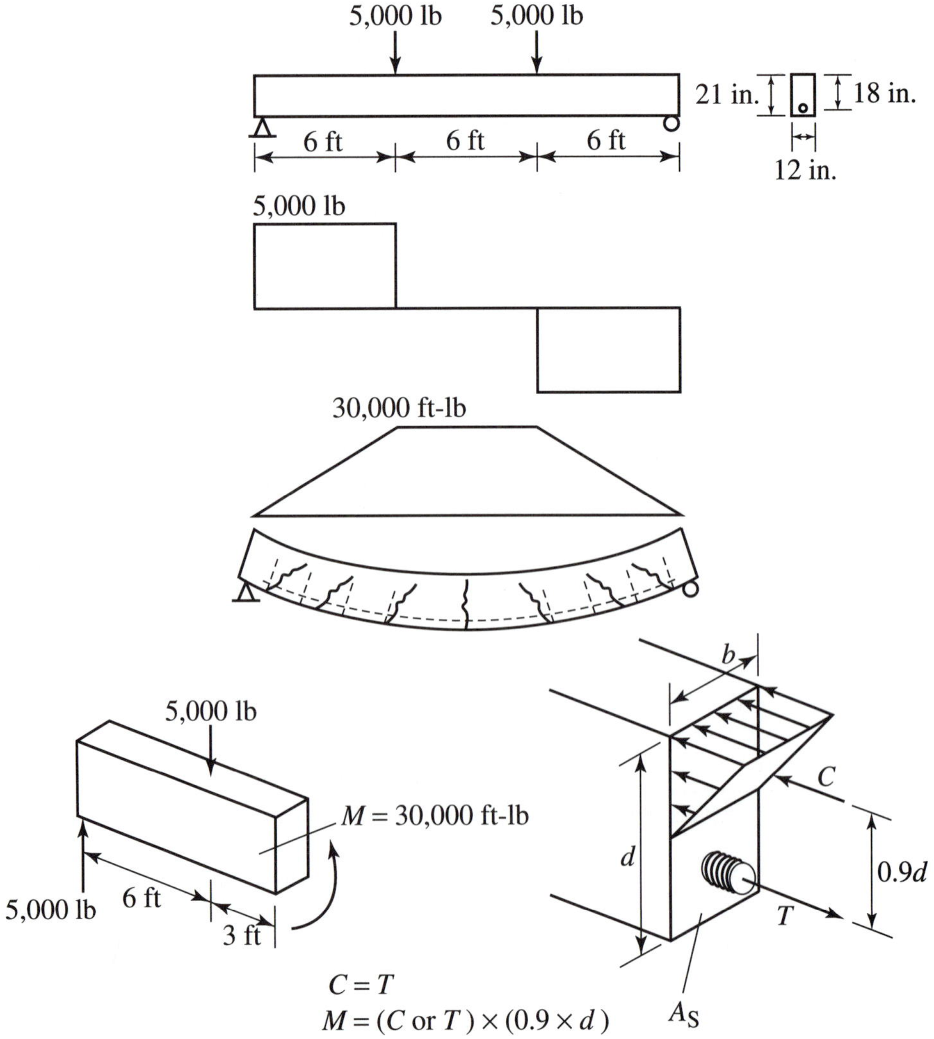

Exercise Assume that the same steel rebar is used to its full tensile capacity. If the beam span is now 3 × 8 ft = 24 ft, what is the new required beam effective depth d? ■

of reinforced concrete is there to resist the tension stresses that the plain concrete cannot.

In this problem, we only focus on the longitudinal reinforcing steel bars, called rebars. The internal moment resisting couple is made up of the compression wedge force C, and the tensile force in the rebars T, separated by a moment arm. The moment arm is usually about 90% of the beam effective depth d, which is the distance from the outer compressive fiber to the center of the reinforcing steel.

The force C is the resultant of the wedge of flexural compressive stress acting on the cross-sectional area above the neutral axis, and T is the tension force in the steel rebar equal to stress times rebar cross-sectional area, A_S, or $T = f \times A_S$. We need to ensure that the concrete and steel stresses are within allowable limits. When the percentage of steel in the cross section is small, as we may assume in this case, the steel stress will be of greatest concern, and we need ensure only that the steel stress is below 24,000 psi.

We will neglect beam weight and see from the figure that the 18-ft simple span has a maximum bending moment, $M = 30{,}000$ ft-lb (360,000 in-lb). The beam width, depth, and effective depth to the steel are $b = 12$ in., $h = 21$ in., and $d = 18$ in. as shown. The single steel rebar has a cross-sectional area of $A_S = 1$ in^2. By equating external applied and internal resisting moments at the beam cross section where the applied moment is at a maximum (all along the middle 6 ft, in this case), we can compute the maximum stress in the steel as follows

$$M = T \times (0.9 \times d)$$

$$360{,}000 = (f \times 1) \times (0.9 \times 18)$$

From this, we get the steel tension stress to be $f = 22{,}000$ psi, which is below the allowable stress, so the beam is OK.

6.7 Propped Cantilever Beam

We know that there are three equations of equilibrium that can be used to determine reactions of determinate structures. In a beam with no horizontal forces acting, there are two equations of equilibrium available to solve for two support reactions. In the case of a cantilever beam, where one end is rigidly fixed to a wall while the other end is free with no support, the two reactions are the moment and the vertical force at the wall. If the free end of a cantilever beam is propped up as shown in Figure 6.8, some of the load that went to the fixed end is now being carried by the prop (the roller support shown). The vertical reaction of the roller becomes a third unknown, yet there are still only two equilibrium equations, so we need to look at compatibility of deformations to generate a third equation before we can solve for all three support reactions.

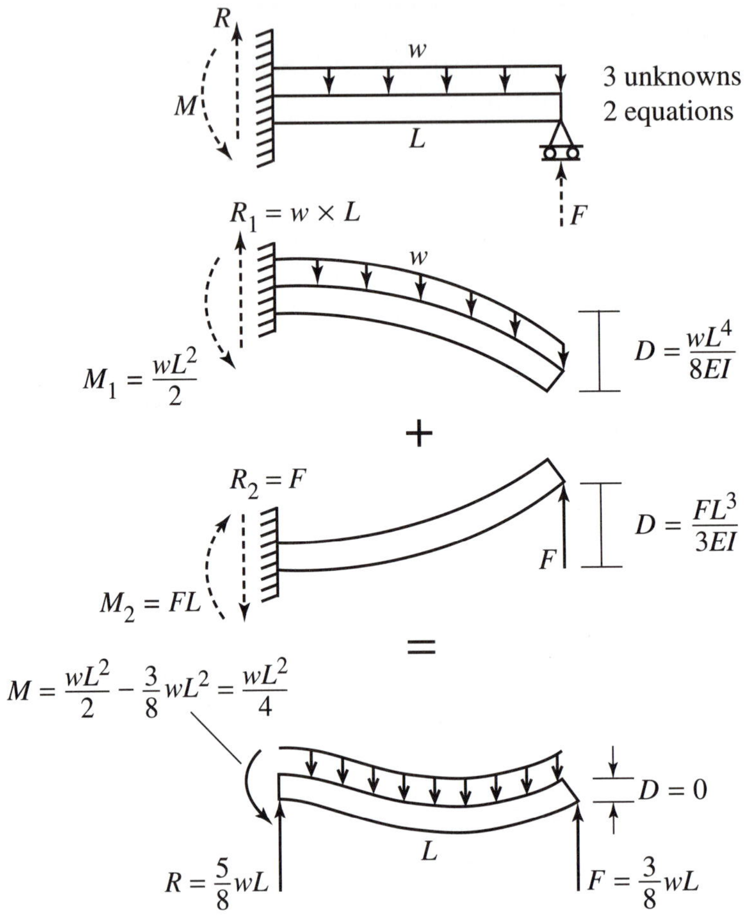

FIGURE 6.8

Let's look at the prop force *F*. Removing this reaction results in a simple uniformly loaded cantilever beam for which the free end deflection is computed by the equation shown. Similarly, the deflection formula for the free end of a cantilever beam with a concentrated force at the free end is also shown. Note that these formulas are specific to their particular case and cannot be used for other situations, such as a simple beam deflection, for which we have developed another formula.

Since the free end does not deflect due to the roller support prop, we see that the downward deflection of the distributed load is negated by the upward deflection of the concentrated load *F*. The two opposing deflection values must be equal in magnitude, so

$$\frac{w \times L^4}{8 \times E \times I} = \frac{F \times L^3}{3 \times E \times I}$$

From this deformation compatibility relationship, we are able to solve one of the three unknown support reactions

$$F = \frac{3}{8} \times w \times L$$

Now, instead of the wall supporting all the vertical load acting on the beam, wL, we see that the prop takes $\frac{3}{8}wL$, or 37.5% of the load, and vertical force equilibrium indicates that the wall now supports the remaining $\frac{5}{8}wL$, or 62.5%.

As can be seen in the figure, we sum moments at the wall to find that the prop has reduced the cantilever beam moment reaction from $\frac{1}{2}wL^2$ to $\frac{1}{4}wL^2$. The free end of a cantilever will have a large deflection, but the propped cantilever deflected shape shows that the deflection will be small (even less than a simple beam).

Exercise Construct a shear and moment diagram for both the cantilever and the propped cantilever beams in this problem if $w = 500$ plf and $L = 14$ ft.

If a 6-in.-wide timber beam with an allowable bending stress of 1,200 psi is used, what beam size is required for both the free and propped end situations? ■

7 Combined Stresses, Columns, and Beam-Columns

7.1 Combined Axial and Bending Stress

It is rare that a structural element supports only axial load or only transverse load. For instance, for an ideal truss whose members are all two-force members, even if the truss loads are applied at the joint pins, the weight of any inclined or horizontal member acts as a uniform load on the element, making it a beam-column. The axial load creates axial stress and the transverse load causes bending stress that both act on the member at the same time. In this section, we look at how these stresses combine, and in the process, confirm the location of the centroid of a triangle. We will later use the principle of superposition of combined stresses to develop beam-column formulas.

A member may be subjected to axial forces in addition to transverse loads that cause flexure. For the case of axial tension and axial compression of short and stocky members that will not buckle, we simply superimpose, or add up, the axial stress, $f = F/A$, with the bending stress, $f = M/S$. This superposition of stress is possible, since both axial and bending stresses similarly act perpendicular to the member cross-sectional area. Thus, the combined stress is

$$f = \frac{F}{A} + \frac{M}{S}$$

In this relationship, if we arbitrarily say that tension stress is positive, then compression stress will be considered negative–if tension is called negative, then compression is positive. If the axial load is compressive and the member is long and slender enough so that buckling is a concern, the member is considered a beam-column, and its slenderness effects necessitate a more rigorous analysis, as we will see later. The superposition principle also holds for axial and bending bearing stresses that exist between a beam and its support or between a footing and the supporting soil.

Figure 7.1 depicts a relatively short and stocky bridge column with a rectangular cross section that is supporting only one girder at a particular phase of construction. The reaction from the girder creates an eccentric load F with an eccentricity e. We see that this force causes axial compression and it creates a moment, $M = F \times e$, with respect to the neutral axis. We can equivalently replace the eccentric force with its separate actions consisting of a force plus a moment as shown. The uniform axial stress of the centric force is f = F/A and the bending stress of the moment is $f = (F \times e)/S$. Using the combined stress formula and recalling that $S = bh^2/6$

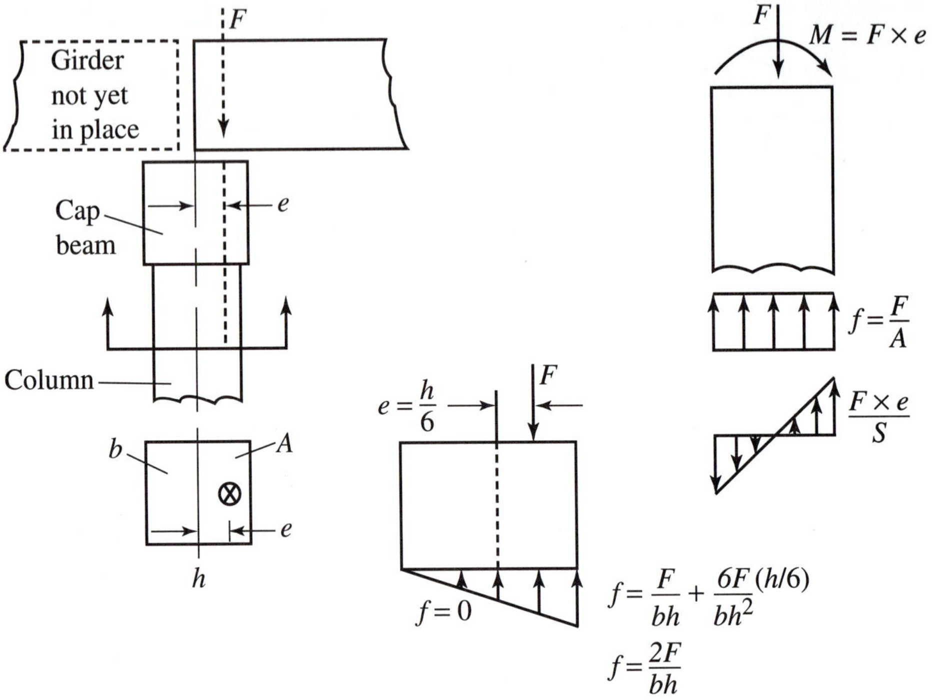

FIGURE 7.1

$$f=\frac{F}{b\times h}+\frac{6\times F\times e}{b\times h^2}$$

Suppose the force has an eccentricity of $e = h/6$; in other words, it is one-third the dimension, h, from the closest edge. From the equation above, we see that the two stress components have equal values when $e = h/6$. At the close edge, the stress on the cross section would be compressive and equal to twice the uniform axial stress of the centric load, which is also the average stress on the cross section. At the far edge, we see that the first component is compression stress and the second is tension, so they cancel one another, and the stress on this edge of the cross section is zero. Thus, a triangular stress wedge is established over the cross section that is equal to the force F.

So we confirm what we have said many times before, that the resultant of a triangular distribution of stress effectively acts at the centroid of the triangle that is located one-third the distance from the side with the maximum stress. If the eccentricity of a force is less than $h/6$, the force acts within the middle third of the cross section ($2\times\frac{1}{6}=\frac{1}{3}$), and the entire cross section will be in compression. If $e > h/6$, there will be both compression and tension stress on the cross section.

Suppose the column is 10 in. × 10 in. and a force of $F = 50{,}000$ lb is applied with a 2.5-in. eccentricity. Would the concrete crack in tension on the far edge?

Concrete has a tensile strength of about 500 psi. The centric stress is

$$\frac{F}{A}=\frac{50{,}000}{10\times 10}=500\text{ psi}$$

The bending stress is

$$\frac{F \times e}{S} = \frac{50{,}000 \times 2.5}{\dfrac{10 \times 10^2}{6}} = 750 \text{ psi}$$

So, on the cross-section edge nearest the load, the compressive stress is

$$f = 500 + 750 = 1{,}250 \text{ psi}$$

For the far edge stress,

$$f = 500 - 750 = -250 = 250 \text{ psi (tension)}$$

This tensile stress is below 500 psi so it should not be enough to cause a crack. Note that when the second girder is in place, the two loads will create a single equivalent centric force of $F = 100{,}000$ lb, which creates a uniform average stress of

$$f = \frac{100{,}000}{10 \times 10} = 1{,}000 \text{ psi}$$

So we find that the column was actually more stressed with one off-centered girder ($f = 1{,}250$ psi) than with two nicely centered to create a centric load.

7.2 Transversely Loaded Truss Chord

A roof system employs a simple parallel chord timber truss with 1,000-lb loads as shown in Figure 7.2. We are concerned with the combined axial stresses in the middle top chord members. These members are made from two full size 2-in. × 8-in. planks and are braced at their ends and at midspan so they will not buckle as slender columns (analysis of column buckling will be discussed shortly). The allowable stress is 1,000 psi. Because a truss is assumed to be loaded only at its joints, in order to perform the truss analysis and determine the axial compression in the top chord, the loads that act transversely to the top chords are equally apportioned to the nearest member joints as shown. The resulting truss analysis indicates that the compression in this member is 4,000 lb.

We then look at the isolated top chord member and treat it as a beam column for which the combined axial load and bending moment will be critical at the middle of the member as shown. The maximum combined stress in the member is the sum of the compressive stresses at the top fibers of the member:

$$f = \frac{F}{A} + \frac{M}{S} = \frac{4{,}000}{2 \times (2 \times 8)} + \frac{2{,}500 \times 12}{\dfrac{4 \times 8^2}{6}} = 125 + 703 = 828 \text{ psi}$$

Since this stress is below the allowable 1,000 psi, the member is OK. The tension stress at the bottom fibers is computed to be

$$f = 703 - 125 = 588 \text{ psi}$$

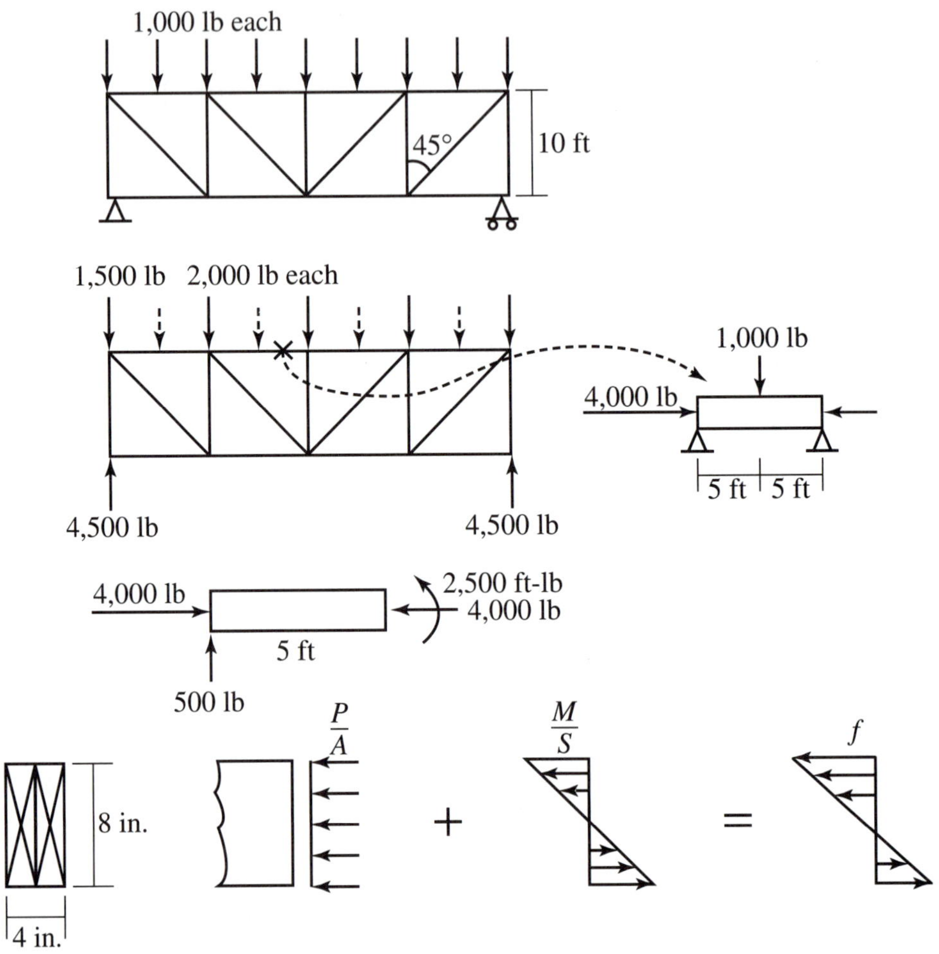

FIGURE 7.2

Exercise Rework this problem assuming that the truss depth is only 6 ft instead of 10 ft. ■

7.3 Nonuniform Stress Distribution Under a Footing

As we have seen in other example problems, the purpose of a footing is to spread out the loads of a structure over a large enough area that the contact pressure between the bottom of the footing and the soil is low enough that the soil can adequately sustain it. The contact pressure is usually reported as pounds per square foot. For instance, the allowable contact pressure for a simple grade footing on clay soil is around 1,000–3,000 psf.

All structural loads must ultimately be grounded through some foundation type, of which square spread footings are very common. Often, the loads that are to be grounded include an axial force and a moment, as shown in Figure 7.3. We wish to determine the relationship between the square footing size, the applied force and moment, and the pressure distribution beneath the footing. The footing measures $B \times B$ and supports axial load P and moment M as shown.

$$f_{\mathrm{H}}, f_{\mathrm{L}} = \frac{P}{A} \pm \frac{M}{S}$$

$$= \frac{P}{B^2} \pm \frac{M}{\dfrac{B \times B^2}{6}}$$

$$f_{\mathrm{H}}, f_{\mathrm{L}} = \frac{P}{B^2} \pm \frac{6M}{B^3}$$

$\dfrac{P}{B^2} > \dfrac{6M}{B^3}$ $\dfrac{P}{B^2} < \dfrac{6M}{B^3}$

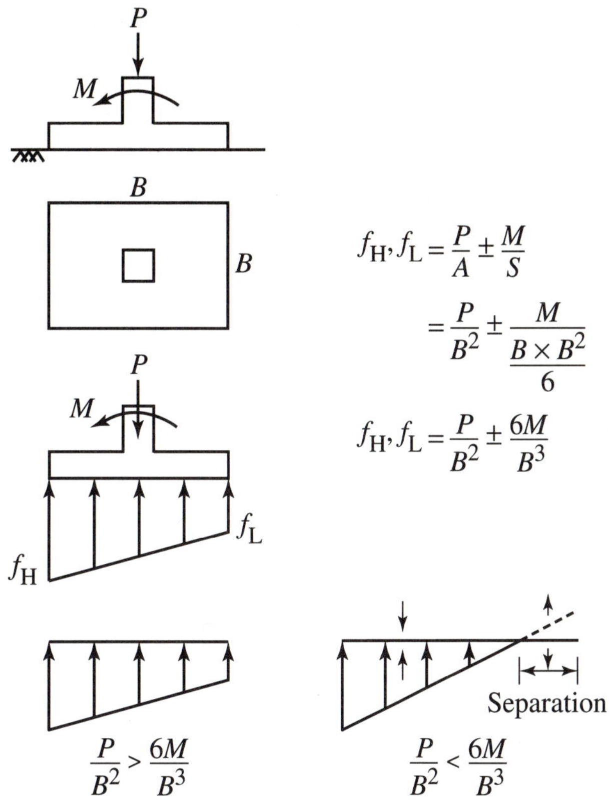

FIGURE 7.3

The contact area between the soil and the footing base may be considered to be basically the same thing as a beam cross section that is subjected to combined axial compression stress, $f = P/A$, and bending stress, $f = M/S$. The combined stresses are actually the contact pressure between the footing and the soil. The "cross section" has an area, $A = B^2$, and a section modulus, $S = (B \times B^2)/6 = B^3/6$. As shown in the figure, using the equation of combined stresses developed earlier, the combined stress equation for this case indicates that the highest and lowest contact stress will be

$$f_{\mathrm{High}}, f_{\mathrm{Low}} = \frac{P}{B^2} \pm \frac{6 \times M}{B^3}$$

As long as the first of these two terms is the larger, the entire area beneath the footing will be in contact with a compressive pressure across the entire base of the footing, as is shown. If the second term is the larger of the two, there will be a loss of contact between the footing and ground, since the two materials are being pulled apart by the combined "tension stress" shown in the figure as a dashed line. Footings are usually sized so as to avoid this situation by ensuring that the vertical reaction falls within the middle third of the base, as we have said.

Exercise If $B = 8$ ft and the allowable soil pressure is 4,000 psf, what is the most bending moment that can act with the axial load, 150,000 lb, without causing separation at the footing heel? ∎

7.4 Buckling of Slender Straight Columns

We are ready now to take a look at the effect of an axial compressive force on a straight slender structural element commonly referred to as a column. As we have said in several previous sections, such a member is prone to failing by lateral buckling.

When a two-force member, such as a truss element, is in tension, the end forces are tending to straighten the element as they cause axial elongation. On the other hand, if the end forces squeeze the member, it is in compression, and in addition to axial deformation that shortens the element, if it is slender enough, the member will also tend to laterally deflect outwards as seen in Figure 7.4. If a large enough compressive load is applied to a slender member (one with a high ratio of length to cross-sectional area), it could cause a buckling failure of the member. To prevent this, compressive elements must have substantial rigidity, $E \times I$, and they require larger stocky cross sections compared to equally loaded tension members.

The term column usually refers to a vertical member that supports loads from above and directs them into the foundation, though horizontal compression members, such as the top chord of simple trusses, are also treated as columns. You see vertical columns everywhere supporting bridges, roofs and upper floors of buildings, and so on. You might even be leaning against one right now as you are reading this. When transverse loads or applied moment couples occur together with an axial compressive force, the member must be analyzed as a beam-column, as we see in later sections.

A "pure column" is perfectly straight and has only centric axial compressive end forces and no other applied loads. Such columns are rare in actual structures, but studying their behavior helps us to gain an understanding of column buckling. Since real columns are rarely perfectly straight, rarely sup-

FIGURE 7.4

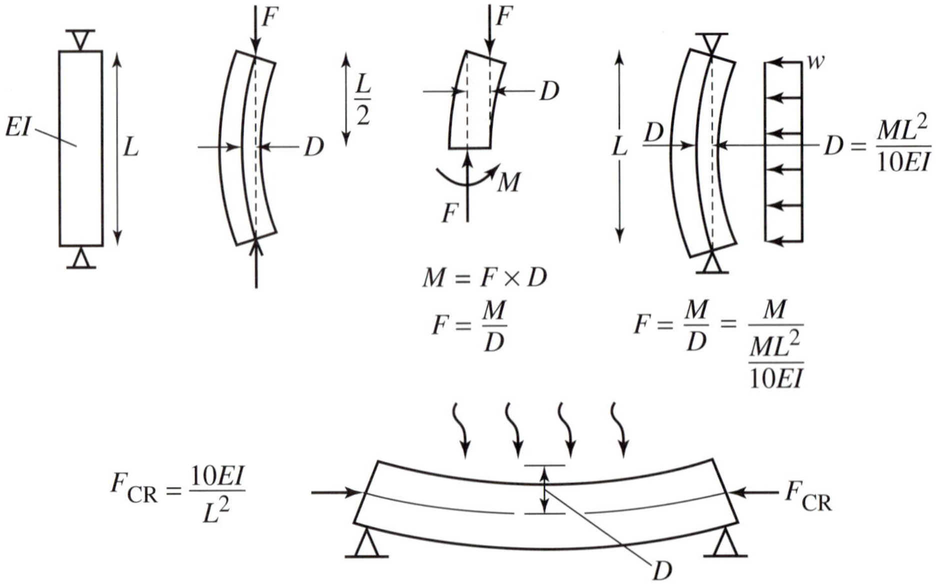

F_{CR} holds beam at deflection D with removal of w.

port perfectly centered loads, and are usually not too slender, we will have to consider the more complex analysis of such columns later.

While applying an increasing axial load on a pure column with pin end connections, any slight applied lateral displacement from a lateral force will vanish upon removing the force–until a critical axial load level is reached. At this critical load, any induced lateral displacement would not vanish when the lateral force is removed. At the critical load, this lateral displacement can even occur with no apparent lateral disturbance. This is called *column buckling*. While the column may maintain equilibrium in a buckled shape under the critical load, any increase in the load will cause unbounded lateral displacement, and thus a buckling failure.

We see in the figure that a column with simple pinned end connections and length L is being compressed with a force F. When the column member is in equilibrium with a lateral deflection, it is subjected to internal bending stresses from moments distributed along the member much the same as for a simple deflected beam supporting a transverse distributed load, as shown. We have previously determined that this simple beam deflection D, which occurs with bending moment M, is approximately

$$D = \frac{M \times L^2}{10 \times E \times I}$$

A section of half of a buckling column shows that a bending moment, $M = F \times D$, is induced in the member and is caused by the axial compressive force F acting with a moment arm of D. We can then say

$$D = M/F$$

Applying moment equilibrium to the column section, we equate the two relationships above, which gives us

$$F_{CR} = \frac{10 \times E \times I}{L^2}$$

This approximate formula provides the critical buckling load, F_{CR}, that is the greatest compressive load, F, for which a slender straight centrically loaded column of length, L, and rigidity, $E \times I$, will not fail by buckling. If $F > F_{CR}$, the applied moment due to lateral deflection, $M = F \times D$, will exceed the internal elastic moment resisting capability of the column member, and the member will experience unchecked lateral deflection leading to a buckling failure. If we replace the number 10 in the formula with $\pi^2(9.87)$ we have the mathematically exact column buckling formula that Leonhard Euler derived in the 1700s using a much more rigorous mathematical approach.

The formula really applies only to long slender columns that buckle at fairly low axial loads and thus low axial stress levels. We define this critical buckling stress as

$$f_{CR} = \frac{F_{CR}}{A} = \frac{10 \times E \times I}{L^2 \times A} = \frac{10 \times E}{(L/r)^2}$$

The term r is a new cross-section property called the radius of gyration and is defined as

$$r = \sqrt{I/A}$$

The term L/r is seen to be a unitless parameter called the column slenderness ratio. As L/r increases, f_{CR} and thus F_{CR} must decrease. The term slender denotes a column with a large L/r value, while stocky denotes a column with a small value of L/r.

Stocky columns carry higher loads than slender ones, since they do not actually buckle. Instead, stocky columns will fail by crushing as the critical axial compressive stress, $f_{CR} = F_{CR}/A$, becomes excessive for the material. Thus, a different relationship exists between the critical stress and the column slenderness for relatively stocky columns than for slender ones. Fortunately, there is a single formula that relates f_{CR} and L/r for all lengths of a column with a given cross section, as we will soon see.

If a column cross section is not the same in the directions of width and height, the member will tend to buckle about the neutral axis having the least value of moment of inertia, I. For example, a yardstick will buckle about the neutral axis that runs parallel with the wider dimension of its cross section. I-beams will buckle about the axis that runs along the centerline of the web.

Actual columns in structures are not always pin-connected at their ends, in which case we replace the member length L with an effective buckling length between locations of effective pins, where the moment is zero. For columns fixed at the base and free at the top, such as a single-pole water tower or some bridge piers, the effective length is doubled. If the column is totally restrained at both ends, the effective length is half the actual length. However, for most situations involving analysis and design, columns may be considered to have simple pin connections at their ends and their effective length equals their actual length L.

For a classic slender column example, what axial load buckles a 1-in. × $\frac{1}{8}$-in. yardstick made of wood with $E = 1{,}600{,}000$ psi? The critical moment of inertia is

$$I = \frac{1}{12} \times 1 \times \left(\frac{1}{8}\right)^3 = 0.000163 \text{ in}^4$$

From the column buckling formula, we find

$$F_{CR} = \frac{10 \times 1{,}600{,}000 \times 0.000163}{36^2} = 2 \text{ lb}$$

If we clamp both ends in our hands and compress the yardstick, its effective length is $\frac{1}{2} \times 36$ in., and $F_{CR} = 4 \times 2 = 8$ lb.

7.5 Increasing the Buckling Load of a Hollow Column

Suppose a hollow rectangular steel tube section is used as a long slender column as seen in Figure 7.5. What percentage increase in the critical buckling load results by filling the tube with concrete and making it a composite member?

Because the rectangular hollow tube has a different moment of inertia about its X and Y axes, it will buckle first about the axis with the least mo-

$$I_Y = \frac{1}{12}(10 \times 6^3 - 9 \times 5^3) = 86.3 \text{ in.}^4$$

$$\frac{9}{n} = 1.08$$

$$I_Y = 86.3 + \frac{1}{12}(1.08)5^3 = 98 \text{ in.}^4$$

All steel

$$10 \times 8.3 = 83$$

$$9 + 2(1/2 \times 8.3) = 17.3$$

$$I_Y = \frac{1}{12}(83 \times 6^3 - (83 - 17.3) \times 5^3) = 810 \text{ in.}^4$$

All concrete

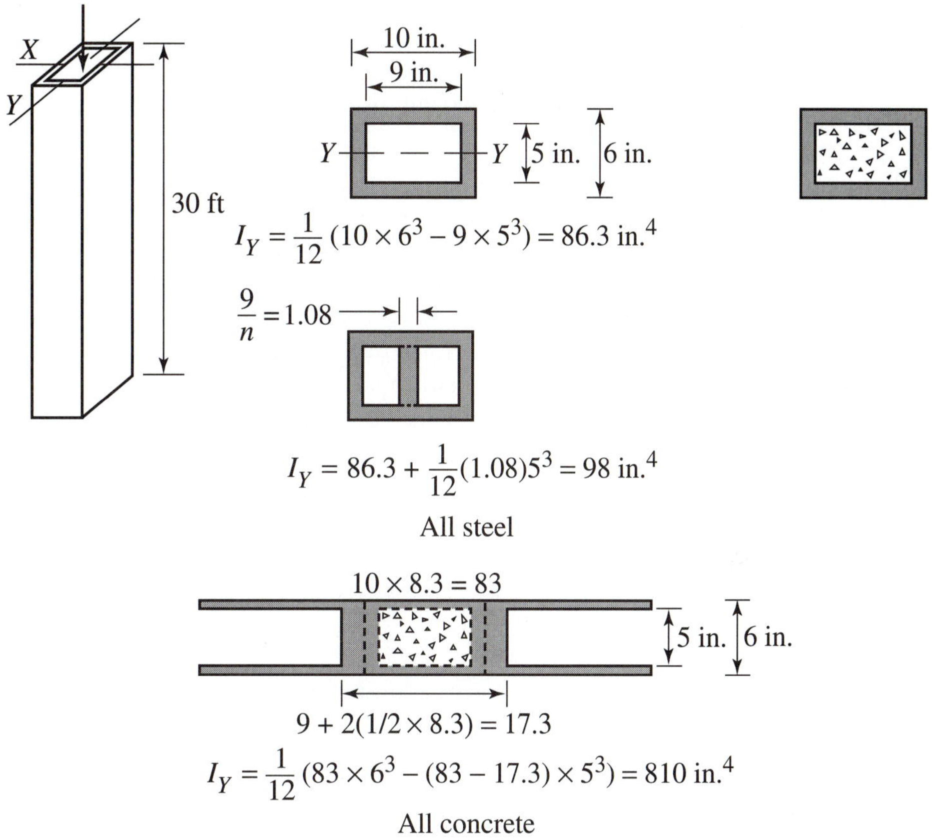

FIGURE 7.5

ment of inertia, so the critical moment of inertia is $I_Y = 86.5$ in⁴ as shown. The buckling load of the steel tube alone is

$$F = \frac{10 \times E \times I}{L^2} = \frac{10 \times 30,000,000 \times 86.3}{(30 \times 12)^2} = 200,000 \text{ lb}$$

When the tube is filled with concrete, buckling will still occur about the weaker Y axis, but the value of I_Y has been increased. In cases where two materials form a composite member, we often transform one of the materials into the structural equivalent of the other and then analyze the member as though it is made of one material. This transformation is performed using the ratio of the moduli of elasticity of each material, called the modular ratio, n. In the case of steel and concrete, n is given by

$$n = \frac{E_S}{E_C} = \frac{30,000,000}{3,600,000} = 8.3$$

When we looked at composite members before, we noted that they formed indeterminate structural elements, the analysis of which required an extra equation based on deformation compatibility. When steel and concrete act as a composite unit, their deformations must be the same. The modular ratio, $n = 8.3$, indicates that the elastic stiffness of steel is over eight times more than that of concrete, and so a square inch of steel carries over eight times the stress as a square inch of concrete.

Exercise What is the buckling load if we double the column height?

Rework this problem using the E value of a higher strength concrete, $E = 5{,}000{,}000$ psi. ■

To compute the moment of inertia of a transformed area about an axis using the modular ratio, we compress or expand the area of the transformed material in the direction of the axis. The transformed sections and moments of inertia, I_Y, are shown for the case of an all-steel section and an all-concrete section. Note that the value $E \times I$ is the same for both the concrete and the steel transformed members:

$$3{,}600{,}000 \times 810 = 30{,}000{,}000 \times 98 = 2{,}900{,}000{,}000 \text{ lb-in}^2$$

Thus, the buckling load for the composite column is

$$F = \frac{10 \times E \times I}{L^2} = \frac{10 \times 2{,}900{,}000{,}000}{(30 \times 12)^2} = 224{,}000 \text{ lb}$$

By adding the concrete to the hollow steel tube column, the buckling load increased about 12% from 200,000 lb to 224,000 lb. Note that this is the ultimate load that the slender column may support, and it contains no factor of safety.

7.6 Eccentrically Loaded Columns and Column Curves

If you are not particularly interested in theoretical derivations, you may choose to skip the derivation and pick up the discussion at the allowable compressive stress versus column slenderness curves of Figure 7.7. The derivations that lead up to the development of these important curves is felt to be worthwhile, particularly because few books present a single equation that can be used to relate allowable compressive stresses (or loads) over the full range of column slenderness ratios (or column lengths).

We have discussed that the critical buckling stress for slender columns is $f_{CR} = 10E/(L/r)^2$, and the critical stress for stocky columns, f_{CR}, is less sensitive to L/r than to material crushing stress. Most real columns fall somewhere between these two conditions. We would like to derive a single formula that relates critical column stress to column slenderness that will aid us later when we analyze and design compression members. In Figure 7.6 we see a pinned column for which the load, $F < F_{CR}$, has an eccentricity e relative to the column centerline at column midlength. The eccentricity is due to initial column crookedness that any real structural elements will have. The eccentricity may also result from an off-centered load placement, which is also very common.

First application of the load creates an initial midcolumn moment of

$$M_0 = F \times e$$

This moment causes deflection, D, and so increases the column lateral displacement, which in turn causes an increased moment, M, as the moment arm of F grows from e to $(e + D)$, where lateral displacements stabilize. For

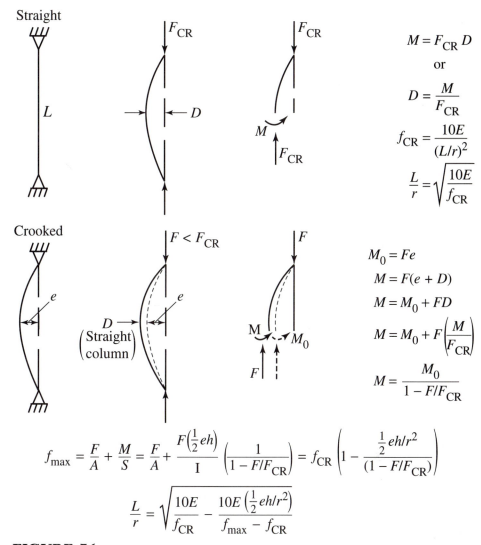

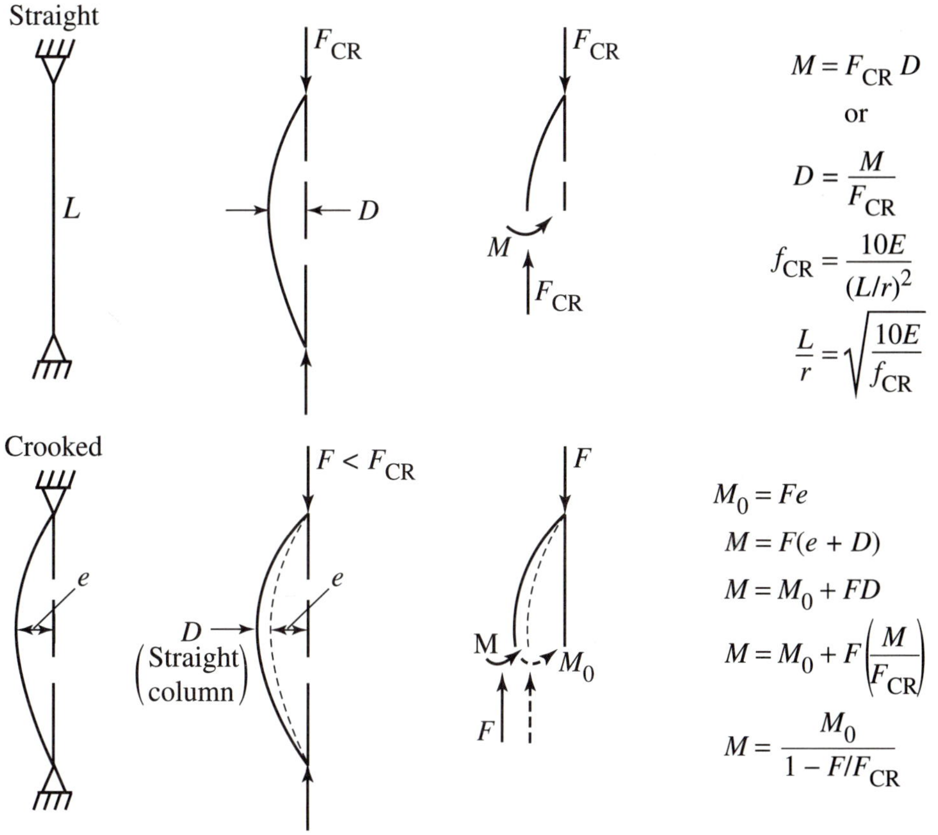

$$f_{max} = \frac{F}{A} + \frac{M}{S} = \frac{F}{A} + \frac{F\left(\frac{1}{2}eh\right)}{I}\left(\frac{1}{1 - F/F_{CR}}\right) = f_{CR}\left(1 - \frac{\frac{1}{2}eh/r^2}{(1 - F/F_{CR})}\right)$$

$$\frac{L}{r} = \sqrt{\frac{10E}{f_{CR}} - \frac{10E\left(\frac{1}{2}eh/r^2\right)}{f_{max} - f_{CR}}}$$

FIGURE 7.6

this stabilization of lateral displacement to occur, the elastic moment capacity of the column member must not be exceeded by the magnified midcolumn moment

$$M = M_0 + F \times D$$

The initial column moment, M_0, is increased an amount, $F \times D$, known as the "$P - \Delta$ effect" (many books use P instead of F and Δ instead of D). The two terms of the magnified moment M indicate the member is responding as a beam to the bending moment effects due to load eccentricity, M_0, and as a straight column to the buckling $P - \Delta$ effect, $F \times D$. If there were no eccentricity ($M_0 = 0$), we have seen that the maximum load that could be in equilibrium with a midcolumn moment capacity, M, would simply be the straight column critical buckling load, $F = F_{CR,}$ and a deflection, $D = M/F_{CR}$. If we substitute this value for D into the amplified moment equation, we have

$$M = M_0 + \frac{F \times M}{F_{CR}}$$

Rearranging this leads to the following expression for the magnified moment:

$$M = \frac{M_0}{1 - F/F_{CR}}$$

This relationship indicates that the initial eccentricity moment is increasingly magnified when the axial load on a member approaches the critical buckling load of the element. If the load F were to equal F_{CR}, the initial moment, M_0, would be magnified to a value of $M =$ infinity.

We must limit the combined column axial and magnified bending stresses to the elastic limit of axial compressive stress (crushing stress), f_{MAX}, and we employ the combined stress concept

$$f_{MAX} = \frac{F}{A} + \frac{M}{S} = \frac{F}{A} + \frac{M_0}{S(1 - F/F_{CR})}$$

which may be arranged in the following form:

$$f_{MAX} = f + \frac{f \times \frac{1}{2}eh/r^2}{1 - (f \div 10E/(L/r)^2)}$$

The unitless term, $\frac{1}{2}eh/r^2$, is called the eccentricity ratio, in which h is the column cross-section depth in the direction of the load eccentricity e. Most columns–even those thought to be centrically loaded–will have an eccentricity ratio of at least 0.3 due to unintended eccentricity from member crookedness and/or off-centered loading. An eccentricity ratio greater than 1 will result in a member with some tension axial stress on the cross section.

Further manipulation of the formula gives us an equation that we may use to generate a plot of the relationship between the slenderness of an eccentrically loaded column and the maximum stress that it can support without buckling:

$$Lr = \sqrt{10E/f_{CR} - \frac{10E \times \frac{1}{2}eh/r^2}{f_{MAX} - f_{CR}}}$$

With a specific material axial stress elastic limit, f_{MAX}, modulus of elasticity, E, and eccentricity ratio, $\frac{1}{2}eh/r^2$, we may generate points to plot the relationship between the maximum compressive stress, f_{CR}, possible in an eccentrically loaded column with different slenderness ratios L/r. We simply substitute numerous values for f_{CR} and solve for L/r until we have enough points to plot the curve. For the graph to begin at the desired value for f_{MAX} when $L/r = 0$, we have to increase f_{MAX} by (1 + eccentricity ratio) in the formula. Notice that the relationship reduces to the straight column case when $e = 0$.

Families of compression member curves for different eccentricity ratios can be plotted for a particular material. As shown in Figure 7.7, curves are plotted for steel and timber. Because reinforced concrete members are composite members, they are handled differently, as we will see when we look at concrete design applications.

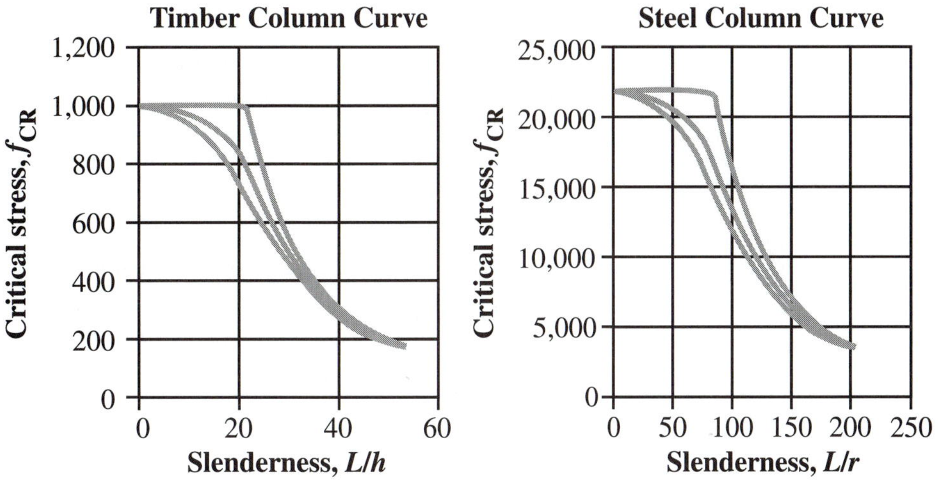

FIGURE 7.7

We model a theoretically straight column by substituting a very small value for the eccentricity ratio ($\frac{1}{2}eh/r^2 = 0.0001$) into the formula and generate the top of the three curves in each graph. This curve very nicely shows the theoretical critical compressive stress for short straight columns is the material maximum compressive stress, while the theoretical maximum compressive stress of slender compression members is dictated by the critical buckling stress, $f_{CR} = 10E/(L/r)^2$. The curve that the horizontal line changes into is a plot of this critical buckling stress, and is often called the Euler buckling curve (with safety factors applied, in this case).

The lower solid curve in each graph is for $\frac{1}{2}eh/r^2 = 0.3$, which provides a curve that accurately models the data of actual columns, which usually have unintended off-centered loads as well as initial crookedness. This is the curve that we will use for any column analysis and/or design.

The middle curve of the graphs is for $\frac{1}{2}eh/r^2 = 0.1$, which splits the difference between pure compression elements, and actual columns. This curve is included to help illustrate the different graphs that result from various eccentricity ratios, but also, as we will see, an eccentricity ratio of 0.1 may be conservatively considered for the analysis of unbraced beam compression flanges. Beam compression flanges behave as horizontal columns that tend to laterally buckle. While the beam flange will have a slight crookedness like column members, the compressive flexural stress is generally uniform across the width of beam compression flanges, so there is essentially no unintended compressive force eccentricity.

The curves presented here are based on typical allowable material stresses for timber and steel with safety factors to ensure that the elastic axial compressive stress limit is not exceeded for stocky columns with small slenderness ratios. For long columns, buckling is prevented by applying a safety factor of between 2 and 3 to the material modulus of elasticity E. For column cross sections that are rectangular, as is typical for timber elements, we conveniently replace L/r with L/h, where h is the cross-section depth in the direction of eccentricity e, and

$$r = \sqrt{\frac{I}{A}} = \sqrt{\frac{bh^3}{12 \div bh}} = 0.29 \times h$$

Thus, $L/h = 0.29 \times L/r$. We will be using these curves to analyze structural members and to generate useful column design graphs and tables for various timber and steel cross sections.

To demonstrate the eccentrically loaded compression element formula, we determine if a $6 \times 6 \times \frac{1}{2}$-in. steel tube is adequate as an axially loaded column. An 80,000-lb axial load is delivered to this 12-ft tall column due to a reaction from a beam that is welded to one of the sides of the top of the member. The axial load has an eccentricity of $e = \frac{6}{2} = 3$ in., and the radius of gyration of the tube is $r_Y = \sqrt{I/A} = \sqrt{\frac{1}{12}(6^4 - 5^4)/(6^2 - 5^2)} = 2.5$ in., so the eccentricity ratio is $\frac{1}{2}eh/r^2 = \frac{1}{2}(3)(6)/(2.5)^2 = 1.44$. This ratio exceeds 1, so there will be some tension induced on the cross section. Since we do not have a plot for this eccentricity ratio, we will use the formula directly to solve for the allowable compressive stress.

The adjusted maximum allowable steel stress is $f_{MAX} = 22{,}000 \times (1 + 1.44) = 53{,}700$ psi and $E = 30{,}000{,}000/2 = 15{,}000{,}000$ psi. The slenderness ratio is $L/r = (12 \times 12)/2.5 = 58$. We substitute into the eccentrically loaded column formula:

$$58 = \sqrt{\frac{10(15{,}000{,}000)}{f} - \frac{10(15{,}000{,}000) \times 1.44}{53{,}700 - f}}$$

By squaring both sides, we solve for the allowable column stress, $f = 16{,}000$ psi, and so the allowable load is $F_{ALL} = 16{,}000 \times (6^2 - 5^2) = 176{,}000$ lb, so the column is adequate to support the eccentric load.

7.7 Column Design Graphs

We can make use of the eccentrically loaded column equation to generate useful design charts for standard column cross sections. For instance, we will benefit from generating a family of graphs that present the allowable axial load, F_{ALL}, versus column length L for the most common timber post sizes: 4×4, 6×6, 8×8, and 10×10. These are nominal sizes, and we deduct $\frac{1}{2}$ in. to determine actual sizes, such as 5.5 in. $\times$ 5.5 in. for the 6×6. Timber columns are not allowed to have a slenderness ratio over 50. Hence, a 4×4 may have only $L/h = 50$, or $L = 3.5(50)/12 = 14$ ft.

Column design charts are usually presented assuming centrically loaded straight columns with some sort of provision being made for unintended eccentricity (crookedness and/or off-centered load), such as assuming an eccentricity ratio of 0.3. We will use an allowable axial compressive stress of $f_{MAX} = 1{,}000$ psi and the safe modulus of elasticity of $E = 580{,}000$ psi. We want to ignore eccentricity and use the full f_{MAX} when $L = 0$, so the maximum allowable stress used in the formula must be $f_{MAX} \times (1 + \text{eccentricity ratio})$. Thus, the eccentrically loaded column equation for timber may be written as

$$L/r = \sqrt{\frac{10(580{,}000)}{f} - \frac{10(580{,}000) \times 0.3}{1{,}300 - f}}$$

which simplifies to

$$L = h^2 \times \sqrt{\frac{487{,}800}{F} - \frac{146{,}300}{1{,}300(h^2) - F}}$$

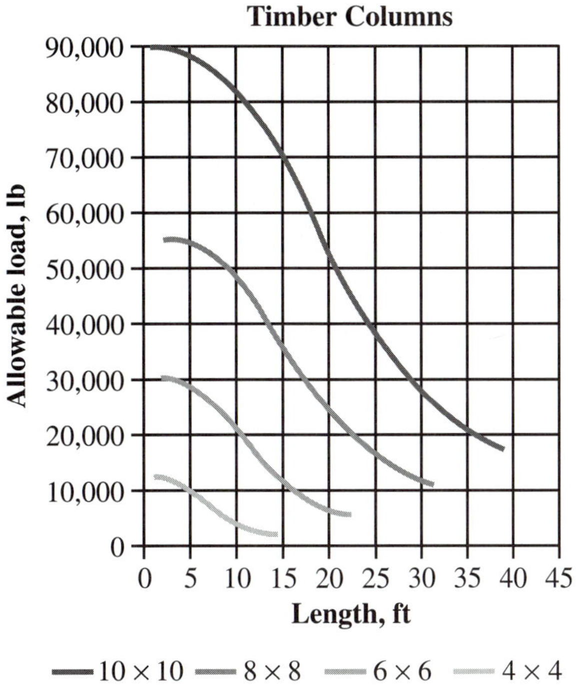

FIGURE 7.8

Exercise Create a similar set of curves for 12 × 12 and 14 × 14 timbers. ■

A simple spreadsheet can be set up with the first column of figures equal to the range of loads from $F = 1{,}000 \times 9.5^2 = 90{,}250$ lb to $F = 0$ using increments of 250 lb. This will be the Y axis of the chart. Then four adjacent columns are created, one for each of the $h \times h$ column cross sections. The cells of these columns contain the column formula with the appropriate value of cross-section h. Each row of these four spreadsheet columns will calculate L associated with the value of F on the same row. The data can be plotted as shown in Figure 7.8. Remember to convert L to feet, and not to show any values for $L/h > 50$. We may now use this chart to determine requited timber column sizes given column length L, and design compressive force F.

7.8 Beam-Column Interaction Equation

When looking at the various elements in structural systems, we find that there are many members that support combined axial compression and bending moment, so that the term beam-column is appropriate for such elements. If the bending moment is due only to load eccentricity, then we can analyze the member using the eccentrically loaded column equation. If the member has an axial compressive load and a transverse load that creates the bending moment, we will need to make use of what is known as the beam-column interaction equation.

We begin with the combined stress equation (which also served as the starting point for developing column curves):

$$f_{MAX} = \frac{F}{A} + \frac{M_0}{S(1 - F/F_{CR})}$$

The axial compressive stress is $f_C = F/A$. M_0 was previously the initial moment due to load eccentricity, and thus it was dependent on the axial force. In the present case, the initial moment being magnified, M_0, is due to transverse load that is independent of the axial force. The bending stress associated with this moment is $f_B = M_0/S$, and we may write

$$f_{MAX} = f_C + \frac{f_B}{(1 - f_C/f_{CR})}$$

which may be rearranged to

$$1.0 = \frac{f_C}{f_{MAX}} + \frac{f_B}{f_{MAX}(1 - f_C/f_{CR})}$$

Because the axial and bending stresses are fairly independent, except for the moment magnification in cases of a large value for f_C/f_{CR}, the allowable maximum stress for axial compression and for bending, f_{MAX}, do not have to be the same value. We may simplify the formula further by noting that the moment magnification effect will usually be negligibly small for practically proportioned beam-columns, and so for this case of beam-columns we may say $(1 - f_C/f_{CR}) = 1$. (*Note:* If the member is a vertical beam-column in a moment resisting frame, the moment magnifier is not negligible, and we will need to consider its effect, as we will see later.) We may then write the general beam-column interaction equation in terms of stress or in terms of force and moment as follows

$$\frac{F}{F_{ALL}} + \frac{M}{M_{ALL}} \leq 1.0$$

The interaction relationship simply tells us that the total capacity of a beam-column can be expressed as a portion available for axial compression and a portion for bending moment. As long as the sum of the fractional portions is less than, or equal to, 1.0, the capacity of the member has not been exceeded. The allowable axial force, F_{ALL}, is determined from column curves or design tables, and the allowable bending moment, M_{ALL}, is the allowable bending stress times the member section modulus, $M = f_B \times S$. (Note that the allowable bending stress is reduced for long unbraced beams in much the same manner as the compressive axial stress is for columns.) We make use of this formula later when analyzing timber, steel, and concrete structural members.

8 Basic Soil Properties

8.1 Overview

Now we switch gears from analyzing the structure above the ground to looking at the ground itself. Later, we return to forces and stresses as we discuss foundation types. Finally we turn our attention back to the structure above the ground as we see how timber, steel, and concrete is fashioned into the constructed environment that surrounds us all.

The gravitational pull of the earth causes the entire weight of any structure on land to bear upon the soil of the earth's surface. Force equilibrium requires that all vertical and horizontal loads that act on a structure must eventually be grounded into the earth through some type of foundation. Hence, a study of structures must also include some of the basic aspects of soil behavior and its analysis. From the work of geologists, we can learn of the natural origins of soil, while from the field of practice known as geotechnical engineering, we have standard procedures for exploring, sampling, and classifying soil and for determining how capable the material is to support structural loads.

To understand the relationships among the three primary constituents of soil–solids, liquid, and gas, we briefly consider typical situations wherein construction site conditions require modifying the existing soil. We consider the basic mechanics of how soil behaves when subjected to loads and how different foundation types ground out these loads. We also look at various ways that separations in grade may be maintained through slopes or soil retaining structures.

8.2 Soil Formation

Soil is formed from rocks and living organisms over eons of time in response to the affects of nature's forces acting from deep within the earth's crust as well as from atmospheric forces. From deep underground, soil masses are radically altered by earthquakes that cause great cracks and landslides at the surface of the earth, as well as through volcanic eruptions that bring forth lava and ash from within the earth's core to form the stuff of new soil.

Above ground, changes in the atmosphere cause weathering of rocks through such means as expansion and contraction cracks, freezing and thawing of rain water in mountain rock crevices, wind- and water-borne abrasives, natural chemical reactions, and so on. Massive rock formations are broken into boulders, stones, and gravel that may be further weathered down into the tiny sand, silt, and clay particles that we call soil. Likewise, living things die and decompose as a result of organic decay and form soft, crumbly particles that mix with weathered rock; this is desirable as fertile topsoil for agricultural use.

The same natural forces that act to create and weather rocks into the smallest of soil particles also act to transport them from one location to another. Residual soil remains at its place of origin, while transported soil is carried by wind, rain, rivers, oceans, glaciers, and landslides to locations thousands of miles away. Thus, at any given location, there will usually be layers of different soil type and size, each representing soil transported from different origins at different times.

There may also be drastic differences in the types of soil that are found existing side by side at a particular construction site. For instance, when a flooding river loaded with eroded soil sediments overtops its banks, the velocity of the flow of water slows, and sand and gravel particles being transported by the swift river current settle out to form sandy banks. Just beyond the banks, the flow rate slows more and eventually ceases, during which time smaller silt and clay particles will settle out of the water onto the floodplain.

The chemical composition of soil is identical to the igneous, sedimentary, or metamorphic rock from which it has weathered. Igneous rocks such as granite and basalt are created from cooled molten lava from deep within the earth. Sedimentary rocks like shale, sandstone, and limestone form as transported soil layers build up and compress lower layers of soil with such pressure that the compressed soil reverts back to rock formations. Metamorphic rocks begin as igneous or sedimentary, but under extreme compression and/or heat from overburden soil layers, these rocks may change into schist, slate, quartzite, and marble.

The materials we have discussed for building structures–the timber from harvested trees, the concrete components of fired pulverized limestone cement and coarse and fine aggregates, and the iron ore and other alloys used in steel–in some sense actually represent the further alteration of soil by human forces. With time, the materials currently in the form of structures will likely be broken down and returned into the earth once again, and so the construction process itself may be seen as quite integral with a naturally changing world.

8.3 Exploration and Sampling

We see from our brief history of soil that the origins and makeup of soil at one site will radically differ from that of another site, as will the mechanical soil properties. Before we build at a site, a geotechnical engineer who is familiar with the general geologic history of the region must explore the subsurface conditions. He or she will make use of considerable engineering judgement backed by indicators that result from standard soil tests to classify the soil and characterize its probable load-carrying behavior. Based on the geotechnical analysis of a site and knowing the proposed structure type and size, the geotechnical engineer can make recommendations as to the type of foundation that is most appropriate.

Subsurface exploration usually involves making several soil borings at locations all around the site. A boring hole is advanced using either a screw-like auger, which is periodically pulled out of the hole to remove the soil, or by using a cutting bit coupled with pressurized water that continuously washes soil up to the surface through the casing that advances with the hole. Sample specimens of the disturbed soil removed while advancing the hole are taken every five feet or so, or whenever a different stratum of soil is encountered. If a rock stratum of unknown thickness is encountered, a rock coring drill tool is used to advance through the layer and rock samples are extracted to determine its strength.

For each soil boring, data is carefully collected so that a record known as the boring log can be created later at the soil laboratory. While advancing the hole of a specific boring, each soil sample specimen retrieved from the hole is specifically labeled and noted along with the depth from which the sample was taken, and any test results or other general observations are also documented for later analysis.

Depending on what is observed from the disturbed soil coming out of the hole, the drilling tool may be removed and replaced with special sampling/testing devices. A device known as a Shelby tube is a hollow and thin-walled stainless steel tube about 2 ft long and 3 in. in diameter that is lowered back into the bottom of the hole and its full length is pushed into the undisturbed soil. Once removed from the hole, the contents of the tube are considered to give a reasonably undisturbed soil sample that can be tested in the lab to provide a good indication of the in situ soil properties of soils that contain a mixture of clay, silt, and/or sand.

If the boring has advanced into a sandy soil layer, the Shelby tube will not work well because granular soil particles will tend to fall out upon removing the tube. Instead, a split spoon device is used. It is similar to the Shelby tube but smaller and it splits longitudinally into two halves to reveal a disturbed sample. This device is widely used as the standard tool for conducting a procedure known as the Standard Penetration Test (SPT). In the SPT, the number of blows delivered via a specific weight dropped a specified height required to drive the split spoon 12 in. into the soil is called the SPT blow count, N (blows per foot). Over the years, empirical data has been collected that accurately correlate N to the density and strength of soils, especially for sands.

8.4 Soil Classification

The field data collected at each of the site soil borings along with the labeled samples are brought to the soils laboratory where further standardized tests are performed on the samples. These tests allow for the various soil layers encountered to be classified and for the boring log reports to be filled in and analyzed as part of the final geotechnical (soils) report. Depending on the structure being considered, there may be several other soil tests performed to determine the soil strength, compressibility, optimum density, and so on. The results of all the lab work are presented in the soils report along with specific recommendations concerning the type of foundation best suited to deliver the load of the structure to the specific soil at the site.

A sample of soil usually reveals a mixture of some or all of the four basic soil particle types–gravel, sand, silt, and clay, and the characteristics of the soil mixture vary according to the fractional presence of each particle type. One of the primary standard classification procedures for characterizing a soil mixture is the sieve analysis, which is conducted to determine the sizes and proportions of the particles in the mixture, in particular, what portion is coarse grained and what portion is fine grained. Particles like gravel and sand that cannot pass through the #200 sieve, which has tiny square mesh openings of only 0.003 in., are termed coarse grained, and their relative sizes and proportions greatly determine the behavior of the soil mix.

The soil particles that pass through the tiny openings of the #200 sieve–silt and clay–are termed fine grained, or simply the fines. If the soil mix contains fines, then their influence on the soil character is gauged using the standard tests known as the *plastic limit* and the *liquid limit* test. The plastic limit is the moisture content at which a sample of the soil will first crumble when rolled into strings of $\frac{1}{8}$-in. diameter, while the higher liquid limit is that moisture content at which the viscosity of the soil becomes liquid. The difference in these two indices provides the soil plasticity index, which determines the nature of the fines that are present in the soil mix. The plasticity index gives an indication of how the soil mix will behave under variable moisture conditions, and how much the soil character is influenced by mutual attractive forces of the fine particles.

Clayey soil particles are very tiny, with diameters of roughly 0.0002 in. or less that cling together as a result of mutually attractive magneticlike forces–this is termed *cohesion.* Gravel, sand, and silt particle sizes are roughly defined to be in the range of 0.1–1 in., 0.004–0.1 in., and 0.0002–0.004 in., respectively. These particles are cohesionless, and they stick together by interlocking through friction among the rough particle surfaces. Organic matter may also be present in the soil mixture, and if there are sufficient amounts of this soft and crumbly matter, it is detrimental to the strength of the soil.

If a soil is predominately composed of gravel and sand, it is termed a granular soil, and will be identified by labels such as well-graded gravel, poorly graded sand, silty gravel, and clayey sand. Such soils have excellent bearing strength with little settlement, and because they also drain well, these soils are useful as backfill for retaining walls. Such a soil mix is largely cohesionless, and internal interparticle friction accounts for most of its strength. The Standard Penetration Test results yield the *material friction angle,* or *angle of repose,* ϕ. This angle may be visualized as the slope of the sides of the material when it is formed into a pile. We discussed this friction angle earlier in the book, where we called the angle z. (You will see that we use different nomenclature to describe things in soils and foundations.)

When fine grains of clay and/or silt dominate a soil mixture, the result is a cohesive soil that is sticky and plastic in nature and may be classified by such identifiers as lean clay, clayey silt, and organic clay. These soils tend to have lower strength than granular soils and may exhibit considerable settlement when supporting load. Highly cohesive soils are often very plastic, having a tendency to shrink and swell considerably with moisture changes and to deform continually under load, and this can cause serious foundation problems in loose, highly saturated clays. Fine-grained soils do not drain well, and so they make poor backfill material, but are useful as the core of earthen dams and levees. Cohesive soils, which tend to be saturated with water, will initially resist structural loads through interparticle cohesion, c, and as time progresses, some water will be expelled under pressure into adjacent soil and some load is then resisted by intergranular friction, as we discussed for sand particles.

Where sufficient fine-grained particles, particularly clay, dominate the soil mix, the mix is termed a cohesive soil, or often simply clay. If there is little or no clay and the mixture is primarily a coarse-grained sand, it is referred to as a cohesionless soil, or simply sand. These two soil classifications are of the greatest concern when analyzing soil behavior for structures.

8.5 Volume-Density Relationships

In addition to tests performed for the purpose of classifying the soil, and to determine its strength, there are numerous other standardized soils tests to determine such soil properties as density, moisture content, void ratio, permeability, optimum dry density, and compressibility. The basis of these tests involves consideration of a sample of soil as a composite of three primary constituents: the solid tiny particles of weathered rock (and perhaps decayed organic matter), water, and air.

When constructing structures on soil, we often need to bring in additional soil (called fill) from another site (often called the borrow pit). The soil must usually be strengthened by compaction, or squeezing the particles closer together. To estimate soil quantities and to gauge the degree of compaction, we need to look at some basic relationships between the volumes and densities of soil's three components, solids, water, and air.

In Figure 8.1, a cubic foot volume of soil is shown with its three components in their natural state, where the solid rock particles are separated by

FIGURE 8.1

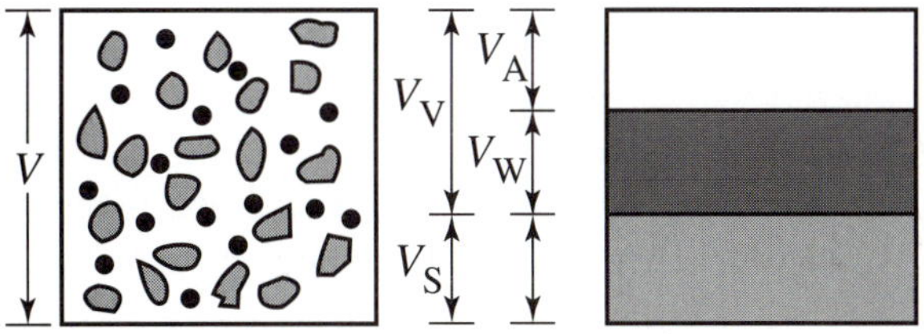

$$V = V_V + V_S$$

$$V_V = V_A + V_W$$

$$V = V_A + V_W + V_S$$

$$W = W_W + W_S$$

$$e = V_V/V_S \qquad \gamma = W/V \qquad \gamma_D = W_S/V \qquad w = W_W/W_S \times 100\%$$

$$\gamma_D = \gamma/(1 + w)$$

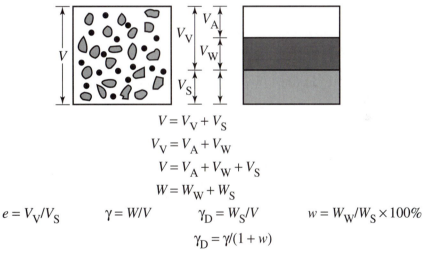

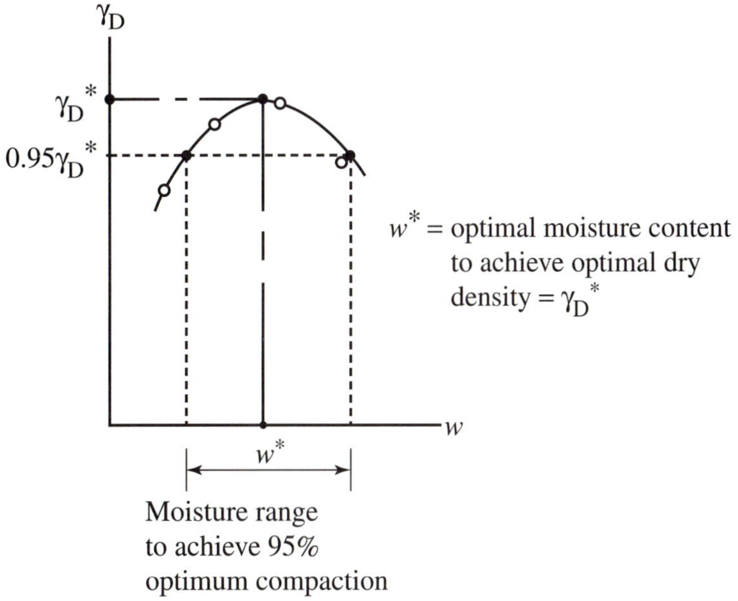

void spaces filled with air and perhaps water. For analysis purposes, we construct an engineer's idea of the cubic foot of soil with volume, $V = 1$ ft^3. We see the volume taken up by the solids of the soil labeled V_S, and we break the volume of void space, V_V, into the volume occupied by water, V_W, and the remaining volume of air, V_A, and

$$V = V_S + V_V = V_S + V_W + V_A = 1$$

The ratio of the volume of voids to the volume of solids is defined as the void ratio, e, so that

$$e = \frac{V_V}{V_S}$$

Typical values of e range from 0.5 to 0.9 for dense sands and from 0.7 to as much as 3 for loose clays. Structures built on soils with relatively large void ratios will exhibit greater settlements than if the soil were denser with a corresponding smaller value of e.

The total weight W of the cubic foot volume of soil equals the weight of the solids, W_S, plus the weight of the water, W_W, with the weight of air being negligible, so we have

$$W = W_S + W_W$$

We can simply use a scale to weigh the sample and determine W, then completely remove the water by oven-drying the sample and weigh it again to determine the weight of solids, W_S. Density, γ, is defined as weight per unit volume

$$\gamma = \frac{W}{V}$$

The weights of our 1-ft^3 sample provide us with the soil density, $\gamma = W/V = W$, and the dry density of the soil that is defined as

$$\gamma_D = \frac{W_S}{V}$$

For a unit volume, $\gamma_D = W_S$.

The weight of water in our sample is merely the difference between the two measured weights, $W_W = W - W_S$. We define the water content (or moisture content), w, as the ratio of the weight of water to the weight of the solids expressed as a percentage

$$w = \frac{W_W}{W_S} \times 100\%$$

The moisture content is highly variable. Typically ranging up to 30%, it may be over 100% for some loose clay deposits.

Suppose the density, moisture content, and void ratio of in situ soil at a borrow pit is $\gamma = 110$ pcf, $w = 15\%$, and $e = 0.9$, respectively, and 100,000 ft^3 of loose fill material is required at a nearby construction site. When digging up and relocating soil, additional air is introduced into the disturbed soil that becomes looser as its volume expands, or swells, maybe as much as 20%. This is sometimes called the fluff factor. What volume of borrow material is taken (that is, what size hole will be created), and what is the density, moisture content, and the void ratio of the loose soil placed in the hauling trucks if the swell factor is 15%?

Since the fill dirt volume is 15% greater than the in situ volume, the ratio of the fill soil volume to the in situ borrow pit soil volumes is simply $V_f/V_i = 1.15$. Therefore, the hole at the borrow pit would have a volume of

$$V_i = \frac{V_f}{1.15} = \frac{100{,}000}{1.15} = 87{,}000 \text{ ft}^3$$

By definition, $V = V_S + V_V = V_S + V_W + V_A$, and it is only the latter term, V_A, that is being altered.

Looking at a sample of in situ soil with unit volume $V_i = 1$ ft^3, and with unit weight of $\gamma_i = W/V_i = 110$ pcf, when this same sample takes on more air voids and expands to occupy a volume, $V_f = 1.15V_i$, its total weight, $W = W_S + W_W$, does not change. However, we see that the unit weight of loose fill must decrease to a density of

$$\gamma_f = \frac{W}{V_f} = \frac{110}{1.15} = 95.6 \text{ ft}^3$$

As we just saw, the volume and density changes from in situ to loose fill states, not the sum of the two weight components, $W_S + W_W$, nor the relative proportions of W_S and W_W. We recall that the water content is defined as $w = W_W/W_S \times 100\%$, and conclude that the water content is unchanged when transporting the soil.

When the in situ soil volume swells, it is the volume of voids, V_{Vf}, that changes while the volume of solids, $V_S = V_{Si} = V_{Sf}$, remains the same. By the definition of void ratio, for the in situ soil, $V_{Vi} = 0.9V_S$. For a unit volume, $V_i = 1$ ft^3:

$$1 = V_S + V_{Vi} = V_S + 0.9V_S$$

From this, we get $V_S = 0.526$ ft^3 and $V_{Vi} = 1 - 0.526 = 0.474$ ft^3. For the fill material, where $V_f = 1.15$ ft^3

$$1.15 = 0.526 + V_{Vf}$$

The volume of voids is $V_{Vf} = 0.624$ ft^3, and the void ratio increases from $e = 0.9$ to

$$e = \frac{V_{Vf}}{V_S} = \frac{0.624}{0.526} = 1.19$$

8.6 Compaction

The increased air volume in the loose fill results in a soil that is much more compressible and more water absorbent than before. If a structure, roadway, or embankment is to be built on this soil, it will have to be improved by compaction.

Compaction of soil involves compressing the material with heavy weights to force the particles into closer contact by squeezing out much of the air voids. The result is a denser, stronger, stiffer, and less pervious material that will better serve as the base for a slab-on-grade, footing, roadbed, or embankment.

Compaction is typically carried out by first spreading fill soil out as one or more 8- to 12-in. layers of fill soil called lifts. Next, measurements of the density and moisture content of the fill soil are taken and used to verify that the material is optimally prepared, as given by results of the Proctor Test, which will be discussed shortly. Then large, heavy, smooth or knobby rollers are moved across the soil lift, much like smoothing pie dough with a rolling pin. After several passes, the rollers compress the lift to about 75% of its original thickness. A roadway subbase may require only one or two lifts, whereas an embankment or levee will necessitate many such lifts.

The compaction process is merely the reverse of the borrow pit situation described above, so that as a result of compaction, fill soil density increases, its volume and void ratios decrease, and no change results in its moisture content due to the action of the rollers. The lift of fill soil must, however, be optimally prepared before compaction, and this involves ensuring that its moisture content is within a range established by lab test results.

There is a single value of moisture content at which several passes of a specific roller weight will achieve the optimum possible density of the lift fill material. If too little moisture is present in the soil, friction prevents the poorly lubricated soil particles from freely and adequately sliding in close together to dispel the most air voids possible. Conversely, with too much water is contained in the lift soil, the particles cannot come into close contact because the excessive liquid already occupies the void spaces.

With a sample of the fill material in the soils lab, a standard test procedure known as the Standard Proctor Test is performed. In this procedure, four or five subsamples are taken from the fill soil sample, and the moisture content of each subsample is varied by adding or removing some moisture from the specimen. Next, for each subsample, several 1-in. layers are compacted inside of a small steel cylinder of specific volume using a certain weight dropped a specific height. Each compacted subsample is removed from the cylinder, weighed, oven-dried, and weighed again to determine its oven-dry density, γ_D, and its moisture content, w (the difference in the two weights divided by the dry weight). A plot similar to that shown in the figure is created from the four or five data points.

The peak of the curve indicates the optimal dry density, γ_D^*, and corresponding optimal moisture content, w^*. The optimal density represents the densest state achievable when compacting the fill soil using routine field procedures. It is nearly impossible to add or remove moisture from the fill material to get the exact optimal moisture content that will allow us to achieve the greatest possible compaction density. Instead, we use the dry density versus moisture plot to determine the range of moisture content values under which we could get an acceptable dry density that is within 95% of the optimal dry density value.

If we consider a unit volume of oven-dry compacted fill soil, its dry density is simply the weight of solids in the cubic foot volume, $\gamma_D = W_S/V$, and thus $\gamma_D/W_S = 1$. A unit volume of compacted fill in the field will contain both solids and water, and by definition, a unit volume of this soil has a density of $\gamma = (W_S + W_W)/V$, so that $\gamma/(W_S + W_W) = 1$. Equating the dry and wet density ratios that are each equal to 1, and noting that $w = W_W/W_S$ (in fractional form), we have the useful relationship

$$\gamma_D = \frac{\gamma}{1 + w}$$

We can use the formula to ensure that the fill has been well compacted and its computed dry density, γ_D, is within 95% of the optimal dry density, γ_D^*, determined from Proctor Test results. A special moisture/density device is available for measuring γ and w in the field. Several moisture density readings are taken, and if the computed dry density is not within 95% of optimum, more compaction is required.

The Modified Proctor Test is similar to the Proctor Test except that more compaction effort is simulated with a larger weight. This test is usually specified when heavier construction equipment is required when building, say, airport runways versus rural two-lane highways. Because greater compaction effort is employed, the Modified Proctor Test will usually result in specification of a higher optimal dry density and a narrower allowable moisture range to achieve it.

8.7 Residential Site Compaction

If a roadbed, building slab, or embankment is to be built directly on the existing grade, the existing soil and/or fill soil can be compacted to serve as a strengthened foundation for the structure being built. We described how the soil being compacted is first subjected to a Standard Proctor Test to determine the optimal dry density and range of moisture contents under which the soil can be compacted to within 95% of optimum density. Depending on the job specifications, the soil is compacted in lifts ranging from 8- to 18-in. thick, and the compacted density of each lift can be field tested and/or a moisture-density measuring device can be used to determine if proper compaction has been achieved.

Suppose a house is to be built with a slab on grade foundation, and that most of the existing grade where the structure will be located needs to be elevated approximately a foot to ensure that it is above the floodplain. To comply with local building codes, the contractor will acquire fill soil from within the local watershed area, which ensures that the flood elevation remains unchanged for the area. The contractor hauls in 3,000 ft^3 of sandy clay fill that will be placed in a 16-in. lift to be compacted to 12 in.

The soils engineer conducts a Standard Proctor Test on a sample taken from the fill from which several dry density versus moisture content values yielded a graph similar to that of Figure 8.1. The resulting optimum dry density and moisture content for the fill soil was determined to be $\gamma_D = 114$ pcf and $w = 15\%$, respectively. The graph also indicated that to achieve 95% optimum dry density, which is $\gamma = 108$ pcf, the lift soil must have a moisture content in the range of $10\% < w < 21\%$ at the time of compaction. Using a moisture meter, if the contractor finds the soil is too wet, it may be loosened with a till and allowed to air-dry a day or so, or if the soil is too dry, water may need to be tilled into the lift.

At midafternoon, the contractor spreads the fill soil and uses a moisture-density meter to measure a density of $\gamma = 105$ pcf and a moisture content, $w = 16\%$ in the lift. At this point, a heavy shower set in for the duration

Exercise To achieve 100% optimum density for a roadway sub-base, how many gallons of water need to be added per foot of the 60-ft-wide road bed if the fill soil forming a 9-in. lift has a 10% moisture content and weighs 110 pcf? From a Modified Proctor Test, the optimum dry density and moisture for the fill was determined to be $\gamma_D = 125$ pcf and $w = 13\%$, respectively. ■

of the afternoon during which time an inch of rainfall was measured. The contractor needs to know whether it will be possible to till the extra moisture into the lift the next morning and immediately compact it, or if it will be necessary to let the soil dry out for a day or two before finishing the job.

The dry density of the fill, which is the weight of solids in a 1-ft³ volume of soil, can be estimated from the measurements taken before the rain:

$$\gamma_D = \frac{\gamma}{1 + w} = \frac{105}{1.16} = 91 \text{ pcf}$$

Each square foot of spread fill occupies a volume of $\frac{16}{12}$ ft³, and an inch of rainwater is added to every square foot of exposed soil, which weighs $\frac{1}{12}$ ft³ of water. Thus, the weight of water per cubic foot is

$$W_W = 62.4 \text{ lb/ft}^3 \times \frac{1}{12} \text{ ft}^3 \div \frac{16}{12} \text{ ft}^3 = 3.9 \text{ lb/ft}^3$$

Therefore, the moisture content of the fill was apparently increased by

$$w = \frac{W_W}{W_S} \times 100\% = \frac{3.9}{91} \times 100 \approx 4\%$$

The moisture content after the rain is apparently $w = 16 + 4 = 20\%$, which is within range for the contractor to try and compact to 95% of optimum density.

The next morning, the contractor tills the lift to thoroughly mix the added rainwater and later that afternoon proceeds to compact the soil to an approximate height of 12 in. The soils engineer takes samples and finds the average moisture and density of the compacted fill are $w = 18.4\%$ and $\gamma = 128$ pcf, respectively. Does the contractor achieve 95% optimum density? Again, we relate dry and actual density to find the compacted dry density is

$$\gamma_D = \frac{\gamma}{1 + w} = \frac{128}{1.184} = 108 \text{ pcf}$$

Thus, the contractor is able to just achieve 95% optimal density. If γ_D in this case had been less than 108 pcf, more compaction would have been required.

8.8 Soil Strength

The strength of soil is unlike the material strengths that we have discussed for timber, steel, and concrete because soil strength is generally not constant–it actually increases with the intensity of active compression stress. Also, the strength of soil is much lower than that of the other materials, so much so that it is usually stated in units of pounds per square foot (psf), versus pounds per square inch (psi). For example, the allowable concrete compressive stress in a column that delivers load to a footing might be 1,000 psi, whereas the allowable bearing stress between the footing and the soil may be 2,000 psf, which is only 14 psi. Of course, it is precisely because of its low stress capacity that we have to reduce the intense stress carried through structural members by spreading them over a large area to deliver the load into the soil. What is the pressure between a car tire and the ground upon which it rests?

By the term, soil strength, we are usually referring to the ultimate shearing stress that a soil mass can withstand before a failure occurs in the form of relative slippage of two portions of the soil mass along a failure surface. Several examples of shear failure planes are shown in Figure 8.2. We see that the active compressive stress of structural loads applied to soil can lead to shear failures, but also, the soil itself may be the activating load that causes shear failures when lateral movements are possible.

The figure shows a small cube of soil with a unit volume of 1 ft^3 located at a depth h below grade that is subjected to vertical and lateral confining stresses. An active vertical stress is exerted on the cube of soil, $q_0 + q_S$. The stress due to the overburden, or weight of soil stacked above the cube is $q_0 = \gamma h$; the density of soil, γ, is usually in the range of 90 to 130 pcf. (The density of soil below the water table is reduced by the density of water,

FIGURE 8.2

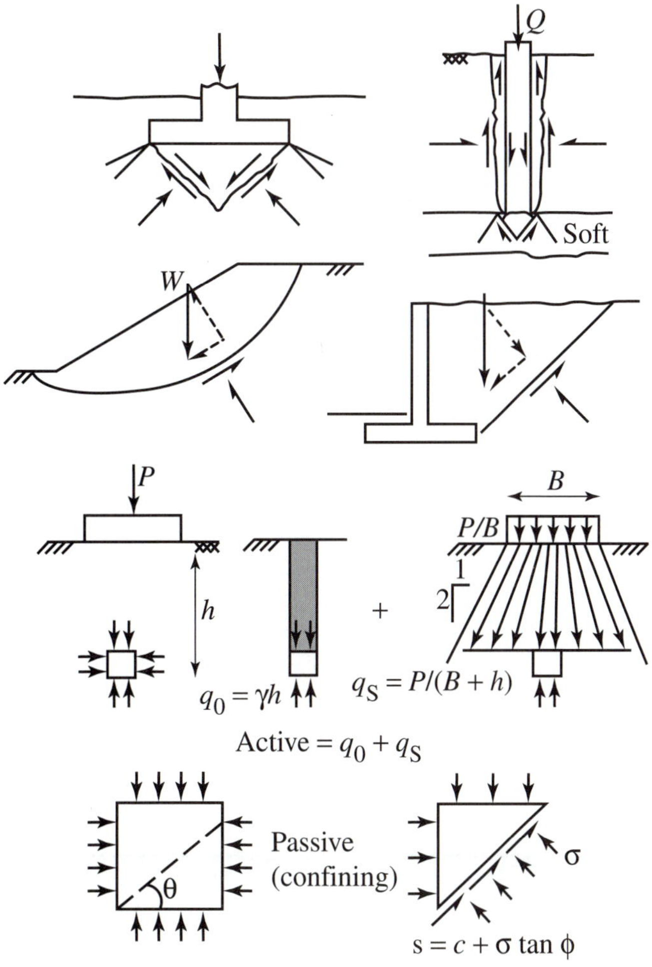

γ_W = 62.4 pcf, because submerged objects have buoyant weight equal to their own weight minus that of the water they displace.) The stress below a structure, q_S, diminishes with increasing depth, as shown, and as a result, soil shear failures are apt to occur fairly close to the base of a structure.

As the active stress vertically squeezes the soil and it tries to bulge laterally, passive lateral stresses due to adjacent soil react to confine the soil as shown. If the difference in the active and passive stresses is great enough, shear failure will occur on a plane oriented at an angle, $\theta = 45° + \phi/2$, from the plane on which the active stress occurs (ϕ is the friction angle of the soil). Looking closer at this failure plane, we see that the stress acting on the plane can be described in terms of the shear stress component, s, and the perpendicular clamping stress component, σ.

The shear strength of soil that resists failure on a critical shear plane comes from two sources: cohesion, the magneticlike mutual attraction of the clayey fines, and the interlocking friction between the granular particles. For a specific soil, the cohesion c is a constant attraction between particles on either side of the failure plane. The intergranular friction, like all friction, increases with the intensity of the clamping stress, σ, that acts perpendicular to the shear plane. As we saw earlier in this book, the coefficient of friction of a specific material (soil, in this case) possessing friction angle, ϕ, is $\tan(\phi)$, and the intergranular soil friction is $\sigma \times \tan(\phi)$. Thus, the shear strength of soil may be written as

$$s = c + \sigma \times \tan(\phi)$$

The terms c and ϕ of this relationship may be experimentally determined by soils lab test procedures such as the direct shear test, the unconfined compression test, and the triaxial compression test, or from in situ tests such as the vane test and the SPT. If the soil is classified as a clay, intergranular friction is generally ignored ($\phi = 0$); if it is classified as a sand, the cohesion is ignored ($c = 0$).

For clays, the simple unconfined compression test is used to determine the axial compressive stress at which a sample cylinder of soil from the Shelby tube fails. This stress is known as the unconfined compressive strength q_U, and the cohesion c may be shown to be

$$c = \frac{q_U}{2}$$

For sands the Standard Penetration Test is generally used to determine soil characteristics. The blow count, N, from the SPT is correlated to empirical data and may be used to predict the soil friction angle, ϕ. The relationship between N and ϕ (degrees) is approximately

$$\phi = \frac{N}{4} + 28$$

8.9 Foundation Settlement and Consolidation

Just as with other materials that we have discussed, when soils must resist some form of loading, they also must deform. Determining the deformations associated with stresses in soil are a bit more involved than for steel, timber, or concrete. Settlement under a footing occurs as the added pressure of a newly constructed structure foundation reduces the void ratio of the soil and squeezes some water out of the soil voids, forcing it into adjacent soil. Structures built on sand will fully settle immediately after construction and initial live loads, because sand is very permeable and allows easy flow of the water through its voids. However, if a particularly loose stratum of clay exists under a foundation, it will continue to settle for many years because the soil is not permeable like sand, so it takes longer for the water in the voids to be extruded.

The settlement that occurs with a compressible clay layer is known as consolidation. The more permeable the soil stratum that underlies a clay layer, the more quickly the water in the clay can be squeezed out. In Figure 8.3 we

FIGURE 8.3

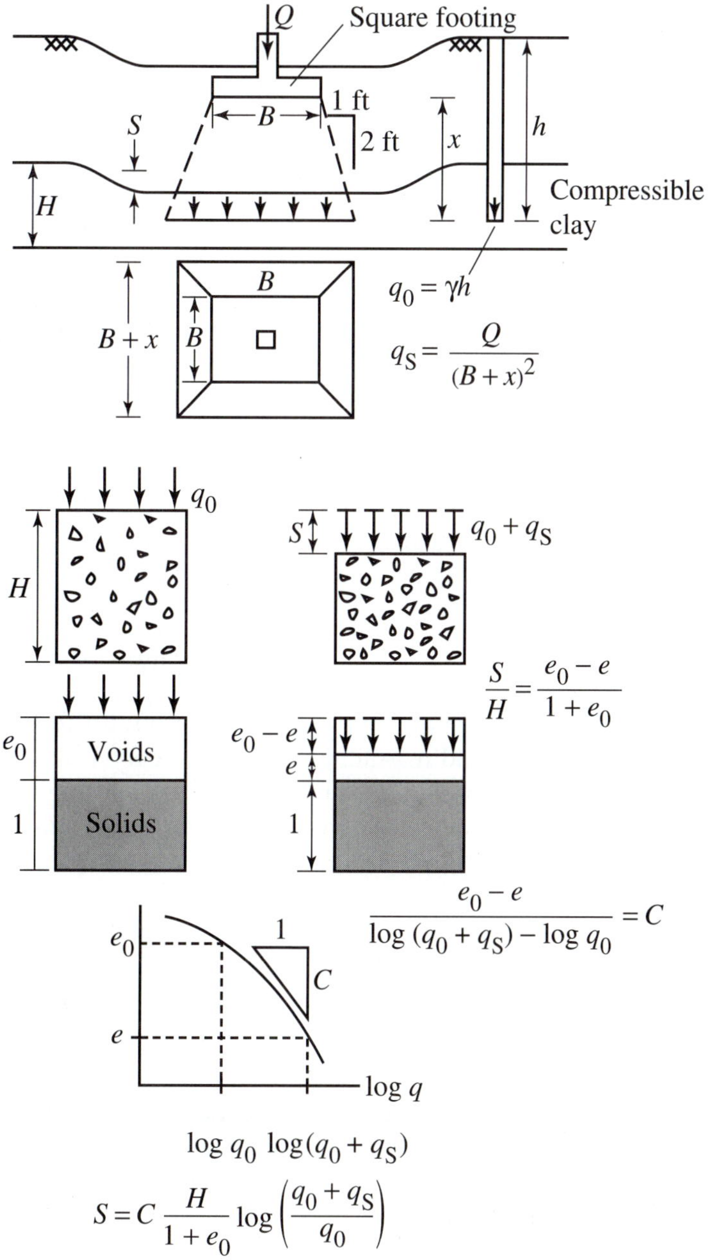

see a compressible clay stratum with a thickness H lying beneath a square footing that experiences a settlement S as a result of the consolidation of the clay.

The soil stress at midstratum (the average stress), which is positioned at depth, h, below grade is shown to be composed of the overburden pressure, $q_0 = \gamma h$, and the added stress at a depth x below the square $B \times B$ footing, q_S. The added soil pressure due to a footing load Q is usually assumed to be spread over an area that expands 1 ft in all four lateral directions for every 2 ft of increased depth below grade, as shown. Thus, at depth x below the footing, the stress due to the footing is

$$q_S = \frac{Q}{(B + x)^2}$$

Under the initial overburden pressure, $q_0 = \gamma h$, the clay layer has long been stabilized to an initial void ratio, e_0. But with added pressure from the newly located footing over a period of months and years, as a result of an average increased pressure, $q_S + q_0$, the void ratio will eventually be reduced to e as water is slowly extruded. In the figure, these relationships are schematically depicted on a soil mass shown to be composed of both solids and voids, and we see that

$$\frac{S}{H} = \frac{e_0 - e}{1 + e_0}$$

Before construction, a Shelby tube sample is taken at midstratum and brought to the soils lab where its initial void ratio, e_0, is determined and a consolidation test is also performed. The consolidation test results in a plot of void ratios versus the logarithm of applied soil pressure similar to that shown. When plotted using the logarithmic scale, a straight-line relationship is typically observed, and the slope of this line is termed the compression index C, which is given by

$$C = \frac{e_0 - e}{\log(q_0 + q_S) - \log(q_0)}$$

The value of C typically ranges from 0.1 to 0.6. By combining the relationship above and rearranging mathematical terms, we get a useful relationship to predict consolidation settlement, S, of a compressible clay layer with thickness H, initial void ratio e_0, overburden pressure q_0, and added footing pressure q_S, (both computed at midstratum), and the compression index, C:

$$S = \frac{C \times H}{1 + e_0} \log \frac{q_0 + q_S}{q_0}$$

Suppose that a 10-ft-thick layer of compressible clay lies 12 ft below grade with a void ratio determined from a Shelby tube sample, $e_0 = 1.1$. Consolidation test results give the compression index as $C = 0.3$. The average soil density is $\gamma = 110$ pcf, and the water table was not encountered during the soil borings. If the footing supports a total load of $Q = 100{,}000$ lb, what consolidation settlement S could be anticipated if the base of a square footing of $B = 7$ ft is located

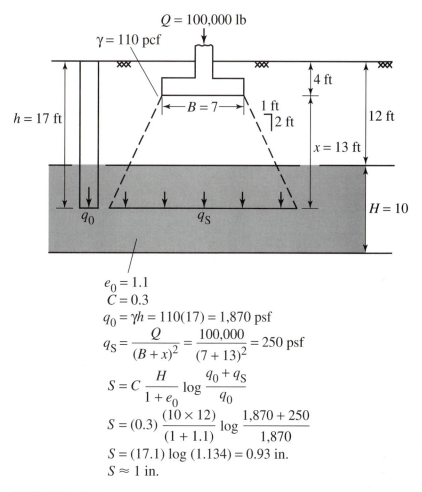

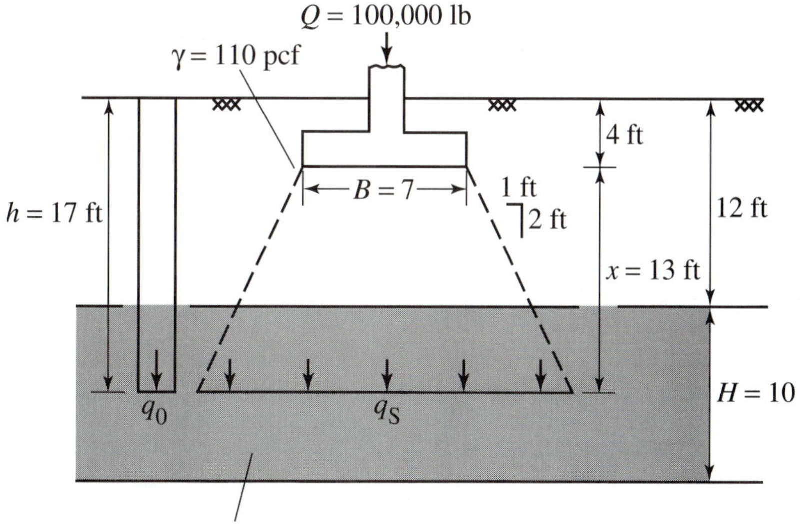

$e_0 = 1.1$

$C = 0.3$

$q_0 = \gamma h = 110(17) = 1{,}870 \text{ psf}$

$$q_S = \frac{Q}{(B+x)^2} = \frac{100{,}000}{(7+13)^2} = 250 \text{ psf}$$

$$S = C\,\frac{H}{1+e_0}\log\frac{q_0+q_S}{q_0}$$

$$S = (0.3)\,\frac{(10\times 12)}{(1+1.1)}\log\frac{1{,}870+250}{1{,}870}$$

$S = (17.1)\log(1.134) = 0.93 \text{ in.}$

$S \approx 1 \text{ in.}$

FIGURE 8.4

Exercise Suppose that a second square footing is located in the same area as that in the problem above. The footing supports Q = 51,000 lb, and its width, B = 5 ft, was selected so that both footings have the same bearing stress at their bases. Will the second footing settle the same amount as the first?

Rework the B = 7 ft problem assuming that the water table is encountered just below the surface. ■

4 ft below grade. The sketch of Figure 8.4 depicts the problem and shows the computations that are needed to determine that S = 1 in. for this case.

8.10 Differential Settlement

As we shall see, the use of conservative allowable bearing stresses for preliminary analysis usually ensures that the footings will have tolerable settlements of under an inch, so settlements usually need not be checked. Regardless, all footings for a structure should be designed to have similar bearing stresses and thereby prevent differential settlement, which means that one footing settles more than another. This differential settlement causes uneven floor and roof lines that can cause windows and doors to stick and cracks to form in plaster ceilings and masonry walls.

In some steel and most cast-in-place concrete structures with beams rigidly attached to columns through moment connections, differential settlements can even cause overstressing of the structural members. In Figure 8.5 we see how no stresses occur in a precast concrete beam and column system with a differential settlement of adjacent columns–the beam merely tilts a bit. In a moment frame, however, we see that the beam is bent in double curvature as a result of relative settlement D of adjacent column lines, and it can be shown that moment M induced in a beam of span L and stiffness EI is

$$M = D \times \frac{6EI}{L^2}$$

For instance, suppose the beam of the moment frame has a 25-ft (300-in.) span and is subjected to a differential settlement of $D = \frac{3}{4}$ in. If the member is a W24 × 84 steel section that has a stiffness of $EI = 30{,}000{,}000 \times 2{,}300 = 69{,}000{,}000{,}000$ lb-in^2, then the induced moment is

$$M = \frac{3}{4} \times \frac{69{,}000{,}000{,}000 \times 6}{300^2} = 3{,}450{,}000 \text{ in-lb}$$

Knowing that bending stress is $f = M/S$, and that $S = 190$ in^3 for the steel shape, the bending stress in the steel girder due to the $\frac{3}{4}$ in. of relative displacement of its ends is $f = 345{,}000/190 = 18{,}200$ psi. If the live and dead loads on the beam were fully stressing it to an allowable value of $f = 24{,}000$ psi, this settlement would cause a 75% overstress.

Building codes provide different limits on tolerable differential settlements depending on the type of framing system used. For simple framing, the

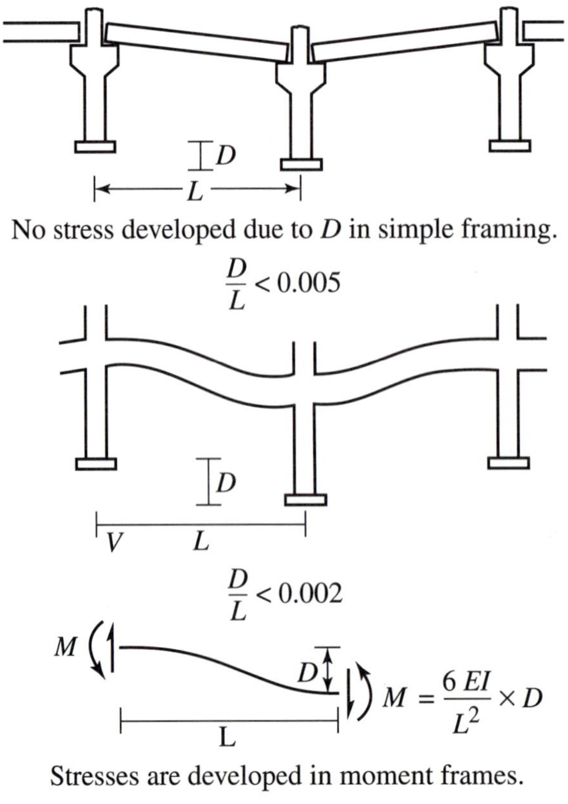

FIGURE 8.5

relative settlement allowed between two footings separated by a distance L is $D/L < 0.005$. For moment frame structures, $D/L < 0.002$.

Exercise How much differential settlement is causing the additional stress of 4,000 psi in a girder that is rigidly attached to columns at either end of its 50-ft span? The moment of inertia of the beam is 15,000 in^4, and it is a 24-in.-deep beam section.

After we cover the concrete chapter you may want to determine what additional steel is required in a concrete beam cast monolithically with its support columns if the span is 24 ft and the girder is 16-in. wide by 30-in. deep ($A_S = M/21{,}600d$). Assume $D/L = 0.002$. ■

9 SOIL STRUCTURES

9.1 SHALLOW AND DEEP FOUNDATIONS

Generally speaking, foundations may be classified as shallow or deep. Shallow foundations are spread footings that usually spread the structure load at a point at or slightly below grade (ground level). By excavating soil and placing the footing below grade and below the frost line, the destructive expansion forces created by freeze-thaw action are avoided, but also, the backfill soil and the flanking soil overburden help confine the footing and thus add to its load-bearing capacity. However, the footing depth will usually be less than 10 ft or so of ground level, since considerable time and labor go in to excavating soil.

Shallow footings may be useful when supporting heavy structures on a solid rock stratum that lies near the surface. They are also commonly used to support moderate loads of medium-rise structures when the soil possesses high bearing capacity, such as in granular soils. Shallow footings are used in clayey soils when the loads are not too great, as for residences and low-rise commercial structures. It is important that the clay is stiff enough to prevent excessive settlement known as consolidation, wherein water in the voids is slowly squeezed out over a period of months and years. A consolidation test is performed in the soils lab if the potential for excessive consolidation exists.

When the soil strata near the surface are insufficient for the support of structural loads or the soil is prone to excessive consolidation, the required footing sizes will become excessive and deep foundations are needed. Either cast-in-place drilled shafts or precast driven piles are used to deliver the structural loads to a strong layer of sand or rock, or else to deliver the load via shear friction between the surface area and soil interface all along the length of the shaft.

Since the holes for the cast-in-place concrete drilled shafts must be augured before placing steel reinforcing and pouring in concrete, their depths are somewhat limited. Depths from 20 to 40 ft may be typical for smaller-diameter shafts, and larger auguring equipment may allow placing the tip of shafts with diameters of 6 ft or more at depths in the 80-ft range. The depth of driven steel, concrete, and timber piles are limited by the structural capacity of the pile, the feasible handling length of the pile, and whether or not the pile sections may be spliced. Driven piles may reach depths up to 200 ft.

9.2 SPREAD FOOTINGS

In Figure 9.1 we see the two main types of shallow foundations–the square isolated footing and the continuous strip footing. The design of these footings entails ensuring that the structure load Q is spread out over an area large enough to prevent soil overstress–hence the name *spread footings*. The total

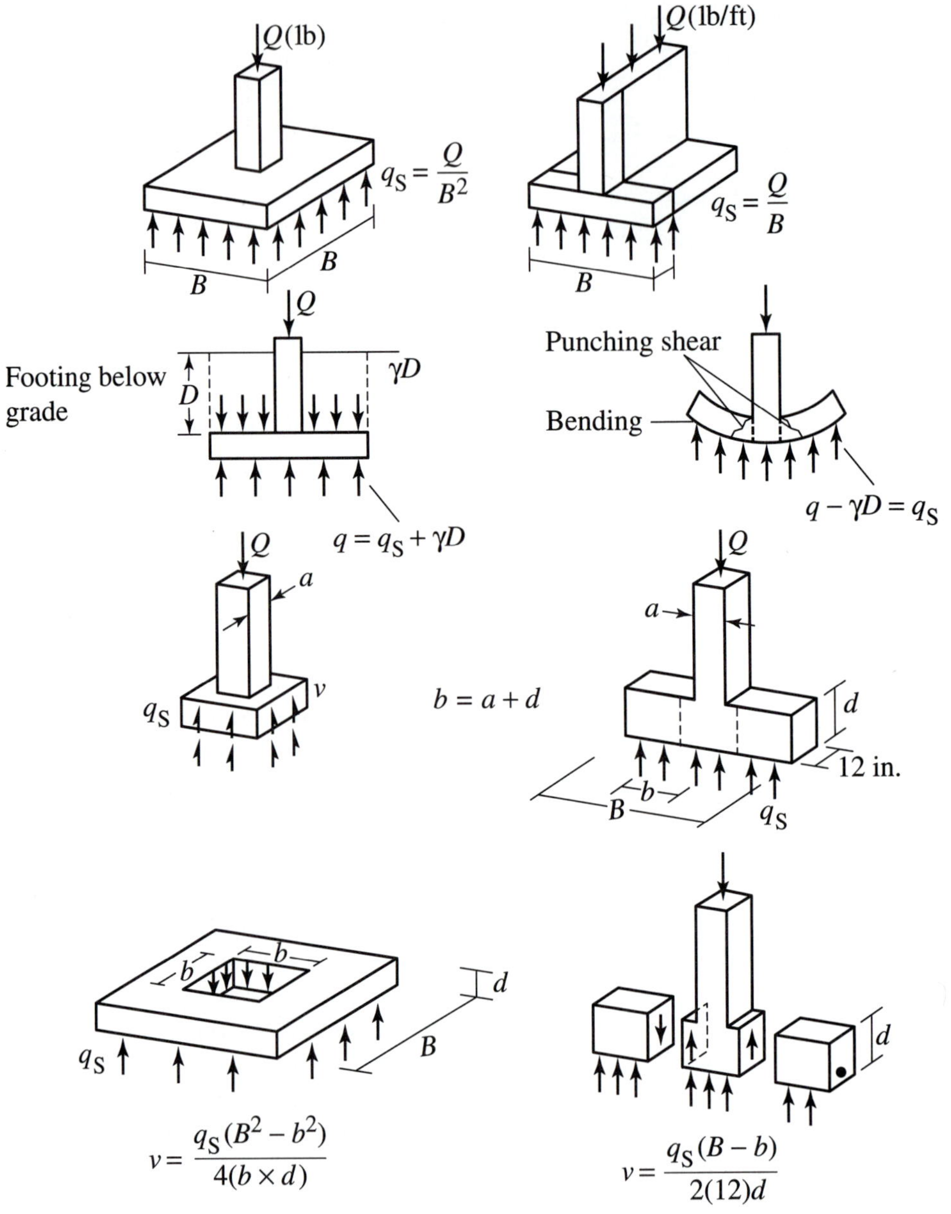

FIGURE 9.1

bearing stress below the footing base is $q = q_S + \gamma D$, where the stress due to the load from the structure is q_S, and the stress created by the surcharge of the backfill of footings placed at a depth D below grade is γD. Based on the allowable bearing stress for the footing, q_{ALL}, we determine the required footing dimension B. Then, we perform a structural design to determine the required thickness and the amount of flexural steel for the footing.

The allowable soil bearing stress q_{ALL} is influenced by many parameters including the footing size and depth, the soil shear strength (a function of cohesion, internal friction, density, and applied load intensity), and the proximity of the water table. The allowable stresses for different types of foundations that may be considered for use on the site for a particular structure type will be stated in the soils report of the geotechnical engineer. There are a variety of analysis methods in the field of geotechnical engineering, and they may yield different results depending on the assumptions of the method, and how closely the site conditions meet these assumptions. Thus soils engineers must use their judgement to apply the most appropriate one of many available analysis procedures that best fits the unique site conditions.

For preliminary designs, we may use conservative values for the allowable bearing stresses of footings on clay and sand. These allowable stresses are based on a safety factor of around 3 with respect to soil shear failure. At these low stress levels, footings should show reasonable settlements of about an inch, and if all footings are sized so as to create the same bearing stress, the problem of differential settlements will be minimized to a certain degree. These allowable soil stresses should be used only as a guide for preliminary work and cannot be a substitute for a thorough soils investigation and analysis.

For clays, the allowable bearing stress under footings turns out to be about twice the soil cohesion. Since cohesion is half of the unconfined compressive strength ($c = q_U/2$), we have $q_{ALL} = q_U$. Typical values are $q_{ALL} = 1{,}000$ psf for soft clays up to $q_{ALL} = 6{,}000$ psf for stiff clay. For sand, the allowable bearing stress is based on the blow count N from the SPT, and it is approximated here as $q_{ALL} = 250N$ (psf). With N values typically ranging from 10 to 50, the range of allowable bearing stresses for footings on sand range from $q_{ALL} = 2{,}500$ psf for loose sand to $q_{ALL} = 12{,}500$ psf for dense granular soil.

Using these values to determine the size of a footing B, we next turn our attention to its structural design. We have previously analyzed a square footing and discussed a formula used to relate punching shear stress to the footing thickness for square footings. In the figure, we repeat the formula needed to compute the punching shear stress for square footings and present a similar relationship for strip footings.

The allowable punching shear stress in the concrete is 70 psi, and this is what determines the thickness of footings on soil, as well as footings that are supported on piles, where they are referred to as pile caps. In Figure 9.2, we see how the flexural analysis of a 1-ft-wide strip of a square and strip footing are identical. Note that flexural bottom steel is required in one direction for the strip footing, whereas it is needed in both directions for the square footing.

In the figure we see a cantilever concrete beam of span L and effective depth d. The beam resists applied bonding moment, $M = q_S L^2/2$, by means of a couple created by concrete compression, C, and the tension force in steel reinforcing rods. If the total cross-sectional area of these rods is A_S, and they are subject to a tensile stress f_S, then the tension couple force is $T = A_S f_S$. The couple moment arm may be taken as 90% of the effective beam depth, $0.9d$. (The reader will find further details of reinforced concrete design in Chapter 12.)

As an example, we will compare the size B of a square footing on grade for soil that is medium clay and soil that is dense sand. The foundation must support a 16-in.-square column carrying a 200,000-lb load. For the footing on clay, we estimate $q_{ALL} = \frac{1}{2}(1{,}000 + 6{,}000) = 3{,}500$ psf, and so the required area is $B^2 = 200{,}000/3{,}500 = 57\ \text{ft}^2$, so $B = 7.5$ ft. For dense sand, the required width is $B = \sqrt{200{,}000/12{,}500} = 4$ ft.

How thick must the footing be? Using the punching shear stress formula for the footing on clay, we may assume a 24-in.-thick footing for which the effective concrete beam depth is $d = t - 4 = 20$ in. (the footing is generally about 4 in. thicker than the effective depth). The dimension b is $\frac{16}{12} + \frac{20}{12} = 36$ in. (3.0 ft). The punching shear stress is computed and compared with the allowable

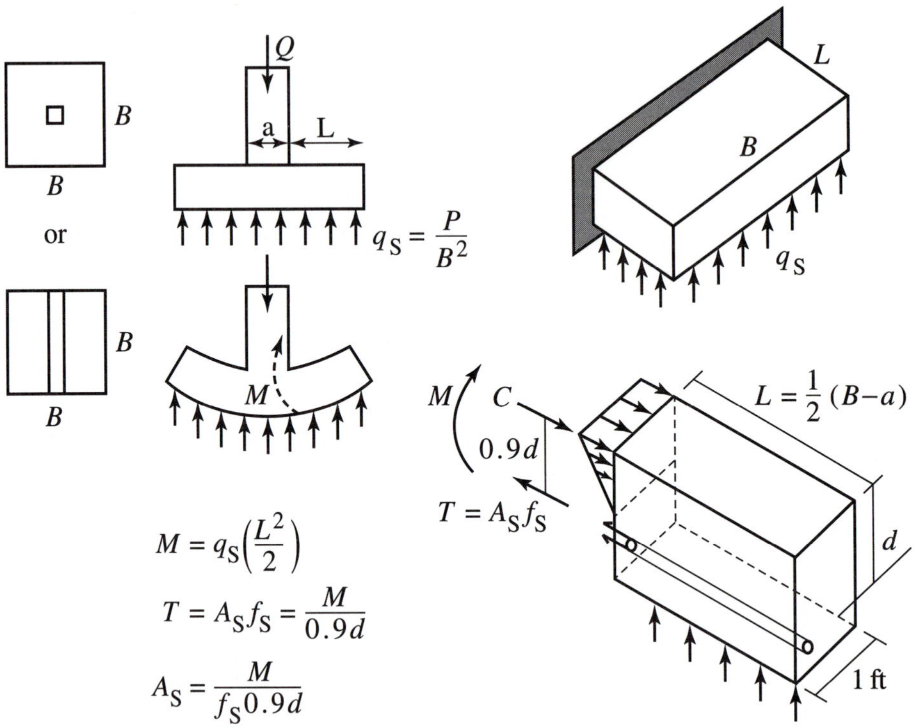

FIGURE 9.2

$$v = \frac{3{,}500(7.5^2 - 3^2)}{4 \times 36 \times 20} = 57 \text{ psi} < 70 \text{ psi}$$

You may further verify that if the thickness is reduced to $t = 20$ in. for both footings, the punching stress will be 84 psi for the footing on clay, and 54 psi for the footing on sand.

9.3 Design of a Strip Footing

Consider the concrete parking garage structure of Figure 9.3 that supports two levels of automobiles above ground and one level on grade. For preliminary analysis, the dead weight of the structure is averaged to be $D = 120$ psf and the nominal live load to simulate the autos is $L = 100$ psf. The linear nature of such a facility allows for the use of a center bearing wall and a strip footing on the sandy soil, as shown. We would like to determine the required footing width B, check the shear stress, and determine the required flexural steel of the footing. A thickness of 18 in. is assumed for both the pedestal and the footing base thickness. The overburden soil weight may be neglected for this shallow foundation.

We may analyze a foot slice of the structure to determine the load Q that is distributed along the footing. Since a slab on grade supports the ground-level autos, the footing along the center of the structure then supports its share of two levels of structure weight and live load

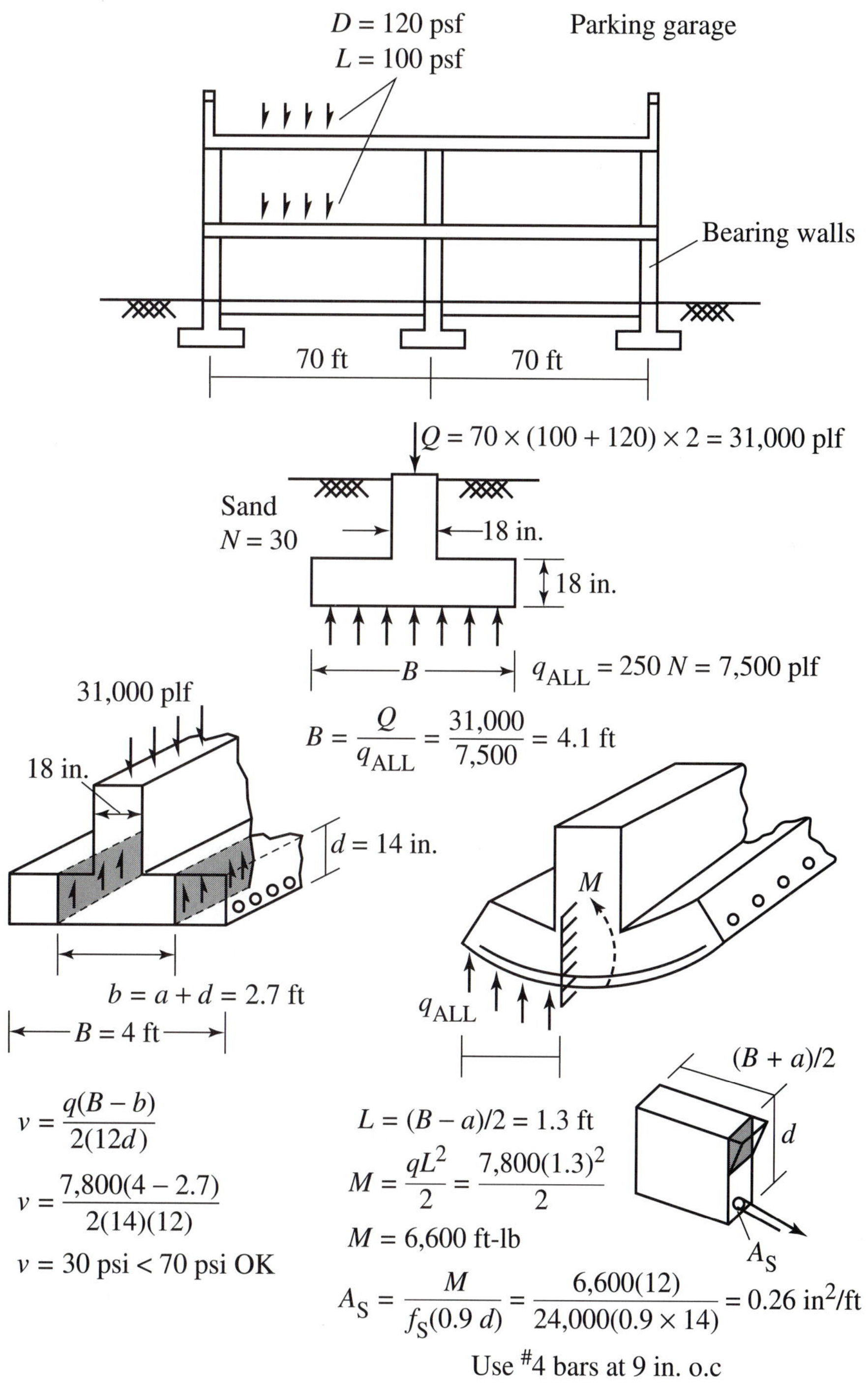

FIGURE 9.3

$$Q = 2 \times \left[\frac{1}{2}(70 + 70) \times (120 + 100)\right] = 31{,}000 \text{ lb/ft}$$

For a sandy soil with an SPT blowcount of $N = 30$, the allowable bearing stress is

$$q_{\mathrm{ALL}} = 250(N) = 250(30) = 7{,}500 \text{ psf}$$

Stress is force per unit area, and the bearing area under a 1-ft length of footing that is B wide is $B \times 1$, or simply B ft^2, and the required footing width becomes

$$B = \frac{Q}{q_{\mathrm{ALL}}} = \frac{31{,}000}{7{,}500} = 4.1 \text{ ft}$$

If we use $B = 4$ ft, the actual bearing stress is

$$q = \frac{Q}{B} = \frac{31{,}000}{4} = 7{,}800 \text{ psf}$$

This is an acceptable overstress of only 3%.

We next check the punching shear stress that occurs on the two assumed failure planes shown, noting that the effective depth of the concrete member is approximately the thickness minus 4 in., or $d = 14$ in. As we have previously discussed, the width of the punch through wall is $b = h + d = 18 + 14 = 32$ in. (2.7 ft), and from the punching shear formula for strip footings

$$v = \frac{q(B - b)}{24d} = \frac{7{,}800(4 - 2.7)}{24 \times 14} = 30 \text{ psi}$$

This shear stress is well below the 70 psi allowed, so the footing thickness is adequate.

Finally, we determine the required flexural steel that runs perpendicular to the wall along the bottom of the footing by analyzing the portion of the footing base from the face of the pedestal to the edge of the base as a cantilever beam. The uniformly distributed load is simply q for the 1-ft-wide beam, and from the formula presented for footing flexure, the moment is

$$M = \frac{q(B/2 - a/2)^2}{2} = \frac{7{,}800(1.3)^2}{2} = 6{,}600 \text{ ft-lb/ft}$$

This moment per foot of wall length requires the flexural steel area per foot

$$A_S = \frac{M}{21{,}600d} = \frac{6{,}600 \times 12}{21{,}600 \times 14} = 0.26 \text{ in}^2/\text{ft}$$

We may use #4 bars spaced 9 ft o.c. to supply the required steel. Note that a #4 bar has a diameter of $\frac{4}{8}$ in. and a cross-sectional area of 0.2 in^2. When spaced 9 in. o.c., the area per foot width (12-in. width) is $12/9 \times 0.2 = 0.27$ in^2.

Exercise Assume that the bearing wall is replaced by 18-in. square columns spaced 20 ft o.c. and design an isolated square footing for one of the columns. ■

9.4 Piles and Drilled Shafts

Often, structural loads are too large to use footing foundations of reasonable size, either because of low soil strength or excessive settlement. In these instances, deep foundations can be used to deliver the structure load into a greater mass of soil, or to deliver the loads to a stiffer soil or bedrock stratum. Deep foundations may be *driven piles* or *augured piles,* also known as *drilled shafts.*

Concrete, steel, or timber driven piles are like large nails that are hammered into the soil with pile drivers. Drilled shafts are cast-in-place concrete members formed by pouring concrete into cylindrical holes drilled with large soil augurs. In general, drilled shafts are used in areas where the dynamic effects of driving piles will likely disturb nearby structures, such as in urban areas or densely developed housing subdivisions.

It is rare that a single driven pile is used to support a foundation. Usually, a clustered group of piles is used to support an isolated footing, or a row of piles is placed beneath a strip footing under a wall. Driven piles are square or circular shafts made from precast concrete, timber, or steel pipe or H sections. The structural capacity of a pile or drilled shaft is determined by its cross-sectional area multiplied by allowable stresses of 1,000 psi for concrete piles and drilled shafts, 1,000 psi for timber piles, and 12,000 psi for steel members. Either the member capacity or the soil strength may govern the allowable pile load.

Concrete piles are usually prestressed members that range in sizes to 36 in. and typical lengths to 60 ft or so, though they can sometimes be field spliced and driven to greater depths. Special high-strength concrete hollow cylindrical segments may be post-tensioned together to create piles with 6-ft diameters that may be driven to depths of more than 100 ft. Timber piles are essentially trees stripped of their limbs. Timber pile sizes are limited to available tree dimensions, with effective diameters of 12 in. and 50-ft lengths being common. The most common steel section used is a special group of W shapes with thick webs and flanges of similar dimensions known as H piles that are available in various lengths and are easily field spliced to reach depths of 100 ft or more. H piles are usually treated as square piles when determining the allowable pile load based on soil capacity.

Because they do not need to be transported to the site, and because they are used instead of a group of piles, drilled shafts typically have the same length as driven piles, but they usually have larger diameters, ranging from 18 in. to 8 ft. If the soil is not stiff enough, the sides of the augured hole must be kept from collapsing by maintaining a dense viscous slurry, often called drilling mud, in the hole. As the denser wet concrete mix is placed in the bottom of the hole using a flexible hose, the concrete slurry displaces the drilling mud from the top of the hole. In many cases, the bottom of the hole is widened to create a bell-bottom shaft for greater bearing capacity.

Generally speaking, driven piles and drilled shafts support load in much the same manner and we will treat them similarly. Because the soil at the tip of a drilled shaft is not densified as for driven piles, the allowable tip bearing stress for drilled shafts is one-third of that for driven piles. It is common practice for the geotechnical engineer to call for one or more test piles to be driven to verify the accuracy of the soil design stresses predicted by soil test results.

Referring to Figure 9.4, we see that a pile of width/diameter d and length L supports a load P by means of skin friction stress f and tip bearing stress q, according to the following relationship:

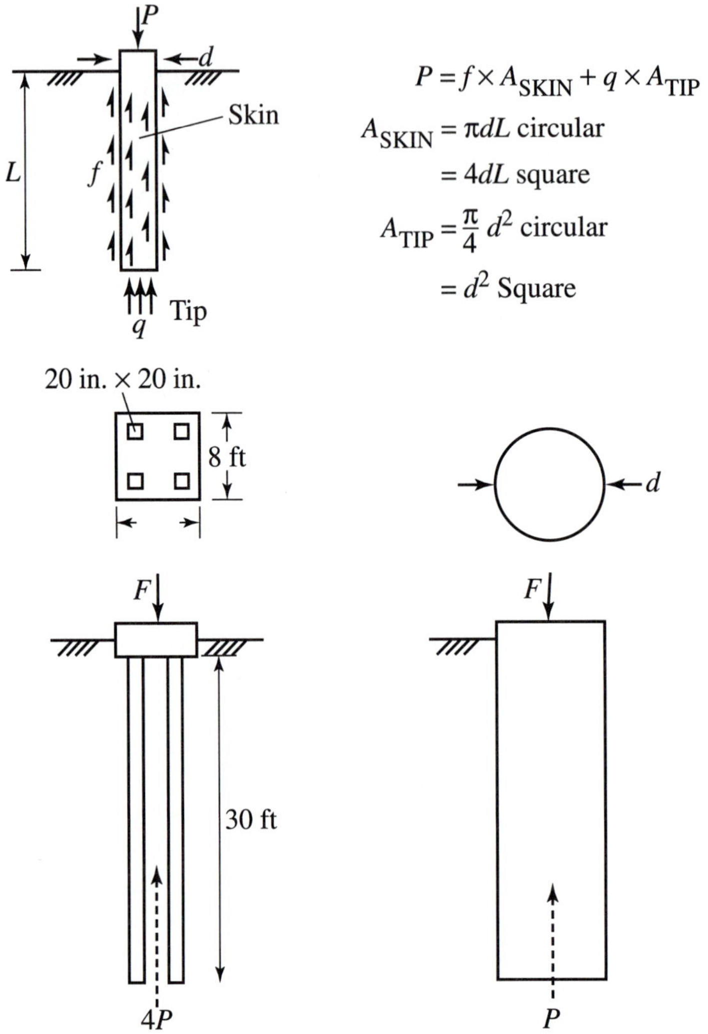

FIGURE 9.4

$$P = f \times A_{SKIN} + q \times A_{TIP}$$

For circular and square piles, the skin friction surface is $A_{SKIN} = \pi dL$ and $4dL$, respectively, and the respective circular and square tip areas are each $A_{TIP} = \pi(d^2/4)$ and d^2.

As we did for footings, we will use a safety factor of about 3 to determine allowable soil stresses, f and q. Skin friction in clays is the adhesion between the soil and the surface of the skin, which is roughly equal to the soil cohesion c, so that the allowable friction stress for a clay of unconfined compressive strength is $f = 0.15q_U$. Tip bearing stress in clays is based on empirical data and is $q = 1.5q_U$ ($0.5q_U$ for drilled shafts). Allowable stresses for piles in sandy soils are empirically correlated to the SPT blow count N, and the allowable stresses (psf) for piles in sand are roughly $f = 8N$ for skin friction, and $q = 2{,}400N$ ($800N$ for drilled shafts) for tip bearing. (For driven piles, these values may be increased 50% if test piles are to be used, thus giving an effective safety factor of 2 instead of 3.)

For example, in the figure, suppose that a change in plans requires that the four 20-in.-square concrete piles driven through 30 ft of clay, with

Exercise How many 60-ft 14-in. × 14-in. square piles are needed to support a load $F = 500{,}000$ lb in a medium clay? For a 40-ft drilled shaft, what diameter is needed? ■

$q_U = 3{,}000$ psf, to a sand stratum, for which $N = 30$, are to be replaced by a single drilled shaft. Assuming that the tip of the drilled shaft will also bear in the sand, what diameter drilled shaft is required to create a foundation of equal load capacity to that allowed for the four driven piles?

The total capacity of the pile group F is simply four times that of one driven pile P. The structural capacity of the pile based on concrete compressive stress is

$$P = 1{,}000(20^2) = 400{,}000 \text{ lb}$$

For allowable pile load based on soil capacity, the allowable skin friction stress in the clay is $f = 0.15(3{,}000) = 450$ psf, and the allowable tip bearing in the sand is $q = 2{,}400(30) = 72{,}000$ psf. The skin and tip areas are $A_{SKIN} = 4(20/12)(30) = 200 \text{ ft}^2$ and $A_{TIP} = (20/12)^2 = 2.8 \text{ ft}^2$, and so the allowable capacity of a single pile based on soil capacity is

$$P = 450(200) + 72{,}000(2.8) = 90{,}000 + 202{,}000 = 292{,}000 \text{ lb}$$

Thus, the allowable foundation load based on the soil capacity is $F = 4 \times 292{,}000 \approx 1{,}170{,}000$ lb. (Notice that this could be used to support the column line of the 10-story building shown in Figure 4.3.)

For the drilled shaft, allowable tip bearing stress q is assumed to be one-third as much as for the piles, or $q = 24{,}000$ psf, and the skin and tip areas are $A_{SKIN} = \pi d(30) = 94d$ and $A_{TIP} = \pi/4(d)^2 = 0.79d^2$ and

$$1{,}170{,}000 = 450 \times 94d + 24{,}000 \times 0.79d^2$$

Using the quadratic equation, or just by trial and error, we find $d = 6.8$ ft. We see that the shaft supports 290,000 lb through friction in the clay, and 880,000 lb by tip bearing in the sand.

9.5 Analysis of a Bridge Pier on Piles

In Figure 9.5 we see a 140-ft-tall concrete bridge pier, usually referred to as the substructure, that supports two 500-ft span steel through truss bridge spans (superstructure) that serve as approach spans to an even longer bridge structure that crosses the Mississippi River. In cross section, the stem of the pier resembles an I-beam with 14-ft × 7-ft flanges and a 26-ft × 2-ft web. The 40-ft-wide stem is seen to flare out to a 70-ft width at the top to support the four-lane roadway truss. The pier load is spread out to 66 supporting piles via the 36-ft × 66-ft rectangular pile cap footing that is 10 ft thick.

The square 18-in. prestressed concrete piles have a structural capacity of $P = 230$ tons each. The piles resist load through skin friction in the upper 80-ft layer of medium clay with unconfined compressive strength, $q_U = 1{,}200$ psf, and tip bearing in the underlying thick strata of dense sand

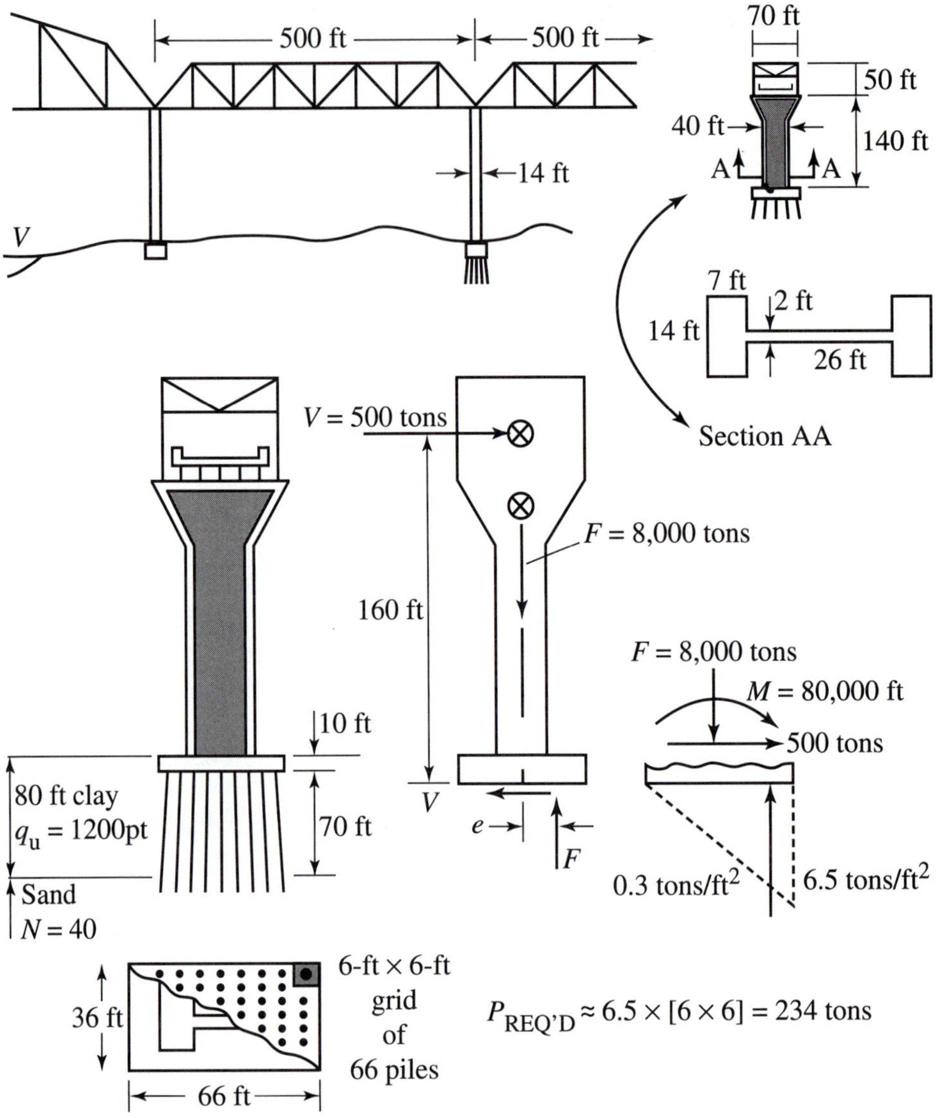

FIGURE 9.5

with SPT blow count, $N = 40$. Note that the perimeter piles are slightly battered (slanted) to resist the lateral force V that the wind applies to the footing.

Bridge design specifications indicate a critical pile loading results from the lateral load caused by hurricane-force wind acting on the projected area of the entire structure plus the vertical dead weight load from the two truss reactions and the pier plus footing. Thus, the pier acts as a cantilever beam-column fixed to the ground by its supporting footing and piles with a vertical load of $F = 8{,}000$ tons, and a lateral wind force of $V = 500$ tons with a centroid located 160 ft above the base of the footing, as shown. These forces create an equivalent axial force, shear, and moment at the top of the piles as shown.

To check the adequacy of the pile group, we first check for any tension on the piles, which occurs if the load eccentricity, $e = M/F$, is greater than $B/6$. We see that $M/F = 80{,}000/8{,}000 = 10$ ft, and $B/6 = 66/6 = 11$ ft,

Exercise Will 20-in. square piles provide the required pile capacity of $P = 234$ tons based on soil strength and a safety factor of 2?

If instead of dense sand, the pile tips bear in a thick stratum of stiff clay with $q_U = 5{,}000$ psf, what length of 20-in. square piles are needed for the bridge substructure (all piles are 20 in.)? ■

so $e < B/6$ and all piles are in compression. We compute the combined bearing stress beneath the footing as though it were on soil instead of piles using the combined stress formula

$$q = \frac{P}{A} \pm \frac{M}{S} = \frac{8{,}000}{36 \times 66} \pm \frac{80{,}000}{36 \times \frac{66^2}{6}} = 3.4 \pm 3.1 \text{ tons/ft}^2$$

Thus the equivalent bearing stress varies from $q = 0.3$ tons/ft^2 on the left to $q = 6.5$ tons/ft^2 on the right side (of course, this reverses when the eye of the hurricane passes and the wind blows from the opposite direction).

Since we are interested in the most heavily loaded pile, we apply the maximum bearing stress to the tributary area and conservatively estimate that the required pile load capacity is

$$P_{\text{REQ'D}} = 6.5 \times (6 \times 6) = 234 \text{ tons}$$

This is close enough to the 230-ton safe structural capacity of the 18-in. (1.5-ft) pile to say it is structurally adequate for the job.

Next, we check the pile capacity based on soil strength. We said that when test piles are to be used, as would be the case for a major structure such as this, the pile capacity may be increased 50%:

$$P = 1.5 \times [0.15q_U \times 4dL + 2{,}400N \times d^2] \text{ lbs}$$

$$P = 1.5[0.15(1{,}200) \times 4(1.5)(80 - 10) + 2{,}400(40)(1.5^2)] = 437{,}000 \text{ lb}$$

Thus, the pile capacity based on soil strength is $P = 219$ tons, which is 6% below the required $P = 234$ tons. Because the critically loaded battered edge piles are also resisting some of the horizontal wind force, $V = 500$ ton load, it may be wise to try a larger pile, such as a square 20-in. member for the battered piles.

9.6 Stability of Grade Separations

It is often necessary or desirable to establish gradual or abrupt changes in the ground elevation, such as for landscape terracing, levees, and highway overpass embankments. If the grade change is gradual, a soil slope or embankment may be created, whereas if significant changes in grade must occur abruptly, soil-retaining structures are usually needed. In grade separations, we need to verify from stability analysis whether a slope will fail, or if a wall will tilt or slide. A safety factor, F.S., of 1.5 to 3 is typically desired.

In Figure 9.6 we see how the safety factor against slope instability is determined for cohesionless and cohesive soils. We have previously mentioned that a granular soil that is poured into a pile will have sides that naturally slope

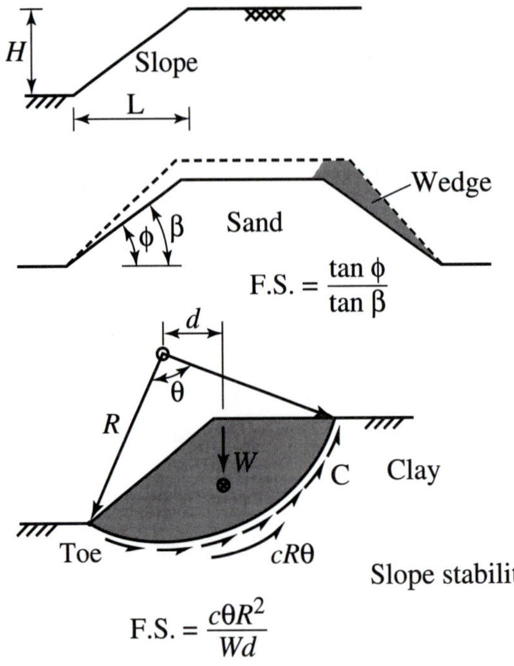

FIGURE 9.6

Slope stability

at the material friction angle, or angle of repose, ϕ. To ensure slope stability with a factor of safety, the side slopes, β, should be less than ϕ. The factor of safety against a slope failure that might take the form of a sliding wedge of sand such as the shaded area in the figure is

$$\text{F.S.} = \frac{\tan(\phi)}{\tan(\beta)}$$

For example, if the sand embankment makes an angle of $\beta = 30°$ with the ground and the soil friction angle is $\phi = 38°$, then we can say that the slope has a safety factor against sliding equal to

$$\text{F.S.} = \frac{\tan(38°)}{\tan(30°)} = \frac{0.781}{0.577} = 1.35$$

This value indicates that the slope is safe, but only marginally.

In a general soil mixture, and especially in clay soils with negligible internal friction, a slope failure usually appears on a plane that forms a circular arc as shown. Such a slope is unstable if the moment about the arc center due to the weight W that acts at the center of gravity of the shaded soil mass exceeds that of the resisting moment of the cohesive shear force, $c \times R \times \theta$, along the arc plane. For the critical failure plane, the factor of safety against instability is

$$\text{F.S.} = \frac{c \times \theta \times R^2}{W \times d}$$

For stability analysis, it is not known which of an infinite number of possible combinations of arc centers and arc radii is the critical one. Thus, a variety of trial arcs must be considered until it is felt that the one with a minimum value for F.S. has been located using the relationship above. This work may be done graphically, or using computer programs.

We will estimate the F.S. for the trial arc of the clay slope in the figure if $H = 10$ ft and $L = 10$ ft. When drawn to scale, the shaded area was determined to be 120 ft^2, and the centroid of the shaded area was determined to occur just below the point where the slope meets the upper level grade. As is common practice, the trial center of an arc was located about midway above the inclined slope plane, from which an arc was created that passes through the toe of the slope. Then we establish arc radius R and subtended angle θ.

In this case, $R = 15$ ft, $\theta = 95°$ (1.7 radians), and $d = L/2 = 5$ ft. The cohesion is $c = 800$ psf and the soil density is $\gamma = 120$ pcf. Since the weight of a 1-ft width of slope is $W = \gamma V = 120(120 \times 1) = 14{,}400$ lb, we have

$$\text{F.S.} = \frac{800 \times 1.7 \times 15^2}{14{,}400 \times 5} = 4.3$$

It is important to remember that several trial arcs must be analyzed before the critical least value for F.S. can be determined.

Another form of grade separation is formed by a retaining wall. To maintain significantly high vertical slopes, concrete retaining walls such as the two types shown in Figure 9.7 can be used. The gravity wall is the simplest retaining structure. It resists the overturning effect of the lateral force caused by a shifted wedge of the retained soil through the stabilizing effect of its own weight spread over a wide base. If water is trapped behind the wall it adds a hydrostatic pressure that reaches a value of $p = \gamma_W H$ at the base of a wall of height H. For this reason, the retained soil is usually a backfill material composed of cohesionless sand or gravel that can drain quickly. Provisions must be made so that water in the backfill can easily drain from behind the wall, such as through a perforated drain pipe placed parallel to the bottom of the wall connected to weep hole openings along the wall base.

Lateral confining pressure of the retained soil pushes outwards on the wall causing a slight wall displacement that activates the wedge of the retained soil, causing it to shift downwards and lean into the wall with significant lateral pressure. Only a little displacement is needed to cause an active shear failure along the plane oriented at $45° + \phi/2$. The lateral pressure at any depth below the top of the wall is a fraction K of the corresponding overburden pressure. For well-drained granular backfill, K can be as low as 0.2, and K can be as high as 1 for saturated cohesive fills. With a typical value of $K = 0.4$, the lateral pressure P at the base of the wall reaches a maximum value of

$$p = K\gamma H = 0.4\gamma H$$

This pressure is distributed in a triangular fashion as shown, and the resulting force per foot of wall width P is the average pressure times the wall height,

$$P = \frac{1}{2}K\gamma H^2$$

This lateral force acts at the centroid of the triangular area defined by the pressure distribution, $H/3$, and creates an overturning moment about the toe equal to $PH/3$. The so-called righting moment about the toe is the weight of the wall times its moment arm, $WB/2$, so the safety factor against overturning is

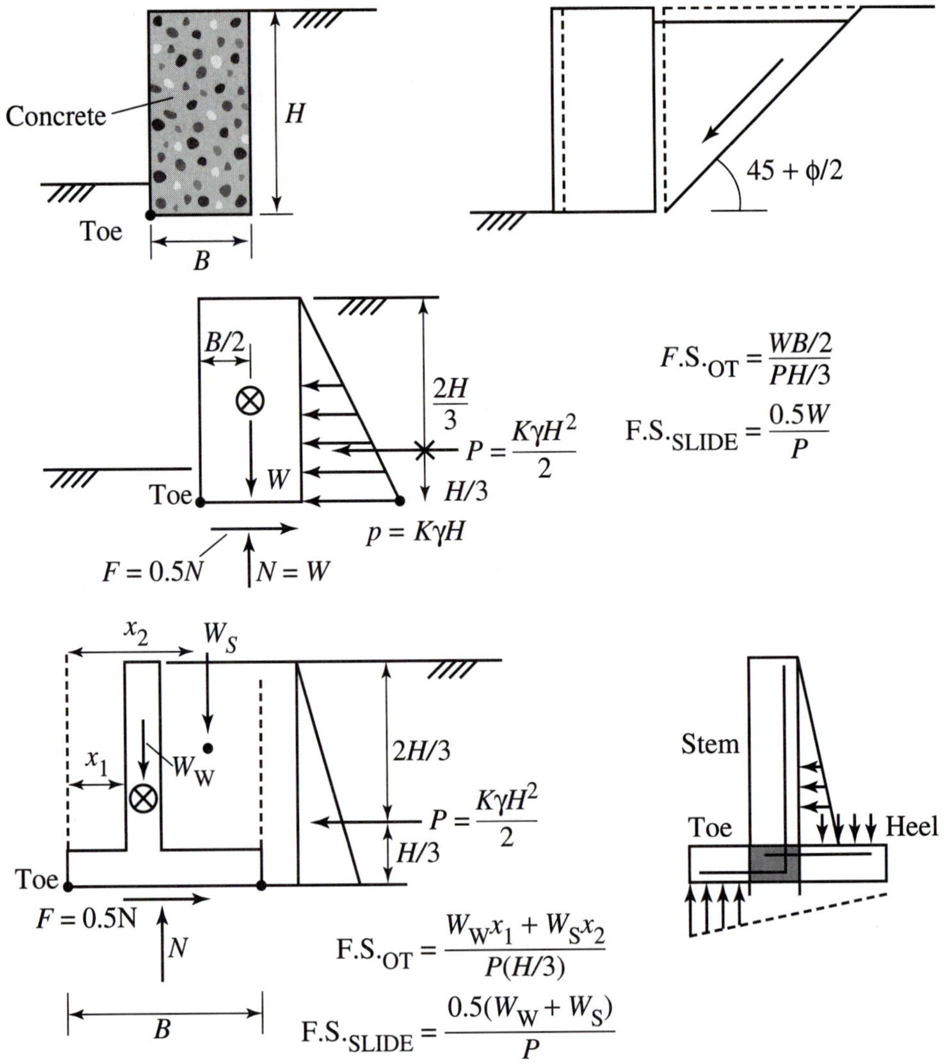

FIGURE 9.7

$$F.S._{OT} = \frac{WB/2}{PH/3}$$

The wall must also resist horizontal sliding due to the effect of the lateral force P by developing a friction force F between its base and the soil equal to the coefficient of friction times the clamping force, $N = W$. The friction coefficient between soil and concrete can be taken as 0.5, so the safety factor against sliding is

$$F.S._{SLIDE} = \frac{0.5W}{P}$$

Suppose the concrete gravity wall in the figure is 12 feet tall and the backfill is a sandy soil with a density of $\gamma = 110$ pcf. What base width B is required to have a safety factor of 2 considering both overturning and sliding? The weight is $W = \gamma_{CONCRETE}BH = 1{,}800B$, and the overturning lateral force is assumed to be $P = \frac{1}{2}(0.4)\gamma H^2 = 3{,}170$ lb, so for a safety factor of 2 against overturning,

$$\text{F.S.}_{\text{OT}} = \frac{WB/2}{PH/3} = 2 = \frac{900B^2}{12{,}700}$$

We find that $B = 5.3$ ft. For safety against sliding

$$\text{F.S.}_{\text{SLIDE}} = 2 = \frac{0.5W}{P} = \frac{900B}{3{,}170}$$

From this, $B = 7$ ft, which governs in this case.

We see from the figure that compared to the massive gravity wall that requires a large weight and wide base to develop a sufficient righting moment, the cantilever retaining wall is constructed of two thinner concrete elements, the stem and the base. This type of retaining structure makes use of the weight of the soil backfill to create sufficient righting moment to safely resist the overturning effects of the lateral pressure. As shown in the figure, the vertical stem and the toe and heel portions of the base each act as cantilever beams that resist distributed loads as the wall reacts to the applied forces, and flexural rebars will be required on the tension side of these beams.

The stability check for the cantilever wall follows that of the gravity wall. Now the righting moment taken about the toe is the sum of that due to the structure weight and that of the soil, so that

$$\text{F.S.}_{\text{OT}} = \frac{W_W(x_1) + W_S(x_2)}{PH/3}$$

The safety factor against sliding is based on the clamping force due to the structure and backfill soil weight

$$\text{F.S.}_{\text{SLIDE}} = \frac{0.5(W_W + W_S)}{P}$$

In addition to checking retaining walls for overall stability, they must also be analyzed as footings with nonuniform bearing pressure. We have pointed out in earlier sections of the book how the base width B needs to be sufficient to prevent a loss of bearing contact beneath the backfill edge of the structure.

9.7 Basement Wall

A basement wall maintains a grade separation like the retaining wall structures we have discussed. After excavation and construction of a concrete slab and concrete or masonry walls, excavated soil or a more permeable granular soil is used as backfill and placed against the walls in the remaining exposed excavation. Since the floor above the basement walls acts as a lateral support preventing the top of the wall from lateral movement, basement walls do not easily move away from the backfill and allow a soil mass failure along a shear plane as do gravity and cantilever walls. Still, there will be lateral stresses exerted by the backfill soil confined by the basement walls, and this lateral pressure may conservatively be estimated to be the same as for retaining walls.

Figure 9.8 shows a cross section of a basement with 10-ft walls that retain a sandy backfill of density $\gamma = 100$ pcf and a lateral stress coefficient of $K = 0.4$. We see that the wall experiences a lateral triangular distributed load having a maximum value at the base of

$$p = K\gamma H = 0.4(100)(10) = 400 \text{ psf}$$

If it were possible for the water table to rise to ground level, the pressure on the walls increases considerably. At the wall base, the lateral pressure is the sum of that due to the soil with buoyant density, $\gamma - \gamma_W$, and that due to hydrostatic pressure, or

FIGURE 9.8

$$p_W = \gamma_W H = 62.4(10) = 620 \text{ psf}$$
$$p = K(\gamma - \gamma_W)H = 0.4(100 - 62.4)(10) = 150 \text{ psf}$$
$$\text{total} = P + P_W = 150 + 620 = 770 \text{ psf}$$

$$M \approx \frac{p_{avg}H^2}{8} = \frac{200(10)^2}{8} = 2500 \text{ ft-lb}$$

$$\frac{1}{2}(400)(10) = 2{,}000 \text{ lb/ft wall}$$

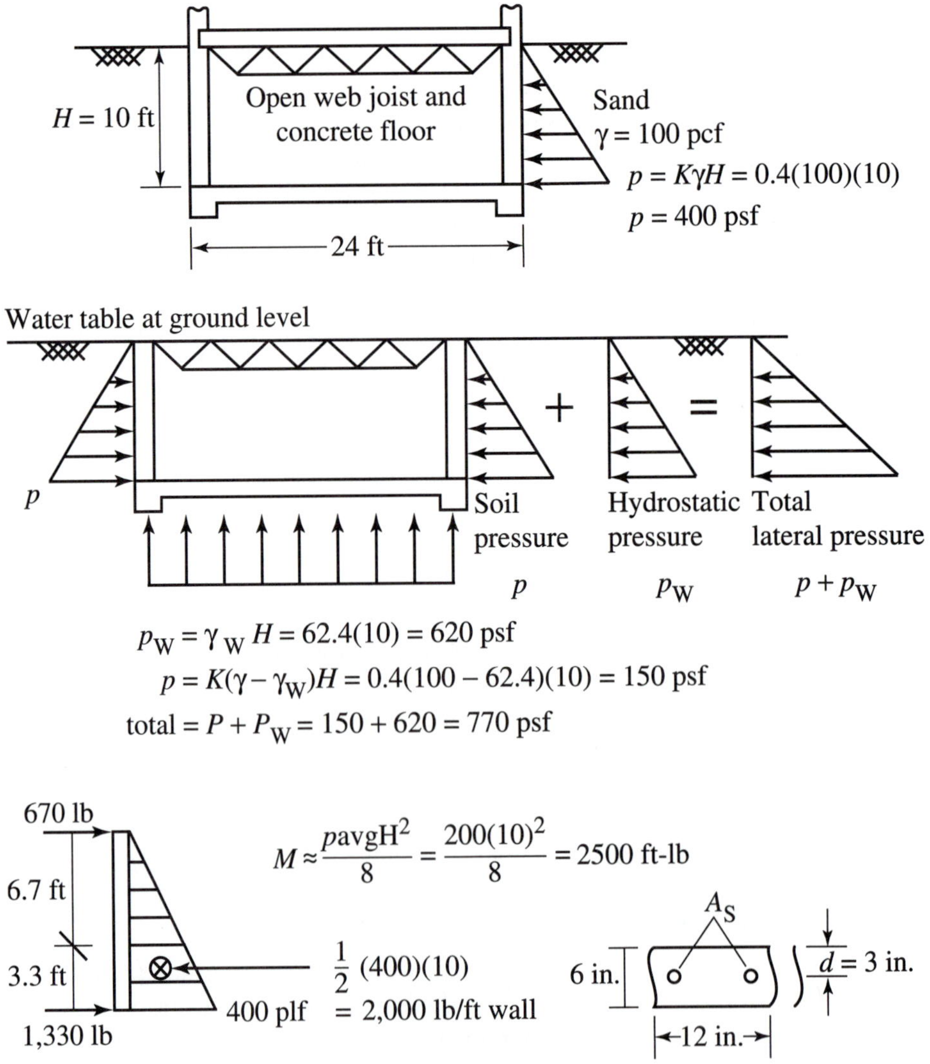

$$A_S = \frac{M}{21{,}600d} = \frac{2{,}500(12)}{21{,}600(3)} = 0.46 \text{ in}^2/\text{ft}$$

Use #6 bars at 12 in. o.c

$$p = K(\gamma - \gamma_W)H + \gamma_W H = 0.4(100 - 62.4)(10) + 62.4(10) = 770 \text{ psf}$$

In addition, since hydrostatic pressure is the same in all directions, there is an uplift pressure beneath the basement slab of $\gamma_W H = 620$ psf that could float the structure out of the ground if sufficient counter weight is not present. For this reason, and because they tend to leak like a sieve, basements are not commonly used where the water table could rise above the basement floor.

We see in the figure that a 1-ft width of the wall is modeled as a 10-ft simple span slab with a triangular distributed load. Notice that the wall self-weight for this vertical wall slab does not contribute to the transverse bending load of the 10-ft beam span. For the case of no water table, the lateral load has a magnitude of

$$P = \frac{1}{2}(p)(H) = \frac{1}{2}(400)(10) = 2{,}000 \text{ plf}$$

This force acts at the centroid of the triangle, as shown, and equilibrium of the beam indicates that the forces holding the top and bottom of each foot of wall in place are 670 lb and 1,330 lb, respectively.

We wish to determine the flexural steel requirements if a single layer of vertical steel rebar is located at the center of the concrete wall that is 6 in. thick. The moment is approximated assuming that the lateral load, $P = 2{,}000$ lb, is uniformly distributed along the 10-ft wall, so that the maximum simple beam moment, $M = wL^2/8$, is given by

$$M = \frac{(P/H)H^2}{8} = \frac{(2{,}000/10)10^2}{8} = 2{,}500 \text{ ft-lb} = 30{,}000 \text{ in-lb}$$

Recall that if the percentage of steel, A_S/bd is less than 1.4%, which would amount to $A_S = 0.014(12 \times 3) = 0.5$ in^2/ft width, then the required steel area is determined as

$$A_S = \frac{M}{21{,}600 \times d} = \frac{30{,}000}{21{,}600 \times 3} = 0.46 \text{ in}^2/\text{ft width}$$

Thus we may use #6 bars spaced 12 in. o.c. at the middle of the basement wall to reinforce it against the lateral soil pressure.

Exercise If the basement must be constructed with the water table at ground level, what is the uplift force on the structure if the basement is 24 ft wide and 34 ft in length.

Assume that the basement floor slab acts as a 24-ft simple span beam to resist the hydrostatic uplift pressure and determine the required slab thickness and flexural steel located near the top of the slab. ■

10 Timber Design Applications

10.1 Allowable Design Stresses for Timber, Steel, and Concrete

In the final chapters of this book we look at common building systems of timber, steel, and reinforced concrete. We have already looked at many such systems throughout the book, and here we go into more detail when discussing some of the unique characteristics of structural members fabricated from these different common building materials.

When analyzing or designing structural elements, we can ensure a margin of safety against structural failure in one of two ways:

1. We can limit the working stresses caused by actual loads to an allowable stress that is about half the value associated with a failure, and thus provide a factor of safety of around two. This is the *working stress method.*
2. We can multiply the actual loads by a load factor of approximately two and design for the structure to fail at the higher-than-actual factored loads. This is the *load factor method.*

In the end, the safety margin would be the same using either method, and there would be no way to tell the two structures apart. Each approach has inherent conceptual limitations that often lead to extra work when analyzing or designing structures. While the use of the load factor method is increasing, many people still use the working stress method and most existing structures were designed by this method. Since it is easier to understand and implement, we will make use of the working stress method to do timber, steel, and concrete analysis and design work, as we have been doing all along.

Structural failure is usually defined as the point when stresses in a member exceed the elastic limit of the material. Increasing the stress beyond this level will cause some permanent inelastic deformation to remain upon removal of the load. By ensuring that working stresses are low, we not only prevent failure, but we also ensure that deformations due to loads recover elastically and the structure thus remains unchanged by the loads. Allowable stresses used in the working stress method vary depending on such things as stress type–tension, compression, bearing, shear, or bending–and on material characteristics like grade and species of timber, alloy chemistry of steel, and mix properties of concrete.

In the case of bending stress, for example, the allowable stress of timber ranges from 900 to 1,800 psi, depending on species of trees from which lumber is cut, and on degree and location of natural wood imperfections (knots, splits, wane, and such). Depending on the elastic limit of steel, also known as steel yield stress, the allowable bending stress of common structural steel is 24,000–33,000 psi. Normal strength concrete will have an allowable bending stress of 1,200–2,200 psi on the compression side of the bending couple, but it is assumed to have no tensile strength so that steel reinforcing bars provide the tension couple force at stress limited to 24,000 psi.

As structural technology has progressed, high-strength versions of all three common building materials have evolved. Layers of thin plies of wood and even dimension lumber can be glued together to form much larger laminated members, known as glulam members, that have considerably higher allowable stresses by dispersing and so minimizing the negative strength effects of natural wood imperfections. Steel is being produced with yield stresses nearly twice that of common A36 steel with its 36,000-psi yield stress, and allowable steel stresses can be increased accordingly. Normal concrete ranges from 2,500 to 4,000 psi compressive strength, but 20,000-psi mixes have been used in special structures. All these advances in building material strength come with some inherent problems. There is considerable added labor expense to laminate wood; steel elements designed for higher working stress are more slender and so more susceptible to compressive buckling; and it is often very difficult to maintain the stricter field-mix quality control measures required of high-strength concrete.

As we close the book with three chapters devoted to analyzing and designing some common structural systems, it may be handy to see a summary of typical allowable working stresses for timber, common steel, and normal strength concrete. The various stress modes of axial tension, axial compression in short stocky members, bearing, shear, and bending are all given in the table below in units of lb/in^2 (psi). For the purpose of easy reference, typical modulus of elasticity, E, values are also provided.

Our discussion of structural systems begins with timber design, since it is the material used in structures that we are most familiar with–our homes. Many of us have likely had hands-on experience with small-scale timber construction projects, and so it is natural to begin a focused look at structural analysis and design with a familiar material.

Timber elements are usually of rectangular cross sections, which are the easiest to analyze. Steel sections are often I-beams that are a bit more complex to design with, particularly when there is the possibility of compressive buckling. Like timber members, reinforced concrete beams and columns are usually rectangular, but because they must be treated as composites of concrete and steel, their analysis requires a bit more rigor than timber or steel.

The basic structural example situations in the remainder of the book were chosen to present some of the most ordinary applications of the three common building materials. You will find that none of our theoretical wanderings of earlier chapters were for naught–everything we have discussed has applicability in the analysis and design of structures.

	Tension	Compression	Bearing	Shear	Bending	E
Timber	800	1,000	500	90	1,200	1,600,000
Steel	22,000	22,000	36,000	14,000	24,000	30,000,000
Concrete	0	1,800	1,000	70	1,800	3,500,000

10.2 WOOD JOISTS, RAFTERS, AND STUDS

Perhaps the simplest and most common structural members are the floor joist, the roof rafter, and wall studs. Joists and rafter beam members and wall stud column members are formed from dimension lumber, which includes boards that are nominally 2 to 4 in. wide and 2 to 14 in. deep, with 2-in. widths and up to 12-in. depths being most common. These are the dimensions of rough lumber, which is typically trimmed and smoothed (sometimes called dressed) to actual dimensions that are $\frac{1}{2}$ in. less for width, $\frac{1}{2}$ in. less for depths to 6 in., and $\frac{3}{4}$ in. less for depths greater than 6 in. Thus, a 2 × 6 is actually 1.5 in. × 5.5 in., while a 2 × 8 is 1.5 in. × 7.25 in. A handy table of section properties based on actual dimensions is easily created where $A = bh$, $S = bh^2/6$, and $Ibh^3/12$.

Individually, these members have relatively low load capacity, but their small sizes permit carpenters to easily handle them without special lifting equipment. By spacing numerous members 12 in., 16 in., or 24 in. apart, floor and roof horizontal spans of up to 20 ft can be created (stud walls are usually 8 or 9 ft tall). While members may be spaced 12 in. o.c. for the longer spans or heavily loaded bearing walls, and 24 in. spacings are often used for lightly loaded elements, most wood joists, rafters, and studs are 16 in. o.c.

Most residential buildings are built totally from dimension lumber. These structures are rarely engineered; rather, local building codes provide standards of construction that lead to rules of thumb that incorporate safe engineering practice. The need for structural analysis usually arises only with unusual situations such as unusually tall load-bearing walls or uncommonly large spans necessary for spacious open areas. Building codes typically provide joist and rafter span tables that incorporate the results of flexural beam analysis for a wide array of possible loads and spans. Wall height and stud spacing limits are also stated for load-bearing walls. We wish to do a simple example that demonstrates what factors go into the development of the code provisions.

In Figure 10.1 we see a cross section of a simple residential structure. We want to determine if the 2 × 10 floor joists, the 2 × 6 roof rafters, and the center 9-ft 2 × 4 load-bearing stud wall are adequate for the loads. (We will check the triple 2 × 10 floor beams in a later example.) We will assume that all surfaces have a 10-psf unit dead weight. Roof live load (LL) is generally 20 psf (more in regions of high annual snowfall), and floor live load is usually 40 psf for residential structures. The roof rafters are toe-nailed to a ridge board at the roof peak and nailed to the side of the ceiling joists, which are toe-nailed to the top plate of the two exterior bearing walls. To prevent wind uplift of the roof, metal tie-down straps connecting the ceiling joists to the top plates of the walls are advisable. A nailed lap-splice connects two ceiling joists where their ends overlap above the center bearing wall.

	$b \times h$	A in^2	S in^3	I in^4
2 × 4	1.5 × 3.5	5.25	3.06	5.4
2 × 6	1.5 × 5.5	8.25	7.56	20.8
2 × 8	1.5 × 7.25	10.9	13.1	47.6
2 × 10	1.5 × 9.25	13.9	21.4	98.9
2 × 12	1.5 × 11.25	16.9	31.6	178

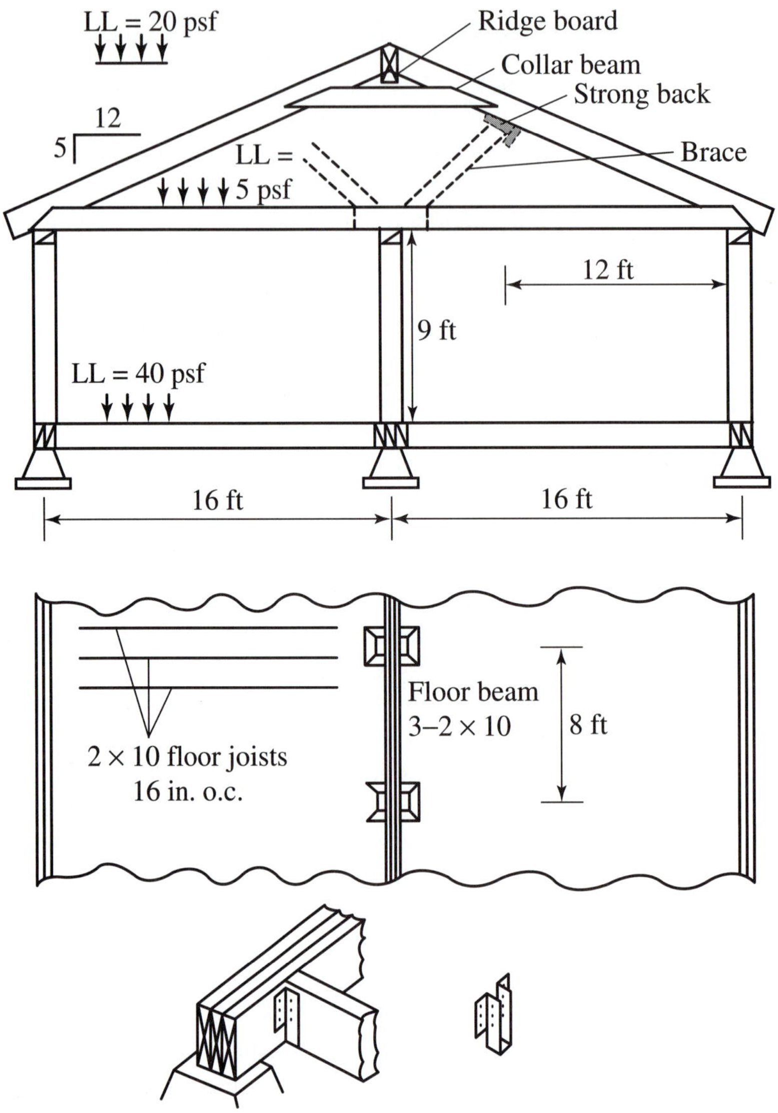

FIGURE 10.1

Note that the collar beam near the roof peak is used only on every third pair of rafters (every 48 in.) and its purpose is to strengthen the connection of the rafters that are toe-nailed to the ridge board. The toe-nailed roof peak connection would otherwise have little resistance to being pulled apart by the uplift pressure from wind or unequally loaded rafters. Note that the peak formed by the two rafters tends to sag as the rafters tend to push outwards on the exterior bearing walls. This thrust must be resisted by a tension force that can be developed in the ceiling joists, provided that these joists are lap-spliced with nails where their ends overlap above the interior bearing wall.

The analysis of rafters usually involves treating them as simple beams with spans equal to the horizontal projection of the maximum length between points where bracing exists. Dead and live loads are assumed to act along this horizontal projection. Rafters are usually selected based on allowable bending stress alone. Each linear foot of horizontal rafter span has a tributary width of $\frac{16}{12}$ ft, so the load per foot is $w = (20 + 10)(\frac{16}{12}) = 40$ plf. In this case, the bending stress in the rafters is $f = M/S$

$$f = \frac{wL^2/8}{bh^2/6} = \frac{40 \times \frac{16^2}{8} \times 12}{7.56} = 2{,}030 \text{ psi}$$

Since this stress exceeds the allowable bending stress of 1,200 psi given for timber in the previous section, we need to try 2 × 8 rafters, or we can reduce the rafter span.

To reduce the span, we first nail a stiffener, or "strongback," made from two 2 × 4 boards running along the underside of all rafters. Next, we use 2 × 4 struts on every other rafter (32 in. o.c.) and brace the strongback to the center bearing wall as shown using dashed lines in the figure. The braces do two things: they reduce the horizontal span from 16 ft to 12 ft, but they also divert the majority of the roof load from the outer walls to the center load-bearing wall, which now supports the center 20 ft of roof. The bending stress in the braced rafters is now

$$f = \frac{40 \times 12^2/8 \times 12}{7.56} = 1{,}143 \text{ psi}$$

Thus the braced 2 × 6 rafters are now acceptable.

The 2 × 10 floor joists are checked for bending stress and a maximum deflection of no more than $L/300 = (16 \times 12)/300 = 0.6$ in. The bending stress is

$$f = \frac{(40 + 10)\left(\frac{16}{12}\right) \times \frac{16^2}{8} \times 12}{21.4} = 1{,}196 \text{ psi}$$

Thus the joists are acceptable for bending stress. The deflection is

$$D = \frac{f \times L^2}{5 \times E \times h} = \frac{1{,}196 \times (16 \times 12)^2}{5 \times 1{,}600{,}000 \times 9.25} = 0.6 \text{ in.}$$

The deflection limit of $L/300$ is not exceeded, so the 2 × 10 floor joists are also acceptable. It is often the case for a selected joist size that the bending stress is acceptable, but the deflection is not, in which case the joist is strong enough, but not stiff enough to be serviceable, and a larger member must be used.

In addition to ceiling load, the center wall now supports roof load delivered through the 2 × 4 braces. Though seldom checked as columns, these braces are compression members that could buckle in the 1.5 in. direction. Focusing on the 2 × 4 studs of the center bearing wall, the studs are treated as 9-ft simple columns. The large sheets of Sheetrock or plywood paneling that cover the studs to provide finished walls are nailed to the studs and prevent them from buckling about the weak axis in the 1.5-in. direction of the stud cross section. However, there is a possibility that the bearing load could cause the entire wall to buckle outwards as the studs buckle in the 3.5 in. direction of their cross section. In the case of a 9-ft wall height, the column slenderness ratio is $L/h = (9 \times 12)/3.5 = 31$. Referring to the timber column stress curve for an eccentricity ratio of = 0.3 of Chapter 7, the allowable column stress is $f_{CR} = 420$ psi.

Thus, the capacity per stud is $F_{ALL} = f \times A = 420 \times 5.25 = 2{,}200$ lb. Since studs are 16 in. = 1.33 ft o.c., the allowable uniform bearing load per foot of wall is $w_{ALL} = 2{,}200/1.33 = 1{,}660$ plf. The tributary load that bears on the center wall amounts to one-half of the ceiling and 20 ft of the roof dead and live load, which is

$$w = [(20 + 10)(20) + (5 + 10)(16)] = 840 \text{ plf}$$

Since $w < w_{ALL}$, the bearing wall is OK. For taller walls and/or for bearing walls supporting upper floors, 2 × 6 studs may be in order.

Exercise Rework this problem, making the house width 36 ft instead of 32 ft. Braces can be used to reduce the rafter span to 14 ft. Check the braces for buckling. Are 2 × 6 ceiling joists adequate for a L/300 deflection limit? (Assume a 5-psf live load.) ■

10.3 Joist Tables

Builders usually rely on tables to select the appropriate size dimension lumber for a particular situation. Joist and rafter span tables allow for quick reference to determine, at a member spacing of 12 in., 16 in., or 24 in., what is the allowable span for a 2 × 4, 2 × 6, 2 × 8, 2 × 10, or 2 × 12. Either bending stress or deflection limits the allowable span. Such tables are often generalized to allow for the checking of members made from different wood species and different grades of lumber.

We will develop a floor joist span table for a specific case where the bending stress is $f = 1{,}200$ psi, and the modulus of elasticity is $E = 1{,}600{,}000$ psi. We will assume 10-pst dead load and 40-psf live load for a total of 50 psf. If we denote member center-to-center spacing in inches as *cc*, then the load per foot on a joist is $w = 50 \times cc/12 = 4.17cc$ plf. We will limit total deflection to $\frac{1}{300}$ × span length, or $L/300$.

The joist section modulus S may be computed or taken directly from the table presented in the previous application problem. With an allowable bending stress, $f = 1{,}200$ psi, we compute a joist moment capacity of $M = f \times S$, or $M = 1{,}200S$ in-lb. The bending moment that the joist must resist is $M = wL^2/8$ ft-lb, or $M = 1.5wL^2$ in-lb. With $w = 4.17cc$ plf, we equate the allowable moment capacity with the moment demand and solve for the allowable span L in feet:

$$L = \sqrt{\frac{192 \times S}{cc}}$$

For a 2 × 10 with $S = 21.4$ in^3, for 16-in. joist spacing, the formula gives an allowable span of $\sqrt{(192 \times 21.4)/16} = 16.0$ ft based on bending stress.

We derived a formula for the deflection of a simple beam in terms of the applied bending moment and member rigidity, $D = ML^2/(10EI)$. We have set an allowable deflection limit of $D = L/300$. If we equate the allowable deflection and the actual deflection, we find that $L = EI/(30M)$. When we substitute $E = 1{,}600{,}000$ psi and $M = 1.5(4.17cc)L^2 = 6.25(cc)L^2$ in-lb and convert the right side to feet by dividing by 12 in./ft, we have

Exercise Develop a rafter allowable horizontal span table for horizontal projected 10-psf dead and 20-psf live loads. Limit total deflection to $L/240$. ■

$$L = \sqrt[3]{\frac{711 \times I}{cc}}$$

For 2 × 10's with $I = 98.9$ in^4 and spaced 16 in., the allowable span is $L = 16.4$ ft based on a limited deflection.

The reported allowable span for a given joist at a given spacing is the lesser of the two computed span lengths, so that the allowable span for 2 × 10 floor joists will be reported as 16 ft in the table. Making use of a spreadsheet and the two allowable span formulas, the following joist table may be developed (values are rounded to the nearest foot for easy recall).

MAXIMUM ALLOWABLE FLOOR JOIST SPAN (FT)

	Joist Spacing		
	12 in.	**16 in.**	**24 in.**
2 × 4	7	6	5
2 × 6	11	10	8
2 × 8	14	13	10
2 × 10	18	16	13
2 × 12	22	20	16

(In this table, deflection controlled the allowable joist spans for 12-in. spacing; otherwise, bending stress controlled this.)

10.4 FLOOR BEAMS

Dimension lumber is handy for carpenters to carry and place, but this convenience of small size means that each element may support only a small tributary area, and thus many pieces must be placed in parallel to capture the full roof, floor, or wall area of a structure. In Figure 10.1, the 8-ft simple span floor beam supports a tributary floor area of 8 ft × 16 ft = 126 ft^2, as well as the load from the bearing wall. The member is made from three 2 × 10 boards nailed together to form a 4.5-in. × 9.25-in. cross section with an area of $A = 3 \times 13.9 = 41.7$ in^2, and a section modulus of $S = 3 \times 21.4 = 64.2$ in^3.

The total uniform load along the 8-ft span of the beam is the floor live and dead load, the bearing wall weight, and the roof and ceiling loads atop the bearing wall:

$$w = (40 + 10) \times 16 + 10 \times 9 + 840 = 1{,}730 \text{ plf}$$

This causes a bending stress of

$$f = \frac{1{,}730 \times 8^2/8 \times 12}{64.2} = 2{,}590 \text{ psi}$$

This indicates that tripled 2 × 10 boards spanning 8 ft are inadequate to meet a working bending stress limit of 1,200 psi. We must reduce the beam span using more foundation piers, and probably use larger joists. If we use tripled 2 × 12 joists ($A = 50.6 \text{ in}^2$ and $S = 94.8 \text{ in}^3$) and a 6-ft span, the bending stress reduces proportionately to

$$f = 2{,}590 \times \frac{64.2}{94.8} \times \frac{6^2}{8^2} = 990 \text{ psi}$$

Since this bending stress meets the 1,200 psi allowable, we will try a triple 2 × 12 floor beam.

Deflection is seldom critical for short spans, and in this case the deflection limit $L/300 = (6 \times 12)/300 = \frac{1}{4}$ in. and the actual deflection is

$$D = \frac{990 \times (6 \times 12)^2}{5 \times 1{,}600{,}000 \times 11.25} = 0.06 \text{ in.}$$

Unlike for lightly loaded long span joists, short heavily loaded beams must be checked for shear and bearing stresses at the supports, where the reaction is half of the entire beam load, $F = \frac{1}{2} \times (1{,}730 \times 6) = 5{,}190$ lb. The shear stress is

$$f_V = 1.5 \times \frac{F}{A} = 1.5 \times \frac{5{,}190}{50.6} = 154 \text{ psi}$$

and assuming the top of the pier is 6 in. × 6 in., the contact area of the two floor beams that it supports is $A = 4.5 \times 6 = 27 \text{ in}^2$, and the bearing stress is

$$f = \frac{2 \times F}{A} = \frac{2 \times 5{,}190}{27} = 384 \text{ psi}$$

We see that the bearing stress is within the 500 psi allowable working stress limit, but the shear stress exceeds the allowable 90 psi by 70%, so that it would take five 2 × 12 boards to provide the required shear area. This is not realistic.

If we try a solid sawn timber beam, which generally has the same allowable stresses as dimension lumber, it would need to have greater section properties than the inadequate triple 2 × 12 beam. Solid timber beams come in nominal sizes typically greater than 5 in. in width with depths over 8 in. Deduct $\frac{1}{2}$ in. from both the nominal width and depth to determine actual dimensions. Since the allowable shear stress is still 90 psi, if we try a 6-in. wide timber, it would need a cross-sectional area of

$$A = \frac{1.5 \times 5{,}190}{90} = 87 \text{ in}^2$$

And so the beam depth would need to be $h = 87/5.5 = 15.7$ in. Accepting a little shear overstress, a 6 × 16 solid timber beam would meet all critical stress limits. However, such timbers are expensive, and tend to be used in places where they are visible and provide rustic aesthetics.

We need to rethink the design of the center floor beam. We could redirect the roof load back to the outer walls using prefabricated trusses. We could use additional floor beam lines and reduce floor joist spans. We may consider eliminating the floor beam span altogether by replacing the individual piers with a continuous concrete strip footing, in which case the floor joists would

Exercise Determine if a triple 2 × 12 floor beam with 6-ft pier spacing is sufficient for the edge floor beams if 32-ft span roof trusses spaced 24 in. o.c. deliver a roof load to the outer two bearing walls. Assume that the total horizontal projection dead plus live roof and ceiling load is 35 psf. Also, determine the required number of 2 × 12 boards needed for the center floor beam now that the center wall does not support any roof load. ■

simply overlap and be toe-nailed to a wood plate fastened to the top of the footing wall. Blocking between the joists would be required to restrain the joists from twisting.

If a continuous footing is not possible, steel beams are often used as floor beams–a common practice where basements are used. We may still consider another timber alternative to our given floor plan: glulam beams, which we discuss in the next application.

10.5 GLULAM RIDGE BEAM

Timber glulam beams offer the advantage of supporting heavy loads with large spans, yet they still allow easy attachment to other wood members using simple nails and bolts. They are not normally used as short span floor beams as in the previous application problem, although they could be so used. In residential and commercial applications, somewhat expensive appearance grade glulam beams provide aesthetics similar to solid sawn timbers. If the appearance of the glulam beam is not so important, industrial grade glulams with a rougher finish are available at a lower cost.

Unlike solid timber beams sawn from large trees, glulam beams are "factory grown." They are fabricated from gluing together multiple laminations of nominal 2-in. or 1-in. thick dimension lumber as shown in Figure 10.2. The

FIGURE 10.2

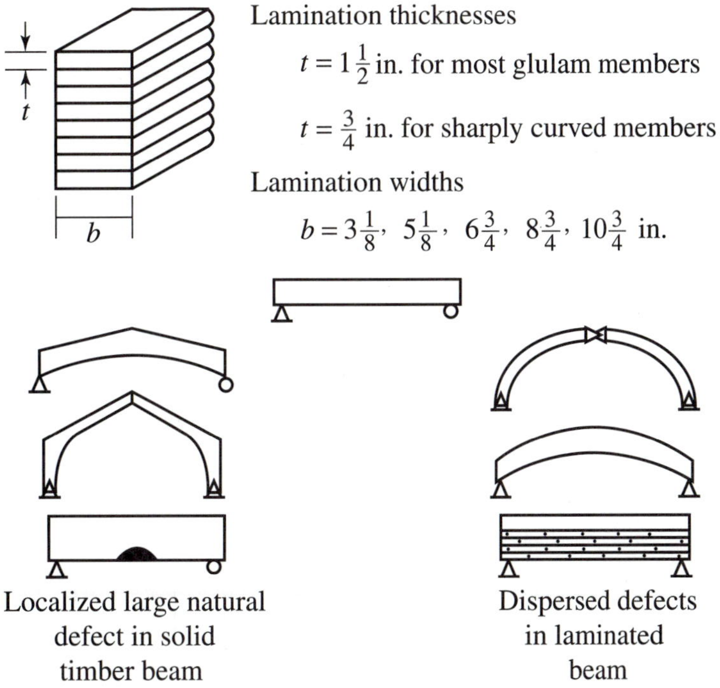

actual lamination thickness is typically 1.5 in., except when members with extreme curvature are created that require the bending of thinner $\frac{3}{4}$-in. boards. The depth of glulam cross sections is simply the number of laminations times the thickness of the boards. The glulam cross-section widths shown in the figure are the slightly reduced original depths of the dimension lumber laminations. This is because the sides of the fabricated glulam member are planed to give a smoother finished appearance to the member.

Compared to the age and size of tree needed to produce large solid timber elements, the dimension lumber used for laminated beams comes from renewable small growth timber that can be planted and harvested on a relatively short time cycle. The small laminations allow great flexibility in creating glulam members that can be fashioned into almost any shape and size, as shown. The allowable bending and shear stresses in glulam members are at least 50% higher than for solid timbers because strength reducing defects are not as severe as for solid timbers, and these defects are evenly dispersed throughout the member as shown. Also, higher-grade wood laminations can be used in the member where stresses are critical, so that the allowable laminated beam bending stress is 1,800 psi, and the allowable shear stress is 150 psi, compared to the respective solid timber stresses of 1,200 psi and 90 psi.

In Figure 10.3 we see a wing of a house that creates a room with an open cathedral ceiling. An exposed appearance grade glulam will be used as an exposed ridge beam with its ends supported by 6 × 6 timber posts. Determine the required number of nominal 2-in. laminations for a nominal 6-in. width glulam beam (actual width = 5.125 in.). To prevent cracks in the finished Sheetrock ceiling, limit the deflection to $L/300$. Assume a horizontal projection roof live and dead load of 20 psf and 10 psf, respectively.

The tributary width of the horizontal roof load is 16 ft, so the uniform beam load is 16 × (20 + 10) = 480 plf. Assume the glulam beam weight is about 20 plf, and so design for w = 500 plf. The bending moment is

$$M = \frac{wL^2}{8} = \frac{500(30)^2}{8} \times 12 \text{ in./ft} = 675{,}000 \text{ in-lb}$$

FIGURE 10.3

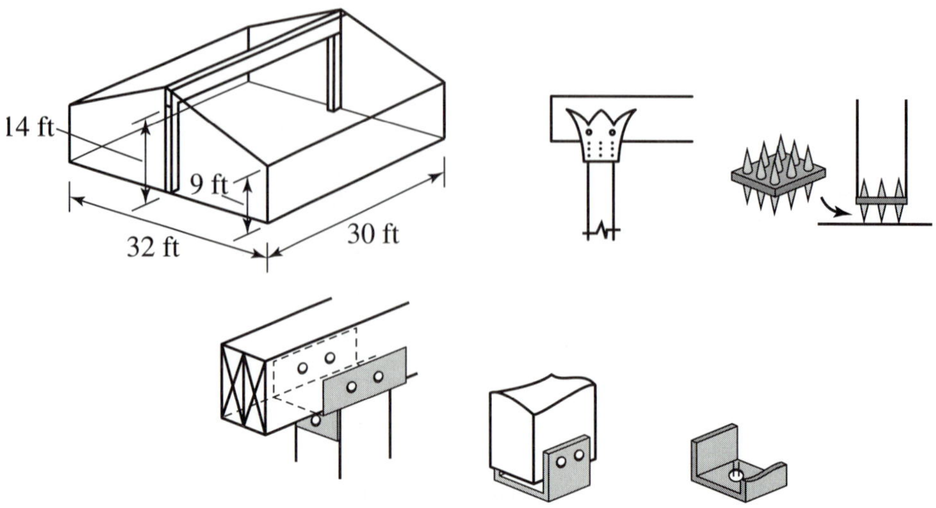

Exercise Rework the problem assuming a 24-ft-span ridge beam. ■

The required section modulus is $S = M/f_{ALL} = 675{,}000/1{,}800 = 375\ \text{in}^3$. Since $S = bh^2/6$ and $b = 5.125$ in., we can solve for the required beam depth

$$h = \sqrt{\frac{6 \times 375}{5.125}} = 21 \text{ in.}$$

So with nominal 2-in. thick dimension lumber, we will require 21/1.5 = 14 laminations. Assuming wood density is 40 lb/ft^3, we see that the beam weight is (5.125 × 21)/144 × 40 = 28 plf, which exceeds our 20-plf estimate, but we can say the 8-plf difference is negligible.

The support reactions are equal to $F = wL/2 = 500 \times 15 = 7{,}500$ lb. The maximum shear stress is

$$f_V = 1.5 \times \frac{F}{A} = 1.5 \times \frac{7{,}500}{5.125 \times 21} = 105 \text{ psi}$$

This is well below the 150-psi allowable stress. The contact area between the glulam and its support columns is $A = 5.125 \times 5.5 = 28.2\ \text{in}^2$, and the bearing stress is

$$f = \frac{F}{A} = \frac{7{,}500}{28.2} = 266 \text{ psi}$$

The bearing stress is below the allowable 500-psi limit. We finally check deflection for the fully stressed beam, which has an allowable deflection $L/300 = \frac{360}{300} = 1.2$ in.

$$D = \frac{1{,}800 \times (30 \times 12)^2}{5 \times 1{,}600{,}000 \times 21} = 1.4 \text{ in.}$$

We have a slight stiffness problem. To meet the 1.2-in. limit, we need a slightly deeper beam. If we add a lamination, the new depth is 22.5 in. and the section modulus is $5.125(22.5)^2/6 = 432\ \text{in}^3$, and the bending stress is 675,000/432 = 1,560 psi. The stiffer beam deflection is now reduced to an acceptable limit of

$$D = \frac{1{,}560 \times (30 \times 12)^2}{5 \times 1{,}600{,}000 \times 22.5} = 1.1 \text{ in.}$$

10.6 Stiffened Floor Beam

A father and his daughter teamed up one summer to construct a vacation home. The remote location of the small house, which included a basement, allowed them to build without building permits, plan checks, or periodic building inspections by local government authorities. After completion of the floor system shown in Figure 10.4, they noticed that it seemed too flexible. Walking along the doubled 2 × 8 floor beam, they could notice a difference in floor stiffness when moving from the 10-ft end spans to the center 12-ft span. They

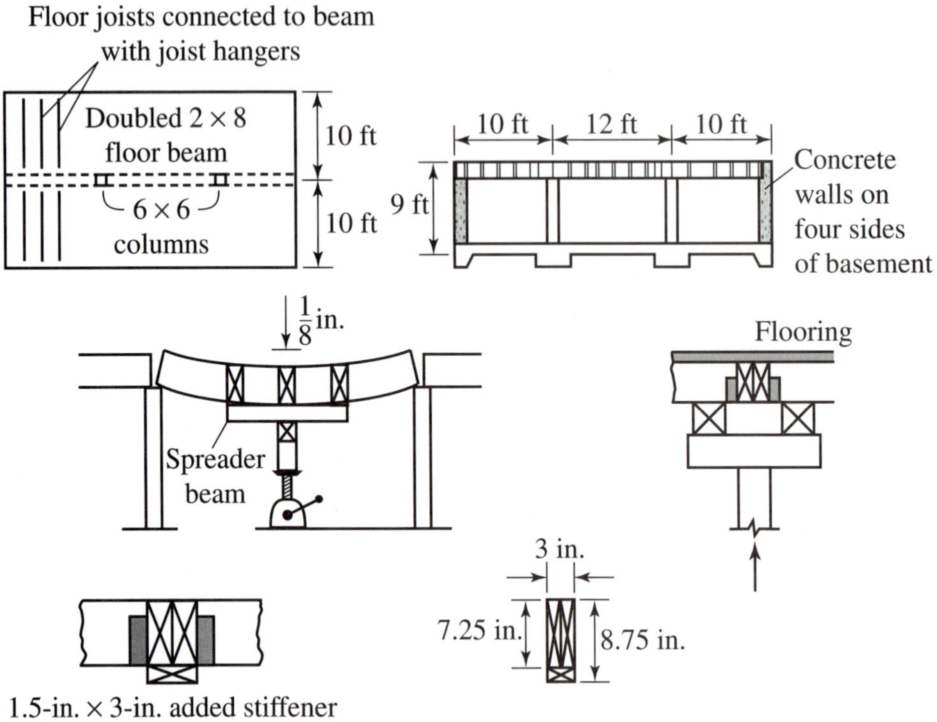

FIGURE 10.4

talked with a neighbor who was a professional carpenter and he indicated that doubled 2 × 10's should have been used instead of the 2 × 8's.

The daughter remembered seeing a home improvement television show where an old sagging basement beam was jacked up and a stiffener was added to the floor beam. The father decided that this would be worth a try before going to the extreme of redoing the center portion of the floor. The two figured that stiff 4 × 4 spreader blocks could engage three floor joists connected to both sides of the doubled floor beam, and a 4 × 4 post would allow them to use their car jack to lift the beam.

Because the 2 × 8 floor joists were the same size as the floor beam, the joist hangers that connected them to the floor beam extended slightly below the bottom edge of the doubled 2 × 8 boards. For this reason, the stiffener that they would attach to the bottom of the floor beam was a trimmed 2 × 4 with actual dimensions of 1.5 in. × 3 in. The deflection of the 12-ft span was measured to be $\frac{1}{8}$ in., so with the jack in place, the floor beam was lifted $\frac{1}{8}$ in. and the stiffener was glued and nailed all along the 12-ft span. After some time, the jack was removed and the resulting stiffened floor system seemed to be adequate so that the two relieved and happy carpenters decided that they would not redo the floor.

We wish to determine the design stresses and deflections for the before and after situations. The dead load of floor joists and a $\frac{3}{4}$-in. plywood floor with carpet is 5 psf, and we will allow for a light 20-psf live load for this situation. The distributed load from the 10-ft-span floor joists is therefore $w = (5 + 20) \times 10 = 250$ plf. The bending stress for the doubled 2 × 8 beam is $f = M/S$

Exercise What increase in stiffness would have resulted if a $\frac{1}{4}$-in. × 3-in. steel plate was lag-bolted to the doubled 2 × 8 floor beam instead of the 1.5-in. × 3-in. wood plate? This creates a composite wood/steel member known as a flitch beam. Use an effective modular ratio, $E_S/E_W = 24$. ■

$$f = \frac{wL^2/8}{S} = \frac{250 \times \dfrac{12^2}{8} \times 12}{2 \times 13.1} = \frac{54{,}000}{26.2} = 2060 \text{ psi}$$

The section modulus of the stiffened beam is $S = bh^2/6 = 3 \times 8.75^2/6 = 38.3 \text{ in}^3$, and the bending stress is $f = 54{,}000/38.3 = 1{,}410$ psi. While this stress exceeds the 1,200-psi allowable timber bending stress, it is a big improvement compared to 2,060 psi, and it is reasonable to allow the overstress in this vacation house.

The deflection of a beam is directly proportional to its moment of inertia. In the case of two rectangular beams with the same width cross sections, the ratio of their relative deflections is simply the ratio of the cube of their cross-section depths. In this case, the stiffened beam is $(8.75/7.25)^3 = 1.76$ times the stiffness of the doubled 2 × 8. The design deflection of the stiffened beam is

$$D = \frac{1{,}410 \times (12 \times 12)^2}{5 \times 1{,}600{,}000 \times 8.75} = 0.4 \text{ in.}$$

The allowable deflection limit $L/300$ is 0.48 in, so the stiffened beam deflection is acceptable.

10.7 COLUMNS

Determine if the 14-ft 6 × 6 timber column supporting the 30-ft-span ridge beam in Figure 10.3 is adequate. Assume that one end of the open cathedral roof space will have a glass wall, so the column is fully unsupported against buckling. The column at the other end is attached to and braced by the wall at that end of the room.

Once we have column curves such as the ones presented in Chapter 7, we have a pretty simple task of checking a column that is subject to axial load alone. In the case of the ridge beam support column, we determined that the support reaction of the 30-ft-span beam supporting a 500-plf uniform load was $F = 500 \times \frac{30}{2} = 7{,}500$ lb. From the column curve for a 6 × 6 post with an unbraced length of 14 ft, the allowable load is $F = 14{,}000$ lb. The column is thus more than adequate.

Note that special hardware may need to be fabricated to make large beam-to-column connections. Some hardware is available off the shelf, such as the support plate shown in Figure 10.3, but special needs, such as adding a rustic look to the structure, may dictate specially crafted connection details, as shown. Also, when columns are attached to concrete foundations, it is recommended that the wood be kept from direct contact with the concrete to

Exercise Determine if a 4×4 timber post would be sufficient for the 9-ft. column supporting the floor beams in Figure 10.4. ■

prevent the wood from rotting due to moisture that could be soaked up by the wood fibers at the cut end. Standard hardware for this purpose is also shown in the figure.

10.8 Bolts and Nails

The most common connectors for timber construction are nails, small wood screws, lag bolts (large wood screws with a bolt head), and bolts. Nails and wood screws have similar connection strength, while lag bolts and single shear bolted connections are also of similar strength. Nails are extensively used to connect dimension lumber, and bolts are used for large timber connections, or when a connection will require a lot of nails to transmit a large concentrated load. In Figure 10.5, we need to transmit the 2,400-lb deck floor load from a pair of 2×12 joists to a 4×4 column.

Nails come in a variety of diameters and lengths. The most commonly used nails to connect dimension boards are the 16d, 20d, 30d, and 40d nails (the d stands for the nail pennyweight). Structural use of smaller pennyweight nails, such as the 6d through 12d sizes, is to connect plywood sheathing in diaphragms, or to connect thin metal members to wood. Nails are used to transmit lateral loads in single shear connections between one member and another as shown in the figure. Connections that rely on the withdrawal strength of nails should be avoided. A longer and fatter diameter nail provides a higher lateral load capacity than a smaller one.

When used to connect a nominal 2-in. dimension board (1.5 in. thick) to some other timber member, the commonly used $3\frac{1}{2}$-in. 16d, 4-in. 20d, and the 5-in. 40d nails have lateral load capacities of 140 lb, 170 lb, and 200 lb, respectively. Assuming each of the 2×12 members delivers half of the floor load to the 4×4 post, it would require $(\frac{1}{2} \times 2{,}400)/170 = 7$ 20d nails to connect each of the two beams to the post.

When we discussed connections earlier in the book, we noted the many stress checks that must be considered in a properly detailed bolted connection. These checks include bearing stress against the connected members, single or double shear stress in bolt, bolt tear-out due to shearing of connected members, member net section versus gross section stress, and stress concentration around holes. In addition to checking stresses, careful consideration must also be given to unique detailing problems. For instance, when steel plates are used in wood connections, natural wood shrinkage due to moisture content changes can cause wood members to split along the grain, since no change occurs in the steel members that are connected to the wood with the unyielding bolts.

We will not get into the many important considerations of proper connection detailing; this task is best left to experienced structural designers and fabricators. We wish only to have a rough idea of the number of bolts required of a connection, and whether there is sufficient room to space the bolts adequately apart. When describing bolted timber connections, we must look at the thickness of connected members; we need to distinguish between single

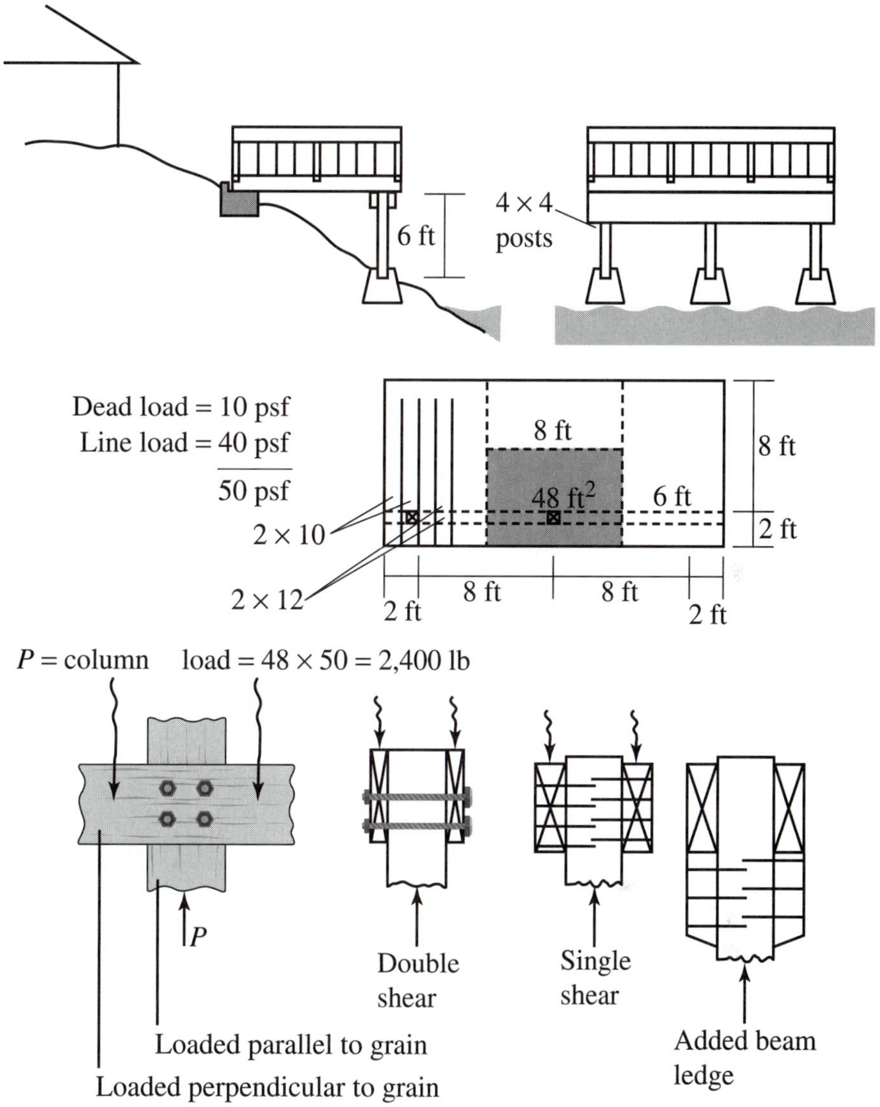

FIGURE 10.5

and double shear connections; and we need to determine whether a member is loaded parallel or perpendicular to its grain.

Common bolt sizes for timber applications range from $\frac{1}{2}$-in. to 1-in. diameters, with the $\frac{3}{4}$-in. bolt being very useful as a substitution for from as few as 2 to as many as 18 nails. We will focus on connections composed only of nominal 2-in. dimension boards, or between nominal 2-in. boards and a larger timber member. Figure 10.6 presents an approximate load capacity for a $\frac{3}{4}$-in. bolt used in various connections. The capacity ranges from 400 lb in a single shear joint between two 1.5-in.-thick members with one member loaded perpendicular to grain, to 2,400 lb for a double shear splice with all members loaded parallel to grain and a main member as thick as both side members. The figure also shows that a row of two bolts that runs perpendicular to the grain of a member requires the member have at least a 5.5-in. actual width if it is loaded parallel to grain. Similarly, the row of two bolts in a member that is loaded perpendicular to grain would need a minimum actual width of 7 in.

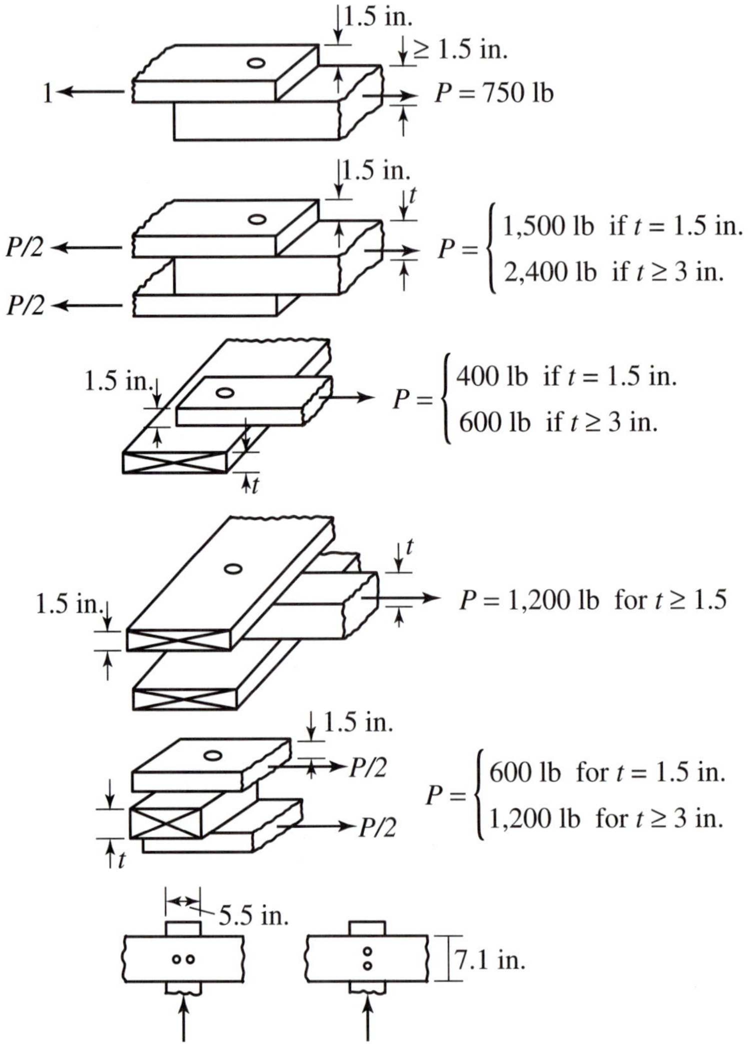

FIGURE 10.6

The connection in Figure 10.5 has a joint load of 2,400 lb. From Figure 10.6, the allowable load per $\frac{3}{4}$-in. bolt in a connection between a 3.5-in. column and 1.5-in. side members loaded perpendicular to grain is 1,200 lb. Thus, we will require 2,400/1,200 = 2 bolts, which will be placed in a single vertical row. If we had needed two rows of two bolts each–four bolts–in our connection as depicted in Figure 10.5, we would need a wider post (at least at the top where the connection is to be made). In this case, we might use a 6 × 6 post instead of our 4 × 4, but the 2 × 12 beams are wide enough for a row of two bolts.

Exercise Rework this problem assuming the 4 × 4 posts are spaced 10 ft apart. Consider bolting or nailing a 2 × 4 beam ledge to the 4 × 4 post (see figure) to take some of the additional load of the larger floor. Check the adequacy of the 6-ft tall 4 × 4 column from the timber column curves. ■

10.9 Glulam Tudor Arch

We want to do a preliminary design of the structural element shown in Figure 10.7, which is a common application of tapered and curved glulam members that form a three-hinged frame in a gabled form known as a Tudor arch. These graceful timber structural elements are often seen in churches, schools, and many other public facilities. The shapes of tailored glulam members vary considerably, with many combinations of tapers and curves. Even the shapes of Tudor arches may vary widely, with spans well over 100 ft, long legs with a relatively low rafter slope, short legs and a high sloping gable shape, symmetrical and unsymmetrical arch halves, and so on. As we have previously noted, sharply curved glulam members may require the use of nominal 1-in.-dimension boards to create $\frac{3}{4}$-in.-thick laminations rather than the nominal 2-in.-thick boards used for straight or slightly curved members.

Tudor arches often directly support deck planks that are 3- to 4-in.-thick tongue-and-groove boards that span transverse to the roof slope from arch to arch and deliver a uniformly distributed vertical roof live and dead load. Alternatively, the arches may support 2-in. roof decking that runs along the roof slope, spanning across secondary glulam purlins that are spaced several feet apart and which themselves span between the arches to deliver concentrated roof loads along the arch rafter. In either case, the roof dead plus live

FIGURE 10.7

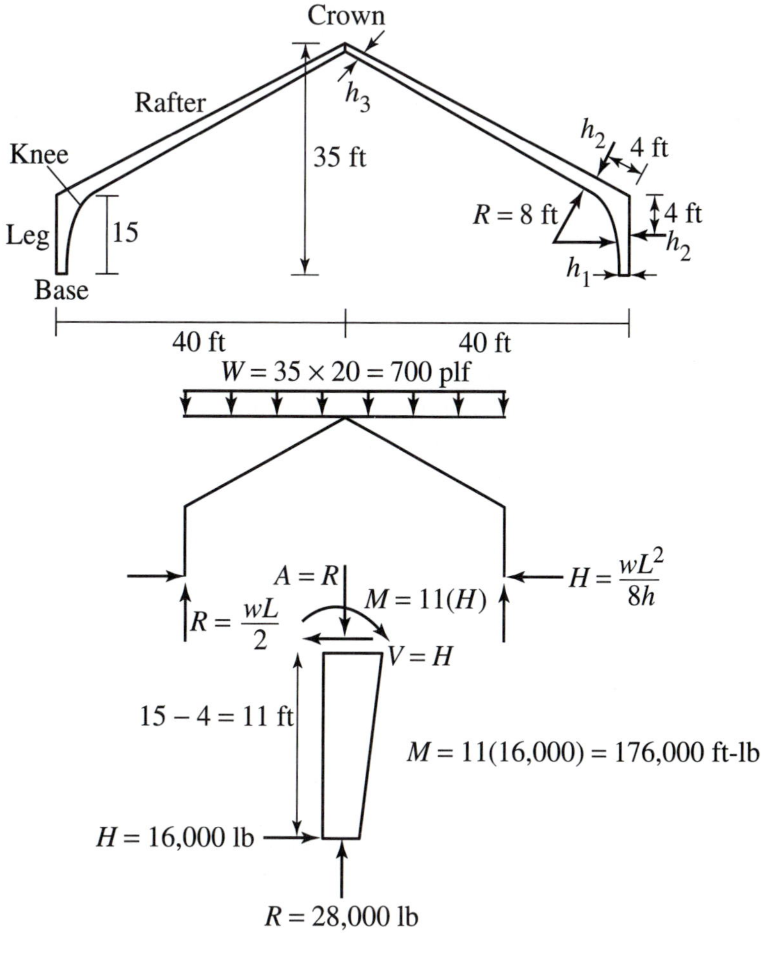

load is assumed to be uniformly distributed over a horizontal projection in a preliminary design check such as this. If the arches are spaced 20 ft apart and the roof dead plus live load is 35 psf, the distributed roof load w is 20 ft $\times$ 35 lb/ft^2 = 700 plf as shown.

Because the two halves of the arch are pin connected, or hinged, at the crown and at the bases of each leg, the structure is a determinate frame with three equilibrium equations available from each half to solve for the six unknown reaction components–two at each pin. However, we may forego a frame analysis by first observing that for this symmetrical uniformly loaded structure, the vertical reactions must each be

$$R = \frac{wL}{2} = \frac{700(80)}{2} = 28{,}000 \text{ lb}$$

Next, we employ the arch horizontal thrust formula

$$H = \frac{wL^2}{8s} = \frac{700(80)^2}{8 \times 35} = 16{,}000 \text{ ft-lb}$$

We have previously used the above formula for uniformly loaded circular arches, but it may also be used to give very good approximations for any uniformly loaded two- and three-hinged arch. Unlike for ideal arches subject to pure compression, the Tudor arch is not ideally shaped as a parabola that follows the bending moment diagram of a corresponding simple beam. As a result, the Tudor arch must resist the combined actions of both axial compression and flexure.

For a symmetrical arch, the two arch member widths are b, which is initially selected on a trial and error basis, with the options being 3.125, 5.125, 6.75, 8.75, and 10.75 in. For preliminary arch sizing, refer to the figure where we see the cross-section depth of the rafter at the crown, h_3, which is typically 1.5 times the member width. The leg cross-section depth at the base, h_1, is determined based on the shear stress due to the thrust force, H.

The knee portion of the arch links together two ends of the rafter and leg elements of one of the two arch members. The member cross sections at these two ends have the same depth, h_2. The location of these cross sections may generally be conservatively estimated to occur 4 ft in either direction from the intersection of the outer faces of the rafter and leg. The actual location depends on the final member cross section depth, h_2, and the inner radius of the knee, which is tangent to the inner sloping rafter and leg faces and typically ranges from 7 to 10 ft.

If we try b = 6.75 in. for the arch member width, the member depth at the crown can be set as

$$h_3 = 1.5 \times 6.75 \approx 10 \text{ in.}$$

The cross-section depth required at the base is determined by limiting the base shear stress, $f_V = 3V/2A$, to the allowable shear stress of 150 psi. Here, $V = H =$ 16,000 lb, and $A = 6.75 \times h_1$, so

$$h_1 = \frac{3(16{,}000)}{2 \times 6.75 \times 150} \approx 24 \text{ in.}$$

We see from the free body diagram of the lower portion of the arch leg in the figure that it is a beam-column subjected to bending and axial compression. We will assume that the outer walls of the structure brace the leg against buckling in the 6.75-in. direction. The bending moment at the junction with the knee segments is $M = (15 - 4)(16{,}000) = 176{,}000$ ft-lb, and the axial compression force is $R = 28{,}000$ lb. We need to select a cross-section dimension that satisfies the beam-column interaction equation

$$\frac{F}{F_{\text{ALL}}} + \frac{M}{M_{\text{ALL}}} \leq 1$$

If we assume that the bending moment takes up the largest share of the member total capacity, then for an allowable bending stress equal to 1,800 psi, the required section modulus is

$$S_{\text{REQ'D}} = \frac{M}{f_{\text{ALL}}} = \frac{176{,}000 \times 12}{1{,}800} = 1{,}170 \text{ in}^3$$

Since $S = bh^2/6$, the required member depth based on moment alone is

$$h = \sqrt{\frac{6 \times 1{,}170}{6.75}} \approx 32 \text{ in.}$$

We may try a slightly larger value, say $h = 36$ in., then check the interaction formula. The allowable axial compression stress for a short braced column is 1,000 psi, and thus $F_{\text{ALL}} = f_{\text{ALL}} \times bh = 1{,}000(6.75 \times 36) = 243{,}000$ lb. Likewise, we find the allowable moment to be $M_{\text{ALL}} = f_{\text{ALL}} \times S = 1{,}800 \times 6.75(36^2)/6 \times \frac{1}{12} = 219{,}000$ ft-lb. The interaction equation becomes

$$\frac{28{,}000}{243{,}000} + \frac{176{,}000}{219{,}000} = 0.12 + 0.80 = 0.92$$

Since the combined ratios are less than 1, the beam column is acceptable, and we may assume that

$$h_3 \approx 36 \text{ in.}$$

If the lower 11 ft of the arch leg is not braced by the outer walls the leg becomes an unbraced compression element with a column slenderness of $L/h = (11 \times 12)/6.75 = 20$. From the timber column stress curve of Chapter 7, $L/h = 20$ gives an allowable axial compressive stress of $f_{\text{ALL}} = 730$ psi, or 73% of that for a braced column. This same reduction should be applied to the allowable bending stress, since the moment also causes flexural compression stress that adds to the tendency to buckle the member in the 6.75 in. direction. Thus, the interaction equation result is increased to $0.92/0.73 = 1.26$, which means there is 26% overstress at the critical section at the leg-knee junction.

To reduce the added stresses due to slenderness effects, we could choose a wider member, say $b = 8.75$ in. This increases the area and section modulus by $8.75/6.75 = 1.3$, or 30%, and at the same time, the new slenderness, $L/h = (11 \times 12)/8.75 = 15$, yields an allowable compression stress of 890 psi, or 89% of a braced column. The interaction equation would now be

$0.92/(1.3 \times 0.89) = 0.80$, which is once again less than 1 (with some room for reducing some of the critical cross section depths.)

It must be remembered that we have performed only a trial design that must be further scrutinized for various load cases, including uplift due to wind. Shear and combined axial compression and bending in the rafter would also need checking. Generally, however, the preliminary Tudor arch design procedure as demonstrated here will result in member dimensions that will satisfy most other stress checks.

Exercise Rework this problem for an arch span of 60 ft instead of 80 ft. Assume the same leg and crown heights. First assume that the walls brace the legs from buckling, then assume that the lower 11 ft of the arch leg is unbraced by the outer walls. ■

11 Steel Design Applications

11.1 Structural Shapes

The slenderness of large steel structures leads to some elegant and dramatic additions to the world's architectural landscape. Long and graceful bridge spans, tall and slim skyscrapers, open and airy public assembly areas, and many other constructed works are but a few forms of aesthetic steel structures.

Steel is a very strong material that is produced with elastic limit (yield) stresses ranging from the common 36,000 psi up to high-strength strands that can resist 270,000 psi in tension. While steel is a dense material with a unit weight of about 500 pcf, when compared to timber and concrete, it has a much higher strength-to-unit weight ratio that allows for long spans with relatively light structures. The high strength-to-weight ratio of steel leads to the fabrication of members with thin cross sections, as shown in Figure 11.1.

We see in the figure that steel mills shape heated steel with rollers configured to form solid elements with a wide variety of shapes and sizes. In turn, these various shapes may be assembled into limitless configurations of built-up structural members. Steel plates, square and round bars, angles, channels, standard I-beams, wide-flange I-beams, rectangular tubes, and circular pipes are commonly available steel cross-sectional shapes. Each of these basic shapes is available in a variety of cross-section sizes, and complete information on all available steel sections may be found in the latest edition of the *Manual of Steel Construction* published by the American Institute of Steel Construction.

Generally speaking, rolled plates are commonly available in sizes up to 108 in. wide and up to 3 in. thick. Square and round bars are available in sizes up to 9 in. Angles, which may have equal or unequal leg dimensions, are available in various thicknesses with sizes ranging from L2 $\times$ 2 $\times$ $\frac{1}{8}$ to L8 $\times$ 8 $\times$ $1\frac{1}{8}$, where the three numbers following the L angle designator are the widths of each leg and the angle thickness in inches. By bending flat plates into rectangles and circles, tube and pipe sections are formed. Pipe diameters range from 1 in. to 12 in. and wall thicknesses from 0.133 in. to 0.675 in. Rectangular tubes come in square sections sized 2 $\times$ 2 $\times$ $\frac{1}{4}$ to 16 $\times$ 16 $\times$ $\frac{1}{2}$, and rectangular tubes from 3 $\times$ 2 $\times$ $\frac{1}{4}$ to 20 $\times$ 12 $\times$ $\frac{1}{2}$.

Channel and standard I-beams share similar characteristics of thick webs and flanges with the latter being somewhat narrow and slightly sloped. Standard I-beams, or S sections, are available in sizes from S3 $\times$ 7.5 to S24 $\times$ 121, where the first number in the section designation is the section depth in inches, and the second number is the weight in pounds per foot of a member with the particular cross section. Similarly for channels, section sizes range from C3 $\times$ 4.1 to C15 $\times$ 50.

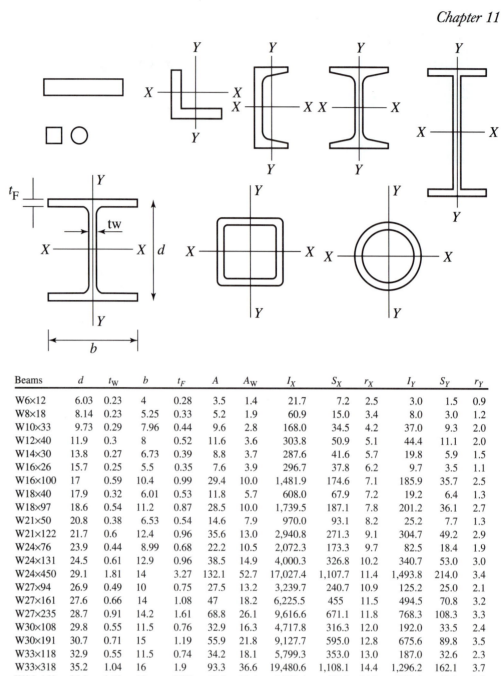

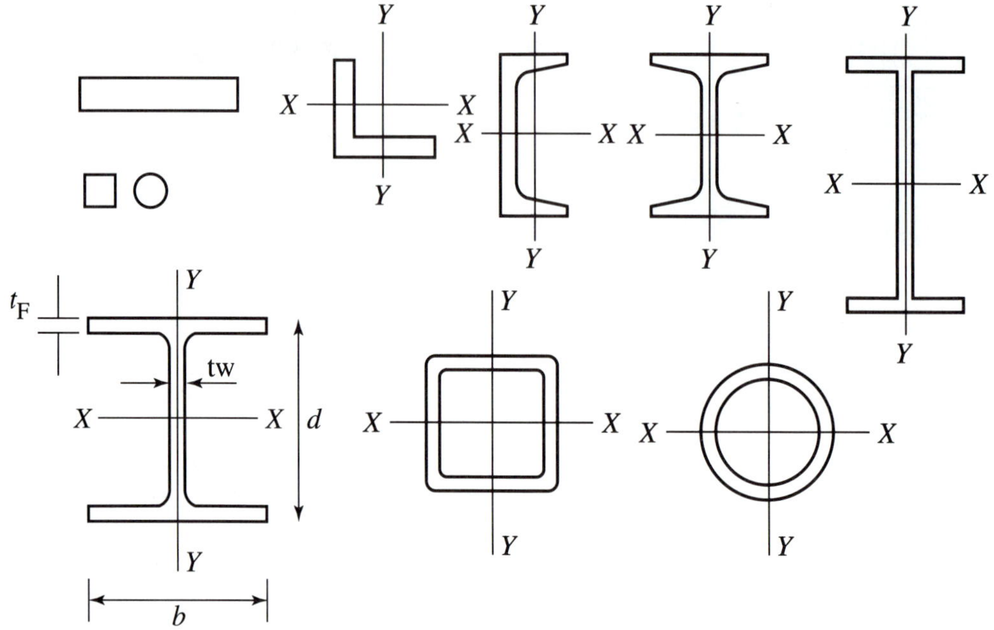

Beams	d	t_W	b	t_F	A	A_W	I_X	S_X	r_X	I_Y	S_Y	r_Y
W6×12	6.03	0.23	4	0.28	3.5	1.4	21.7	7.2	2.5	3.0	1.5	0.9
W8×18	8.14	0.23	5.25	0.33	5.2	1.9	60.9	15.0	3.4	8.0	3.0	1.2
W10×33	9.73	0.29	7.96	0.44	9.6	2.8	168.0	34.5	4.2	37.0	9.3	2.0
W12×40	11.9	0.3	8	0.52	11.6	3.6	303.8	50.9	5.1	44.4	11.1	2.0
W14×30	13.8	0.27	6.73	0.39	8.8	3.7	287.6	41.6	5.7	19.8	5.9	1.5
W16×26	15.7	0.25	5.5	0.35	7.6	3.9	296.7	37.8	6.2	9.7	3.5	1.1
W16×100	17	0.59	10.4	0.99	29.4	10.0	1,481.9	174.6	7.1	185.9	35.7	2.5
W18×40	17.9	0.32	6.01	0.53	11.8	5.7	608.0	67.9	7.2	19.2	6.4	1.3
W18×97	18.6	0.54	11.2	0.87	28.5	10.0	1,739.5	187.1	7.8	201.2	36.1	2.7
W21×50	20.8	0.38	6.53	0.54	14.6	7.9	970.0	93.1	8.2	25.2	7.7	1.3
W21×122	21.7	0.6	12.4	0.96	35.6	13.0	2,940.8	271.3	9.1	304.7	49.2	2.9
W24×76	23.9	0.44	8.99	0.68	22.2	10.5	2,072.3	173.3	9.7	82.5	18.4	1.9
W24×131	24.5	0.61	12.9	0.96	38.5	14.9	4,000.3	326.8	10.2	340.7	53.0	3.0
W24×450	29.1	1.81	14	3.27	132.1	52.7	17,027.4	1,107.7	11.4	1,493.8	214.0	3.4
W27×94	26.9	0.49	10	0.75	27.5	13.2	3,239.7	240.7	10.9	125.2	25.0	2.1
W27×161	27.6	0.66	14	1.08	47	18.2	6,225.5	455	11.5	494.5	70.8	3.2
W27×235	28.7	0.91	14.2	1.61	68.8	26.1	9,616.6	671.1	11.8	768.3	108.3	3.3
W30×108	29.8	0.55	11.5	0.76	32.9	16.3	4,717.8	316.3	12.0	192.0	33.5	2.4
W30×191	30.7	0.71	15	1.19	55.9	21.8	9,127.7	595.0	12.8	675.6	89.8	3.5
W33×118	32.9	0.55	11.5	0.74	34.2	18.1	5,799.3	353.0	13.0	187.0	32.6	2.3
W33×318	35.2	1.04	16	1.9	93.3	36.6	19,480.6	1,108.1	14.4	1,296.2	162.1	3.7
W36×150	35.9	0.63	12	0.94	43.8	22.4	8,905.4	496.8	14.3	270.1	45.1	2.5
W36×300	36.7	0.95	16.7	1.68	87.7	34.9	20,159.6	1,097.4	15.2	1,297.1	155.7	3.8
W40×244	39.1	0.71	17.7	1.26	70.6	27.7	18,834.5	964.4	16.3	1,167.6	131.9	4.1
W40×436	41.3	1.34	16.2	2.4	126.9	55.4	35,035.4	1,695.0	16.6	1,720.6	211.9	3.7
W44×285	44	1.02	11.8	1.77	83.3	45.1	24,328.4	1,105.3	17.1	489.5	82.9	2.4
Columns	d	t_W	b	t_F	A	A_W	I_X	S_X	r_X	I_Y	S_Y	r_Y
W5×19	5.2	0.27	5	0.43	5.5	1.4	26.4	10.1	2.2	9.0	3.6	1.3
W6×25	6.4	0.32	6	0.46	7.3	2.0	53.2	16.6	2.7	16.6	5.5	1.5
W8×40	8.3	0.36	8.1	0.56	11.7	3.0	147.2	35.5	3.6	49.6	12.3	2.1
W8×58	8.75	0.51	8.2	0.81	16.9	4.5	225.5	51.5	3.7	74.5	18.2	2.1
W10×60	10.2	0.42	10.1	0.68	17.4	4.3	335.9	65.9	4.4	116.8	23.1	2.6
W10×100	11.1	0.68	10.3	1.1	28.7	7.5	608.7	109.7	4.6	200.6	38.9	2.6
W12×87	12.5	0.51	12.1	0.81	25.2	6.4	729.4	116.4	5.4	239.3	39.6	3.1
W12×120	13.1	0.71	12.3	1.11	35.0	9.3	1,060.4	161.9	5.5	344.6	56.0	3.1
W14×120	14.5	0.59	14.7	0.94	35.1	8.6	1,371.2	189.1	6.3	497.9	67.7	3.8
W14×159	15	0.75	15.6	1.2	46.9	11.3	1,912.0	254.9	6.4	759.7	97.4	4.0
W14×428	18.7	1.88	16.7	3.04	125.1	35.0	6,591.2	706.1	7.3	2,366.7	283.4	4.3
W14×730	22.4	3.07	17.9	4.91	214.4	68.8	14,330.6	1,278.4	8.2	4,715.9	527.2	4.7

FIGURE 11.1

Of the different steel member cross-section shapes available, the I-shaped wide-flange section–usually referred to as W sections–is the most commonly used section both for beams and for columns. Because there are more than 100 different standard wide-flange sections available, structural designers have great flexibility when fitting structural members together. The flange width b_F and thickness t_F, the section depth d, and the web thickness t_W, are given for a few of the common W sections used for beams and for columns as the first four columns of the table of Figure 11.1.

Using a simple spreadsheet and the formulas below, the four given dimensions were used to compute approximate values for the section area A, web area A_W, the moment of inertia I, section modulus S, and radius of gyration r, about both the X-X and Y-Y axes. These values are slightly approximate, since the fillets at the four corners of the web element were neglected. Based on definitions of section properties previously presented in this book, the reader should be able to easily verify the following formulas

$$A = 2b_F t_F + t_W(d - 2t_F)$$

$$A_W = dt_W$$

$$I_X = \frac{b_F d^3}{12} - \frac{(b_F - t_W)(d - 2t_F)^3}{12}$$

$$S_X = \frac{2I_X}{d}$$

$$r_X = \sqrt{\frac{I_X}{A}}$$

$$I_Y = \frac{2t_F b_F^3}{12} + \frac{(d - 2t_F)(t_W)^3}{12}$$

$$S_Y = \frac{2I_Y}{b_F}$$

$$r_Y = \sqrt{\frac{I_Y}{A}}$$

For example, if we choose the W8 × 40, which has the reported dimensions $b_F = 8.07$ in., $t_F = 0.560$ in., $d = 8.25$ in., and $t_W = 0.360$ in., we compute the remaining values in the table as follows:

$$A = 2(8.07)(0.560) + (0.360)[8.25 - 2(0.56)] = 11.6 \text{ in}^2$$

$$A_W = 8.25(0.360) = 2.97 \text{ in}^2$$

$$I_X = \frac{8.07(8.25^3)}{12} - \frac{(8.07 - 0.036)[8.25 - 2(0.560)]^3}{12} = 145 \text{ in}^4$$

$$S_X = \frac{2(145)}{8.25} = 35.2 \text{ in}^3$$

$$r_X = \sqrt{\frac{145}{11.6}} = 3.54 \text{ in.}$$

Exercise An I-shaped cross section is made up from three plates welded together, which is referred to as a built-up member or plate girder. The flange plates are each 16 in. × 1.5 in. and the web plate is 60 in. × 0.5 in. Determine the area properties of this cross section. Repeat the exercise if the top flange is 12 in. × 0.75 in. For this case, the formulas must be modified since the centroidal axis is not in the center of the web. (A useful formula for the moment of inertia of a rectangular area about the axis that coincides with the base of the rectangle of width b and depth h is given as $I = bh^3/3$.) ■

$$I_Y = \frac{2(0.560)(8.07^3)}{12} + \frac{[8.25 - 2(0.560)](0.360^3)}{12} = 49.1 \text{ in}^4$$

$$S_Y = \frac{2(49.1)}{8.07} = 12.2 \text{ in}^3$$

$$r_Y = \sqrt{\frac{49.1}{11.6}} = 2.06 \text{ in.}$$

The W section is optimally shaped for use as a beam resisting flexure about its strong *X-X* axis, but is relatively weak about its *Y-Y* axis. This is verified from the table of section properties where the strong *X-X* axis section properties are seen to be much greater than those for the weak *Y-Y* axis. The difference in strong and weak axis area properties is more pronounced for sections with small flange-width to section-depth ratios, and this gives rise to the need for lateral bracing of beams. Lateral beam buckling is of particular concern with steel structures where long unbraced compression flanges are more likely to be encountered, and because the lateral *Y-Y* stiffness of W sections is much less than that of their strong *X-X* axis.

W sections are also commonly used as compression members, but closed shapes like rectangular tubes and circular pipes are the most efficient cross-section shapes for columns because the cross section provides similar slenderness ratios about *X-X* and *Y-Y* axes. To approach the efficiency inherent in closed cross sections, the W sections that are commonly used as columns are selected to have thick web and flange elements with flange widths and section depths that are nearly equal. As a result, the strong and weak axis section properties are somewhat closer in value, so the column will not buckle about the weak axis at very low compressive stress values.

Generally speaking, with long members whose cross sections are composed of thin elements and subject to high stress levels, steel members tend to be more slender than their timber or concrete counterparts and the required size of steel members is more likely to be governed by compression buckling stress limits. Also, the cross-sectional plate elements of a steel member are sometimes so slender that localized high compressive stresses require adding stiffener plates to prevent buckling of the thin steel plates.

11.2 Open Web Joist and Rolled Beam Floor Deck

When used as beams, W sections are often referred to as "rolled beams," which refers to their one-piece construction due to the steel mill rolling process as opposed to the I-shaped plate girders built up by welding separate web and flange

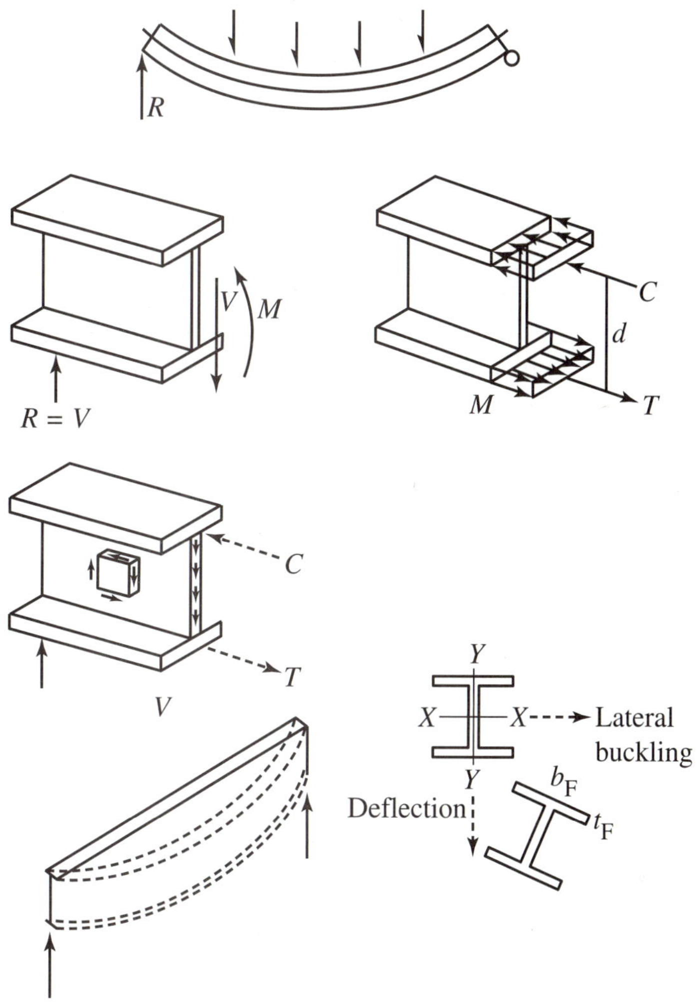

FIGURE 11.2

plates. In Figure 11.2, we see a W section being used as a simple beam. The majority of the W section area is located away from the *X-X* centroidal axis in the flanges where the bending stress, $f = M/S_X$, is highest. The flanges essentially resist all the bending stress and they form a moment couple composed of a compression force in the top flange *C* and a bottom flange tension force *T*.

The web depth plus half-flange thicknesses become the couple moment arm as the web holds the two equal and opposite couple forces apart. We see that in the process of connecting the two flanges, the web is being sheared, and we have previously stated that the magnitude of the equal horizontal and vertical flexural shear stress is $f_V = V/A_W$. The allowable shear stress is $f_V = 14{,}000$ psi.

Bending about the *X-X* axis of the W section causes the vertical beam deflection indicated in the figure. We naturally associate this deformation with a beam in flexure and we usually limit it to a fraction of the beam span, such as $L/300$. We have previously shown that simple beam deflection is $D = fL^2/(5Eh)$.

As we see in the figure, a laterally unbraced compression flange allows a beam the opportunity to shed its transverse load as the top compression flange of the member lateral buckles. This lateral buckling about the *Y-Y* axis of the W section may occur suddenly for a slender top flange behaving like a horizontal column, and the allowable bending stress in the flange must be reduced to prevent this buckling. To minimize the reduction in allowable bending stress due to an unbraced compression flange, we try to use W shapes with wide compression flanges. Fortunately, beams may usually be lateral braced by welding or bolting the closely spaced roof or floor joists to the flange of the supporting beam, or through the use of shear connectors that tie the compression flange of the beam to the concrete deck that it supports. Provided that the compression flange of the beam is laterally braced, the allowable bending stress is $f = 24{,}000$ psi.

In Figure 11.3 we see a plan view of the framing layout used for the roof and floor decks of a three-story office building. A possible alternate layout is also shown for use as a later exercise. Simple shear connections are used to connect girders to girders and girders to columns, so all spans act as simple beams. As shown in the Detail 1 sketch, the deck is formed by pouring 2 in. of concrete onto corrugated metal sheets that run transversely with the supporting open web joists, which are in turn supported by rolled beams.

FIGURE 11.3

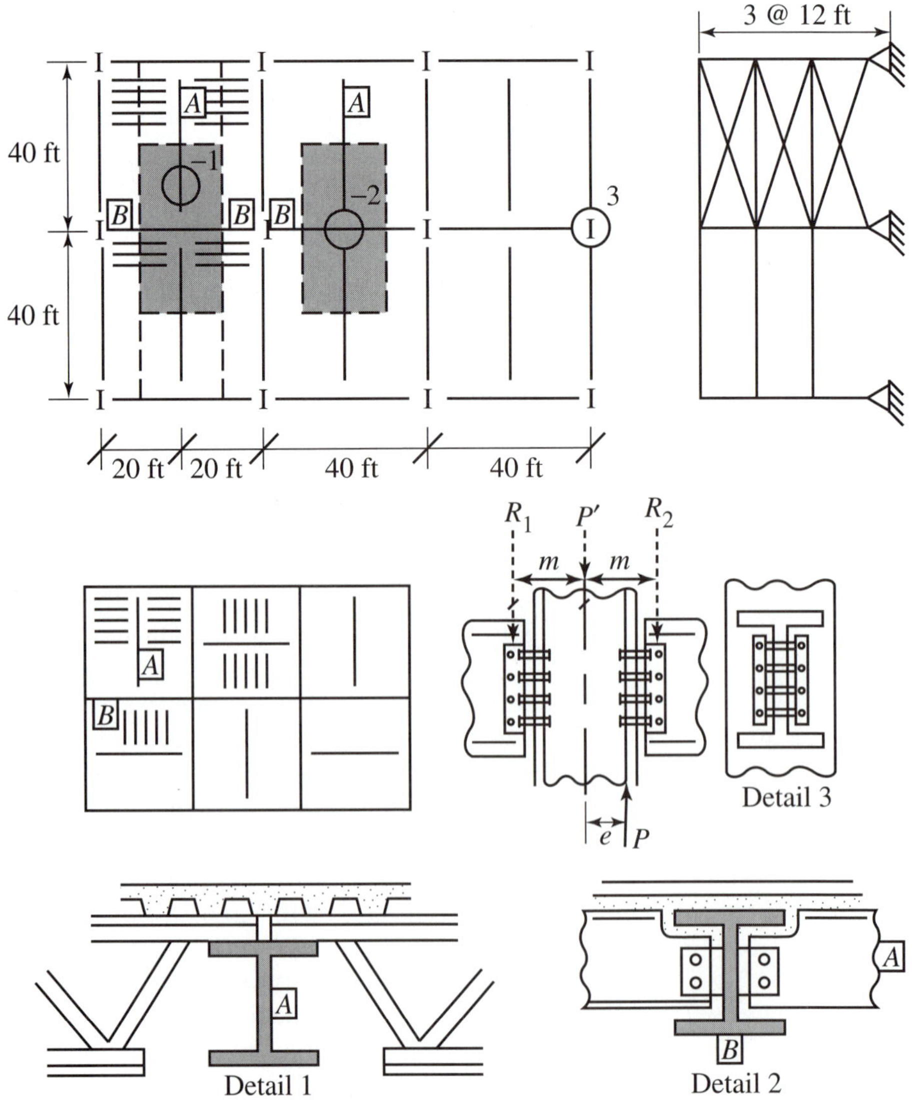

Open web joists are typically fabricated with double angles used as the top compression chord and smaller angles or even steel bars that are shaped and welded together to form light-duty trusses that are commonly used for roof and floor decks. The term *open web* indicates that the shear-resisting element is not a solid web as for rolled beams, and the term joist reflects the fact that these members are used as secondary span members. These trusses are very light, usually weighing from 5 to 10 plf, with the result that a single joist can usually support a distributed deck load of only 150 to 500 plf. Thus, open web steel joists, like their timber dimension lumber counterparts, must be closely spaced, typically being placed from 3 to 5 ft apart.

Open web joist trusses are not normally individually designed and the stresses in the member are not computed as they are for rolled beams. Instead, manufacturers provide span tables that give the distributed load capacity for various span lengths for the different available sizes of prefabricated joists. The manufacturer usually provides span information regarding sheet metal decking, as well.

We want to select appropriate-sized girders to support the floor and roof decks. In this case, the roof will be used as an open balcony, and will thus be designed for the same loads as the floor, which for this building are 40-psf dead load, and 60-psf live load, for a total design load of 100 psf. We focus on the two typical interior members marked *A* and *B*. Note that the weight of the outer walls of the structure would contribute to the distributed load of the exterior girders.

The tributary area for girder *A* is the $20 \times 40 = 800$ ft^2 shown cross-hatched in the figure. The total load on girder *A* is the design load times the tributary area, 100 lb/ft^2 $\times$ 800 ft^2 = 80,000 lb. This load is uniformly distributed along the 40-ft span of girder *A* by the closely spaced joists that are welded to the top compression flange of the W shape, and is given by the design load times the tributary area width, $w = 100 \times 20 = 2{,}000$ plf. The uniform load creates a simple beam moment, $M = wL^2/8 = 2{,}000(40^2)/8 = 400{,}000$ ft-lb.

Since the joists continuously brace the compression flange, the allowable bending stress for girder *A* is 24,000 psi, so we need a section modulus

$$S_{\text{REQ'D}} = \frac{400{,}000 \times 12}{24{,}000} = 200 \text{ in}^3$$

We look in the table of W shapes for beams and find that the lightest section with a strong axis section modulus of about 200 in^3 is a W24 $\times$ 84. We check the shear stress as $f_V = V/A_W = \frac{1}{2} \times 80{,}000/11.3 = 3{,}500$ psi, well below the allowable shear stress of 14,000 psi. For a fully stressed steel beam such as this, the deflection is $D = 24{,}000(40 \times 12)^2/(5 \times 30{,}000{,}000 \times 24.1) = 1.5$ in., which we find is under the allowable $L/300 = 1.6$ in. (You might try to verify that for fully stressed braced beams of A36 steel, deflections will be OK if the ratio, L/h, is below 21.)

Next, we look at girder *B*, which is also a 40-ft simple span beam, but which carries a single concentrated load equal to the reactions of two *A* girders connected to *B* as shown in the Detail 2 sketch. Notice in the figure how the cross-hatched tributary area of B is the same 800 ft^2 as for girder A, so the concentrated midspan load on girder B is the same as the total load on girder A, $P = 80{,}000$ lb. We have seen that for this single point load, $M = PL/4 = 80{,}000(40)/4 = 800{,}000$ ft-lb, which is twice that of girder A, because when a midspan load is distributed over a beam, it causes half as much bending moment.

We will need a W shape with a section modulus well over twice that for girder A, because the moment is twice as high, but also because the allowable bending stress must be reduced due to compressive flange buckling. For girder A, the floor deck was attached to the top flange through the joists that continuously brace the compression element. For girder B, however, the compression flange is braced only at its ends and at midspan, and the 20-ft unbraced length of flange will tend to laterally buckle about the weak axis of the W section.

If a W shape beam must have a large unbraced length of compression flange, we need to use a W shape with a wide and stocky flange to minimize the flange slenderness. The complete analysis of laterally buckling beam members is quite complex, as it involves the combined effects of axial compression stresses, torsional warping axial stresses, and torsional shear. We may very conservatively ignore the torsional strength of unbraced W shapes to approximate their moment capacity. We analyze the flange as a horizontal column subjected to compressive stress, $f = M/S$, having a slenderness ratio, L/r, where L is the unbraced flange length and r is the radius of gyration of the flange about the Y-Y axis of the W section. This approximation is pretty good for narrow flanged sections, but quite conservative for W sections with wide and stocky flanges.

If girder A has a 20-ft (240-in.) unbraced flange, the 9-in.-wide rectangular flange plate of the W24 $\times$ 84 section has a radius of gyration, $r = 0.29(9) = 2.61$ in., so the flange slenderness ratio is $L/r = 240/2.61 = 92$. From the steel compression stress curve of Chapter 7 with eccentricity ratio of 0.1, for a slenderness ratio of 92, the allowable compression stress is 15,000 psi. This would be a big reduction from the fullest possible allowable bending stress of 24,000 psi.

We will say more about unbraced compression flanges (and Figure 11.3) when we discuss steel beam-columns. For now, for basic design purposes we will assume a reduced value for the allowable bending stress in the flange of a laterally unsupported beam. For fully braced flanges, the allowable bending stress is $f_{ALL} = 24{,}000$ psi, so let us assume $f_{ALL} = 20{,}000$ psi, which corresponds with a compression member slenderness of $L/r = 65$ from the steel compression stress curve with an eccentricity ratio of 0.1. For girder B, the required section modulus would then be determined as $S = 800{,}000(12)/20{,}000 = 480\ in^3$, and we select a W27 $\times$ 161 from the table with $S = 455\ in^3$. The flange width is 14 in., so its radius of gyration is $r = 0.29(14) = 4.1$ in. and the unbraced flange slenderness ratio is $240/4.1 = 59$.

From the compression stress curve with $L/r = 59$, the allowable flange stress is about 21,000 psi, so the moment capacity is $M = f_{ALL} \times S = 21{,}000(455)/12 = 796{,}000$ ft-lb, which is acceptable. By observation, the shear stress and deflection of girder B will be less than for girder A. Why?

Exercise Rework the problem and select interior girder sizes for the alternate girder layout shown in the figure. Determine the exterior girder size assuming a uniform wall load of 250 plf. Where they support a girder, the exterior girders are only laterally supported at their ends and at midspan. ■

11.3 Columns

W sections are commonly used as columns, even though they are not the optimal shapes for column cross sections, since they are far more slender about their weak axis compared to their strong axis ($L/r_Y > L/r_X$). However, this drawback is more than overcome by the advantage offered by the open flange and web plates of the W section that allow for easy connections with beams, as we mentioned when discussing connections. Using the steel column curve that relates the allowable compressive stress versus column slenderness of Chapter 7, a family of specific column curves can be derived for various W sections as well as for the many available sizes of tubes and pipes.

For example, similar to what we did for timber columns, we want to create a graph that gives the allowable axial load F versus the unbraced column length L for a few of the W sections listed as column shapes in Figure 11.1. We may assume that the column is pinned at both ends and is unbraced in both weak and strong directions, so that the column maximum slenderness ratio for each section is L/r_Y. For the eccentrically loaded column formula, the eccentricity ratio may be assumed to be 0.3, the bottom of the three curves plotted, as previously discussed. We convert stress terms to axial compressive forces using the area A of the W section. A safety factor of 2 is applied to the modulus of elasticity, so that $E = 15{,}000{,}000$ psi, and the maximum short column compressive force is limited to $F_{MAX} = 22{,}000 \times A$. If we ignore eccentricity and use the full F_{MAX} when $L = 0$, the maximum allowable force used in the formula must be $F_{MAX} \times$ (1 + eccentricity ratio, or 1.3). Substituting these values into the eccentrically loaded column formula, we have

$$L = r_Y \times \sqrt{\frac{150{,}000{,}000(A)}{F_{ALL}} - \frac{45{,}000{,}000(A)}{22{,}000(A) \times 1.3 - F_{ALL}}}$$

For each selected W column section with its specific values of r_Y and A, we set up a spreadsheet that solves for L using a range of F values in the formula. If we limit column slenderness to no more than $L/r = 200$, then the maximum length for each is $L = 200r_Y$. Figure 11.4 shows the resulting graph for a W8 × 40, W10 × 60, W12 × 87, W14 × 120, and a W12 × 120. The W12 × 120 is plotted as the light dotted line in the figure. It is included because it has the same cross-sectional area and short column strength as the W14 × 120, but since its area is closer to its centric axis, it is more slender and thus carries comparative less load as its slenderness increases.

We may use this column graph to determine the allowable first-floor height based on the allowable compressive load of a W10 × 60 used for an interior column of the structure in Figure 11.3. The reader should verify that the tributary area for an interior column is 40 ft × 40 ft = 1,600 ft^2, and for three levels it is 4,800 ft^2. With the roof and floor design loads of 40 psf dead

FIGURE 11.4

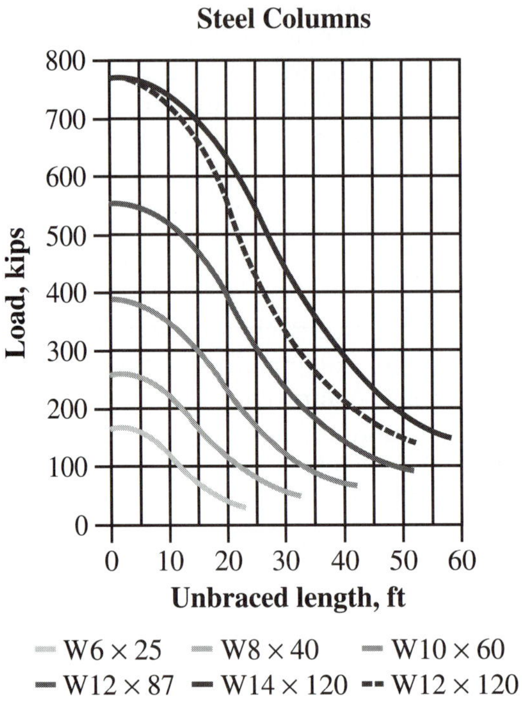

and 60 psf live, for a total 100 psf, the total column load from the roof and upper two floors is $F = 100 \times 4{,}800 = 480$ kips. From the graph, we see that for $F = 480$ kips, the W10 × 60 is inadequate regardless of floor height. However, a W12 × 87 could be used with a 15-ft story height, a W12 × 120 for a 22-ft height, and the W14 × 120 could be used for a 27-ft ground-floor height.

It is very improbable that all three upper levels are fully loaded with 60-psf live load over all 1,600 ft^2 per level at one time. We have previously discussed how, because of this improbably high loading, building design codes allow for live load reduction when the area that influences the load on a single member becomes very large. This is more likely to occur with columns than with beams, since a typical interior beam influences the two bays that it supports at one level, while an interior column usually supports four bays from every level above it. For typical interior columns (and their foundations), we can reduce the design live load of a column member by a maximum of 50% when its tributary area exceeds about 1,000 ft^2. For exterior columns not at a corner, the cumulative tributary area needed to take a full 50% live load reduction is 2,000 ft^2, and it is 4,000 ft^2 for corner columns.

It may trouble you to think that we are not designing for the full nominal 60-psf live load. Rest assured that we are still designing for a significant live load when $\frac{1}{2} \times 60 = 30$ psf is simultaneously applied over all 4,800 ft^2 of the column tributary area. With a live load reduction of 50%, the column load is $F = (40 + \frac{1}{2} \times 60)(4{,}800) = 336$ kips, and from the steel column graph, we see that a W10 × 60 can support this load with an unbraced height of 12.5 ft. From Figure 11.1, we see that we require only a 12-ft height, so the W10 × 60 shape will suffice as an interior column.

We may also use the formula to generate column tables instead of graphs for all of the W column sections, as well as pipe and tube shapes. The tables could present the allowable loads for unbraced lengths from 4 ft to 48 ft in increments of 4 ft or so. This will be left as an exercise for the reader.

Exercise Using Figure 11.4, what is the minimum-size exterior column for the ground floor of Figure 11.3 if its unbraced height is 16 ft? What about a typical interior column of the upper floor? Are the column loads different for the alternate floor girder layout?

The procedure to develop column design graphs can be applied to the W shapes in Figure 11.1 that are not covered in Figure 11.4, or to any of the many other available W sections listed in any edition of the AISC *Manual of Steel Construction.* A graph could also be developed for square tube or pipe columns ranging in size from 4 in. to 12 in. with 2-in. increments and wall thickness of $\frac{1}{4}$ in., $\frac{3}{8}$ in., and $\frac{1}{2}$ in. for each size. ■

11.4 BEAM-COLUMNS

As we have seen, when a W shape is used as a column in axial compression, it tends to buckle and its allowable load, F_{ALL}, is a function of its unbraced length L, as shown in Figure 11.4. Also, when a W shape beam member is subjected to bending moment, it may or may not tend to buckle depending on whether or not its compression flange is laterally unbraced for an appreciable length, and its moment capacity reduces with increasing unbraced flange length. When a W shape is used for a member that is subjected to axial compression and bending moment, it is called a beam-column, and we use the interaction formula

$$\frac{F}{F_{ALL}} + \frac{M}{M_{ALL}} \leq 1$$

As we did for W shape columns, to use the interaction formula, we need to create a graph that gives the allowable beam moment, M_{ALL}, versus the unbraced compression flange length, L, for W sections. As we mentioned when designing an unbraced floor girder, by analyzing the compression flange as a column, we conservatively ignore the torsional strength that is quite significant with W shapes having very wide and stocky flanges. We have previously treated the unbraced flange as a column and checked the steel compression stress curve with $f = M/S_X$ and a slenderness ratio, L/r, where r is the flange radius of gyration about the Y-Y axis of the W section. You may note that the radius of gyration of the top flange is almost equal to r_Y for the entire W section, since the web contributes very little to this cross-section property.

The eccentrically loaded column formula will be used to generate the M_{ALL} versus L graphs. Since the bending stress on the compression flange is uniform, an eccentricity ratio of 0.1 is assumed to account only for flange plate out-of-straightness, whereas 0.3 was used for columns for which both crookedness and nonuniform stress due to off-centered loads are assumed. The stress terms are replaced by moments, and a safety factor of 1.5 is applied to the modulus of elasticity, so E = 20,000,000 psi. The 1.5 safety factor is justifiably lower than the factor of 2 used for the steel compression stress curve, since we are already conservatively ignoring torsional strength of the laterally deflecting section.

The maximum compressive stress for columns is 22,000 psi, but for bending, the maximum allowable stress is 24,000 psi for fully braced beams.

As for column curves, for the maximum moment that corresponds to $L = 0$ to be $M_{MAX} = 24{,}000 \times S_X$, we must multiply it by 1 + eccentricity ratio, or 1.1, in the formula. The critical slenderness is still L/r_Y, and so we have

$$L = r_Y \times \sqrt{\frac{200{,}000{,}000(S_X)}{M_{ALL}} - \frac{20{,}000{,}000(S_X)}{24{,}000(S_X)(1.1) - M_{ALL}}}$$

Figure 11.5 presents the results of using the formula for a pair of W sections with similar section modulus values, but with different flange widths. We see that with a typical column section, the W10 × 60 with its 10-in. flange, and with a typical beam section, the W18 × 40 with a 6-in. flange, there is a reduction in moment capacity with increasing unbraced flange lengths. The reduction in M_{ALL} is much greater for the narrow-flanged W18 shape. We see that the wider-flanged W10 section can carry the same moment as the narrow-flanged beam with double the unbraced flange length of the W18. (But what about their deflections?)

Note that when fully braced, the lighter W18 × 40 can support the same moment as the W10 × 60 using only two-thirds as much steel, so it is clearly more efficient for braced beam applications. Also, since vertical deflection is inversely proportional to section depth, when both sections are equally stressed in bending, the ratio of the W18 deflection to the W10 section is $\frac{10}{18} = 0.56$. Thus, we tend to use deep and relatively narrower flange shapes for beams and reduce unbraced flange lengths as much as possible. We

FIGURE 11.5

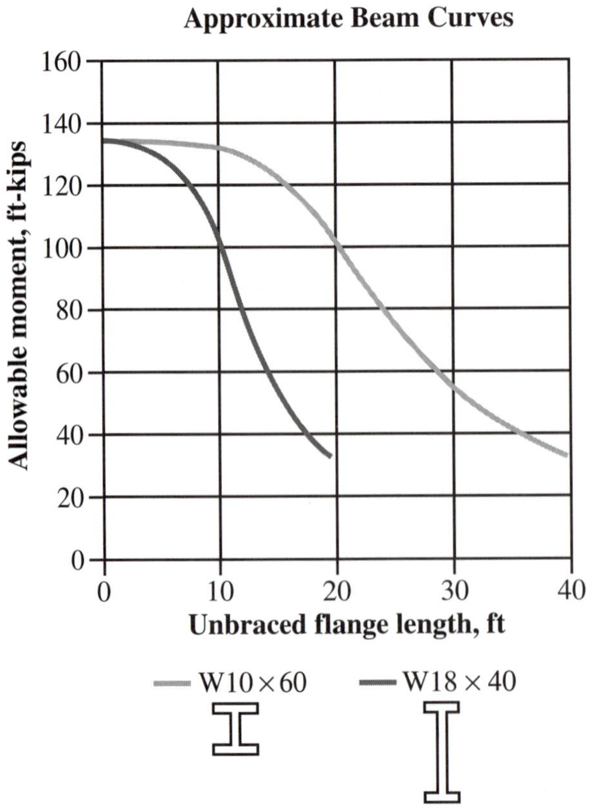

see shallower stocky sections used as vertical columns and beam-columns, since these members are usually fully unbraced.

Suppose a beam-column that is a 20-ft W10 × 60 member pinned at both ends and simultaneously resisting an axial compression force of $F = 120$ kips and a bending moment about the strong axis equal to $M = 50$ ft-kips. To check the adequacy of this member using the interaction formula, with an unbraced length, $L = 20$ ft, we find $F_{ALL} = 220$ kips from Figure 11.4 and $M_{ALL} = 82$ ft-kips from Figure 11.5. From the beam-column interaction formula

$$\frac{120}{220} + \frac{50}{100} = 0.55 + 0.50 = 1.05$$

When the interaction equation exceeds a value of 1, the stress demand on the member exceeds its capacity, as in this situation.

Suppose we can brace the member at midheight so that its unbraced column length and compression flange length are cut in half to $L = 10$ ft. From Figure 11.5 with $L = 10$ ft, $M_{ALL} = 130$ ft-kips. We need to determine if as a column the member will first buckle about the weak axis with a 10-ft length, or about the strong axis with the full 20-ft unbraced length. The two slenderness ratios are $L/r_Y = 120/2.6 = 46$ and $L/r_X = 240/4.4 = 55$, so the member is being forced to buckle about the strong axis. Since Figure 11.4 is for a fully unbraced member that buckles about the weak axis, we must go to the steel compression stress versus slenderness graph with $L/r = 55$ and get $f_{ALL} = 17{,}000$ psi. Therefore, $F_{ALL} = f_{ALL} \times A = 17{,}000 \times 17.4 = 296$ kips, and the interaction equation is

$$\frac{120}{296} + \frac{50}{130} = 0.41 + 0.38 = 0.79$$

Now, only 79% of the member capacity is being used and the braced W10 × 60 is adequate. Bracing is everything to steel members in compression because of the susceptibility of the thin plate elements to buckling.

Exercise In Detail 3 of Figure 11.3, we see that the axial load from upper levels, P', and two additional unequal beam reactions, R_1 and smaller R_2, result in an equivalent load, $P = P' + R_1 + R_2$, with an eccentricity of

$$e = \frac{(R_2 - R_1) \times m}{P}$$

If the 336-kip load on the interior column of the previous section has a 4-in. eccentricity with respect to its strong axis and the W10 × 60 is used with an unbraced story height of 12 ft, is the member adequate?

Suppose a W18 × 40 is used as a floor beam that is a compressive chord of a truss and spans 20 ft, supporting a midspan load of 8 kips and an axial compressive force of 80 kips. The member is braced at its ends and at midspan. Is it adequate as a beam-column? What is the moment magnifier for this beam-column? ■

11.5 Wind Bracing

We have discussed the vertical loads on the three-story building of Figure 11.3, and now want to examine lateral wind loading. Figure 11.6 shows diagonal wind bracing that will be located in the two outer north-south direction frames of the building. Of course, wind bracing must also be provided in the east-west direction as well. As shown, the diagonal braces form stable triangles that prevent the parallelograms formed by the pin-connected beams and columns from extreme racking.

The diagonal bracing at each floor level forms a vertical truss that prevents the three diaphragm elements–the roof, the third floor, and the second floor–from collapsing atop one another as the wind pressure on the broad face of the building causes a large lateral load. The X truss is an indeterminate structure, having more members than are absolutely required to support load without collapse. Because wind loads are less for relatively low-rise structures with

FIGURE 11.6

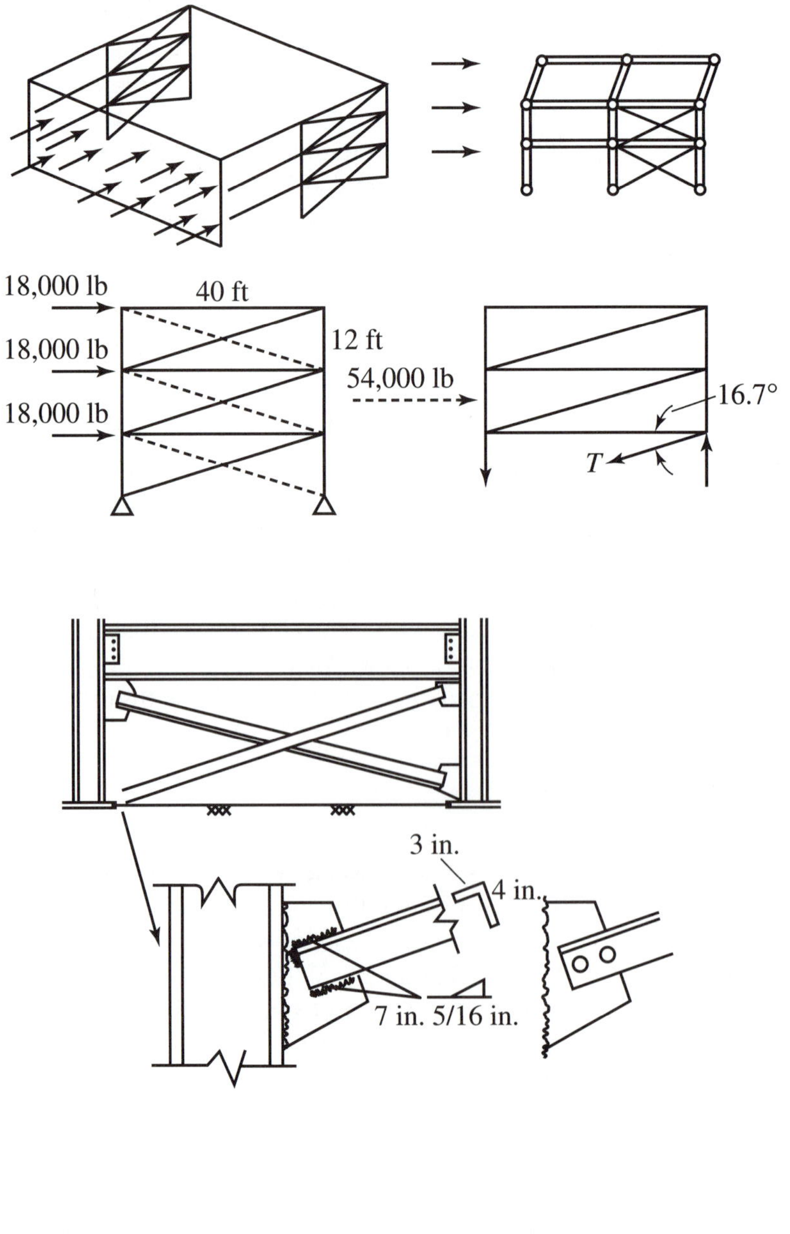

only a few floor levels, they may be braced for wind with only slender angles or even cables, which because of their slenderness will elastically buckle in compression. Since the compression truss diagonals go limp and may be ignored, the vertical truss becomes a determinate structure that is quite simple to analyze.

The wind pressure that results from a 100-mph design wind speed is $q = 0.003(100)^2 = 25$ psf. The projected area of the building is $A = 120 \times 36 = 4{,}320$ ft^2, so the total lateral load on the structure from a north-south wind is $F = 25 \times 4{,}320 = 108{,}000$ lb. We may simply divide this load evenly between each truss, and then evenly among the three levels above grade, so that the horizontal wind load at the roof and the third- and second-floor levels is $(\frac{1}{2} \times 108{,}000)/3 = 18{,}000$ lb. Remember that the wind may blow from either direction, which is why the truss tension diagonals for either loading are provided and form the X brace.

We see from the figure that we may analyze the vertical truss by the method of sections to determine the force in the most critically loaded ground-floor diagonal brace. We determine the angle of the brace as arc $\tan(12/40) = 16.7°$, and equilibrium of horizontal forces tells us that the horizontal force in the brace T must equal the total lateral load on a vertical truss

$$3 \times 18{,}000 = T \times \cos(16.7°)$$

From this equation, we see that $T = 56{,}400$ lb, and if the allowable tension stress of steel is 14,000 psi, we see that we need a brace member with a cross-sectional area of $A = 56{,}400/14{,}000 = 4$ in^2. The figure shows how the X brace at each floor level is formed using a pair of L4 $\times$ 3 $\times$ $\frac{5}{8}$ sections that may be field-bolted or welded to plates that were shop-welded to the columns. We recall that the strength of a $\frac{5}{16}$-in. fillet weld is 4,000 lb/in., so a weld length of $L = 56{,}400/4{,}000 = 14$ in., is needed to connect the angles to the columns.

For high-rise structures, building codes specify that wind and earthquake lateral loads increase at higher floor levels. For these structures, more beefy bracing is required, especially at the lower floor levels, where heavy K trusses or massive shearwalls may be used. The elevator core may also be used as part of a lateral load-resisting system. For extremely tall buildings of 30 to more than 100 stories, unique systems for lateral load resistance have been devised. For instance, by bundling all exterior columns with X braces to form a solid perimeter exoskeleton, a 100-story laterally loaded structure is designed to resist lateral load as a vertical cantilever beam that effectively has the cross section of a hollow tube.

Exercise Rework this building with the wind acting on two vertical trusses that resist east-west direction loading.

Suppose that the X bracing is replaced by a shearwall made from 8 $\times$ 8 $\times$ 16 in. solid block concrete masonry units (CMU) with a rated shear strength of 20 psi (based on the mortar strength). Is a 40-ft length shearwall adequate? What if a lower strength mortar is used and the allowable stress is only 12 psi? ■

11.6 Plate Girder Bridges

Let's look a little closer at how the thin plate elements of steel members must act to resist stresses, and then move into a discussion of big bridge girders. We see in Figure 11.7 that the flanges primarily resist the bending moment in a wide-flange beam section, since that is where the majority of section area is located in order to coincide with the greatest intensity of bending stress, and the web primarily carries the shear stress. Though there is some bending stress resisted by the web, the percentage of the bending moment resisted by the web amounts only to 10% or so of the total moment. Try to prove this for yourself.

We can increase the moment capacity of a wide-flange member by cutting it along its neutral surface and separating the two Tee sections that are formed. By locating the Tees away from their centroidal axis, a cross-sectional

FIGURE 11.7

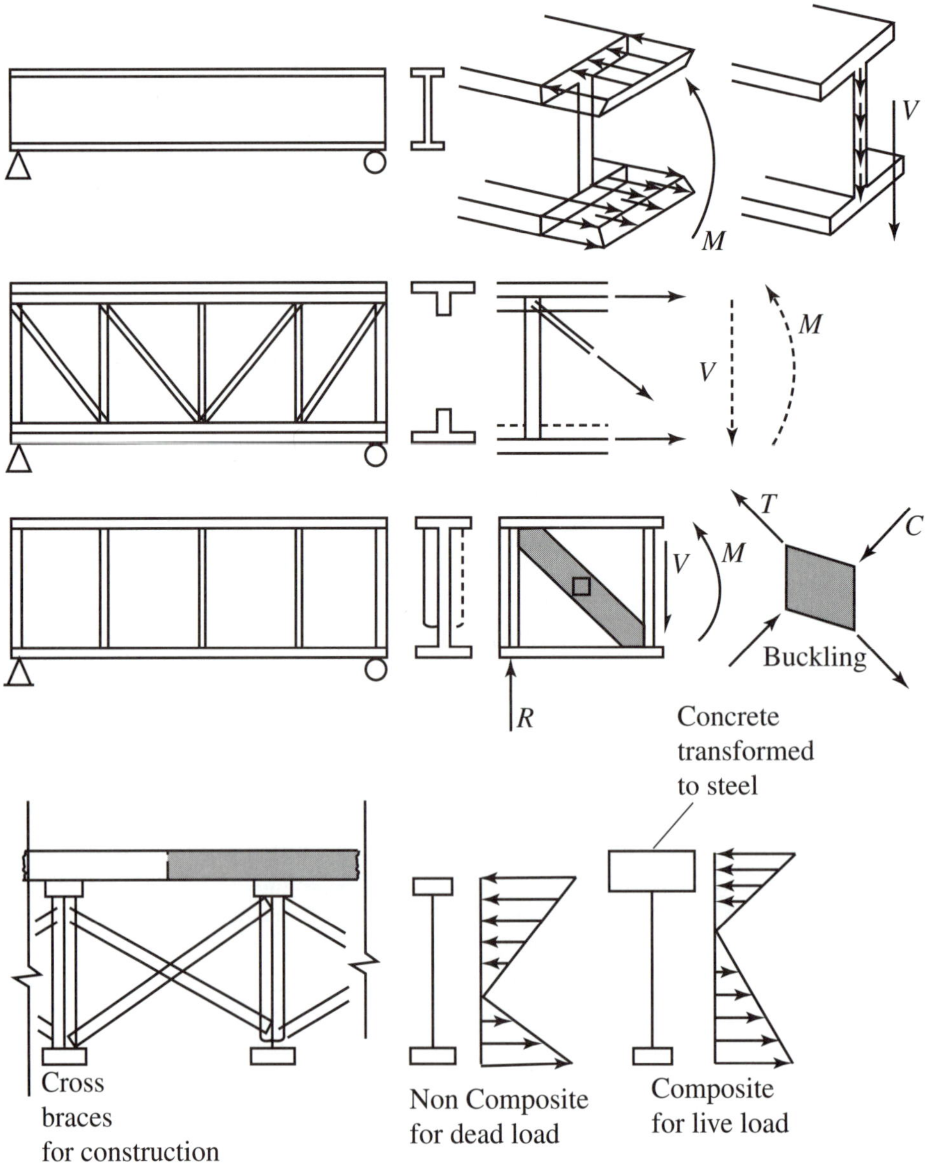

area with a much larger moment of inertia and section modulus is created. By connecting the two Tee sections with vertical and diagonal members, we create a truss element that is capable of quite large spans. The truss is essentially a large I-beam with top and bottom chords that act as flanges and verticals and diagonals that together function like a web. The chords carry the couple forces and the verticals and diagonals carry the shear.

Plate girders such as those shown in the figure are commonly used for long-span bridge structures instead of trusses. Plate girders are built-up I-beams formed by welding together three steel plates, and unlike rolled beams that are produced in shapes less than 4 ft in depth, plate girders may be fabricated with depths of up to 15 ft or more. They may be chosen instead of trusses because they are simpler to fabricate and their appearance may be more aesthetically compatible with the girders of the approach spans in many situations.

Plate girders are somewhat of a hybrid between rolled wide-flange beams and trusses. While they look like rolled beams, plate girders are much larger with trusslike spans of up to several hundred feet. Moreover, the solid thin steel plate web of plate girders resists flexural shear in a manner resembling the structural behavior of truss diagonals and verticals. Notice how small vertical stiffener plates are welded to the tall, thin web plate of the girder. These stiffeners prevent the thin web from buckling wherever there are compressive stresses. Full-depth bearing stiffeners are added to the web at the girder ends to create a sort of column that transmits the concentrated beam reaction, R, into the support.

We see that rectangular panels are formed along the span by single stiffener plates welded to the web. These stiffener plates prevent the web from failing due to buckling diagonally as a result of compression formed by the racking effect of the beam shear. Each stiffener acts with some of the web plate to form a vertical compressive strut in the web that resists the vertical component of the diagonal web compression. As seen in the figure, in the opposite diagonal direction, the shaded region of the web plate resists tension caused by shear racking of the panel.

Thus, a trusslike system of compression verticals and tension diagonals forms within the web of plate girders. We may imagine the intersection of vertical stiffeners with the ends of the shaded bands as the joints of a parallel chord truss. The analysis of stiffened web shear capacity is fairly involved, and we will not go in to the details of this subject matter. Suffice it to say that the closer the spacing of the stiffeners, the greater is the web shear-resisting ability.

We see in the figure that bridges with steel girders and concrete decks consist of multiple steel plate girders (or rolled beams for smaller spans) positioned side by side and spanning longitudinally in the roadway direction. These girders, in turn, support a concrete deck slab that itself is a slab beam spanning from girder to girder in the transverse direction. X-braces, called diaphragms, are field-bolted to stiffener plates that are shop-welded to the girder webs. These diaphragms are typically spaced 25 ft apart along the span to provide lateral stability of the steel girders during construction, especially for the top girder flanges that resist compressive bending stress caused by the dead weight of the bridge and concrete deck formwork.

If shear studs, which are essentially 4-in. long bolts, are welded every foot or so along the top flanges before pouring the concrete deck, when the deck hardens, the steel section and concrete deck will become connected together. Now the bridge will resist vehicular live loads as a composite steel and concrete structure. The main advantage of composite bridges is that the live load stresses and deflections are reduced, since the section properties of steel cross section plus composite concrete flange are somewhat larger than for the steel girder alone, so less steel is required to keep stresses within limits.

Making the top flange of the steel section much smaller than the bottom tension flange is a common means of optimizing steel use because it needs to be only large enough to support deck formwork and stocky enough to resist lateral buckling during construction. When the deck hardens, the large composite compression flange that is coupled with the large bottom tension flange via the web resists live load bending stresses.

To check bending stresses of a plate girder bridge, we focus on a single girder. We determine its dead load by observing its tributary deck area, and we determine the bending stress that this load creates in the steel cross section using its centroidal strong axis area properties–the moment of inertia I and the section modulus S. Next, we locate the design live load truck(s) longitudinally and transversely so as to cause the greatest live load moment and compute the stresses due to this moment. The total bending stress in the girder is simply the superposition of the dead and live load stresses.

If the deck is made composite with the steel section, we would divide the concrete flange evenly to each of the steel girders and compute the area properties of the composite section and determine the live load bending stresses created in the composite section. To determine the composite girder section properties, the concrete is transformed into steel using the modular ratio, $n = E_S/E_C \approx 8$. Since the cross section is not vertically symmetrical, we locate the centroidal axis and determine the section properties, I and S, about this axis. To compute the actual bending stress in the concrete flange that was transformed into steel, we divide the computed stresses in the transformed area by the modular ratio.

For example, we could replace one of the bridge trusses that we discussed in Chapter 3 with plate girders having 20-in. × 1-in. flanges and a 60-in. × $\frac{1}{2}$-in. web as shown in Figure 11.8. The two noncomposite girders are connected by cross-brace diaphragms spaced every 22.5 ft for construction stability and to provide overall stiffness to the structure. We assume the concrete deck and steel weight is still 160 psf of deck area, but instead of concentrated truss joint loads, it now creates a distributed load along the 90-ft span of w = 1,280 plf as shown. We also assume that the portion of vehicle live load resisted by one of the two girders is the same as for a single truss, and as shown in the figure, the live loads have been converted from tons to pounds.

The reader should verify the dead and live load moments presented in the figure, as well as the reported section properties of S = 1,490 in^3, and I = 46,200 in^4, and the computed stresses. The maximum total dead plus live load bending stress is f = 10,500 + 6,650 = 17,150 psi in the flanges, which is acceptable for an allowable tension flange stress of 22,000 psi for plate girders.

Even if shear studs are not used, as for noncomposite construction, the hardened concrete deck usually encases the top flange and fully braces it from buckling. However, we must investigate whether the dead load compressive flange stress, f = 10,500 psi, that exists in the unbraced top flange is below the

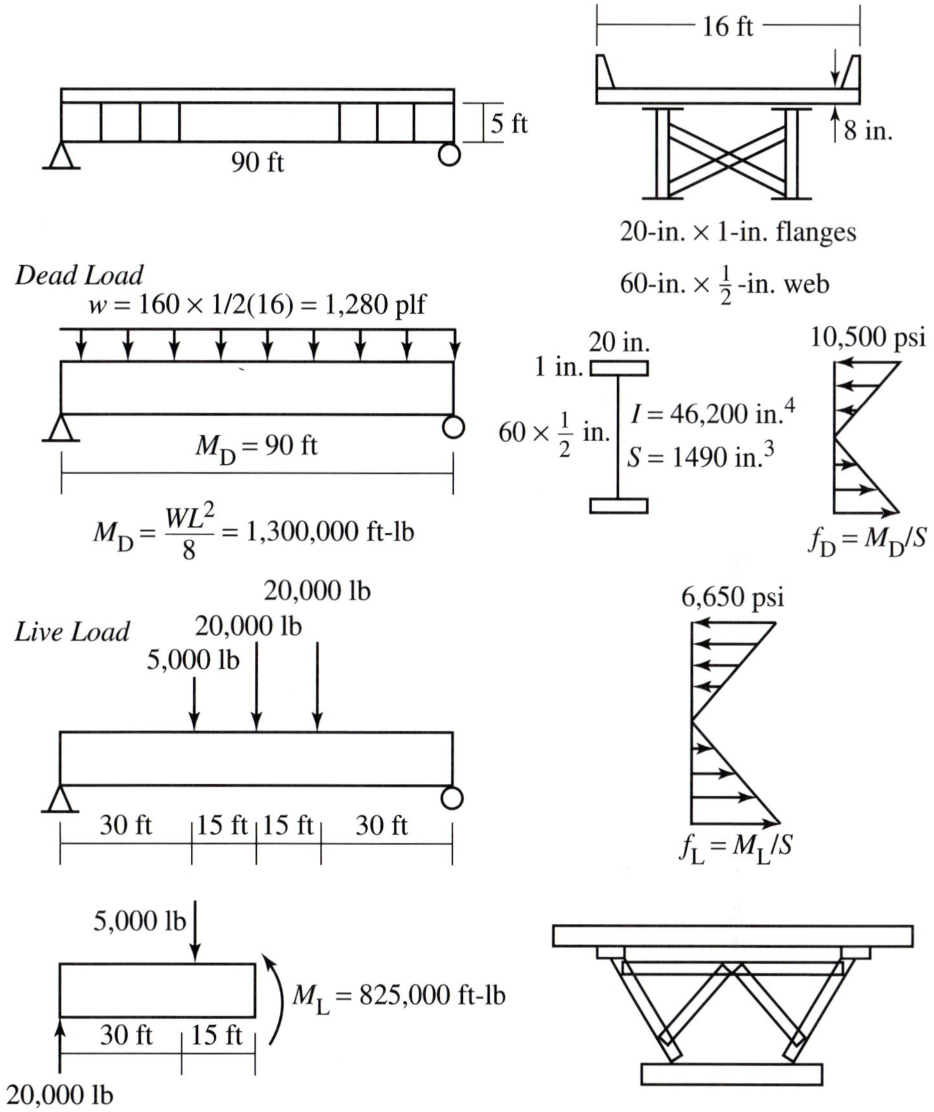

FIGURE 11.8

allowable compression stress. During construction, the flange is a slender compression member with an unbraced length of 22.5 ft between diaphragm frames. The top flange tends to laterally buckle about the weak axis of the I-shaped girder with a slenderness ratio, $L/r = (22.5 \times 12)/(0.29 \times 20) = 47$. From the steel compressive stress curve, $f_{ALL} = 21{,}000$ psi, so the plate girder bending stresses all seem to be OK.

Another form of steel bridge uses a box girder section, which may have vertical webs, or slanted webs that form a trapezoidal box, as shown in the figure. Essentially, the box girder may be considered to be two plate girders that share a common bottom flange, and the same need for web stiffeners and diaphragm bracing still exists. Besides the aesthetics of the smooth lines presented by closed box sections, such shapes are inherently torsionally stiffer, which makes them very desirable for use in horizontally curved structures.

Exercise Rework the plate girder problem using 15-in.-width flanges. Compare the live load deflection of the 90-ft span to an allowable limit of $L/1000$.

For a bigger challenge, determine the stresses in the 20-in. flanged plate girder if it is composite with an 8-in.-thick deck.

You will need to use the parallel axis theorem, which states that the moment of inertia I of an area A taken about an axis other than its centroidal axis is

$$I = I_{NA} + A(d^2)$$

In this formula, I_{NA}, is the moment of inertia of the area taken about its own centroidal axis, and d is the distance between the two parallel axes.

We know that for symmetrical cross sections, the section modulus, $S = I/(\frac{1}{2} \times h)$, is used to compute the bending stress, $f = M/S$, at the top and bottom of the cross-section height. In the case of unsymmetrical cross sections, the distance in the denominator $(\frac{1}{2} \times h)$ is replaced with the distance from the centroidal axis to the point along the cross-section height where the stress $f = M/S$ is to be computed. ■

12 Concrete Design Applications

12.1 Flexural Analysis of Beams

When we covered soil structures in Chapter 9, we discussed reinforced concrete design in some detail. Throughout this chapter, we look at essential components of cast-in-place concrete structures, slabs, joists, beams, and beam-columns, all of which are usually monolithically cast into removable formwork. What results is a rigid frame through which continuously attached members share loads amongst themselves through their moment connections. Reinforced concrete structures can be formed into an infinite number of shapes, but the linear column and beam building system is so commonplace that any basic presentation of concrete structures technology must address this subject.

Another form of concrete structure is that of precast construction, in which the individual slab, beam, and column members are formed at a fabrication plant and delivered to the site, much as for I-beams and columns of a steel structure. Usually, the connections among members of precast concrete structures are simple pin connections that transfer no moments among the joined members. Lateral bracing of such structures is often accomplished by fashioning diaphragm systems, and/or bracing the frame against elevator shaft cores that act as rigid vertical cantilever beams. Because they are formed under controlled conditions at fabrication yards, it is possible to employ prestressing to achieve lighter and stronger members, as we discuss later.

We begin with the main ingredient of concrete, cement, which is a fine powdery material formed by pulverizing limestone and clay that has been fired in a kiln. Concrete is a mixture of cement, water, sand and gravel aggregates, and sometimes chemical admixtures that alter the strength and/or workability of the mix. These materials are mixed into a wet concrete slurry that can be formed into beams, columns, slabs, footings, arches, walls, retaining walls, and domes.

Concrete strength is normally reported as the compressive failure strength of a test cylinder that has been allowed to cure and harden for 28 days. Concrete 28-day compressive strengths range anywhere from 3,000 psi to 20,000 psi, depending on mix proportions and admixtures, with 4,000 psi being the normal compressive strength of concrete. Concrete is weak in tension, and will experience a sudden brittle failure at a tensile stress of about 400 to 500 psi.

When we use the term *concrete structure,* we usually are referring to a structure with composite members made up of steel reinforcing bars and hardened concrete. Since concrete has a negligibly small tensile rupture strength, it must be reinforced with a material that can take tension stress such as steel. Grade 60 steel reinforcing bars, called rebars, are fabricated from steel with an elastic limit (yield) stress of 60,000 psi and are the most common type of steel reinforcing for concrete structures.

Grade 60 bars have raised bumps circling their perimeter surface that allow them to form excellent slip-free bonds with the concrete that encases them, so that the two materials act compositely when stressed. Rebars used for beams come in nominal sizes of #3 through #9 bars, and their nominal size is the number of $\frac{1}{8}$-in. increments of the bar diameter, so the #3 bar has a $\frac{3}{8}$-in. diameter, the #9 has a $\frac{9}{8}$-in. diameter, and so on. Using many small reinforcing bars instead of a few large ones will provide better flexural crack control. The larger available bar sizes, #10, #11, #14, and #18, are typically used in column reinforcing applications where a greater percentage of steel reinforcing is desirable and tensile flexural cracking is not as much of an issue.

We want to develop some basic relationships between the moment capacity of concrete beams and their cross-sectional makeup. The design of a concrete beam involves primarily determining what width b, depth h, and area of longitudinal steel A_S are required to resist the maximum design bending moment without exceeding the material allowable stresses. The allowable flexural compressive stress for normal concrete is 1,800 psi, while for Grade 60 rebars, the allowable flexural tension stress is 24,000 psi.

Figure 12.1 depicts a simple span concrete beam. For the simple span, the bottom portion of the beam is subject to flexural tension caused by the positive bending moment, and longitudinal rebars are needed to run all along the bottom and be embedded at the ends, perhaps by simply hooking the bars, as shown. Longitudinal bars intercept the vertical flexural cracking that predominately occurs in the beam midspan region, which is caused by the lower wedge of bending tension stress in the direction of the bars. We look at the need for shear stirrup reinforcing to intercept inclined cracks in the next section.

In the figure we see the cross section of a concrete beam at the section where the design moment is causing maximum stress, such as the midspan section of a simple beam. We know that flexural compression and tension stresses are created in the cross section of a beam, which increase with distance from the neutral axis. As we see in the figure, when we assume that the concrete subject to tensile stress is cracked and thus ineffective, all the tension stress is transferred into the longitudinal rebars.

The wedge of flexural compressive stresses acting above the neutral axis creates a compressive force, $C = \frac{1}{2} f_C b(kd)$, which acts at the wedge centroid located $kd/3$ from the top of the section. The beam section resists bending moment, M, through the action of the C-T couple, as shown. The tension couple force, $T = f_S A_S$, must be equal to and oppose the compressive force C, and the two forces are separated by a moment arm, $jd = (1 - k/3)d$. Thus, the moment capacity of the beam is $M = C(jd)$, or the more useful $M = T(jd) = f_S A_S(jd)$, and we have $A_S = M/(f_S jd)$.

Next we define the steel ratio (steel percentage when multiplied by 100%) in the effective concrete cross section as $p = A_S/bd$. For steel ratios below $p = 0.0141$, the moment capacity is governed by the allowable tensile stress of steel, $f_S = 24{,}000$ psi, and the concrete compressive stress is less than the allowable, $f_C = 1{,}800$ psi. Also, the couple moment arm is approximately $jd = 0.9d$, so we have

$$A_S = \frac{M}{21{,}600 \times d}$$

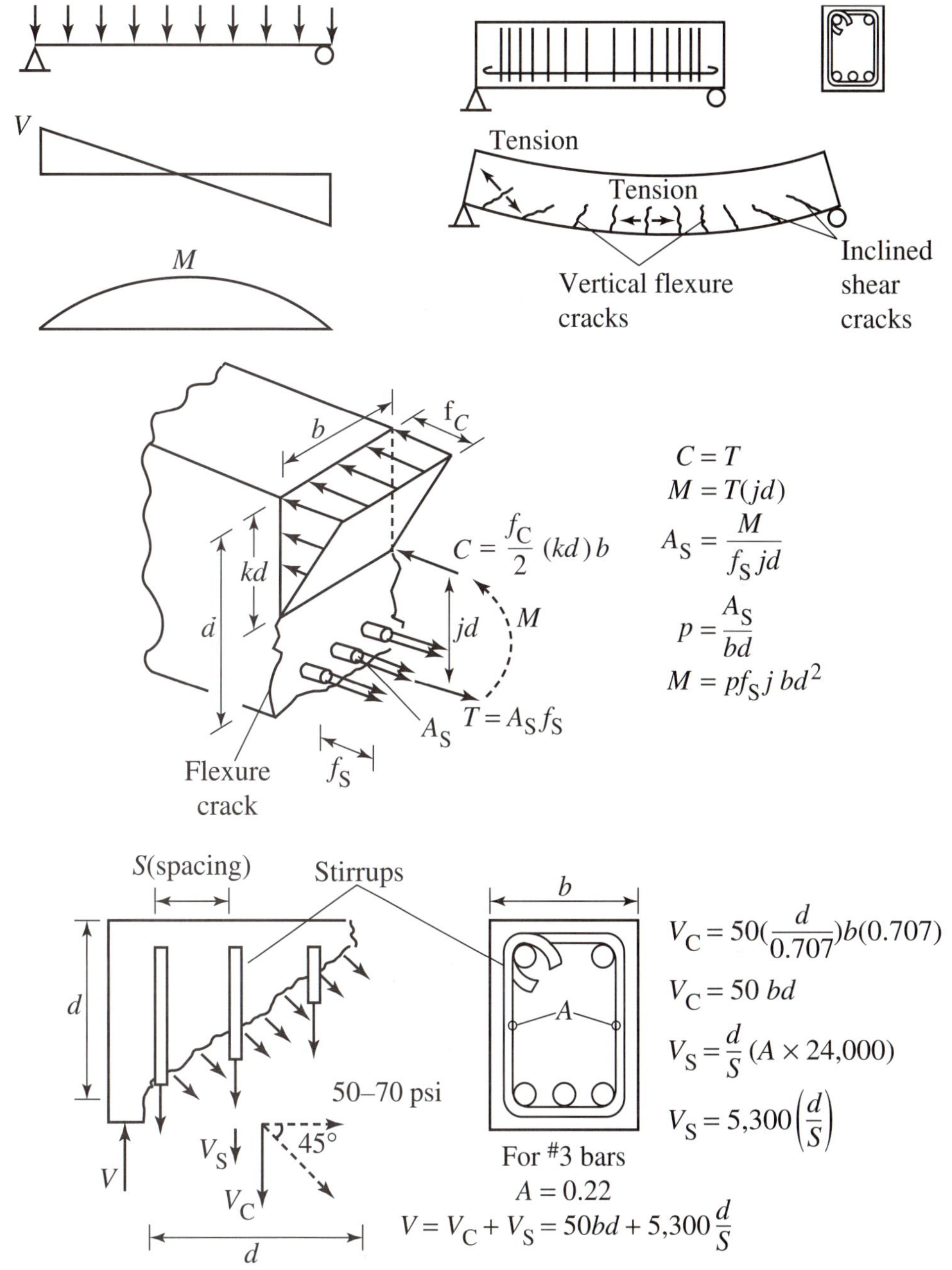

FIGURE 12.1

This formula is used to determine the required area of rebars needed to resist moment in a beam with a known effective depth *d*, which is very often determined based on deflection limits.

Optimally, we would like to design a beam with a percentage of steel such that the moment capacity is reached when both the steel and concrete are simultaneously stressed to their full allowable limits. This is called a balanced beam, and its steel percentage is 1.41%. The reader should verify that when $p = A_S/bd = 0.0141$, $f_C = 1{,}800$ psi, $f_S = 24{,}000$ psi, $k = 0.375$, and $j = 0.875$. Since $M = f_S A_S(jd) = pf_S jbd^2$, the balanced beam moment capacity is given by

$$M = (0.0141)(24{,}000)(0.875) \times bd^2 \approx 300 \times bd^2$$

This may be considered to be the maximum allowable moment for rectangular concrete beams that has at least 1.4% steel. So for beam designs, we can loosely say that the effective allowable flexural stress is 300 psi for cracked rectangular concrete beams with an effective section modulus, bd^2.

It is generally disadvantageous to design beams for steel ratios over 1.4%, since incremental increases in the steel ratio p do not bring about as high an increment in the moment capacity as for values of $p < 0.014$. Also, the steel is underutilized, and the extra percentage of steel in the cross section is difficult to fit in the forms and it is harder to get the concrete slurry to fully encase the tightly spaced bars.

Suppose the simple beam in the figure spans 24 ft and supports a distributed load, $w = 2{,}000$ plf. The beam is supported by 16-in.-square columns, and column widths usually dictate beam width b. We will estimate a beam size of 16 in. × 24 in., so a 1-ft length of the beam weighs 150 lb/ft × $\frac{16}{12}$ ft × $\frac{24}{12}$ ft × 1 ft = 400 lb per foot. Thus we estimate that $w = 2{,}400$ plf, and the design moment is $M = 2{,}400(24^2)/8 = 172{,}800$ ft-lb, or 2,074,000 in-lb. Since beam capacity is $M = 300bd^2$, we have

$$d = \sqrt{\frac{2{,}074{,}000}{300 \times 16}} = 21 \text{ in.}$$

So the required effective depth from the top of the beam section to the center of the longitudinal rebars is $d = 21$ in., but the overall beam depth h is usually $d + (2.5 - 3.5)$ in. This extra space is needed to provide space for the rebar radius, the stirrup diameter, and 1.5-in. concrete cover for any steel in the beam. The cover primarily ensures that the steel is bonded to the concrete and also well protected from fire. We will use $h = 24$ in. and note that our beam weight estimate is accurate.

Since we are designing a balanced beam, we need 1.4% flexural steel rebar area, so

$$A_S = pbd = (0.014)(16 \times 21) = 4.7 \text{ in}^2$$

The size and number of rebars we select to provide this area must account for the fact that the space between the inside of the vertical legs of the stirrups is limited to the beam width minus two times the stirrup diameter plus two times the 1.5 in. of cover. In addition, we need at least an inch between each rebar to allow the large aggregate in the concrete slurry to easily flow around and encase the rebars when the concrete is poured and vibrated into the formwork.

We prefer to use only one layer of rebars and to place as many smaller bars as possible, rather than a lesser number of larger rebars, and so we find that six #8 bars provide $A_S = 4.71$ in^2. If #3 stirrups are used, the required beam width for the six 1-in. diameter bars with five 1-in. spaces between them is $2 \times (\frac{3}{8} + 1.5) + 6 + 5 = 14.8$ in., which is less than 16 in. We try to use beam widths that allow us to use only one layer of rebars; however, sometimes we are forced to use two. In this example, we could place two layers of eight #5 bars separated by an inch or so with their centroid still at 21 in. from the top of the beam, but the added time and complexity of placing 16 bars in this manner is not called for.

Exercise Verify that for a steel ratio of $p = 0.0141$ in a rectangular beam cross section, $k = 0.375$, $j = 0.875$, and $M = 295(bd^2)$ for a balanced design.

Design a simple beam to span 18 ft and support a live load $w = 1{,}500$ plf, assuming that the beam width is one-third its depth.

Determine the number of #7 rebars needed for a 20-ft simple span bridge precast slab panel that is 4 ft wide and 1 ft deep. The design load is the slab panel self-weight plus a midspan 16,000-lb force equal to half the rear axle load of a truck. Stirrups are not used here, and the cover requirement is only $\frac{3}{4}$ in., so assume $d = h - 1$ in. If the balanced steel percentage is used, what is the allowable midspan load? ■

Suppose we want to use a 14 × 28 beam instead of the 16 × 24. Now we have a situation where the dimensions and the moment are set, and we need to determine the steel rebar area that is required. We have $A_S = M/(21{,}600 \times d)$, and assuming $d = 25$

$$A_S = \frac{2{,}074{,}000}{21{,}600 \times 25} = 3.84 \text{ in}^2$$

We can use five #8 bars, with $A_S = 3.93$ in^2, and required beam width of 12.8 in.

12.2 Shear Reinforcement

Once a beam cross-section width and height and its longitudinal reinforcing requirements are established, the shear reinforcing needs to be determined. We see in the figure that the racking effect of the shear, which is worst at the ends, causes tension in the diagonal direction, which creates diagonal cracks. Small diameter bars (#3 or #4 bars) are tied around the longitudinal rebars (and some top rebars, which are usually present) to provide the shear reinforcement. These ties are called stirrups, and they must be spaced closely enough to stitch together the inclined cracks that form where the shear stresses are high enough to exceed the allowable flexural shear capacity of concrete, which is around 50-70 psi.

Just as for stiffeners along the web of steel plate girders, the closer that stirrups are spaced in a concrete beam, the higher the shear capacity of the beam, and so required stirrup spacings vary with the beam shear diagram. For a reinforced concrete member of width b and effective depth d, we say that the shear stress due to shear at a section V, is

$$f_V = \frac{V}{bd}$$

Generally speaking, when the computed beam shear stress, $f_V = V/bd$, is in the range of (50-70) psi, stirrups are needed and should be spaced no closer than 4 in. apart, nor more than half the beam effective depth d. Even when the computed shear stress f_V is below 50 psi and the concrete alone can carry the shear, it is good practice, especially in seismic regions, to place stirrups at a spacing of no more than the beam effective depth d.

Instead of looking at stress, we may look at the overall shear-resisting forces in a beam. We see in the figure that the shear capacity of a beam is the

Exercise How much shear capacity is provided by #3 stirrups spaced $d/2$? What about #4 stirrups?

A 24-ft simple span beam with a 14-in. × 28 in. cross section and #3 stirrups supports a midspan live load of 24,000 lb. What is the required stirrup spacing at the supports? Does the required spacing vary much along the span?

What is the shear stress in a 20-ft × 4-ft × 1-ft bridge slab panel supporting a 16,000-lb midspan load. What about when the load moves to within a foot of the support? ■

sum of the concrete strength, V_C, and the strength of the stirrups spaced s apart, V_S, and for #3 stirrups, the shear capacity of a rectangular concrete beam is

$$V = V_C + V_S = 50bd + 5{,}300(d/s)$$

For a 24-ft simple span 16-in. × 24-in. beam supporting $w = 2{,}400$ plf, the maximum shear at the supports is $V = wL/2 = 2{,}400(24/2) = 28{,}800$ lb. The capacity of the concrete alone is $V_C = 50(16)(21) = 16{,}800$ lb, so the required stirrup capacity is $V_S = 28{,}800 - 16{,}800 = 12{,}000$ lb. Equating this with $V_S = 5{,}300(d/s)$, we find that the required stirrup spacing near the supports is $s = 5{,}300(21)/12{,}000 = 9.3$ in.

This is a conservatively close spacing of stirrups because we used the shear at the support, while building codes specify that the lower shear computed at a distance d from the support face may be used. The required stirrup spacing of beams with distributed loads varies along the length of the beam, and a schedule of stirrup spacings may be determined by solving for new spacings every few feet.

12.3 Continuous Frames

Figure 12.2 shows, among other things, a continuous span beam that is part of a concrete moment frame. The continuous frame is quite common for cast-in-place concrete structures, since these structures can be molded into any shape that can be created with formwork. Thus it is easy to create monolithic beams and beam to column connections. Such frames are indeterminate structures, and we must make simplifying assumptions to render them determinate. These rigid frames (also called moment frames) are more difficult to analyze, and they can become overstressed under some situations of differential settlement or thermal changes. Still, rigid frames make a lot of sense, as continuity typically creates stiffer structures with less deflection and lateral sway. Continuity also has the effect of reducing the maximum beam moments 20% or more by distributing the load-carrying task of a beam span to its attached adjacent spans and even to its supporting columns.

Continuous beams experience both positive and negative bending moments, so instead of a $wL^2/8$ simple span positive design moment, continuous beams are designed for both a midspan positive and an end span negative design moment of $wL^2/10$, as shown. This design moment conservatively accounts for many factors that enter a rigorous indeterminate analysis of a rigid frame, such as joint rotation, patterned load placement, assumed member stiffness, and inelastic load redistribution.

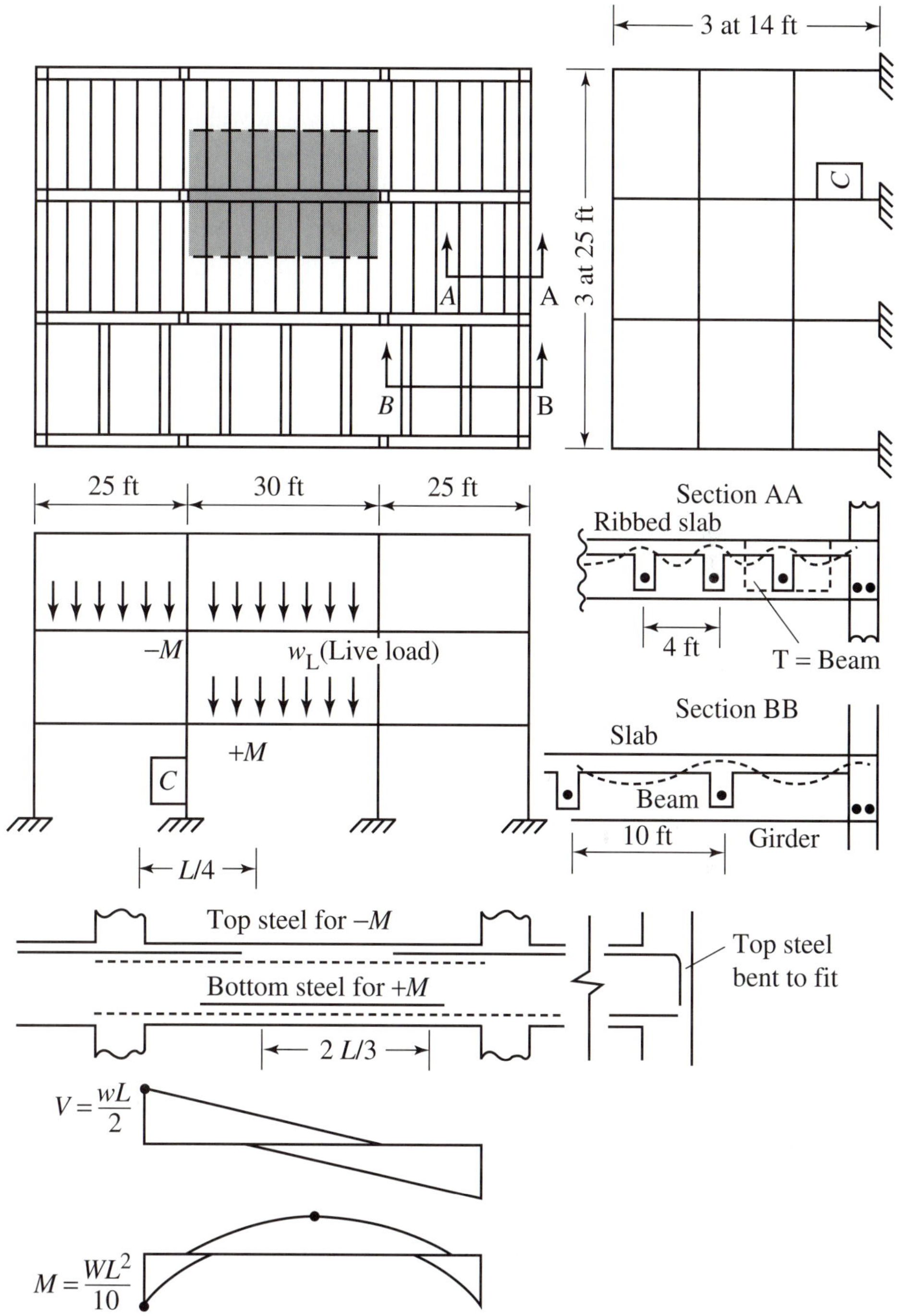

FIGURE 12.2

A patterned placement of live loads gives rise to the unusual looking shear and moment diagrams shown in the figure. As shown, live loads are arranged in various patterns throughout a continuous frame because the load pattern that places the beam in the worst positive moment situation is not the same as the load pattern that creates the maximum negative moment. Live load in adjacent spans creates the highest negative beam end moment, while live load only on the span creates the highest midspan positive moment. By enveloping all the highest positive and negative shears and moments that occur at each section along a beam, we create the diagrams called *shear and moment envelopes.* These envelopes provide the designers with the maximum design shear and moment values as well as a good picture of where steel reinforcing can be reduced. These shear and moment envelopes are critical for designing bridges, where the worst possible effect of the moving truck loads must be accounted for.

With the reverse bending in continuous beam members, there is tension along the bottom as well as tension at the top of the beam at its ends. Longitudinal rebars are needed to run all along flexural tension regions and be embedded a few feet into adjacent compression zones. The figure shows where steel is typically located along a continuous beam.

We are going to design the typical east-west interior girder shown in the figure. Column size usually determines the width of the girders in a monolithically formed concrete frame, since it is easier to form columns and beam connections when they are of equal widths. We will see that the effective allowable stress for a reinforced column is about 1,000 psi. Suppose that all the concrete used for the slab and girders of the floor (and open balcony roof) decks averages to 8 in. for the three-story structure in the figure, so the unit floor dead load is $(\frac{8}{12})150 = 100$ psf.

Suppose the live load is 60 psf for this university classroom building. The typical interior ground-floor column supports a tributary area of $3 \times [(30 + 25)/2 \times 25] = 2{,}060 \text{ ft}^2$. As discussed in Section 11.3, we can reduce the nominal design live load by 50% since the tributary area exceeds $1{,}000 \text{ ft}^2$. So the total design load for the column is $(100 + \frac{60}{2}) \times 2{,}060 = 268{,}000$ lb, and the required dimensions of a square column are $\sqrt{268{,}000/1{,}000} = 16.4$ in. Because this estimate does not include load eccentricity or lateral load moments, we will assume slightly larger 18-in. × 18-in. columns and thus we have 18-in.-wide floor girders.

For the design of floor girders, which are more likely to experience the full live load over their tributary area (which is much smaller than the area supported by a lower-level column), we use the full dead plus live load of $100 + 60 = 160$ psf. The floor system for this structure consists of what is known as a one-way ribbed slab, which acts much like a plywood deck and timber joist system, where a uniform thin slab of concrete is stiffened with webs as shown in Section AA of the figure. (We look at the design of the floor slabs in the next section.) The triburary area of the 30-ft girder is shown in the figure, and with a 25-ft tributary width, the uniform load is $w = 160 \times 25 = 4{,}000$ plf. Remember that the dead load represented an average of all concrete members of the floor system, so we need not add in a beam weight estimate.

The design moment of the continuous girder in the positive and negative bending regions is $M = 4{,}000(30^2)/10 \times 12 = 4{,}320{,}000$ in-lb, and so for a balanced beam design, the required effective depth is

$$d = \sqrt{4{,}320{,}000/(300 \times 18)} = 28 \text{ in.}$$

We will assume a 32-in. girder depth. The required area of steel is

$$A_S = (0.014)(18 \times 28) = 7.1 \text{ in}^2$$

We select seven #9 bars with an area of $A_S = 7\text{ in}^2$. When using bars larger than #8 size, the required space between bars equals the bar diameter, so we have a required beam width (assuming #3 stirrups) of $2 \times (\frac{3}{8} + 1.5) + 7(\frac{9}{8}) + 6(\frac{9}{8}) = 18.4$ in., which we will say is OK.

We typically run the top steel continuously through the columns and one-fourth the span distance into the two adjoining spans. When the span frames into an exterior column, the top steel must run several feet into the column to develop its tension force, so the bars must be bent to fit as shown. In addition, building codes require that about one-fourth of all bottom rebars should be run continuously along the entire member. It is general practice to run at least a couple of small rebars all along the top and bottom of the beam, especially in seismic regions where added ductility is provided by the steel. These continuous bars also provide a frame to which the shear stirrups can be wrapped around and tied. Shear stirrup spacing is much the same for continuous spans as for simple beams.

Looking ahead to Figure 12.3 for a moment, we see the columns of a continuous moment frame work with the girders to resist the negative moments at support joints, as shown in Figure 12.3. We first look at an exterior column into which a girder is framed from only one side and brings a girder support negative moment of $M = wL^2/10 = 100$ to the joint, as shown. When this unbalanced moment is applied, all three monolithically attached members essentially share the load equally as the clockwise rotation action of $M = 100$ rotates the joint an imperceptible amount. This rotation forces the three attached members to bend and they resist this bending with three equal countermoments of $\frac{100}{3}$. The joint is brought into equilibrium with the girder moment reduced to $M = 100 - \frac{100}{3} = 66.6$, and the two columns each resist with a moment of $M = 33.3$, as shown. It is by this process that load is shared among members rigidly connected.

When two girders frame from either side at a monolithic joint, the unbalanced moment taken by the columns is usually not as much as for the exterior column case just described, especially if both spans are of equal length. However, if the two spans have different lengths, and we place full live load on the longer span, a considerably unbalanced joint moment may be created. We see at an interior joint of Figure 12.2 where a 25-ft and a 30-ft girder meet. The end moment of the shorter span with only dead load is $M = 2{,}500(25^2)/10 = 156{,}000$ ft-lb, and $M = 4{,}000(30^2)/10 = 360{,}000$ ft-lb for the longer span with full dead and live load. As shown in Figure 12.3, this results in column moments of 51,000 ft-lb, or 51 ft-kips.

These column moments due to vertical dead and live loads are called gravity moments, to distinguish them from lateral load moments induced in an unbraced frame by wind or earthquakes.

Exercise Determine the steel requirements of a typical exterior east-west girder that retains the same 18 × 32 dimensions. What is the required stirrup spacing at the support?

What is the minimum depth exterior girder required using a balanced design? What size bars and spacing are needed? What is the required stirrup spacing at the support?

What is the gravity moment in the exterior column of an interior frame? ■

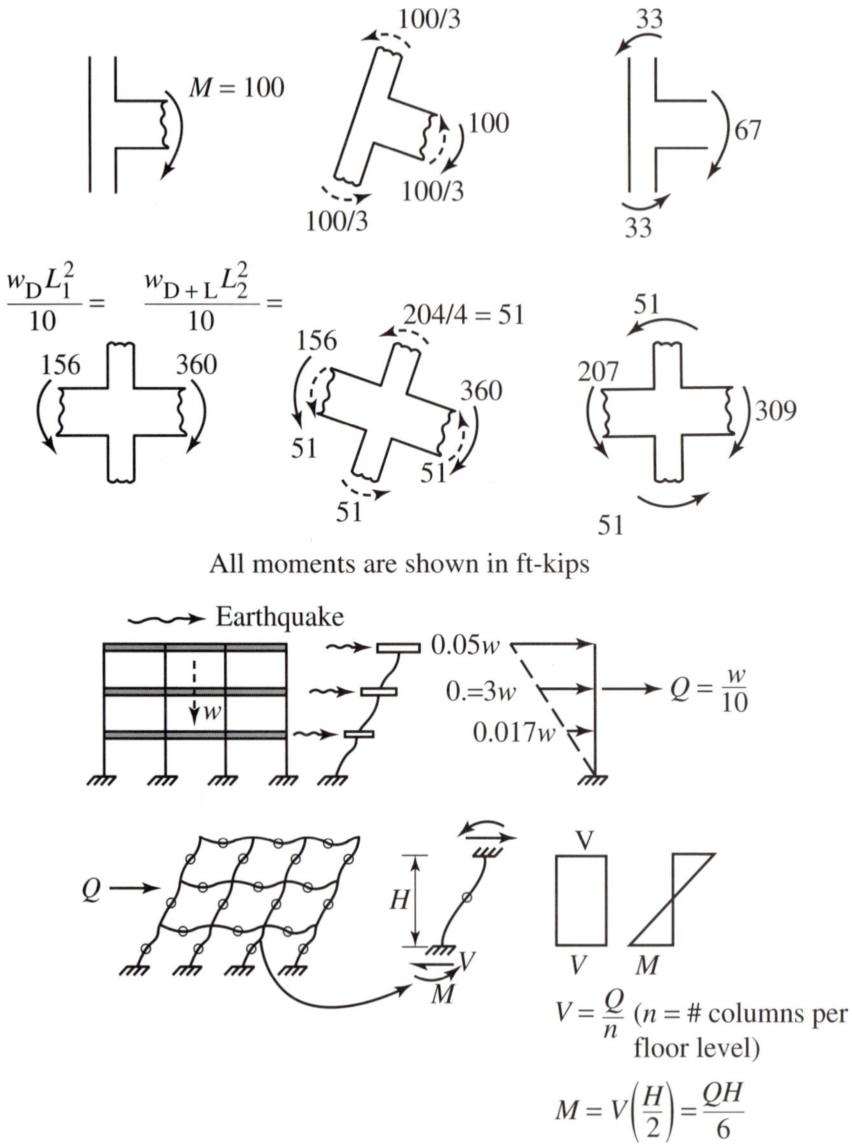

FIGURE 12.3

12.4 Slabs and Floor Systems

One of the most common concrete structural elements is the reinforced slab that acts as a beam to support a uniform dead plus live load per square foot w over span distances from several feet to 60 ft or more, depending on how it is supported and reinforced. When used in roof and floor deck systems, most slabs are made continuous over several spans, as shown in Sections AA and BB of Figure 12.2. Typically, because a slab is so wide, we analyze a 1-ft-wide strip to form a concrete beam of the same span as the slab with a cross-section width, $b = 12$ in., and a depth h. The thickness h of a slab with a span L is normally limited to prevent excessive deflections, and should be at least $L/25$ for continuous spans, or $L/20$ for simple spans. Since the beam is 12 in., or 1 ft wide, its tributary load per foot is simply w, and the design moment is $M = wL^2/8$ for simple spans, and $M = wL^2/10$ for continuous spans.

Instead of the 1.5-in. steel reinforcement cover required of girders, only $\frac{3}{4}$ in. of cover is required of formed slab reinforcing. Also, unlike for girders in which the load from a large tributary area is concentrated, the support reactions of slabs are distributed along their large width, so shear stresses are low enough in slabs that stirrups are not usually needed. Thus, the centers of the steel reinforcing bars are set about 1 in. above the bottom form or below the top of the slab, so the effective depth of the beam is approximately $d = h - 1$ in. If the slab is fairly thin, such as when it transversely spans across numerous closely spaced ribs, as in Section AA, a single layer of steel may be located in the middle of the slab thickness to serve as positive and negative steel. The analysis of the slab beam, with its fixed dimensions and design moment, is simply a matter of determining how much steel is required per foot of slab width.

Building codes require that about 0.2% longitudinal steel be provided in both the width and span directions of a slab to intercept any cracks that form as the concrete slab shrinks with time and with temperature fluctuations. This so-called temperature and shrinkage (T&S) steel requirement is based on actual slab depth, so that $A_S = 0.002(bh) = 0.024(h)$ in^2/ft width. It is commonly the case that the flexural steel requirements are less than 0.2% longitudinal rebars, especially for short spans, so T&S steel requirements may govern the design. Since steel is required in both directions of the slab, it is convenient to construct slabs using welded wire mesh formed by small-diameter steel rebars spaced about 6–12 in. o.c. Reinforcing bars should normally be spaced no more than 12 in. apart.

For the 10-ft continuous span slab shown as Section BB in the figure, we want to determine the slab thickness, top and bottom flexural steel, and the T&S steel requirements. To prevent excessive deflection, the slab should have a thickness of at least $h = L/25 = 10(12)/25 = 6$ in., and so the effective depth is $6 - 1 = 5$ in. for the top and bottom steel layers. The uniform load is $w = 160$ plf on a 1-ft-wide beam with continuous 10-ft spans, so the positive and negative design moments are $M = 160(10^2)/10 \times 12 = 19{,}200$-in-lb/ft slab width.

The required flexural top and bottom steel per foot width of slab is $A_S = M/(21{,}600 \times d) = 19{,}200/(21{,}500 \times 5) = 0.18$-in^2/ft width. The T&S steel requirement of $A_S = 0.024(6) = 0.14$-in^2/ft width. The reader may verify that the flexural steel may be #4 bars spaced 12 in. apart in the direction of the slab span, and the T&S steel requirements are met with #3 bars 9 in. o.c. in the transverse direction.

The joists of Section AA and BB, which span in the transverse direction of the slabs that they support, are best designed as continuous rectangular beams supporting a tributary floor width equal to the joist spacing. To provide sufficient stiffness and thus small deflections, the overall depth of the joists and girders should be at least $L/20$ for continuous spans and $L/16$ for simple spans. When these joists are closely spaced, they may have widths as small as 4 in., depending on shear requirements. Note that a 4-in.-wide web would allow only a single vertical stirrup bar in the beam cross section. A deck system with these closely spaced joists is often referred to as a ribbed slab.

If the joists are simple spans, then each joist can be analyzed as a T-beam as shown by the dashed lines in Section AA, and for simple span

Exercise Design the 4-ft continuous slab of Section AA. Note that a single layer of steel should be sufficient here.

Determine the flexural and shear steel requirements for the 25-ft continuous span rib joists of Sections AA and BB.

Suppose that the joist of Section BB is a simple span. Design the ribs using a T-beam analysis. Assume the web is 8 in. and that the effective flange width is 12 times the slab thickness, or $12 \times 6 = 72$ in. ■

beams, excessive deflection is prevented when the member depth is at least $L/16$. The T-shaped section may be analyzed as a rectangular beam that is as wide as the rib spacing, but for which all the flexural steel must be placed within the narrow width of the rib. The ribbed slab is in essence a thick solid slab spanning in the rib directions, but with the excess tension concrete removed. However, the narrow ribs provide a more limited area to locate all the required flexural rebars and also carry the concentrated shear stress. When the ribs form continuous span joists, the negative moment at the joist ends governs the steel requirements because the Tee (top) flange is in tension and ineffective. In this case, a rectangular continuous beam analysis is required.

With the $L/25$ thickness requirement for solid slabs, a 25-ft slab span would need to be 12 in., and it represents a practical upper limit for slabs that span in only one direction. However, if the columns of a building are spaced on a nearly square grid, then two-way slabs may be constructed. If the width and length of a slab panel are approximately the same, then flexural steel may be run in both directions with the result that half the load is carried in either direction. The two-way spanning slab is inherently stiffer than a one-way span, and so it has a thickness limit of about half that of a one-way slab. Thus, two-way slabs have greater spanning capability as compared to one-way slabs of equivalent thickness, so that they are useful when a larger column-free space is essential.

Two-way slabs can be supported by girders that span along the column lines, or else girder-free two-way slabs known as flat plates are connected directly to the columns. In the latter case, the high loads that result from the relatively large tributary areas of flat plate systems require that the slab be thickened where it connects to the columns (the thickened area is called a drop panel). Otherwise, the large load from the expansive thin deck may shear off of the column in the same way that a column will punch through a footing that is too thin.

12.5 Earthquake Loads on a Rigid Frame

As we have previously discussed, when subsurface slippage of massive plates of the earth's crust occurs, violent side-to-side movements result at the earth's surface that place tremendous lateral loads on a structure that may nearly equal one-half the vertical weight of the structure. As depicted in Figure 12.3, the massive floors of a building resist the dynamic forces equal to the floor masses times their respective accelerations, which are greater at higher levels. In a moment-resisting frame, the members must be capable of resisting the bending that results from these loads.

Shown in the figure is the case where a particular moderate earthquake causes lateral loads equal to 10% of the vertical weight of the structure. The

Exercise What is the wind load moment on the interior column for an east-west wind creating a pressure of 25 psf? ■

moment frame columns at each level are resisting lateral racking shear that forces them into double curvature, along with the building girders to which they are rigidly attached. The exaggerated depiction of a deformed rigid frame shows how girders and columns resist lateral loads through reverse bending moments shown that cause the double curvature. The moment frame is an indeterminate structure, yet we can make two assumptions that allow us to fully analyze the frame.

First, we assume that the ground-floor columns equally resist the horizontal racking shear. For the second assumption, we look at the shear and moment diagram of an interior column, and we see that the member in double curvature must have a point of zero moment at its midsection, called a point of contraflexure. At this point, as for the contraflexure points of all the girders and columns of the frame, we assume that a pin connection exists, since there is no moment at a pin. The approximate analysis we are performing is based on the portal analysis method, which before computers, was the primary method for designing high-rise structures, and it is still widely used today.

Since we are most concerned with the interior columns of the ground floor, which are the critical elements in an earthquake (as we may visualize in the column stack depicted in the figure), we can perform a focused analysis on one column alone. If the floor and roof diaphragms are rigid enough, as they are for concrete structures, we may assume that all columns at one floor level equally resist lateral load. With the 100-psf dead load over three levels of the building of Figure 12.2, the total vertical weight is $W = 100 \text{ psf} \times 3 \times (80 \times 75) \text{ ft}^2 = 1{,}800{,}000 \text{ lb}$, the lateral load (from either a north-south or an east-west quake) is $Q = W/10 = 180{,}000 \text{ lb}$, and for one of the 16 equally loaded ground-floor columns the lateral load is $V = 180{,}000/16 = 11{,}250 \text{ lb}$. The column height is measured as the clear distance between the floor level and the bottom of the upper level girder, or $L = 14 - 32/12 = 11.3 \text{ ft}$. Thus, the lateral load moment is then $M = 11{,}250 \times 11.3/2 = 64{,}000 \text{ ft-lb}$.

12.6 Beam-Columns

As we have been discussing, the vertical column members of concrete rigid frames are subjected to bending moments as well as axial loads; hence the term beam-column more accurately describes the type of load resistance provided by these members. Still, it is common to simply call them columns.

Reinforced concrete columns are generally either rectangular or circular in cross section, although other cross-sectional shapes may also be used. Columns must have at least four longitudinal rebars, which may be as large as #18 bars, as well as small-diameter lateral reinforcing ties, typically #3 or #4 bars. Ties contain the longitudinal steel from buckling in compression, and create a strong inner core column in the event of a loss of the required 1.5 in. of concrete cover for the reinforcing.

The term *tied column* refers to rectangular or circular column cross sections with a minimum of four longitudinal rebars, and with ties forming closed loops around the longitudinal steel spaced every 12 to 18 inches or so along the column, similar to beam stirrups. If the ties take the form of a continuous helical coil wrapping around a minimum of six rebars with a 3- to 4-in. spiral pitch, the member is called a *spiral column.* Though they are less common than tied columns because of their higher fabrication costs, spiral columns are often used in highly seismic regions because they afford greater ductility and durability when overstressed, even when the cover has broken away.

The allowable percentage of longitudinal column steel ranges from 1% to 8% of the cross-sectional area. Because the modular ratio is 8, every 1% of steel adds the equivalent of 8% of concrete column cross-sectional area, and more significantly, when there is considerable load eccentricity, the steel will resist tension, thus allowing the concrete member to properly behave as a beam-column. Because of this, building codes specify that all concrete columns be designed as beam-columns with a minimum eccentricity, $e = 0.1 \times h$, where h is the column width in the direction of eccentricity.

We must analyze reinforced concrete beam-columns as composite members, and so the analysis is not as straightforward as for steel and timber. As was the case when we developed the allowable compression stress versus slenderness ratio curves for timber and steel sections, you may want to skip over the development presented in the following paragraphs. Based on the formulas of Figure 12.4, we will end up developing a family of beam-column curves for various longitudinal steel percentages shown in Figure 12.5, and thus you may choose to pick up the discussion around there.

We first determine the allowable axial force and bending moment of a short, stocky member by analyzing the distribution of steel and concrete stresses over the cross-sectional area, as shown for the tied square column in Figure 12.4. We limit our discussion to short members with $L/n < 10$. A bending moment with an axial force may be expressed as an equivalent eccentric load P, where the moment is $M = P \times e$. The column has a percentage of steel, $p = A_S/bh$, with equal amounts, $p/2$, on the cross-section faces farthest from the neutral bending axis, as shown. With at least 1.5 in. of concrete cover, #4 tie diameter, and the radius of the longitudinal steel bars, the location of the center of the rebars is approximately $0.2h$ from the outer column face.

Because they are usually rigidly connected with beams and are rarely perfectly straight, concrete beam-columns must be designed with a minimum load eccentricity, $e \geq 0.1h$. The general distribution of combined stresses that occurs with an eccentric load is shown in the figure where half of the steel is in tension, and half is in compression, with a wedge of compression stress acting over a portion of the column cross section, $b \times kh$. Flexural stresses in the cross section increase with increased distance from the neutral bending axis. Also, from our investigation of composite members, we know that the stress in the steel at a point is $n = E_S/E_C = 8$ times the stress in the concrete at the same location.

From these observations, we use similar triangles to develop relationships for the three internal forces, F_1, F_2, and F_3, which resist the eccentric load. These three forces may be expressed in terms of the maximum allowable concrete flexural stress, $f = 1{,}800$ psi, the steel percentage p, the cross-sectional area bh, and the variable depth of the compression wedge kh. The maximum allowable steel tension stress of 24,000 psi will govern only the force F_1 when the steel percentage is less than 2% and the member is acting more as a beam than a column. This occurs if the member supports a small load P with a high eccentricity moment, $P \times e$.

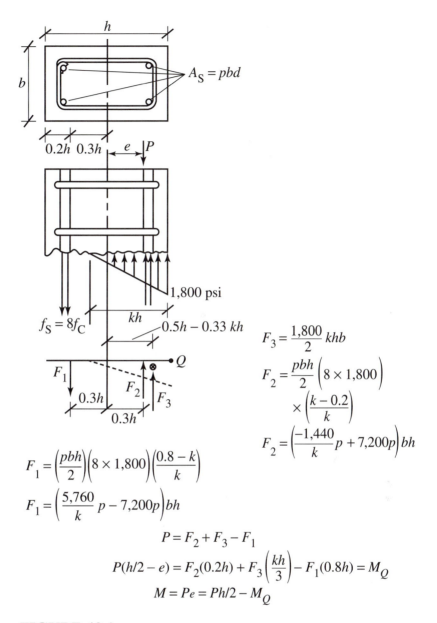

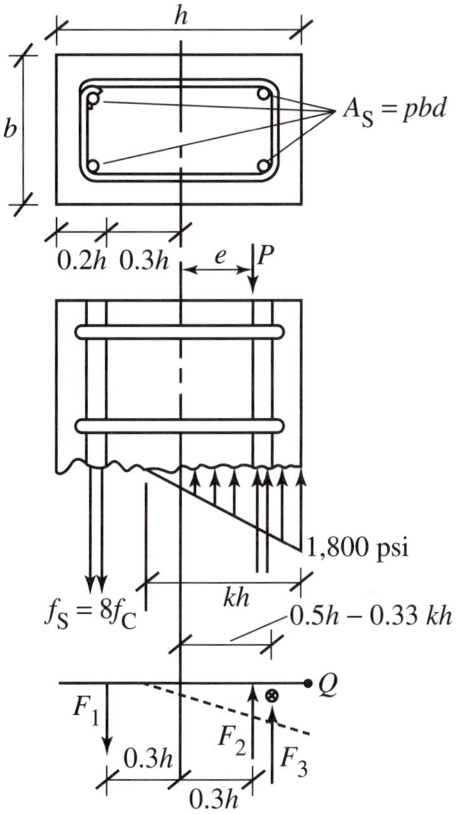

$$F_3 = \frac{1{,}800}{2} khb$$

$$F_2 = \frac{pbh}{2}\left(8 \times 1{,}800\right) \times \left(\frac{k - 0.2}{k}\right)$$

$$F_2 = \left(\frac{-1{,}440}{k} p + 7{,}200p\right) bh$$

$$F_1 = \left(\frac{pbh}{2}\right)\left(8 \times 1{,}800\right)\left(\frac{0.8 - k}{k}\right)$$

$$F_1 = \left(\frac{5{,}760}{k} p - 7{,}200p\right) bh$$

$$P = F_2 + F_3 - F_1$$

$$P(h/2 - e) = F_2(0.2h) + F_3\left(\frac{kh}{3}\right) - F_1(0.8h) = M_Q$$

$$M = Pe = Ph/2 - M_Q$$

FIGURE 12.4

We may set up a spreadsheet using a range of k values from about 1.2 to 0.3, for several values of the steel percentage p. For any value of k in this range, we compute the axial load P, as the sum of the three forces, and by taking moments at an arbitrary point Q, we get $M = P \times e$, as shown in the figure. Note that when $k > 0.8$, all the steel will be in compression, and when $k \geq 1$, all of the cross section is in compression.

The results from such a spreadsheet for steel percentages of 2%, 4%, 6%, and 8% are shown in Figure 12.5, where values of P are divided by the column area bh, and the corresponding eccentricity moments are divided by bh^2. Thus the vertical and horizontal axes correspond to the allowable axial stress, f_A, and the allowable bending stress, f_B, for concrete beam-columns, respectively. Therefore, the set of all points between one of the curves and the origin point (0,0) is the range of allowable axial and bending stress combinations (f_B, f_A) that the column member with a certain steel percentage may support.

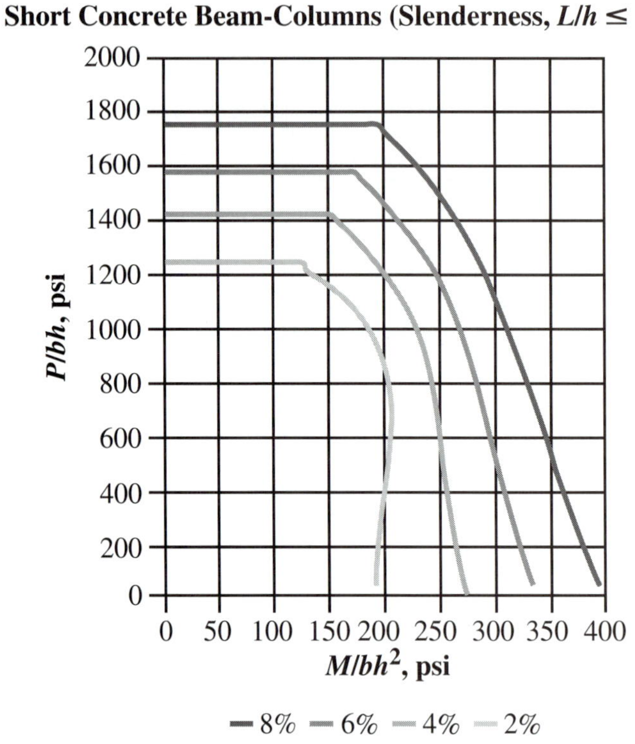

FIGURE 12.5

The location of a point allows us to interpolate between the curves to determine what percentage of steel p is required for a given (f_B, f_A) combination.

The requirement of a minimum eccentricity, $e = 0.1h$ gives the curves their "flattops" and thus the range of (f_B, f_A) combinations is somewhat truncated. When using the graphs for slender concrete columns, especially for columns in unbraced moment frames, the moment should be multiplied by the moment magnifier, $1/(1 - F/F_{CR})$. As we have discussed, F_{CR} is the buckling load of a straight column with a centric load and for concrete columns it is divided by a safety factor of 2, or $F_{CR} = 5EI/L^2$. (P and F are interchangeable here.)

For instance, in the case of the 11.3-ft clear height 18-in. × 18-in. interior column in Figure 12.2, $F_{CR} = (5 \times 3{,}500{,}000 \times 18^4/12)/(11.3 \times 12)^2 =$ 8,330,000 lb. The member is subjected to an axial load of 268,000 lb, and so the moments must be magnified by a factor of $1/(1 - 268/8.330) = 1.03$. The column has a gravity moment of 51,000 ft-lb, and an earthquake moment of 64,000 ft-lb. The axial stress is $P/bh = 268{,}000/(18^2) = 830$ psi, and the effective bending stress is $M/bh^2 = (1.03)(51{,}000 + 64{,}000)(12)/(18^3) = 244$ psi. The point (244,830) lies on the $p = 4\%$ curve, so we see that we need $A_S = 0.04(18)^2 = 13$ in.^{2} steel, or ten #10 bars (five bars in each column face). Note that the moment magnification of 1.03 could have been neglected, which is usually true of short columns to which we limit our discussion. The analysis of concrete columns with slenderness of $L/h > 10$ is complex; fortunately, most columns have $L/h < 10$.

If we assume a small likelihood of the full live load occurring simultaneously with a major earthquake event, then we could justify using the 18-in. × 18-in. section with $A_S = 0.08 \times 18^2 = 26$ in^2, which amounts to 12 #14 bars. Otherwise, a larger column section is needed, or else we must consider bracing the frame using a concrete elevator shaft and/or the use of shearwalls.

Exercise Will an 18-in. × 18-in. column work for the second-floor interior column of Figure 12.2? If so, what area of steel is needed?

If we brace the frame, will the 18-in. × 18-in. column be adequate? What minimum-size square exterior column is required if the frame is braced? ■

If we were to use a 20 × 20 column instead, $P/bh = 670$ psi, and $M/bh^2 = 73$ psi. From the diagram we see that the point (173,670) lies close to the $p = 2\%$ curve. We then conclude that the required area of longitudinal steel is $A_S = 0.02(20^2) = 8\ \text{in}^2$, or four #9 bars in each face. If the building is also unbraced against earthquakes in the north-south direction, then another similar column analysis is needed to determine what steel is needed in the alternate two column faces.

Before leaving the subject of beam-columns, it is interesting to take note of what happens when $P = 0$, and the member is acting only as a beam. The corresponding points (f_B, 0) on the beam-column interaction diagrams provide the allowable stress for beam sections that have reinforcing on both the tension and compression sides of the neutral axis, and these beams are called *doubly reinforced sections.* Recall that for a balanced beam with 1.4% steel in only the tension face of the beam section, the effective allowable stress is, $M/bd^2 = 300$ psi.

If we put the same amount of steel in the compression face and create a doubly reinforced member with $2(1.4) \approx 3\%$ steel, we interpolate between the 2% and 4% curves of the diagram to find $M/bh^2 = 230$ psi. Since $d = 0.8h$, $M/bh^2 = 230$ psi is equivalent to $M/bd^2 = 360$ psi, which is 20% greater than $M/bd^2 = 300$ psi for the singly reinforced section. This additional moment capacity of doubly reinforced members can be useful when the size of a beam is limited and the moment requirement is high, such as at the ends of continuous joists in ribbed slabs.

12.7 Post-Tensioning and Prestressing Girders

Suppose that instead of using a normally reinforced concrete beam with its cracked cross section, we could use the full-uncracked cross section of the member. We would have a greater moment capacity from the same member as well as having a much stiffer beam. The result would be that we could use the same member to span a greater distance, provided that we ensure that allowable stresses are not exceeded and that the deflection is less than $L/300$.

This is accomplished by employing the process of either post-tensioning or prestressing high-strength steel strands in the tension side of the beam. With either method, we prevent tension stress in the concrete cross section and the full cross section works to support load. The special high-strength steel strands have nominal $\frac{1}{2}$-in. diameters and an allowable stress of 150,000 psi (the same type of strands we used to prevent cracking in residential floor slabs).

As we have previously seen for slabs on grade, post-tensioning girders involves the process of placing steel strands encased in sheathing in the formwork of a beam and later stretching them with a tension force after the poured concrete has cured and hardened. Stretching the free end of a strand while the far end is anchored in the concrete member creates a tension force that may be transferred to the member by clamping a device to the strand, which then bears against the end face of the girder when the strands are released. As the stretched strands that are now anchored to the two ends of the girder try to shorten back to a state of no stress, their tension force acts to compress the girder as the strands pull the two ends together.

With prestressing, unsheathed strands are placed in the beam forms and stretched in tension before the wet concrete mix is poured and allowed to harden. Once the concrete hardens and bonds to the stressed strands, the strands are cut flush with either end of the girder. As the stretched cables try to shorten back to a state of no stress, their tension force is transferred into the girder as compression via the bond between the steel and concrete. Compressing the girder through prestressing yields the same result as for post-tensioning, with the difference being that the transfer of tension to compression takes place through bond along the girder length for prestressing, instead of through end anchorage with post-tensioning.

Post-tensioning is usually done one member at a time with the member in place at the field site. Prestressed girders are produced at a fabrication yard and then shipped to the field. Usually the forms for several girders are lined up so that continuous strands may be stretched through all the forms at once. When the concrete is poured and has hardened, the continuous strands are cut at the ends of each girder, and the tension transfers into the girder as compression.

At transfer, the girders are not yet carrying their full loads, and the compressed bottom half of the girder causes the member to arch upwards slightly. This upward deflection is called *camber;* it must be controlled in bridge girders to provide a smooth riding surface. Care must be taken to avoid the member snapping in two from excessive tension at the top of the member. For this reason, when mass-producing several girders each day, it is critical that designers and fabricators work carefully together to ensure the right balance of member length, number of strands, concrete strength at the time of transfer, and member cross-sectional area.

We have seen that when a simple beam designed with a balanced steel percentage ($p = 1.4\%$), is loaded to its full moment capacity, $M = 300bd^2$, and over half the section is cracked with the neutral axis located $0.375(d)$ from the top of the section. To prevent excessive deflections we usually specify a depth limit, such as $h > L/16$ for simple span girders, in lieu of actually computing the deflection, $D = ML^2/10EI$, where the moment of inertia of the cracked section I is about half that of the full uncracked section.

In Figure 12.6 we see the effective cross section and material stresses created in a fully stressed 12-in. × 24-in. normally reinforced balanced beam. We note that the depth of the top uncracked portion of the cross section is $0.375d = 8$ in., or only a third of the full section. For the case of balanced beams, the allowable moment is

$$M = 300(12)(21.5)^2 = 1{,}660{,}000 \text{ in-lb} = 139{,}000 \text{ ft-lb}$$

Since $M = wL^2/8$ for simple spans, the allowable uniform load using this balanced normally reinforced beam over a 24-ft simple span is

$$w = 8M/L^2 = 8(139{,}000)/24^2 = 1{,}900 \text{ plf}$$

If we assume that the cracked beam has about half the stiffness of an uncracked member, the deflection is

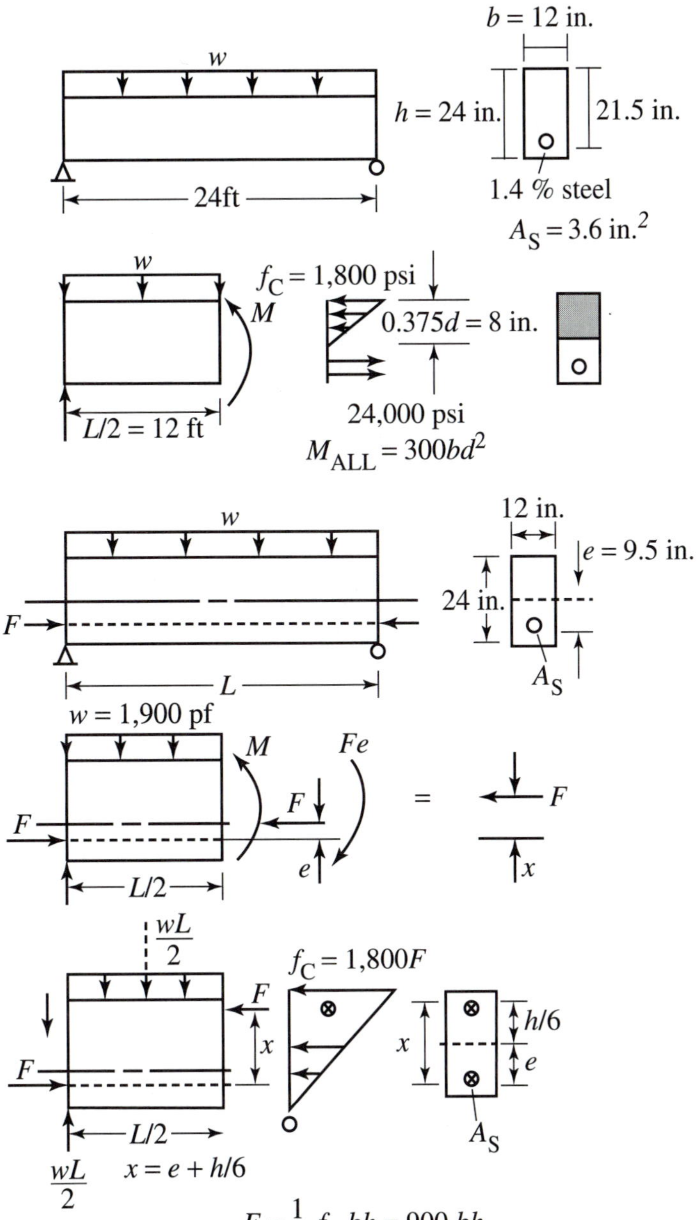

$$F = \frac{1}{2} f_C\, bh = 900\, bh$$

$$M_{ALL} = Fx$$

$$M_{ALL} = 900bhe + 150bh^2$$

FIGURE 12.6

$$D = \frac{1{,}660{,}000 \times (24 \times 12)^2}{10 \times \frac{1}{2}\left(3{,}500{,}000 \times \frac{12(24)^3}{12}\right)} = 0.6 \text{ in.}$$

This is well within the allowable $L/300 = 1$ in.

We see in the figure the same cross-sectional area used with externally stressed strands (either prestressed or post-tensioned) located a distance, $e = 9.5$ in., from the neutral axis at the center of the uncracked section. For a cross section with a given strand location e, area, $A = bh$, and section modulus, $S = bh^2/6$, there is a unique combination of applied moment M and strand force F that will create the optimal compressive stress distribution on an uncracked cross section. Such a section will have a wedge of compression stress acting on the section with zero tension stress at the bottom, and the full allowable concrete compressive stress at the top, $f_C = 1{,}800$ psi.

At the midspan girder section, there is the applied moment M and the applied force in the strands F. The two applied load effects can be reduced to a single force F, which is moved from its line of action along the strands by an amount x such that it creates the same moment effect, $M = Fx$. We observe that the wedge of compression stress on the uncracked section has its centroid at $h/6$ from the section centerline, and this locates the force F, so we have

$$x = e + h/6$$

Horizontal force equilibrium of the half section of the beam indicates that the force in the strands, F, must equal the resultant force created by the stress wedge:

$$F = \frac{1}{2} f_C bh = 900bh$$

Finally, moment equilibrium of the half beam section tells us that the moment applied to the beam, $wL^2/8$, is equal and opposite to the resisting couple, Fx, and so the allowable moment that may be applied to a post-tensioned or prestressed girder is

$$M_{ALL} = Fx = 900bhe + 150bh^2$$

We want to first determine how much steel strand area, A_S, is needed to keep the entire cross section in compression. Then, using the same uniform load, $w = 1{,}900$ plf, as for the normally reinforced 24-ft span, we want to see what additional span length is made possible by external stressed strands. We will need to check the deflection of the longer span using the full uncracked member stiffness EI.

To first determine the steel area, we need to know the required force in the strands, F, which equals the product of the allowable stress and strand area, $F = 150{,}000(A_S)$ as well as the wedge compression force, $F = 900(12 \times 24) = 259{,}000$ lb, so we have

$$A_S = \frac{F}{150{,}000} = \frac{259{,}000}{150{,}000} = 1.73 \text{ in}^2$$

The actual area of a single strand is not $\pi/4 \times (\frac{1}{2})^2 = 0.2$ in^2, because the strands are not round, but are formed by a bundled helix of several small wires, with an actual cross-sectional area per strand of 0.144 in^2. So, we need $1.73/0.144 = 12$ high-strength strands. We could use two rows of six strands each.

To determine the allowable span, we first compute the moment capacity of the stressed strand beam. We note that $e = 9.5 = 0.4h$ and that $d = 21.5 = 0.9h$, and so

$$M_{ALL} = 900bhe + 150bh^2 = 640bd^2$$

We see that this moment capacity is 110% greater than that for a balanced normally reinforced beam, where $M_{ALL} = 300bd^2$. The moment capacity is

$$M_{ALL} = 640(12 \times 21.5^2) = 3{,}550{,}000 \text{ in-lb} = 296{,}000 \text{ ft-lb}$$

For the distributed load, $w = 1{,}900$ plf, we solve for the allowable span

$$L = \sqrt{\frac{8M}{w}} = \sqrt{\frac{8(296{,}000)}{1{,}900}} = 35 \text{ ft}$$

This represents nearly 50% more spanning capability through the use of prestressed or post-tensioned tendons in concrete beams.

We need to make sure that the deflection of the more slender member is not excessive. The deflection of a prestressed or post-tensioned beam is based on that due to the positive moment created by the distributed load, $D = ML^2/10EI$, and the upward camber created by the constant negative moment applied along the girder, $Fe = 259{,}000 \times 9.5 = 2{,}460{,}000$ in-lb, for which $D = (Fe)L^2/8EI$, so

$$D = \frac{(3{,}550{,}000/10 - 2{,}460{,}000/8)(35 \times 12)^2}{3{,}500{,}000 \times 12(24)^3/12} = 0.2 \text{ in.}$$

There is no problem meeting deflection requirements, since the allowable deflection is $L/300 = 1.4$ in.

Exercise Rework the problem assuming a 16-in. × 60-in. section where the centroid of the steel strands is 5 in. from the bottom of the beam.

What is the required spacing of stirrups for the normally reinforced beam and for the 12 × 24 prestressed beam presented above?

A concrete I-beam is made from flanges both 10 in. wide by 8 in. deep and a connecting web that is 4 in. thick and 32 in. deep. The cross-sectional area of this member is the same as for the 12 × 24 section we have discussed above. What is the maximum span possible if $w = 1{,}900$ plf and the lower stress is to be zero and the maximum stress at the top is 1,800 psi? The centroid of the strands is located 4 in. from the bottom of the beam. ■

INDEX

R

S

T

U

V

W

X